The Economics of Climate Change Mitigation

POLICIES AND OPTIONS FOR GLOBAL ACTION BEYOND 2012

Indian edition 2011
published by arrangement with the
Organisation for Economic Co-operation and Development

ISBN: 978-93-80574-20-2

Indian edition 2011, published by:

BOOKWELL

Head Office:

3/79, Nirankari Colony, Delhi-110009, India
Ph: 91-11-27601283, 27604536.
Fax: 91-11-23281315
E-mail: bkwell@nde.vsnl.net.in
Website: www.bookwellindia.com

Sales Office:

24/4800, Ansari Road, Darya Ganj,
New Delhi-110002, India
Ph: 91-11-23268786, 23257264
E-mail: bookwell@vsnl.net

Printed at:
D K Fine Art Press P Ltd.
Delhi-110052

Foreword

The analysis presented in this book aims to support countries in developing and implementing an ambitious, cost-effective, equitable, and comprehensive approach to global climate change mitigation. It is part of a broader and long-standing programme of work that aims to assist countries in their efforts to build sustainable economies.

At the 15th Conference of Parties to the UN Framework Convention on Climate Change (COP15) in Copenhagen in December 2009, governments will need to demonstrate the political will and ambition required to collectively tackle the challenge of climate change. Only a few months before COP15, many challenges still remain before a successful agreement can be reached. At the July 2009 G8 l'Aquila Summit, leaders of all major emitting countries reiterated the importance of keeping the increase in average global temperature below 2°C. This means a maximum concentration of greenhouse gas emissions in the atmosphere of around 450 parts per million CO_2 equivalent. Leaders also suggested that developed countries should lead the way by reducing their emissions by 80% by 2050.

But there remains considerable uncertainty on the resolution of other key issues that will be critical for reaching a successful agreement in Copenhagen. These include: identification of the mid-term emission reductions needed by individual developed countries to move towards these long-term goals, the actions that large developing economies might take, and how finance and technology can be scaled-up to support emission reductions and adaptation to climate change, in particular in developing countries.

Critical to achieving the 2°C target will be an ambitious and comprehensive agreement, including the participation of as many countries and sectors as possible. Broad participation is also critical for ensuring that the target is met at the least possible economic cost. This book presents the range of policy instruments that can be used to reduce emissions, and how they can best be combined in policy mixes that are both environmentally and cost effective. An understanding of the various policy instruments in the mix – including the removal of subsidies, cap-and-trade schemes, carbon taxes, support to R&D, standards and regulations – is essential for each country to gauge, in an international context, the emission reduction commitments they can take on and how to best translate these commitments into action. The analysis presented in this book, for example, shows that removal of energy subsidies can help to both reduce emissions and increase economic efficiency. This type of low-cost or even net-benefit mitigation action could constitute an important contribution to achieving global climate goals.

Globally, the most cost-effective approach to tackling climate change is to put a price on greenhouse gas emissions, that is, to make polluters pay, across all sectors, emission sources and countries. This would provide crucial incentives to the private sector for moving towards a low carbon society. This book shows how a global carbon price can be built up gradually, from the existing piecemeal and scattered approaches. It also shows how governments can encourage climate-friendly economic growth. This includes expanding the use of cap-and-trade schemes to reduce emissions and linking them together; complementing these with taxes and other policy instruments, including support for R&D, regulations and standards; scaling-up and reforming the use of the Clean Development Mechanism (CDM); and possibly introducing sectoral approaches and incentives to reduce emissions from the forestry sector in developing countries.

It is important to start now to build such a global carbon market. In the near- to medium-term developed countries will need to take on ambitious targets if we are to stay within a 2°C temperature increase limit. This book examines the emissions reductions and the costs associated with the mid-term targets already declared or suggested by a number of developed countries, providing some of the information that can help countries compare their proposed efforts with those of others as well as an estimate of the impact of these efforts. Overall, while many of the mid-term targets declared thus far look ambitious, our analysis suggests that the combined developed country targets would lead to only about a 8 to 14% reduction in their emissions by 2020 compared with 1990. This is significantly less stringent than the 25 to 40% reduction in developed country emissions, which is suggested by the IPCC as the pathway consistent with a 450 parts per million CO_2 equivalent concentration level. These targets will need to be scaled up significantly if we are to stay within the 2°C limit.

Finally, while broad participation is essential, reaching a successful international agreement will also require scaled-up and sustainable financing and technology support for developing countries, including both public support and private financing such as through the carbon market. Some decoupling of mitigation action from its cost will be needed, to ensure a fair sharing of the burden of action while respecting the principle of common but differentiated responsibility and the respective capabilities of countries. The analysis presented here looks critically at the incentives for different countries to participate in a global approach to climate change, and at how financing and technology can help to support action in developing countries.

The challenge of tackling climate change can seem even greater now, as countries around the world struggle to recover from recession and rebuild their economies and financial sectors. But the economic crisis is no excuse to delay action on climate change. Such delay would only increase the global costs to be faced in the future for mitigating climate change. Instead, ambitious policies to move toward a low-carbon economy should be an essential element in the strategy to recover from the crisis. At the recent Meeting of the OECD Council at Ministerial Level in June 2009, Ministers from thirty-four countries requested the OECD to develop a Green Growth Strategy. Our efforts in this policy area will be intensified in the coming years and will aim to support countries to achieve economic recovery and environmentally and socially sustainable economic growth.

By applying economic analysis to environmental policies and instruments, by looking at ways to spur eco-innovation and by addressing other aspects of the green economy such as financing, taxation, governance and skills development, the OECD can continue to show the way to make a cleaner, low carbon world compatible with economic growth. By doing so, it can also help countries identify the policy choices that are needed to build a solid economic foundation for the post-2012 international climate agreement.

Angel Gurría

Secretary-General

Acknowledgements

This book is the product of a joint effort by the Economics Department and the Environment Directorate of the OECD. Preliminary versions of the chapters were presented at meetings of the Working Party No 1 (WP1) of the Economic Policy Committee and the Environment Policy Committee's Working Party on Global and Structural Policies (WPGSP). Participants to these meetings provided valuable comments and suggestions.

The chapters were mainly written by Jean-Marc Burniaux, Jean Chateau, Rob Dellink, Romain Duval, Stéphanie Jamet and Alain de Serres, under the supervision of Helen Mountford and Giuseppe Nicoletti. Jan Corfee-Morlot, Christine de la Maisonneuve and Bruno Guay contributed to Working Papers that were inputs to the book. Extensive comments and suggestions were provided by a number of OECD colleagues, in particular Jane Ellis, Jorgen Elmeskov, Katia Karousakis, Lorents G. Lorentsen and Jean-Luc Schneider.

The preparation of the book has benefited from the information and expertise provided by the International Energy Agency. It has also benefited from contributions by external consultants, notably Johannes Bollen, Adriana Ignaciuk, Bill Whitesell, as well as from a team of researchers from the Foundation Eni Enrico Mattei (FEEM) led by Professor Carlo Carraro, and including Valentina Bosetti, Enrica DeCian, Emanuele Massetti, Massimo Tavoni and Alessandra Sgobbi.

Statistical assistance was provided by Cuauhtemoc Rebolledo-Gómez. Fiona Hall edited the report, and Jane Kynaston, Patricia Nilsson and Irene Sinha provided administrative assistance and formatted the publication.

Table of Contents

 THE ECONOMICS OF CLIMATE CHANGE MITIGATION – ISBN: 978-92-64-05606-0 – © OECD 2009

Acronyms and Abbreviations

BAU	Business as usual
BRIC	Brazil, Russia, India and China
CAC	Command-and-control
CCS	Carbon capture and storage
CER	Certified emissions reductions
CDM	Clean Development Mechanism
CH_4	Methane
CO_2	Carbon dioxide
CO_2eq	Carbon dioxide equivalent
EFTA	European Free Trade Association
EII	Energy intensive industry
ETS	Emissions trading scheme
EU-ETS	European Union emissions trading scheme
FAO	United Nation's Food and Agriculture Organization
FDI	Foreign direct investment
GHG	Greenhouse gas
Gt	Gigatonnes
GWP	Global warming potential
HFCs	Hydrofluorocarbons
IEA	International Energy Agency
IMF	International Monetary Fund
IPCC	Intergovernmental Panel on Climate Change
IPR	Intellectual property rights
ITC	Induced technological change
JI	Joint implementation
LAP	Local air pollution
LBD	Learning by doing
LULUCF	Land use, land use change and forestry
MRV	Monitoring, reporting and verifying
N_2O	Nitrous oxide
OPEC	Organization of the Petroleum Exporting Countries

PEC	Potentially effective coalition
PFCs	Perfluorocarbons
$PM_{2.5}$	Particulate matter, particles of 2.5 micrometres (μm) or less
PPM	Parts per million
PPP	Purchasing power parity
R&D	Research and development
REDD	Reducing emissions from deforestation and forest degradation
SF_6	Sulphur hexafluoride
TFP	Total factor productivity
UNFCCC	United Nations Framework Convention on Climate Change
USD	United States dollar
VA	Voluntary agreement
VAT	Value added tax
WITCH	World Induced Technological Change Hybrid model

THE ECONOMICS OF CLIMATE CHANGE MITIGATION – ISBN: 978-92-64-05606-0 – © OECD 2009

Executive Summary

The climate challenge: business as usual is not an option

The global climate is changing, and the release of greenhouse gases (GHGs) from human activity has contributed to global warming. While there is significant uncertainty about the costs of inaction, it is generally agreed that failing to tackle climate change will have significant implications for the world economy, especially in developing countries, where reduced agricultural yields, sea level rise, extreme weather events and the greater prevalence of some infectious diseases are likely to be particularly disruptive (OECD, 2008a). Furthermore, there are significant risks of unpredictable, potentially large and irreversible, damage worldwide. The exact economic and welfare costs of policy inaction could equate to as much as a permanent 14.4% loss in average world consumption per capita (Stern, 2007), when both market and non-market impacts are included.

To understand how to best tackle these challenges, Chapter 1 provides a picture of what emissions and temperatures would be like over the next half century in the absence of new policy action. This is referred to as the business-as-usual (BAU) baseline.[1] This is not meant to be a realistic course of events, but provides a basis against which the economic implications of climate change mitigation efforts can be assessed. Under this business-as-usual scenario, world GHG emissions, which have roughly doubled since the early 1970s, would nearly double again between 2008 and 2050. As a result, atmospheric concentrations of CO_2 and GHGs more broadly would increase to about 525 parts per million (ppm) and 650 ppm CO_2 equivalent (CO_2eq) in 2050, respectively, and continue to rise thereafter. This could cause mean global temperatures to be about 2°C higher than they were in pre-industrial times[2] in 2050, about 4-6°C higher by 2100, and higher still beyond that.

The current economic crisis provides no room for complacency. Although it is expected to result in a non-negligible reduction in global emissions, the impact is likely to be temporary, with the upward trend resuming as the economic recovery gets underway. The crisis is not a reason to delay action on climate change; delaying mitigation action would mean that larger cuts would be needed later to achieve the same target, and would ultimately be more expensive than taking a more gradual approach. Instead, if well-designed climate mitigation policies are phased-in gradually over the coming years this will avoid unnecessary scrapping of capital, and initial costs should be very low. In the short term, there may be scope for stimulating the depressed economy by bringing forward some low-carbon investment expenditures. In the longer term, the crisis has also created sizeable government funding shortfalls in many OECD countries, which prospective fiscal revenues from carbon pricing could help reduce at low, if any, welfare costs.

Examining scenarios for a low-emission future

Wide economic and environmental uncertainties surround the expected damage from the business-as-usual scenario, but there is a significant probability of very large losses. Given these uncertainties, an economically rational response would be to reduce global emissions to levels which ensure a "low" probability of extreme, irreversible damage from climate change.

The size of reductions and the timeframe over which they should be achieved are two of the key issues in current discussions leading up to an international agreement at the UN Framework Convention on Climate Change (UNFCCC) conference in Copenhagen at the end of 2009. It is widely accepted that cuts should be large enough to stabilise GHG concentrations at a level that would "prevent dangerous anthropogenic interference with the climate system" (IPCC, 2007). A global mean temperature increase of around 2-3°C has been considered by many to be the maximum for avoiding such interference, and this would mean stabilising overall GHG concentration in the atmosphere at no more than about 450-550 ppm. Reflecting the uncertainties and risks involved with any global temperature increase, a number of both developing and developed nations have recently rallied around the more ambitious objective of limiting temperature rises to 2°C. However, for illustrative purposes only, the analysis presented in this book is mostly based on a 3°C objective. It is not an endorsement of such a target.

Given the magnitude of emission cuts required to achieve this objectives (a reduction in world emissions by at least 30% by 2050), it is essential to minimise the costs involved. Different scenarios built around this objective are also assessed and discussed in more details in Chapter 1. While they mainly differ in terms of their timeframe, most scenarios imply substantial worldwide emission cuts compared both to the situation today and the baseline level in 2050. The results show that if these cuts can be achieved through the global pricing of carbon, the economic cost (lost GDP) could be relatively modest.

This is especially the case when some overshooting of the long-term concentration target is allowed. For instance, achieving stabilisation of GHG concentrations at 550 ppm according to a pathway that allows for global emissions to continue rising until around 2025 would reduce average annual world GDP growth projected over 2012-2050 by 0.11 percentage points – resulting in world GDP being lower by about 4% in 2050, compared to the BAU baseline scenario. This is despite a sharp increase in the carbon price, from less than USD 30 in 2008 to around USD 280 in 2050. The reason for the GDP loss relative to the BAU scenario is that substantial human and capital resources will have to be reallocated to GHG mitigation, thus reducing the resources available for producing other goods and services. To put this loss in perspective, world GDP would still be expected to grow by more than 250% over the same period, even if significant mitigation action is undertaken. Thus, citizens would still be financially better off on average in three or four decades than they are today. Furthermore, the large benefits from mitigation, in the form of reduced damages from climate change, are not taken into account in this calculation.

The cost from mitigation policies are expected to be unevenly distributed across countries. Those using carbon more intensively and/or exporting fossil fuel, such as Russia and major oil-exporting countries would face the largest GDP costs. In general, despite their cheaper emission abatement opportunities, emerging economies and developing countries are more affected than developed countries because the level and growth of their production is more intensive in fossil fuels.[3] Likewise, the mitigation efforts in terms of percentage reductions in GHG emissions per capita relative to the BAU scenario is also generally higher in developing countries, in this case owing in part to cheaper abatement opportunities.[4] Again, these estimated mitigation costs are assumed to take place in the context of a global, broadly-based carbon market with relatively few distortions or imperfections. Without this precondition, costs would be higher. In order for such cost-efficient mitigation action to be feasible, a number of policy instruments must be put in place or expanded so as to create the proper incentives to ensure that emissions are reduced first where it is cheapest to do so.

What policies are best for cost-effective emissions cuts?

There is a variety of national and international policy instruments available for tackling climate change. But what are the pros and cons of each, and can they be integrated into a coherent policy framework? Carbon taxes, emissions trading (or cap-and-trade) schemes, standards and technology-support policies (R&D and clean technology deployment) are all examined in Chapter 2 according to three broad cost-effectiveness criteria:

- Is the instrument cost-effective, and does it provide sufficient political incentives for wide adoption (static efficiency)?
- Does it encourage innovation and diffusion of clean technologies in order to lower future abatement costs (dynamic efficiency)?
- Can it cope effectively with climate and economic uncertainties?

A mix of policy instruments will be required

In principle, putting a price on GHG emissions through price mechanisms such as carbon taxes, emissions trading (cap-and-trade) systems (ETS), or a hybrid system combining features of both, can go a long way towards building up a cost-effective climate policy framework. Although taxes and ETS differ in a number of respects, both are intrinsically cost-effective and give emitters continuing incentives to search for cheaper abatement options through both existing and new technologies. They can also be designed and adjusted to minimise short-term uncertainty about emission abatement costs (*e.g.* through the use of banking and borrowing provisions and price caps in the case of permits) and longer-term uncertainty about environmental outcomes.

However, market mechanisms are unable to deal with all the market imperfections (monitoring, enforcement and asymmetric information problems) which prevent some emitters from responding to price signals. Furthermore, it might not be politically feasible currently to achieve a global carbon price. Thus, a broad mix of policy instruments in addition to emissions pricing will be needed. These could include the targeted use of complementary instruments, including standards (*e.g.* building codes, electrical appliance standards, diffusion of best practices) and information instruments (*e.g.* eco-labeling). Furthermore, R&D and technology adoption instruments could encourage innovation and diffusion of emissions-reducing technologies, beyond the incentives provided by the pricing of carbon.

But while multiple market failures arguably call for multiple policy instruments, poorly-designed policy mixes could result in undesirable overlaps, which would undermine cost-effectiveness and, in some cases, environmental integrity. For example, if a price is put on carbon, applying other policy tools such as renewable, energy efficiency or biofuel targets in addition to the carbon price can lead to overlap and might lock-in inefficient technologies. While these policies may be motivated by other objectives, in many OECD countries the side benefits for innovation and/or energy security do not seem to justify the very high implicit carbon abatement prices currently embedded in renewable and biofuel subsidies and targets. As a general rule, different instruments should address different market imperfections and/or cover different emission sources.

What are the implications of incomplete mitigation policy coverage?

Despite the fact that more and more cap-and-trade systems are put in place or envisaged, it will be a while before their coverage reaches the levels assumed in the various scenarios examined. Furthermore, most of these systems exclude certain important emission sources and sectors (especially transport and forestry). The costs, environmental consequences and competitiveness implications of this incomplete coverage are assessed in Chapter 3:

- Exempting *energy-intensive industries* from policy action could increase the costs of achieving the illustrative 550 ppm CO_2eq scenario by over half in 2050 compared to a situation where all sectors were to participate.
- If policies only target *CO_2 emissions*, rather than all GHGs, costs also increase significantly. If the illustrative stabilisation scenario were to be achieved through CO_2 emission cuts only, the costs in 2050 would amount to 7% of world GDP rather than 4% of world GDP as reported above.
- An incomplete *country coverage* of GHG mitigation policies would not achieve much. All but the laxest (*e.g.* 750 ppm CO_2eq) of GHG concentration targets are found to be virtually out of reach if Annex I countries act alone, either because they simply do not emit enough to make a big enough difference – for concentrations below 650 ppm – or else, because of the very high costs of action concentrated on such a narrow base.

Fears of carbon leakage should not be exaggerated

However, while incomplete country coverage raises the costs of achieving any global target, it does not necessarily imply significant carbon leakage – *i.e.* that emission cuts in a limited number of participating countries might be partly offset by increases elsewhere. Unless only a few countries take action against climate change, for instance the European Union acting alone, leakage rates are found to be almost negligible. For example, if the European Union acted alone (*i.e.* no other countries put in place climate policies), almost 12% of their emission reductions would be offset by emission increases in other countries. However, if all developed countries were to act, this leakage rate would be reduced to below 2%.

If the coalition of acting countries is very small, imposing countervailing tariffs (border tax adjustments) on the carbon content of imports from non-participating countries could be one way to prevent leakage. However, such tariffs would imply potentially large costs for both participating and non-participating countries, is likely to be administratively burdensome, and could provoke trade retaliation, while not necessarily reducing the output losses incurred by energy-intensive industries in participating countries.

Integrating forest protection in the international climate framework is desirable but challenging

The various scenarios to stabilise GHG concentration referred to so far do not take account of the potential from forest protection. Yet, emissions from deforestation are thought to amount to about 17% of global emissions. The implications of incorporating forestry into an international climate policy framework are therefore treated separately in Chapter 3 as part of the discussion on incomplete coverage. Reducing Emissions from Deforestation and forest Degradation (REDD) could potentially reduce the cost of global action by 40% (although there could be an impact on land and food prices). However, one

THE ECONOMICS OF CLIMATE CHANGE MITIGATION – ISBN: 978-92-64-05606-0 – © OECD 2009

reason why the abatement potential from forest protection is left out from most scenarios examined in the book is that the measurement of this potential is still in its infancy.

Furthermore, incorporating forest protection in a global policy framework raises a number of implementation issues, including how to certify performance and ultimately compliance, limiting emissions leakage – as deforestation may shift to areas not subject to control – and addressing non-permanence, as emissions may simply be delayed. These risks can be better addressed if a REDD mechanism is implemented and performance overseen at the national, rather than the individual project, level. Applying any REDD mechanism as widely as possible across forest nations will also help to manage the risk of international leakage.

Clear and robust eligibility criteria for environmental integrity will need to be developed if a REDD mechanism is linked to the international carbon market. Access to the carbon market might be limited to only those countries that meet these well-designed eligibility criteria and funding from developed countries could help some developing countries to build the capacities needed to meet those criteria.

Several approaches could be envisaged during the transition towards integration of a REDD market in the international carbon market, all of which have pros and cons. One approach, could be to establish a REDD market that is separate from other carbon markets. Alternatively, a fund-based approach would rely on voluntary or institutionalised contributions to a Fund from developed country governments and other sources but this approach may not provide adequate incentives to significantly reduce the rate of deforestation.

What are the key steps towards a global carbon market?

A broad-based international carbon market will only be achieved gradually. A number of concrete steps towards achieving this objective are thoroughly reviewed in Chapter 4, and the main findings are summarised here:

Removing environmentally-harmful energy subsidies

Fossil fuel energy subsidies are currently high in several non-OECD countries. OECD countries also provide subsidies to energy production and/or consumption, but it is estimated that they are small in comparison to non-OECD countries, and they are often provided through channels that are harder to measure, thus they are not reflected in the modelling analysis presented here (IEA, 1999). In the latter case, they are particularly substantial in Russia, other non-EU Eastern European countries, and a number of large developing countries, particularly India. These subsidies amount to a negative carbon price that keeps fossil fuel consumption, and hence GHG emissions, higher than they would otherwise be. Thus, removing them is a necessary, though politically difficult, step towards broad-based international carbon pricing. It would also free up finances for more direct reallocation to the social objectives being supported by the subsidies. Removing energy subsidies in non-OECD countries will have positive effects:

- Closing the gap between domestic and international fossil fuel prices could cut GHG emissions drastically in the subsidising countries, in some cases by over 30% relative to BAU levels by 2050, and globally by 10%. Nonetheless, broad-based energy subsidy removal would lower the demand for, and thereby the world prices of, fossil fuels. As a result, emissions would rise in other (mainly developed) countries, limiting the decline in world emissions. However, with binding emission caps in developed countries, such leakage would be contained, and world emission reductions would be even larger.

- Energy subsidy removal would also raise GDP per capita in most of the countries concerned, including India and, to a lesser extent, China. Conversely, broad-based energy subsidy removal would imply terms-of-trade and output losses for producing countries. Still, the global GDP effect would be positive.

Linking and harmonising carbon markets

Given the political and institutional challenges of achieving a global carbon price, less ambitious interim arrangements will be needed for the coming years. The increase in domestic/regional ETSs and discussions on reform of the Clean Development Mechanism (CDM) present some opportunities. A global carbon market could be gradually built up through direct linking of domestic/regional ETSs, and/or indirect linking via a scaled up CDM or other mechanisms that provide credits for mitigation action in developing countries to offset emission reduction commitments in developed countries. Compared with a fragmented approach under which a number of regions would meet their emission reduction objectives in isolation, this gradual path towards global carbon pricing could reduce mitigation costs, and possibly carbon leakage:

- Linking could be an important step towards the emergence of a single international carbon price. By equalising carbon prices, and thus marginal abatement costs, across different ETSs, the cost of achieving a joint target will be reduced. Other significant, but difficult to quantify, gains arise from the enhanced liquidity of permit markets.

- The greater the difference in carbon prices across countries prior to linking, the larger the cost savings from linking (Box 0.1). Countries with higher pre-linking carbon prices gain from abating less and buying cheaper permits. Countries with lower pre-linking prices benefit from abating more and selling permits, although their economy may be negatively affected by the real exchange rate appreciation triggered by the large permit exports (the Dutch disease effect). If domestic Annex I ETSs were linked, permit buyers would include Canada, Australia and New Zealand and, to a lesser extent, the European Union and Japan. Russia would be the main seller.

Box 0.1 The impacts of linking Annex I emission trading schemes

In the absence of linking, a scenario in which each region of Annex I (industrialised) countries is assumed to cut its GHG emissions unilaterally by 50% below 1990 levels by 2050 is estimated to reduce average Annex I income by 1.5% and 2.75% relative to BAU by 2020 and 2050. Linking ETSs would lower these cost estimates by just under 10%, or about 0.25% percentage points of income. Mitigation cost saving achieved through linking is found in this analysis to be quite low because there is relatively little heterogeneity in carbon prices across countries before linking. Furthermore, if some degree of carbon price convergence is already achieved through indirect linking of ETSs via the use of crediting mechanisms, the (additional) gains from explicit linking are reduced.

Linking ETSs enhances emission reductions in those schemes which had lower marginal abatement costs before linking (especially Russia), but these increases are offset by lower emission reductions in the others. On the whole, a scenario in which Annex I (industrialised) GHG emissions are cut unilaterally by 50% below 1990 levels by 2050, without or with linking, would still lead to increases in world emissions relative to 2005 levels and would, therefore, need to be rapidly tightened and/or supplemented with further action in non-Annex I countries in order to achieve ambitious emission reduction targets.

 THE ECONOMICS OF CLIMATE CHANGE MITIGATION – ISBN: 978-92-64-05606-0 – © OECD 2009

- National intensity targets could increase GHG mitigation action by fast-growing emerging economies as they catch up with developed countries, without unduly constraining their economic growth prospects. Unlike absolute targets, intensity targets are measured in emissions per unit of output and are linked to future GDP. They would automatically adjust to unexpected growth trends and insure countries against the risk of unexpected increases in mitigation costs. Within a linked system, they would therefore stabilise the carbon price. However, they would require frequent government intervention to be met and would imply greater uncertainty about overall emission abatement. Over the longer term (in the context of a world ETS), another way to reflect economic development concerns would be to allocate absolute targets across countries linked to actual output and expected economic growth rates and to adjust them over time.

- However, although direct linking across schemes could be very beneficial for mitigation costs, it also creates incentives for participating countries to relax their target for future compliance periods (in order to become a permit seller). Also, when systems are linked, different design features (links to other emission trading and crediting schemes, safety valves, banking and borrowing provisions) can spread to the others, undermining environmental integrity. While some of these problems could be reduced by limiting linking for regions with low-quality permits or offsets (*e.g* by imposing discount factors on sellers, allowance import quota or tariffs), this could have several drawbacks. For example, it could trigger retaliation, and such mechanisms would need to be progressively removed as environmental integrity improved. A more cost-effective approach would be for all parties involved to reach agreement on key issues prior to linking, including on levels and/or procedures for setting future emission caps, the adoption of safety valves, and rules about future linking to other ETSs or crediting mechanisms.

Expanding the role of crediting mechanisms

A more indirect way of gradually building up an integrated world carbon market and lowering mitigation costs occurs when an ETS allows part of a region's emission reductions to be achieved in countries outside the ETS. This can occur through a crediting mechanism such as the Clean Development Mechanism (CDM), which is one of the flexibility mechanisms of the Kyoto Protocol. The CDM allows emission reduction projects in non-Annex I countries – *i.e.* developing countries, which have no GHG emission constraints – to earn certified emission reduction (CER) credits (or offsets), each equivalent to one tonne of CO_2eq. Annex I countries can buy these CERs and used them to meet part of their emission reduction commitments:

- The cost-saving potential for developed countries of well-functioning crediting mechanisms appears to be very large, reflecting the vast low-cost abatement potential in a number of developing countries. The same benchmark scenario as above was examined (each region of Annex I countries cuts its GHG emissions unilaterally by 50% below 1990 levels by 2050). This time 20% of Annex I emission reduction commitments were allowed to be met through cuts in non-Annex I countries. This would nearly halve mitigation costs in Annex I countries, and raising this cap on offset credit use from 20% to 50% would bring further benefits. Cost savings would be largest for the more carbon-intensive Annex I economies, such as Australia, New Zealand, Canada and Russia. China has the potential to be by far the largest seller, and the United States the largest buyer in the offset credit market, each of them accounting for about half of transactions by 2020.

- In theory, by lowering the carbon price differential between participating and non-participating countries, crediting mechanisms can also reduce carbon leakage and reduce competitiveness concerns. However, whether crediting mechanisms reduce leakage in practice depends in part on how the baseline against which credits are granted is set.

These gains are unlikely to be fully reaped under the current CDM. Concerns about the latter include its environmental integrity (the difficulty of establishing that emission cuts are indeed "real, additional and verifiable"), and the fact that it may create perverse incentives for developing countries to increase emissions. Existing proposals to scale up the CDM, such as "programmatic", "sectoral" or even possibly "policy" CDMs, could reduce other problems, such as transaction costs and bottlenecks, but may not address these deeper problems. One approach might be to negotiate baselines today for the largest possible number of sectors for a sufficiently long time period (*e.g.* a decade), and to set these baselines below BAU emission levels. A long-term baseline would address the perverse incentive issue by ruling out the possibility that any future increase in emissions might, if offset by subsequent reductions, deliver CERs. It would also minimise the risk of leakage, especially if the number of countries and sectors covered would be large. Setting baselines below BAU levels might insure against over-estimating baseline emissions and the excess supply of CERs. The main weakness of this approach is that estimating and negotiating baselines simultaneously across a wide range of countries and sectors would involve significant methodological and political obstacles.

Another incentive problem is that the large financial inflows from which developing countries may benefit under a future CDM could undermine their willingness to take on binding emission commitments at a later stage. Agreement on CDM reform could therefore incorporate built-in phasing-out mechanisms under which developing countries would commit to increasingly stringent actions as their income levels increase. For instance, the sectoral and/or national baselines negotiated in the context of scaled-up CDM might be gradually tightened, and eventually converted into binding emission caps which could be expanded across sectors and lowered as financing for action through crediting mechanisms is removed.

A role for sectoral approaches

Sectoral approaches have been put forward as a way to broaden participation in emission reductions to developing countries. They could lower overall mitigation costs, facilitate international technology transfers, and are likely to require less institutional capacity than nation-wide targets. The argument is that a narrowly-focused agreement covering firms that share some characteristics and compete among themselves may be easier to achieve than broader agreements. Indeed, a relatively small number of sectors account for a large share of world emissions. For instance, the emissions of energy-intensive industries (EIIs) and the power sector together account for almost half of current world GHG emissions from fossil fuel combustion. International shipping and air transport, due to their transnational character, are another two industries where a sectoral approach could be useful.

Two types of sectoral approaches could play a useful role:

- *Binding sectoral targets,* under which some developing countries might cap the emissions or the emission intensity of key GHG-emitting sectors. A binding sectoral cap covering EIIs and the power sector in non-Annex I countries could substantially reduce emissions worldwide. Owing to the fast emissions growth expected in non-Annex I countries, a 20% emissions cut in these countries would achieve a larger reduction in world emissions (compared to a BAU scenario) than a 50% cut in Annex I countries. Linking a sectoral scheme covering non-Annex I countries to an Annex I economy-wide ETS would also bring an economic gain to participating countries as a whole, but could generate winners and losers. In order to ensure that the overall gain from linking is shared widely across participants, permit allocation rules might need to be adjusted upon linking.

 THE ECONOMICS OF CLIMATE CHANGE MITIGATION – ISBN: 978-92-64-05606-0 –

- *Sectoral crediting mechanisms,* which would reward emission cuts below a baseline in a specific sector. Given the rapid projected BAU emission growth in most developing countries, meeting ambitious world targets through sectoral crediting alone would not be feasible. Therefore sectoral crediting would have to evolve gradually into more binding arrangements such as sectoral caps, at least for key developing country emitters. In the transitory period during which sectoral crediting operates, baselines could be progressively tightened – *i.e.* set further below BAU emission levels – from one commitment period to the next. Sectoral crediting could even increase the income of developing countries and may, therefore, be easier to adopt. At the same time, it would raise many of the same limitations as other CDM reform options. If credits are granted to governments, ways would also need to be found to ensure that the price signal is effectively transferred to firms.

In the long run, however, to achieve ambitious global emission reductions at low cost, such approaches will need to be integrated in a unified, global carbon market, such as through the use of binding national caps with trading. By exploiting low-cost abatement opportunities in developing countries, both sectoral caps and sectoral crediting mechanisms have the potential to lower the cost of achieving a given global emissions target. If appropriately designed, they can also curb leakage and the competitiveness and output losses of EIIs in developed countries. Even so, both approaches would need to be ambitious in order to be environmentally effective. Other sectoral initiatives, such as voluntary, technology-oriented approaches can help diffuse cleaner technologies, but are unlikely to provide sufficient emission reduction incentives to individual firms as they put no explicit opportunity cost on carbon.

Regulating carbon markets

Carbon markets will naturally develop as more and more countries undertake mitigation actions. As they become large, institutions and rules will be needed to foster their development and to reduce the problems of linked systems of multiple independent and varied cap-and-trade schemes:

- An *ad hoc* framework may fail to reduce global emissions sufficiently. This environmental risk will ultimately have to be addressed through agreement on longer-term targets. Centralised institutions created to implement the UNFCCC and the Kyoto Protocol have a key role to play in building consensus.
- Compliance mechanisms at the national or regional level will also be needed. For example: i) a system of performance bonds under which governments would put some of their own bonds before the start of a compliance period into the hands of a compliance committee, which would then have the right to sell those bonds in the market in the event of compliance failure; or ii) a system of buyer liability, under which buyers would be liable for the poor quality of the permits or offsets they hold while, as a result, sellers would also face costs in the form of price discounts on future sales. This system ultimately rests on the willingness of (net) buying countries to enforce penalties on their domestic emitters, and would also require an independent international institution to assess permit and offset quality.
- The financial market institutions in charge of monitoring and regulating these markets need to be clearly identified. If inadequately regulated, the development of carbon derivative markets could become a source of financial instability. Unlike in other commodity markets, a majority of regulated firms will tend to hedge against the (one-sided) risk of carbon price increases. Therefore, financial traders will have to take the reverse position, bearing some of the net risk and playing a major role in the development of derivative markets. At the same time, one open issue is whether existing limits on the size of short positions in spot and derivative commodity

markets should also be set in emission permit markets, in order to limit the risk of sudden and/or unwarranted carbon price fluctuations. The creation of a working group of regulators could facilitate exchange of information about regulations, risks and harmonisation needs.

- Liquid spot markets and credible commitments on future emission levels or mitigation policies can foster the development of derivative markets, and lower the cost of insurance against carbon price uncertainty. Market liquidity risks could be limited by regular spot sales of permits that could be banked between compliance periods. Releasing longer-dated permits could signal the strength of government commitment and build a political constituency to support the continuation of mitigation action. However, it could also fragment the market and should, therefore, be only considered if the credibility of the scheme cannot be established otherwise.
- With a large proportion of transactions taking place in over-the-counter markets, the counterparty risk in carbon markets could become significant. Options to address this include expanding access to clearing houses and exchange trading, or specifying penalties for performance failures in contracts. If delivery failures were nevertheless to develop, they might reflect imbalances between supply and demand, which could be addressed though temporary lending of allowances by governments. More broadly, limiting the uncertainty around long-term commitments and the associated supply and demand for permits would also contain this risk.

How can the cost of abatement be lowered through technology policies?

Speeding up the emergence and deployment of low-carbon technologies will ultimately require increases in – and reallocation of – the financial resources channelled into energy-related R&D. However, average public energy-related R&D expenditure has declined dramatically across the OECD.

The impact of technological development on mitigation costs hinges crucially on the nature of R&D. When R&D leads to only minor improvements in energy efficiency, impacts on mitigation costs are only modest, especially under less stringent concentration targets which provide a lower stimulus to innovation. This reflects the declining marginal returns to R&D and low-carbon technology deployment, and the current availability of low-carbon options in the electricity sector (such as nuclear and, soon, carbon capture and storage). By contrast, if R&D were to lead to major new technologies – especially in transport and the non-electricity sector more broadly, where marginal abatement costs are higher – future mitigation costs could fall dramatically, by as much as 50% in 2050.

These issues are explored in Chapter 5 and the main conclusions are as follows:

- Pricing GHG emissions – including removing implicit emission subsidies such as fossil fuel energy subsidies – would increase the expected returns from R&D in low-carbon technologies. Future increases in carbon prices will have powerful effects on R&D spending and clean technology diffusion. For instance, setting a world carbon price path to stabilise overall GHG concentration at about 550 ppm CO_2eq in 2050 is estimated to quadruple energy R&D expenditures and investments in installing renewable power generation. Future carbon price expectations – and, therefore, climate policy credibility – are also crucial. R&D investment will be much higher under more stringent long-run concentration objectives, because these reflect higher expected future price increases.
- Specific policies aimed at boosting climate-friendly R&D may be needed in addition to carbon pricing for major breakthroughs in low-carbon technologies to occur. Carbon pricing does not

address the large market failures undermining R&D in climate mitigation, such as incompatibility with existing infrastructure and weak intellectual property rights protection. Possible policies could include rewarding innovation through the use of "innovation prizes", and/or establishing a global fund for helping with technology transfers and rewarding innovations, *e.g.* by buying out the associated patents. A global fund to support R&D and/or low-carbon technology deployment could further reduce mitigation costs, in particular if it is a complement to pricing carbon. However, as indicated above, there is a risk that public support for installing existing technologies will lock-in potentially inefficient technologies for years to come.

- Relying on R&D policy *alone* (in the absence of a carbon price) would not be enough to reduce emissions sufficiently. Model simulations indicate that even under very large increases in spending and very high returns to R&D, CO_2 concentration would still rise continuously, reaching over 650 ppm by the end of the century, with overall GHG concentrations reaching more than 750 ppm CO_2eq.

How big are the regional incentives to participate in global mitigation action?

Ambitious mitigation action at the world level will require a coalition of countries to be built that is, i) environmentally effective (*i.e.* that can, in principle, achieve ambitious world targets even if non-participating countries take no mitigation action); ii) economically feasible (*i.e.* that can meet the target without inducing excessive mitigation costs); iii) delivers a net benefit to its member countries as a whole; and iv) provides each member country with sufficient incentives to participate. In Chapter 6, modeling analysis is used, first to identify the minimal size of a coalition for achieving a global GHG concentration target, and then to study the incentives for the main emitting regions to participate in the coalition. The main results are:

- Ambitious mitigation action would have net global benefits. This is the case even though the analysis does not include the large likely co-benefits from mitigation action (the positive implications of mitigation policies on other policy domains such as for instance, the reduction in local air pollution and its impact for human health, and the improvement of energy security and of biodiversity).
- Given the current emissions growth of a number of developing regions, achieving an overall GHG concentration target equal to (or below) 550 ppm CO_2eq will require significant action by all developed countries, as well as by China and India, by 2050. The coalition would also need to expand to the entire world (with the possible exception of Africa) by 2100. Smaller coalitions would not achieve that target.
- From an economic perspective, ensuring incentives for all emitting regions to participate in action will be challenging, because most of them are found to gain less individually from participating than from staying outside and benefiting from the abatement efforts of others ("free riding"). This is especially the case for countries where the mitigation costs from a world carbon price are relatively high and/or the expected damages from climate change are relatively low (Russia and other carbon-intensive, fossil fuel producing Eastern-European economies, Middle-Eastern countries and China).
- One powerful way to broaden country participation is through international financial transfers or other support (including financing for mitigation, R&D, and climate change adaptation, as well as through technology transfers and international trade policies). However, even with international transfers, it will be difficult to convince countries who gain the least to participate, while ensuring that nobody else incurs net losses. In order for the incentives to free ride to be

broadly overcome, it may therefore be necessary that a set of key regions be willing to accept relatively minor losses.

- In a situation where national emission caps were to be adopted by all participants, financial incentives to free-ride could be reduced through the allocation or negotiation of emission reduction commitments. For instance, compared with a world carbon tax (or a full permit auctioning) scenario, developing countries could gain significantly by 2050 from allocation rules under which their emission rights cover their business-as-usual emissions ("BAU" rule), or else are inversely related to their contribution to past cumulative emissions ("historical responsibility" rule). Developing countries would also usually benefit from rules based on population size ("per capita" rule) or GDP per capita ("ability to pay" rule), albeit to a somewhat lesser extent. All four rules – in particular the former two – would impose significant costs on developed countries, although these vary widely from country to country. Allocating emission rights across countries in a way that separates where the action occurs from who pays for it could help to secure participation of all major emitters. This would also help to ensure that abatement takes place wherever it is cheapest.

How to build political support for action?

In the lead up to the UNFCCC conference in Copenhagen at the end of 2009, several countries and the European Union have adopted, declared or suggested emission reduction targets for 2020. These targets, as well as the main instruments used currently to limit GHG emissions are reviewed in Chapter 7. Assuming that the more ambitious targets are implemented in a context of fully harmonised emissions trading schemes, they would together imply a 14% reduction of emissions in Annex I countries by 2020 from 1990 levels (including emission reductions through offsets in developing countries). Given projected growth in emissions in non-Annex I countries, world emissions in 2020 would still rise by more than 20% above their 2005 levels (compared to +35% in the BAU projection).

The declared targets and actions are therefore insufficient to put emissions onto a pathway that could keep temperature increases within 2°C above pre-industrial level, which is the objective recently supported by major developing and developed countries. And, even though ambitious stabilisation targets might still be achievable, they might imply far more significant efforts after 2020, at a higher cost and with a greater risk of potentially irreversible climate impacts. Hence, international climate policy action will need to evolve gradually to achieve more ambitious emissions reductions, including possibly through tighter targets as well as enhanced actions or commitments by developing country emitters. As also discussed in more details in Chapter 7, one way to support this evolution would be by improving international financial transfer mechanisms across countries. In addition to the allocation rules for emission rights mentioned above, such devices could include:

- International public funding to support mitigation actions in developing countries has gained prominence recently with a proliferation of multilateral funds and a number of bilateral initiatives. To enhance their effectiveness, these funds should be rationalised and targeted primarily at those emission sources and/or market imperfections not covered by other market-based financing mechanisms, and in a way to help leverage private sector investments.
- A cost-effective way to boost international deployment of clean technologies would be to remove policies that work against mitigation efforts, such as barriers to trade and foreign direct investment and weak intellectual property rights.
- Compared with technology transfers, R&D policies have received only limited attention in the international context thus far. Yet, previous analysis has found the rationale for policy

intervention to be particularly strong in this area, due to both their large potential impact on future mitigation costs and the multiple market failures undermining them. Climate-related R&D could thus be better incorporated in the portfolio of activities of existing multilateral funds.

- Adaptation financing could be increased through a mix of domestic policy reforms, such as adequate pricing of water and ecosystems, and through international and national financing for relevant local public goods, including sea walls, flood defences, and disaster relief. For least developed countries, the Adaptation Fund will be particularly important to support these investments.

Political support for action will also likely be influenced by the perceived comparability of mitigation efforts across countries. Even though a broad range of factors need to be taken into account in comparing efforts, one way to do so is by assessing the emission reductions and the associated cost of action over a range of carbon taxes applied uniformly across all Annex 1 countries. The results reported in Chapter 7 suggest that both total costs and emission reductions achieved in 2020 compared with 1990 levels for a given uniform carbon price vary substantially across countries. Put differently, the carbon price required to bring emissions back to the 1990 level would be much higher in some countries than others.

A global post-2012 international climate policy framework

Countries are currently working together to agree how they might address climate change globally after 2012, when the first commitment period of the Kyoto Protocol comes to an end. A broad framework for international action is expected to be agreed at the UNFCCC Conference in Copenhagen. The main elements of the post-2012 framework are likely to include: quantified economy-wide targets for emissions reductions by developed countries; nationally appropriate actions to reduce GHG emissions by developing countries, reflecting the principle of common but differentiated responsibilities and respective capabilities; support for GHG mitigation action in developing countries, including finance, technology and capacity development; and measures to help countries, especially the most vulnerable least developed countries, to adapt to the climate change that is already locked-in.

How can the work reported in this book inform the climate policy framework? To summarise:

- Significant and cost-effective emission reductions in a post-2012 framework will require a mix of policy instruments. A carbon price should be applied as widely as possible across the major emitting countries and sectors, starting with the removal of fossil fuel subsidies. This book discusses the instruments and approaches that can be used to gradually build such an international carbon price, as well as the financing and support that might be provided to assist developing countries in their efforts to reduce emissions. But it also describes the other policies that will also be needed, such as support for R&D and technology diffusion, or targeted standards and regulations to help address market and information barriers.

- Developed countries have acknowledged that they should take the lead in reducing emissions, and a number of them have already declared or suggested emission reduction targets. However, on their own, these will be insufficient to achieve the ambitious reductions required to achieve a pathway consistent with keeping temperature increases below 2°C.

- Developing countries will need to increase their mitigation action and reduce their reliance on external financing as their national circumstances evolve. The post-2012 international framework will need to evolve over time to reflect changes in emission sources as well as the capability of different countries to undertake mitigation action. The future framework will need to be sufficiently flexible to adjust over time to reflect changing national circumstances, sectoral developments, and the developing understanding of the science of climate change.

- To ensure the political acceptability of any agreement, it will be essential to ensure a distribution of the burden of action that addresses free-riding incentives while being perceived as fair and equitable. This may imply that support for action is prioritised to those areas where it has the largest impact on world emissions and to those that need it most.

Notes

1. More specifically, the BAU projection assumes that no further action is taken to limit emissions beyond what had been done or planned by 2005. Hence, the baseline incorporates the effect of the EU emission trading scheme and assumes that it will be sustained in the future.
2. Including the 0.5°C rise above pre-industrial levels already observed.
3. For instance, under the same scenario that stabilises GHG concentration at 550 ppm, the cost in terms of lower GDP in 2050 relative to BAU would be around 15% in major oil-exporting countries, Russia and other non-EU Eastern European countries, and nearly 10% in China, as compared to around 2% or less in the United States, the European Union and Japan.
4. One exception is the United States, where the percentage reduction in GHG emissions per capita under this scenario would be comparable to that of Russia and China (around 70-75% below the BAU reference in 2050), and significantly higher than in the European Union or Japan (around 50%).

THE ECONOMICS OF CLIMATE CHANGE MITIGATION – ISBN: 978-92-64-05606-0 – © OECD 2009

ISBN: 978-92-64-05606-0
The Economics of Climate Change Mitigation
Policies and Options for Global Action beyond 2012

Chapter 1

Greenhouse Gas Emissions and the Impact of Climate Change

This chapter describes past trends in greenhouse gas emissions, and future projections. It presents the potential consequences of climate change when no action is taken, and discusses the associated risks and uncertainties. The chapter assesses four different scenarios for stabilising greenhouse gas concentrations, and examines how differences in the stabilisation target, peaking year and level of overshooting of the target affect the costs of action. These scenarios all assume that mitigation policies are cost-effective, i.e. *that all carbon emission sources can be priced globally, to provide a benchmark for more realistic scenarios examined in later chapters.*

Key Messages

- *World greenhouse gas (GHG) emissions have roughly doubled since the early 1970s and are likely to double again over 2008-2050 if no further action is taken to reduce them. In this case, CO_2 concentrations would increase to about 525 parts per million (ppm) and overall GHG concentration to 650 ppm of CO_2 equivalent in 2050, and continue to rise thereafter, causing average temperature to increase by at least 4-6°C by 2100 and more in the following decades.*
- *Wide economic and environmental uncertainties surround the expected damage from this scenario, but very large losses cannot be ruled out, with developing countries likely to suffer the greatest damages. Given these uncertainties, an economically rational response would be to reduce global emissions to levels which ensure a "low" probability of extreme, irreversible damage from climate change.*
- *Four global scenarios for stabilising GHG concentration in the atmosphere are assessed. While these mainly differ in terms of their timeframe, most imply substantial worldwide emission cuts compared both to the situation today and the baseline level in 2050 if no new policy action is taken.*
- *The results show that if ambitious GHG cuts can be achieved in a cost-effective way through the global pricing of carbon, the economic cost (lost GDP) could be relatively modest. This is because global carbon pricing would allow emission cuts to first be made where it is least costly to do so. For instance, stabilising long-run CO_2 concentrations at about 450 ppm and overall GHG concentrations at about 550 ppm CO_2 equivalent, and allowing some modest overshooting of the target, is projected to reduce average annual world GDP growth between 2012 and 2050 by around 0.1 percentage points. This would result in world GDP being about 4% lower in 2050 than in the baseline scenario. This is despite a sharp increase in the carbon price, from less than USD 30 in 2008 to around USD 280 in 2050. The 4% GDP loss in 2050 relative to the baseline would be in a context where world GDP is projected to rise by more than 250% over the same period.*
- *This projected GDP growth would leave citizens financially better off, on average, in three or four decades than they are today. But if GHG emissions continue to accumulate in the atmosphere at current rates, the cost of reducing concentrations to an acceptable level later will be prohibitively high. Developing low-carbon technologies will also take time, and investors need a clear and credible long-term price signal now to make the appropriate investment decisions.*

Introduction

The pace of greenhouse gas emissions to the atmosphere has picked-up sharply since the mid-1990s, driven mainly by strong economic growth in developing countries. While the on-going economic crisis – and the likely contraction of world output in 2009 – can be expected to reduce global emissions somewhat, the impact on the build-up of GHG concentration is by itself likely to be only temporary. In fact, based on recent trends, and in the absence of any major climate change mitigation policy, emissions are set to nearly double by 2050 and beyond, contributing to continued global warming.

THE ECONOMICS OF CLIMATE CHANGE MITIGATION – ISBN: 978-92-64-05606-0 – © OECD 2009

This chapter explores recent trends in emissions by type of gas, by regions and by sector. It then outlines a business-as-usual (BAU) baseline scenario, against which policy scenarios aimed at achieving emission cuts can be assessed. This BAU scenario assumes that there are no new climate change policies implemented, and projects future emissions on the basis of assumptions on the long-term evolution of output growth, relative prices of fossil fuels and potential gains in energy efficiency (details in Annex 1). The chapter also briefly reviews the likely main consequences of climate change on various aspects of human well-being, especially economic activities, with some differences across major regions of the world. Different scenarios involving substantial reductions in worldwide emissions between now and 2050 are then explored. These all assume that a global price for carbon can be established. All these scenarios are assessed with the use of a global computable general equilibrium model (ENV-Linkages), which can disaggregate effects by production sectors (details in Annex 2).

1.1. Past emission trends

World GHG emissions have roughly doubled since the early 1970s, reaching about 47 gigatons CO_2 equivalent (Gt CO_2eq) in 2005 (Figure 1.1). Carbon dioxide (CO_2), methane (CH_4) and nitrous oxide (N_2O) together account for over 99% of all current anthropogenic GHG emissions, with hydro fluorocarbons (HFCs), per fluorocarbons (PFCs) and sulphur hexafluoride (SF_6) accounting for the remaining 1%. Non-CO_2 emissions include those from agriculture (rice cultivation, livestock, fertiliser use), coal and gas extraction, landfills and various chemical processes involved in the production of steel and chemical products. While the bulk of CO_2 emissions are energy-related, a substantial share (more than 20%) results from land-use changes, including deforestation, although cement production is another significant source of non energy-related CO_2 emissions.

Figure 1.1. World emission trends by gas[1]

(1970-2005)

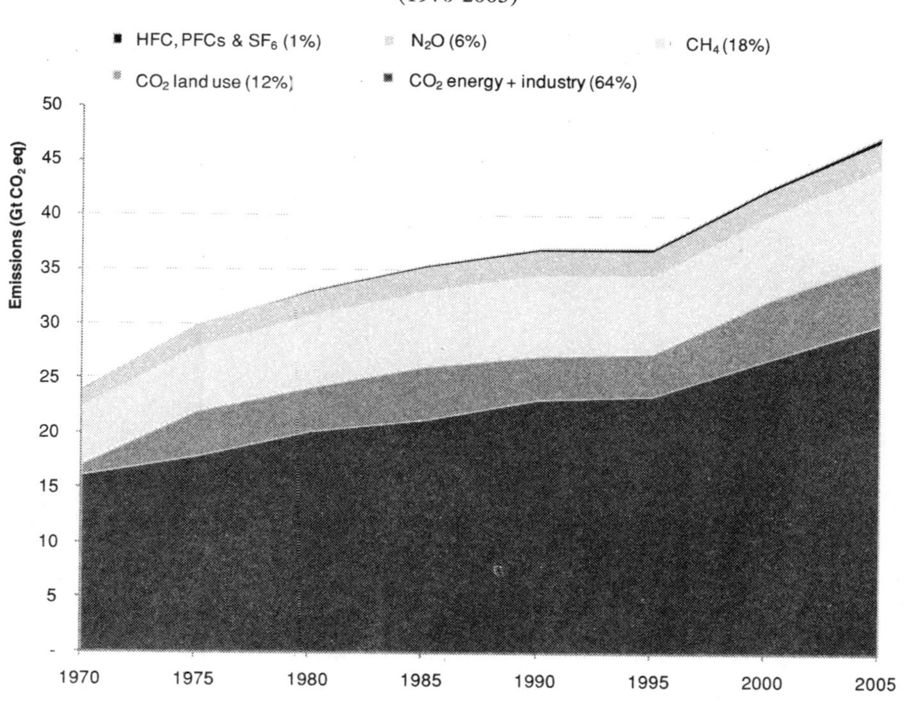

1. Number in brackets represents percentage share of total emissions in 2005.

Source: OECD Environmental Outlook to 2030 (2008b).

After two decades of slowing,[1] emissions have accelerated sharply since 1995, growing at about 2.5% a year on average between 1995 and 2005. Non-OECD countries have accounted for most of the growth in world emissions over the past four decades, including the recent acceleration (Figure 1.2). However, emissions rose in virtually all major regions between 1990 and 2005 (apart from Western Europe, where a slight decline was recorded).[2] As a result of these trends, OECD countries now contribute to just over 35% of world GHGs emissions, down from 55% in 1970. Power generation and transport have contributed most to the recent pick-up in world emissions growth, reflecting fast output increases in these sectors in developing countries (Figure 1.3).

Despite the fall in their share of world emissions, OECD countries still emit much more in per capita terms than most other world regions (Figure 1.4). Compared with China, India, oil-exporting countries and the rest of the world, emissions per capita remain almost twice as high in Japan and the European Union, three times as high in Russia and four to six times as high in Canada, Australia, New Zealand and the United States. To a large extent, this reflects the much higher level of GDP per capita in these advanced economies. A rather different picture emerges when countries and regions are ranked according to the CO_2 intensity of output (Figure 1.5), reflecting in general the greater energy efficiency and/or less carbon-intensive energy mix of more developed economies. However, there are substantial differences in the CO_2 intensity of output within these economies, with Japan and Europe having production structures that are significantly less CO_2-intensive than the United States, Canada and Australia. Lower energy efficiency in emerging countries, combined with their rising contribution to world GDP growth, has contributed to the slowing in energy – and CO_2 – efficiency gains observed at the world level in recent years.

Figure 1.2. World emission trends by country/regions[1]

(1970-2005)

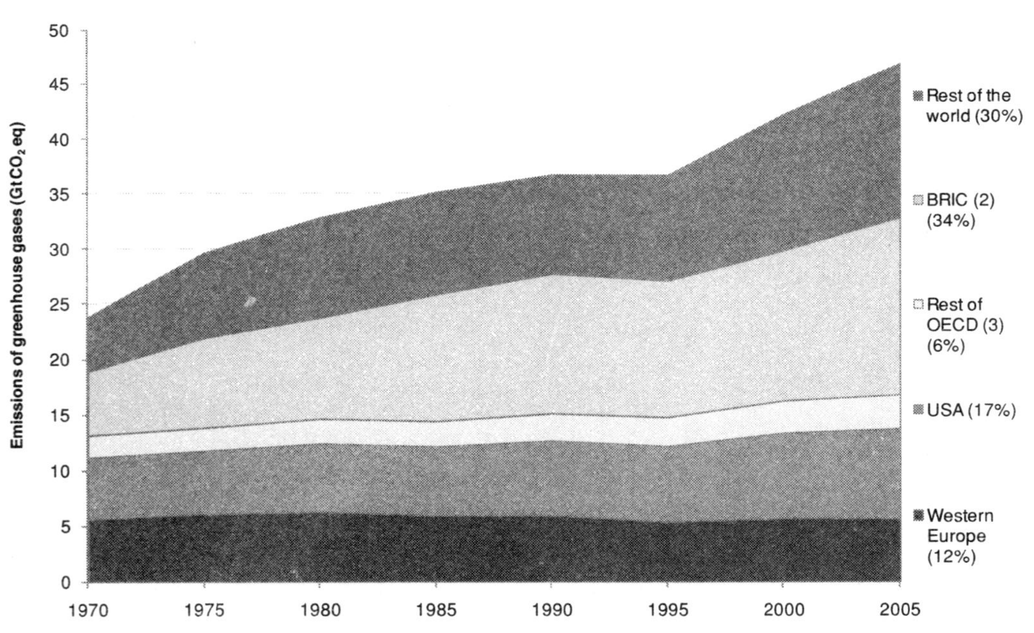

1. Including emissions from Land Use, Land-Use Change and Forestry. Number in brackets represents percentage share of total emissions in 2005.
2. Brazil, Russia, India and China.
3. Rest of OECD does not include Korea, Mexico and Turkey, which are aggregated in Rest of the World (ROW).

Source: OECD Environmental Outlook to 2030 (2008b).

Figure 1.3. World energy-related CO_2 emission trends by sector[1]

(1970-2005)

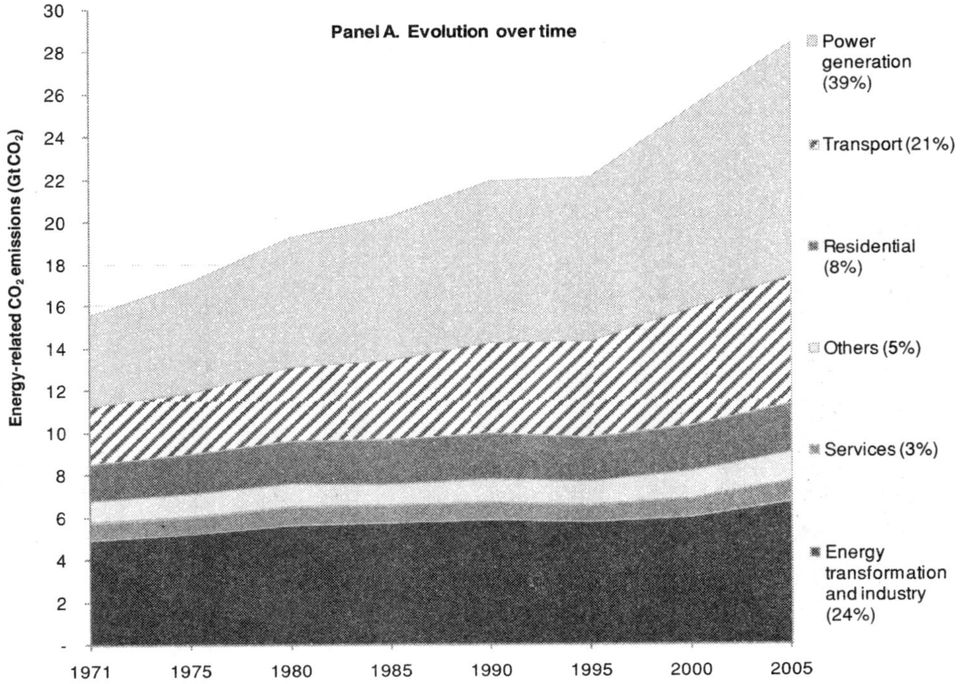

Panel A. Evolution over time
Energy-related CO_2 emissions (Gt CO_2)
30
28
26
24
22
20
18
16
14
12
10
8
6
4
2
-
1971
1975
1980
1985
1990
1995
2000
2005
Power generation (39%)
Transport (21%)
Residential (8%)
Others (5%)
Services (3%)
Energy transformation and industry (24%)

1. Number in brackets represents percentage share of total emissions in 2005.

Source: OECD Environmental Outlook to 2030 (2008b).

Figure 1.4. GHG emissions per capita, by country/region, 2005

Emissions per capita (t CO_2 eq.)
30.0
25.0
20.0
15.0
10.0
5.0
0.0
Non-CO_2
CO_2
Australia & New Zealand
United States
Canada
Russia
Japan
EU27 & EFTA
Brazil
Non-EU Eastern European countries
Oil-exporting countries
China
Rest of the World
India

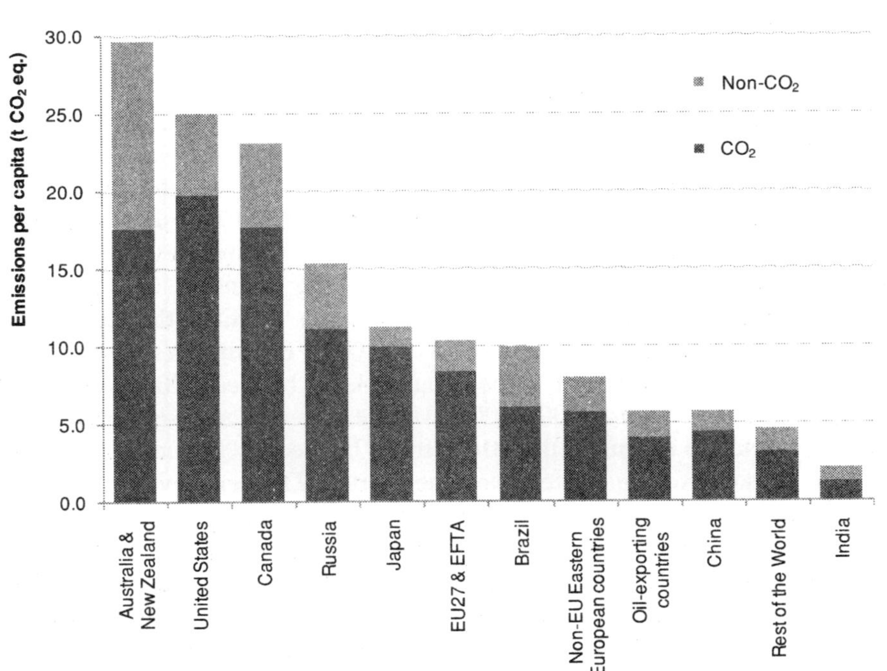

Source: IEA.

Figure 1.5. GHG emissions per unit of GDP, by country/region, 2005

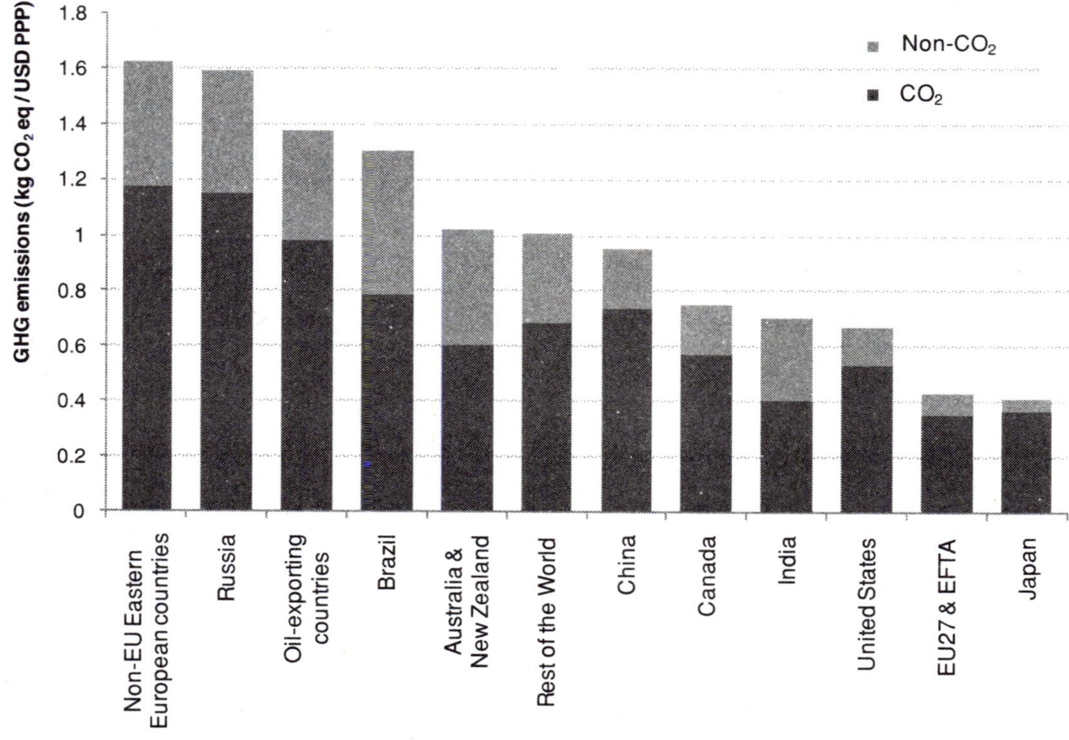

Source: IEA.

1.2. Projected emission trends

In order to assess the costs and effects of mitigation policies, it is necessary to first evaluate what emission trends would look like in the absence of any new policies. The "baseline" or BAU projection therefore assumes that no further action is taken to limit emissions beyond what had been done or planned by 2005. A profile is generated for the period 2005-2050 using a computable general equilibrium model highly disaggregated by sector (the OECD ENV-Linkages model, see Annex 2). The BAU projection also assumes that income levels in developing countries converge towards those in developed countries over the coming decades (Box 1.1 and Annex 1). Since the scenario was constructed before the world recession in 2009, average annual world GDP growth (in constant purchasing power parity – PPP – in 2005 USD) is assumed to be around 3.5% between 2006 and 2050 (Table A1.2, Annex 1). This is slightly lower than the 2000-2006 average. Overall, average world GDP per capita in constant PPP USD is expected to rise more than three times between 2006 and 2050. When expressed in constant 2005 USD at market exchange rates, baseline world GDP per capita growth up to 2030 falls roughly in the middle of the range of estimates provided in the Intergovernmental Panel on Climate Change's (IPCC) *Special Report on Emission Scenarios* (Nakicenovic *et al.* 2000). Critical drivers of projected emissions other than GDP growth include assumptions about future fossil fuel prices and energy efficiency gains (Box 1.1 and Annex 2). Finally, the BAU projection assumes that the EU Emissions Trading Scheme (EU-ETS) will be sustained in the future (see Chapter 7), with a gradual convergence in the carbon price to USD 25 per tonne of CO_2 and a stabilisation at this level (in real terms) beyond 2012.

Box 1.1 Methodology of construction of the BAU economic scenario

Assumptions about drivers of GDP

Baseline economic scenarios underlying climate change projections – such as those developed for the IPCC (Nakicenovic et al. 2000) – typically assume that there will be some gradual convergence of income levels towards those of most developed economies. A similar approach is taken here, but special emphasis is put on integrating some of the current theoretical and empirical knowledge on long-term economic growth, and making transparent assumptions about the drivers of GDP growth over the projection period (for discussion of assumptions, detailed results and data sources, see Annex 1).

As with previous OECD work (OECD, 2004), a "conditional convergence" hypothesis is incorporated into the projections. Following past research (*e.g.* Hall and Jones, 1999; Easterly and Levine, 2001), and based on a standard aggregate Cobb-Douglas production function with physical capital, human capital, labour and labour-augmenting technological progress, GDP per capita is first decomposed as follows for 2005:

$$Y_t / Pop_t = (K_t / Y_t)^{\alpha/(1-\alpha)} A_t h_t (L_t / Pop_t)$$

where Yt/Popt, Kt/Yt, At, ht, and Lt/Popt denote the level of GDP per capita (using PPP exchange rates to convert national GDPs into a common currency), the capital/output ratio, total factor productivity (TFP), human capital per worker and the employment rate, respectively. α is the capital share in aggregate output.

Based on this, long-term projections are then made for each of the four components so as to project the future path of GDP per capita:

- Long-term annual TFP growth at the "frontier", defined as the average of the "high-TFP" OECD countries, is 1.5%. The speed at which other countries converge to that frontier is assumed to tend gradually towards 2% annually.
- Where it is currently highest, the human capital of the 25-29 age group is assumed to level off based on past experience. The speed at which other countries converge to that frontier is assumed to tend gradually towards a world average between 1960 and 2000. The human capital of the working-age population is then projected by cohorts.
- Capital/output ratios in all countries gradually converge to current levels in the United States, which is implicitly assumed to be on a balanced growth path. In other words, marginal returns to capital converge across countries over the very long term in a world where international capital is mobile.
- Employment projections combine population, participation and unemployment scenarios. We have used the United Nations population projections (baseline scenario). In those OECD countries where participation is currently highest, future retirement ages are partially indexed to life expectancy. Elsewhere, participation rates gradually converge to the average in "frontier" countries. Unemployment rates converge to 5%.

This framework was applied to 76 countries, covering 90% of the world's GDP and population in 2005. For all other countries, the productivity convergence scenario to labour productivity or GDP per capita was applied instead of TFP.

The approach followed addresses recent criticisms of economic projections using market exchange rates, which form the vast majority of scenarios in the literature (Castles and Henderson, 2003a, 2003b; Henderson, 2005). This is achieved in two ways: (i) By using purchasing power parities (PPPs), not market exchange rates, to compare initial income per capita levels; (ii) by assuming faster future productivity growth in tradable than in non-tradable industries, in line with historical patterns. Reflecting this "Baumol-Balassa-Samuelson" effect, the real exchange rate of fast-growing countries typically appreciates. Therefore, the GDP PPP per worker path produced by the ENV-Linkages model combines both a volume effect (GDP growth in constant national currency) and a relative price effect (the real exchange rate appreciation), with the former being the main driver of emissions.

Box 1.1 continued on next page.

Box 1.1 Methodology of construction of the BAU economic scenario

(continued)

Assumptions about other drivers of emissions

The BAU scenario was developed on the basis of the pre-crisis surge of the international crude oil price, and therefore assumed that it would culminate at USD 100 per barrel (in real 2007 prices) in 2008, stay constant in real terms up to 2020 and increase steadily thereafter up to USD 122 per barrel in 2030. Beyond that horizon, oil exporters' crude oil supply is projected to decelerate gradually, roughly reflecting reserve constraints, and resulting in a sustained rise in the real crude oil price beyond 2030 at 1% annually between 2030 and 2050 (see Annex 2 for more details). The international price of natural gas is assumed to follow the international crude oil price up to 2030, but this link then weakens somewhat, reflecting a higher assumed long-term supply elasticity for natural gas than for oil. Coal prices are projected to rise only modestly (in real terms) beyond their recent levels. The price of steam coal is assumed to reach USD 100 per tonne in 2008, in line with the assumption of a high long-term supply elasticity. International Energy Agency (IEA) energy demand projections were used to calibrate future energy efficiency gains. These assume a gradual weakening of the relationship between economic growth and energy demand growth, especially after 2030.

Figure 1.6. Projected GHG emissions[1] by country/region[1]

(2005-2050, Gt CO_2eq)

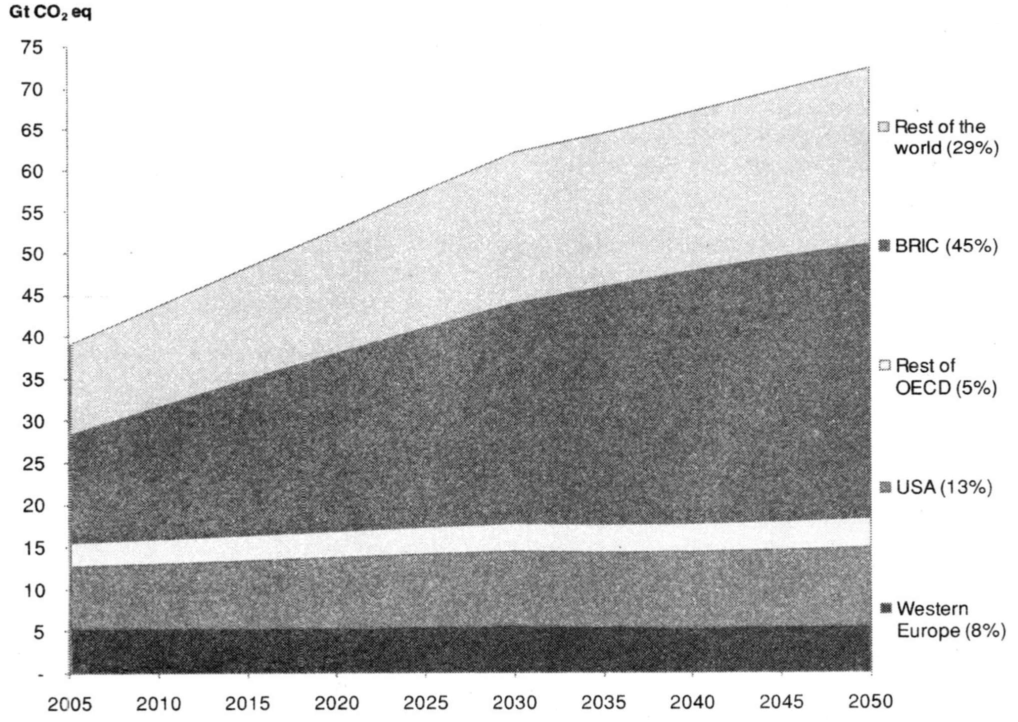

Note: Countries/regions in this figure are based on the 12-regions aggregation of the ENV-Linkages model. Korea, Mexico and Turkey are included in the Rest of the World (ROW).

1. Excluding emissions from Land Use, Land-Use Change and Forestry. Number in brackets represents percentage share of total emissions in 2050.

Source: OECD, ENV-Linkages model.

THE ECONOMICS OF CLIMATE CHANGE MITIGATION – ISBN: 978-92-64-05606-0 – © OECD 2009

According to the BAU projection, annual world GHG emissions – including non-CO_2 gases but, importantly, excluding CO_2 from land use changes – would almost double between 2005-2050, rising from 39 Gt CO_2eq to about 72 Gt CO_2eq (Figure 1.6). This would occur despite the assumption of sizeable energy efficiency gains to be achieved and, to a lesser extent, that there will be a gradual switch to an energy mix that is less intensive in GHG emissions.[3] Brazil, China, India and other developing countries would account for most of the rise in world emissions, with yearly emission growth rates typically exceeding 2% in many of these countries (Figure 1.7). The projected increase in GHG emission in developing countries is accounted for by population growth and increases in GDP per capita which, under unchanged policies, would lead to further rises in GHG emissions per head over the period (Figure 1.8). Emissions growth would be low in OECD regions, even staying flat or slightly declining in Japan and the European Union, partly reflecting demographic decline. As a result, the contribution of OECD countries to annual world emissions would shrink further to about 25% in 2050. Overall, projected world emissions growth from fossil fuel combustion falls well within the range of similar exercises reported by the IPCC.

Figure 1.7. Past and future projected emission growth rates by country/region

(Average annual growth rates)

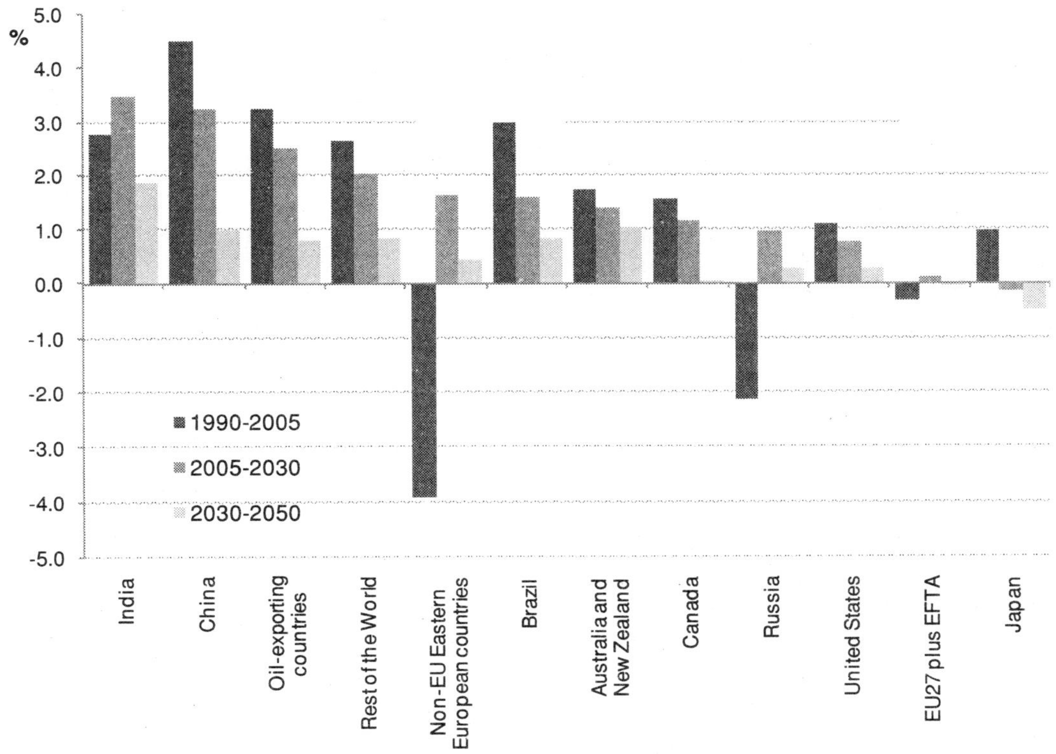

Source: IEA and OECD, ENV-Linkages model.

Figure 1.8. Sources of growth in GHG emissions per capita by country/region[1]

Business-as-usual (BAU) scenario, % change over the period 2005-2050

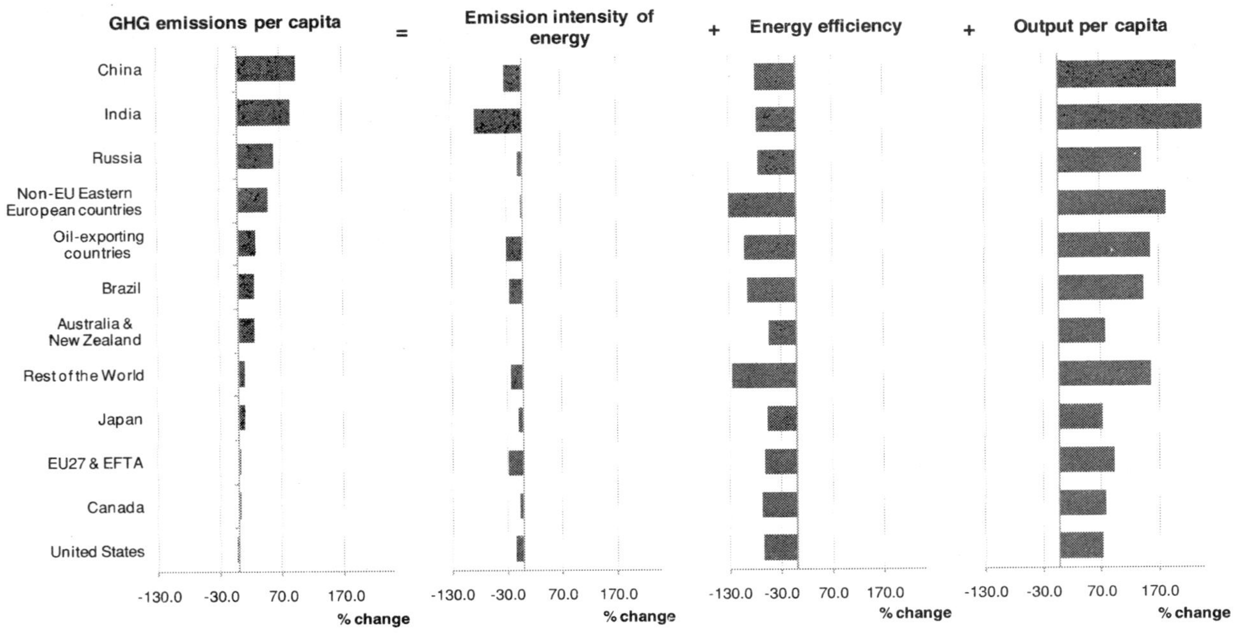

GHG emissions per capita = Emission intensity of energy + Energy efficiency + Output per capita

China
India
Russia
Non-EU Eastern European countries
Oil-exporting countries
Brazil
Australia & New Zealand
Rest of the World
Japan
EU27 & EFTA
Canada
United States

-130.0 -30.0 70.0 170.0
% change

1. Note that not all emissions are linked to the production of energy used to generate output. Hence, a change in the structure of the economy could lead to changes in GHG/energy that are not necessarily linked to a switch to lower-emission technologies or source of energy.

Source: OECD, ENV-Linkages model.

1.3. The consequences of climate change

The projected increase in emissions over the coming decades is expected to have major effects on atmospheric concentrations of GHGs and thereby the global climate. According to the baseline scenario, CO_2 concentration would rise to about 520 parts per million (ppm) in 2050, and overall GHG concentration to about 690 ppm CO_2eq. This is almost twice the concentration of the pre-industrial era (estimated to be 270 ppm), and falls roughly in the mid-range of previous studies (IPCC, 2007). The resulting rise in global mean temperature could be over 2°C by 2050, including the 0.5°C increase already observed (Figure 1.9).[4] The long-term rise in temperatures will depend on the level at which the GHG concentration stabilises. However, without any further policy action or major technological breakthroughs, GHG concentration would rise continuously and global mean temperature could increase by about 4°C by 2100 – within a wide range of possible outcomes[5] – and further beyond.

Figure 1.9. Projected temperature increases in the baseline scenario (relative to pre-industrial levels)

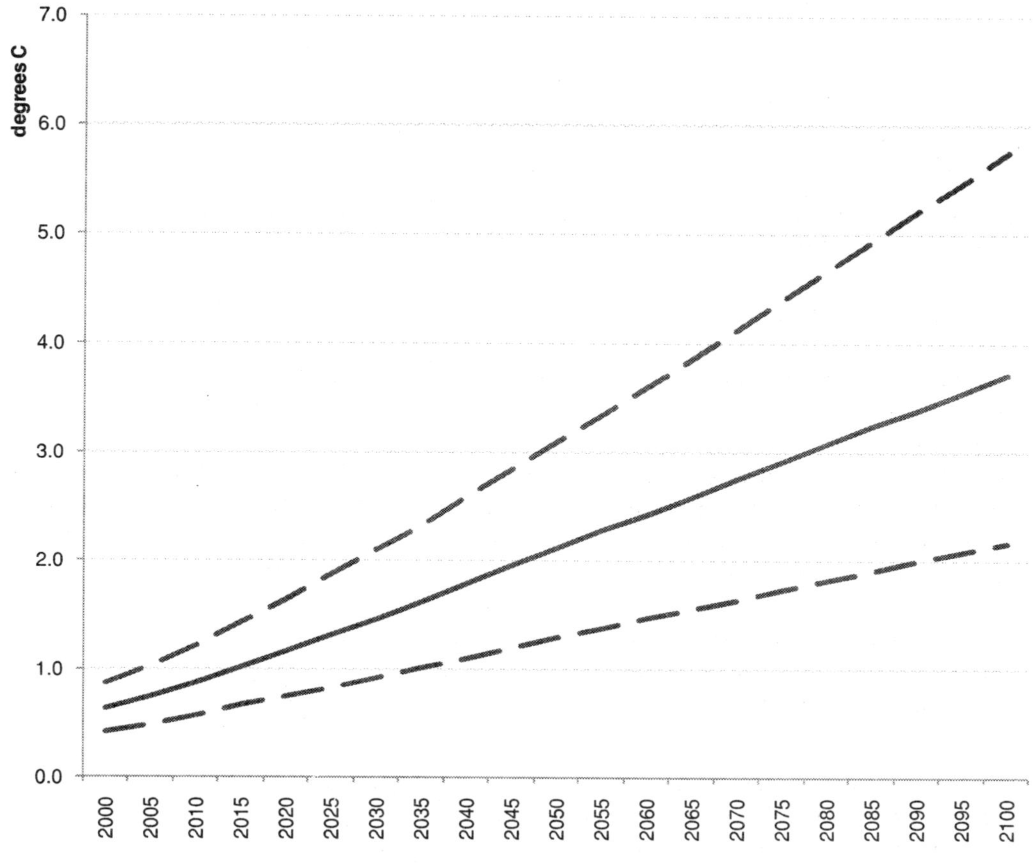

Note: lower and upper bounds corresponding to lower and upper values of the climate sensitivity parameter.

Sources: Magicc 5.3 and OECD ENV-Linkages model.

A relatively large number of studies published in the mid to late 1990s have attempted to estimate the impacts of climate change in specific areas using various methodologies. The impacts of climate change are often classified in two broad categories depending on whether they directly affect the economy such as for instance agriculture production, energy consumption, called "market" impacts or whether they more broadly affect humans and society (health, environment), then called "non-market" impacts. The typical approach of early studies combined a climate model that projects climate change from CO_2 concentrations (generally a doubling from pre-industrial level) with either an "economic" model that captures the market impacts or another type of model that incorporates non-market impacts. These studies estimate *static* and *physical* impacts of climate change on "today's world", *i.e.* on an economy with the current production and consumption structure, mainly for modest increases in temperatures, and cover a limited number of regions, often only the United States. A number of conclusions emerge from these studies (Fankhauser, 1995; Nordhaus, 1991; Tol, 2002):

- One of the most important impacts from climate change is likely to be on health. However, the extent of impacts may be understated since the estimates are largely incomplete. The number of additional deaths coming from an increase in temperatures has been estimated only for specific diseases (malaria, heat- and cold-related cardiovascular mortality, heat-related respiratory mortality). Furthermore, the indirect consequences of climate change on health through food availability, water constraints, air quality or conflicts induced by climate change are largely unknown.[6]

- Climate change can lead to a significant rise in sea level and catastrophic events with implications for migration and infrastructure. Some of these impacts could be avoided or partly offset through adaptation policies.

- Climate change would also have a negative impact on biodiversity and the ecosystem, although these effects are still partly unknown.

- The impact on agriculture is uncertain, at least for moderate increases in temperatures. The main challenges here come from the limited knowledge of the impact of climate change on precipitation. Furthermore, there are also debates about whether CO_2 fertilisation occurs, whereby the increase in CO_2 concentration in the atmosphere enhances photosynthesis rates, allowing stronger plant growth and more effective carbon fixation; this could mitigate or even offset the negative impact of climate change in the agriculture and forestry sector.[7] Adaptation could also mitigate the impact of climate change in this sector, but estimates suggest that without adaptation, climate change would lower gross agricultural production in most countries (but not in Central and Eastern Europe and in some Asian countries).

- Climate change could either increase or decrease energy consumption, water resource availability and demand depending on location, with warm regions being more negatively affected than cooler ones.

Even abstracting from uncertainty and potential catastrophic events (see below), the impacts of a mean temperature increase of 2°C or more would affect a wide range of human activities. Market-related impacts on agriculture production and, possibly, energy consumption and water resources would directly affect GDP. Non-market impacts (on health, biodiversity or migration) would affect human welfare more broadly (for details, see Jamet and Corfee-Morlot, 2009). According to current knowledge, the impact on GDP would be limited for a moderate rise in temperatures (*i.e.* a 2.5°C increase would reduce GDP by less than 3%), but could be much larger for the higher temperature increases projected beyond the 2050 horizon (Figure 1.10). Also, the economic impacts of climate change are projected to be unevenly distributed across countries. As a general rule, developing countries – especially in Africa, Southeast Asia and the Middle East – are expected to face greater damage, although the range of estimates also tends to be wider for these regions (Figure 1.11).

Figure 1.10. Global economic impacts of climate change from various studies[1]

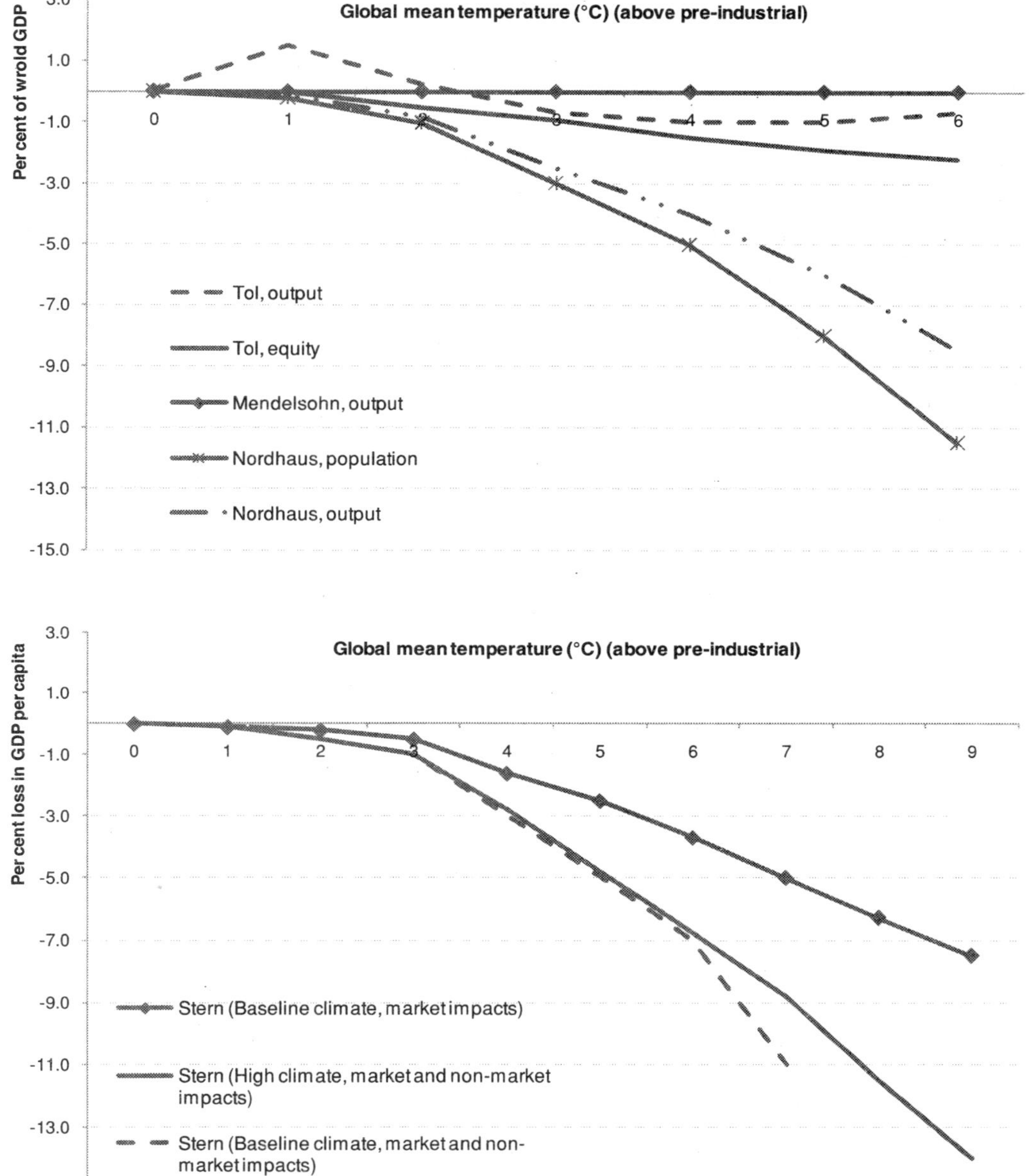

1. Estimates represent the annual GDP impact (relative to a no-climate-change scenario) of a given increase in temperature, as observed at the time when this increase in temperature is reached. They come from studies by Tol (2002), Mendelsohn (1998), Nordhaus and Boyer (2000) and Stern (2007). There are several ways to aggregate impacts across regions. In "Tol, output", impacts across regions are simply added while in "Tol, equity", they are weighted by regional per capita income. In "Nordhaus output", impacts are weighted by GDP while in "Nordhaus equity", they are weighted by population. Weighting by population or GDP per capita attributes more weight to impacts in developing countries, which are expected to be higher than in developed countries, hence increasing the estimate of global impacts. Finally, "Stern (High climate, market and non-market impacts)" includes, in addition to market and non-market impacts that are covered in the "baseline climate" scenario, the impacts of catastrophic events. "High climate" scenarios explore the impact of large increases in temperatures on GDP.

Source: IPCC (2007) and Stern (2007).

Figure 1.11. Regional economic impacts of climate change

(% of GDP)

Dispersion of long-run impacts across countries of a 2.0-2.5°C increase in temperature above its pre-industrial level

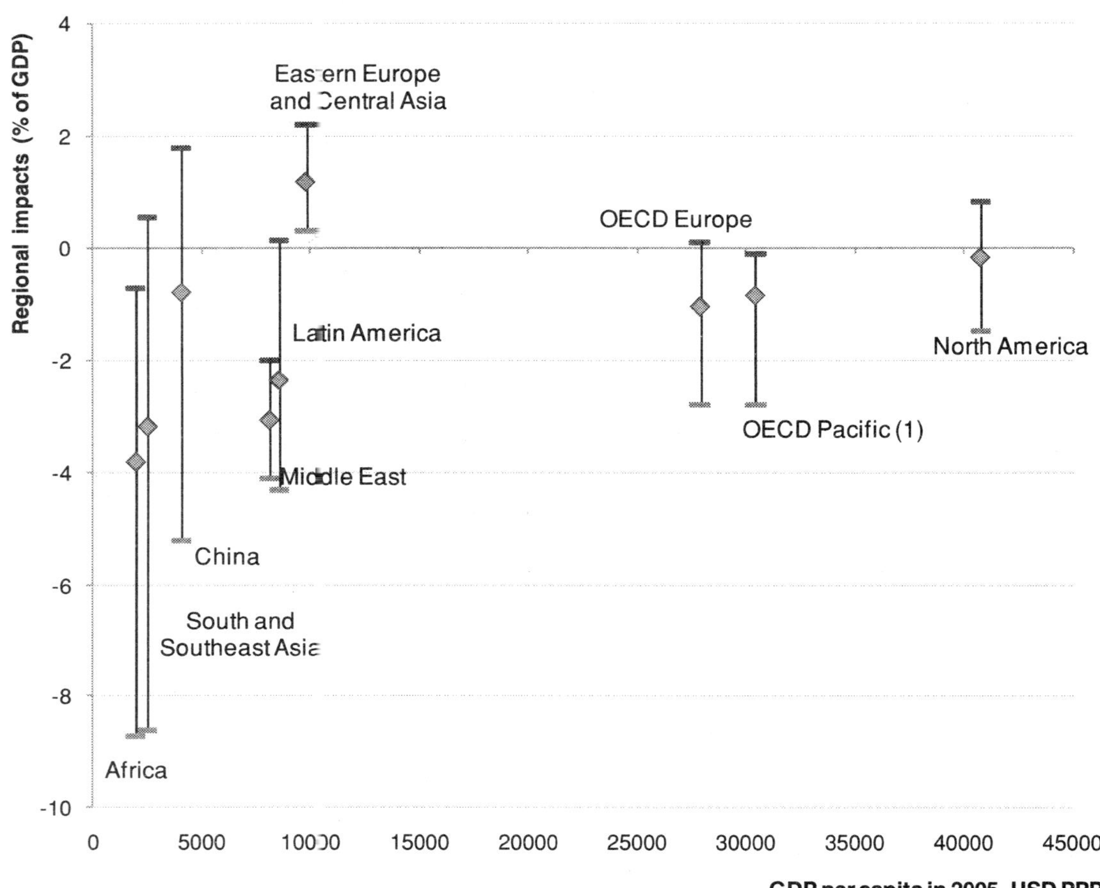

Note: Estimates come from different sources that are not entirely comparable. Those by Mendelsohn *et al.* (2000) and Nordhaus and Boyer (2000) represent the annual GDP impact (relative to a no-climate-change scenario) observed at the time when a +2.5°C increase in temperature is reached (i.e. in 2100 in both exercises). They are not entirely comparable to first-generation estimates surveyed by IPCC (1995), which are static estimates representing the annual GDP impact of a +2.5°C rise in temperature based on 1990 economic structures. The figure should be read as follows: For example, for Africa, the impacts of a warming of 2-2.5°C is expected to fall within the range of -1% to -9% of GDP according to existing estimates, with an average value of about -4% of GDP.

1. The OECD Pacific region includes Japan, which could not be featured separately due to the geographical aggregation of the underlying models. However, a few available estimates point to costs for Japan alone of -0.1 to -0.5% .

Source: Nordhaus and Boyer (2000), Mendelsohn *et al.* (2000) and IPCC (1995).

1.4. Risks and uncertainties

Wide economic and environmental uncertainties surround the expected damage from a business-as-usual scenario; but very large losses cannot be ruled out. Uncertainties include:

- *Future GHG emissions*, which in the BAU projection are driven by a number of hard-to-predict factors (*e.g.* demographic growth, productivity gains, fossil fuel prices and energy efficiency gains). In particular, labour productivity growth matters, considering both its historical variability and its important contribution to emissions growth (OECD, 2006a).[8] Other influential factors include assumptions about current and future crude oil and natural gas reserves.[9]

- *The links between emissions, GHG concentration and global temperature.* The so-called climate sensitivity, which measures the impact on temperature of a doubling of concentrations in the atmosphere, is very uncertain (Figure 1.12). A best estimate is 3°C (IPCC, 2007), but its 66% confidence interval is 2°C-4.5°C, and values above 5°C cannot be excluded (Meinshausen, 2006).

- *The physical impacts of a rise in global temperature, especially for a large increase.* Damage estimates may not fully account for adaptation, *i.e.* defensive actions to reduce the damage from climate change as it occurs, though these actions would also be costly. But existing estimates are likely to understate the effects of any global temperature increase, because they do not fully cover the non-market impacts, which are increasingly seen as likely to dominate (Watkiss and Downing, 2008; and Yohe, 2006). Furthermore, the severity of the effects is likely to increase more dramatically if temperature increases contribute to the melting of the Greenland and West Antarctic ice sheets, thereby leading to large sea level rise, and possibly altering global thermohaline circulation (*e.g.* the Gulf Stream). Such "extreme", largely irreversible events are seldom, if ever, explicitly factored into climate change damage cost estimates.

- *The valuation of physical impacts from climate change.* Economic analysis faces several methodological challenges, including the valuation of non-market physical impacts (such as valuing life loss) and the aggregation of regional effects into global impact estimates (Jamet and Corfee-Morlot, 2009).

- *The valuation of damages that are distant in time.* In this case, the choice of a rate at which society discounts future losses is contentious and is a major influence on (the present value of) damage estimates. For instance, the discounted impact of climate change in terms of per cent loss in permanent consumption can vary from 3.3% to over 10% according to whether future damages are discounted at a relatively high rate (2.8%) or a low one (1.3%) (Stern, 2007).[10]

Figure 1.12. Link between long-run GHG concentration and global temperature

Increases in temperature with concentration for the "likely" range of climate sensitivity values

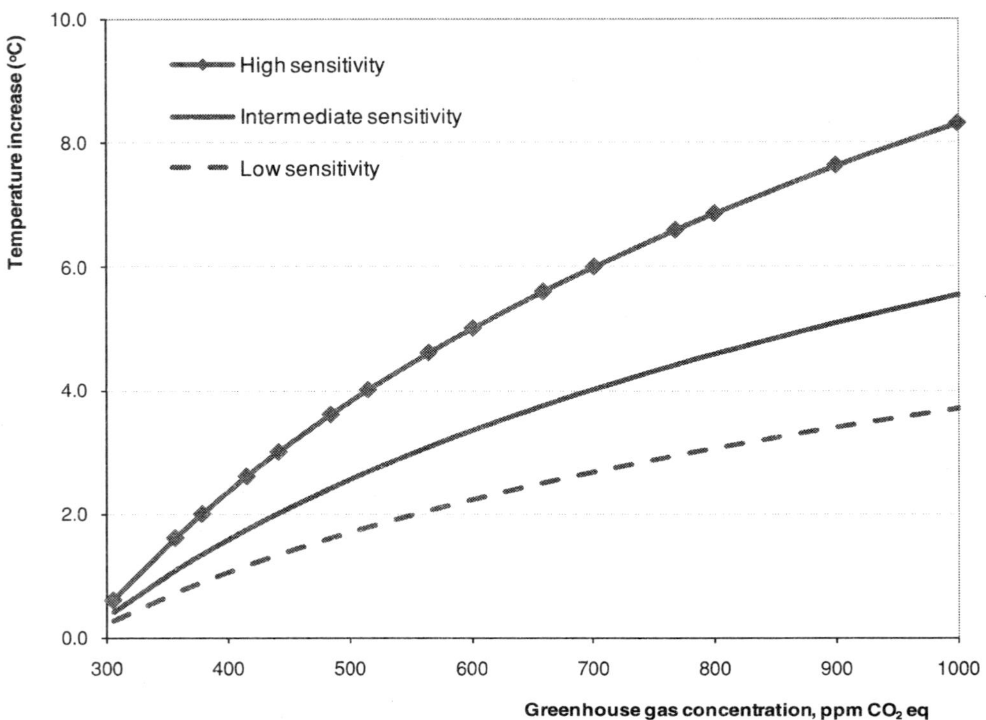

Note: The climate sensitivity parameter measures the impact on temperature of a doubling of concentration and determines the link between long-run GHG concentration and global temperature at the steady state. Because of the inertia of the system, steady-state temperatures may be reached several decades after concentration stabilisation. This parameter equals 4.5 in the "high sensitivity" scenario, 3 in the "intermediate sensitivity" scenario, and 2 in the "low sensitivity" scenario.

Source: IPCC (2007), AR4.

The high level of risks and uncertainties suggests that strong early action against climate change may partly be justified as an insurance policy against large unforeseen adverse climate developments. From this perspective, the most advisable global climate policy objective may not be to balance (marginal) damages and costs, as standard economic theory would suggest, but rather to follow a risk-based approach and set a GHG concentration objective and a timing of action consistent with a "low" probability of "dangerous" climate change (see *e.g.* Stern, 2008). Such objectives are hard to determine, however.[11] Based on existing estimates of the link between GHG concentrations and temperature increases (discussed above), a number of scenarios are next examined in which the rise in temperature is kept within the 2 to 4°C range by pricing carbon globally.

THE ECONOMICS OF CLIMATE CHANGE MITIGATION – ISBN: 978-92-64-05606-0 – © OECD 2009

1.5. Scenarios for stabilising GHG concentration

This section examines the economic costs associated with four global scenarios for stabilising GHG concentration at different levels and over different timeframes. Costs are evaluated in terms of GDP losses relative to the levels of GDP that are projected in the absence of climate change mitigation policies. It is important to note, however, that abatement also obviously generates benefits in terms of avoided climate change, and these benefits are not captured in the conventional GDP estimates reported here. Economic costs of achieving any concentration target depend on the instruments in place, as well as on their coverage in terms of countries, sectors and emission sources. In general, policies aimed at minimising the overall economic cost of mitigating climate change would have to meet four broad criteria:

i) Fully exploit all existing opportunities for low-cost GHG emission reductions. In economic terms, this would require that policies equalise marginal abatement costs across all emission sources. To this end, the set of policy instruments should be not only cost-effective *per se*, but also would have to be applied as widely as possible across countries, sectors and GHGs.

ii) Obtaining such wide coverage requires in turn that sufficient political incentives for adoption and compliance be provided, both across and within countries.

iii) Cope effectively with risks and uncertainties, *i.e.* the set of instruments should be responsive to risks and uncertainties surrounding both climate change and abatement costs.

iv) Foster an efficient level of innovation and deployment of emissions-reducing technologies in order to lower future marginal abatement costs.[12] For an environmental problem like climate change, which is of great magnitude (in terms of mitigation costs) and has a long time horizon, this criterion plays an important role in assessing alternative policy instruments.

The scenarios examined in this section assume that criteria i) to iii) are met so that marginal abatement costs are equalised and risks and uncertainties regarding climate change are effectively dealt with. This is achieved through a unique world price, which is settled for each unit of carbon emission and which encourages all emitters to adopt the cheaper abatement options that are available until marginal abatement costs across all individual emitters are equalised to the level of this carbon price. Policy instruments that put a price on carbon include emissions trading schemes (ETS) and carbon taxes although these two instruments differ in a number of respects (see Chapter 2). From this perspective, a tax instrument is intrinsically cost-effective (sometimes called the "static efficiency" property of the tax). However, when there are other market failures, a carbon price needs to be complemented by other policy instruments (see Chapter 2). Although highly stylised, scenarios which put a world price on GHG emissions are useful benchmarks, as they provide lower bound estimates of aggregate emission reduction costs.[13] It is important to note that these scenarios should be considered as intellectual experiments aimed at providing a cost effective benchmark against which to assess the more realistic policy scenarios analysed in later chapters.

Illustrative simulations were therefore run with the ENV-Linkages model assuming that a world carbon tax (or a set of harmonised domestic taxes) is applied to all countries, industries and GHGs. Ignoring transaction costs and uncertainties, this world carbon tax policy is equivalent to an ETS with full permit auctioning. Four such cost-effective scenarios were considered (Figure 1.13):[14]

- **Scenario A**: Long-run CO_2 concentration is stabilised at 450 ppm, and overall GHG concentration at about 550 ppm CO_2eq, with modest overshooting of the target before 2050.[15] Stabilisation of overall GHG concentration at about 550 ppm would be consistent with a temperature increase (relative to pre-industrial levels) not exceeding 3°C over the longer term.

- **Scenario B**: Long-run CO_2 concentration is stabilised at 450 ppm, and overall GHG concentration at about 550 ppm CO_2eq, allowing for significantly higher overshooting of the target. In order to reach the same long-term target as in Scenario A, this scenario will require greater emission reductions after 2050. While scenarios A and B, as well as other emission pathways for the next decades, can be compatible with overall GHG concentration stabilisation at about 550 ppm CO_2eq sufficiently far in the future, GHG emissions will have to be reduced by at least 30% by 2050 relative to their 2005 level and ultimately to fall to about one-fourth by 2100 if such a target is to be met.
- **Scenario C**: A 50% cut in total world GHG emissions (expressed in CO_2eq) in 2050 relative to 2005 levels, starting in 2013 and phased in gradually so that world emissions peak in 2020. This illustrative scenario would be consistent with stabilisation of CO_2 concentration in the atmosphere below 450 ppm in the long run, and stabilisation of overall GHG concentration below 550 ppm CO_2eq, without any overshooting.[16]
- **Scenario D**: Long-run CO_2 concentration is stabilised at 550 ppm, and overall GHG concentration slightly above 650 ppm CO_2eq.

Figure 1.13. GHG emissions in alternative cost-effective policy scenarios

(2005-2100)

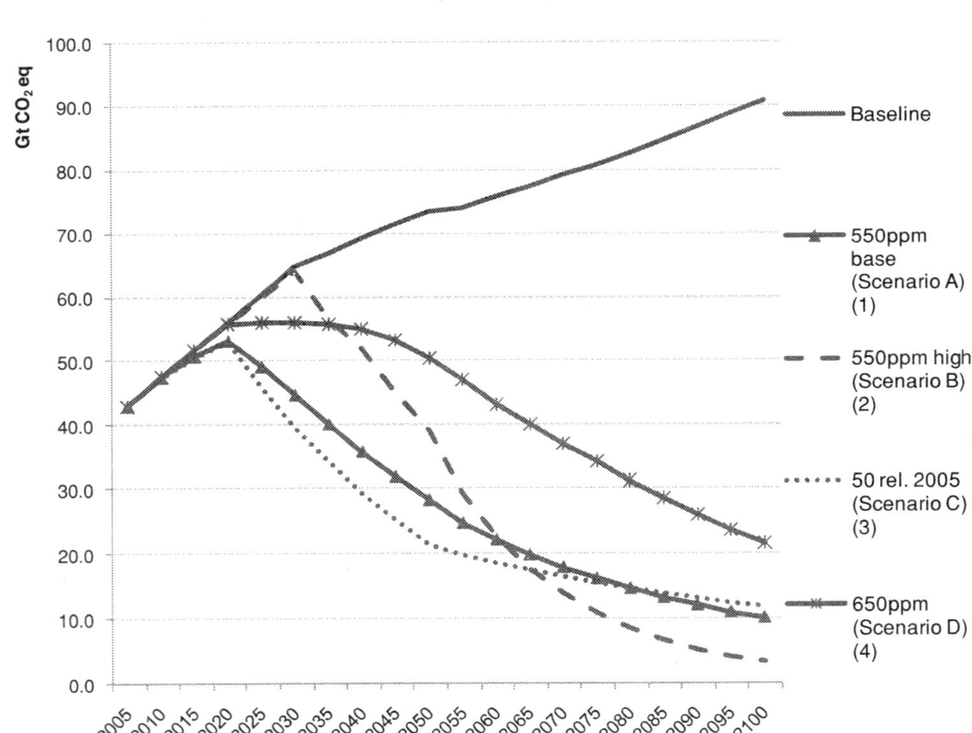

1. Stabilisation of CO_2 concentration at 450ppm, and of overall GHG concentration at about 550ppm CO_2 eq, with modest overshooting.
2. Stabilisation of CO_2 concentration at 450ppm, and of overall GHG concentration at about 550ppm CO_2 eq, with high overshooting.
3. 50% GHG emission cut in 2050 with respect to 2005 levels.
4. Stabilisation of CO_2 concentration at 550ppm, and of overall GHG concentration at about 650ppm CO_2 eq, without overshooting.

Source: OECD, ENV-Linkages model.

It should be stressed a concentration level of 550 ppm CO_2eq was chosen as the most stringent potential target, but this choice is solely for illustrative purposes and is not intended as an endorsement of such target. While this level is broadly viewed as the minimum required to limit the damage from climate change, more ambitious targets are feasible and indeed have recently been supported by the international community.

1.5.1. Emissions under cost effective policy scenarios

As cheaper abatement opportunities are exhausted, the world economy faces sharply rising marginal abatement costs and any further abatement would have to be achieved by reducing overall energy intensity, as in Scenario A. Indeed, the contribution from energy efficiency to the overall emission reduction in 2050 is much higher in Scenario A than in Scenario D, where reductions are primarily achieved through cleaner sources of energy (Table 1.1).

Table 1.1. Decomposition of world GHG emission trends under alternative scenarios[1]

(index 2005 = 100)

	2025			2050		
	Baseline	650ppm (Scenario D)[3]	550ppm-base (Scenario A)[4]	Baseline	650ppm (Scenario D)[3]	550ppm-base (Scenario A)[4]
GHG emissions	146.9	135.4	117.8	184.3	124.7	68.6
Population	122.9	122.9	122.9	140.9	140.9	140.9
GDP/Population	154.3	154.2	153.8	278.2	276.5	267.3
Energy[2]/GDP	67.5	66.5	63.6	33.9	29.7	18.7
GHG/Energy[2]	114.7	107.4	98.0	138.6	107.6	97.2

1. The amount of GHG emissions at any point in time can be decomposed as the product of population, GDP per capita, energy intensity and the GHG intensity of energy. This is commonly known as the so-called "Kaya identity".
2. Primary energy demand.
3. Stabilisation of CO_2 concentration at 550ppm, and of overall GHG concentration at about 650ppm CO_2eq, without overshooting.
4. Stabilisation of CO_2 concentration at 450ppm, and of overall GHG concentration at about 550ppm CO_2eq, with modest overshooting.

Source: OECD, ENV-Linkages model.

Scenario A would imply a lower level of emissions per capita in all major countries/regions in 2050 compared to 2005 (Figure 1.14). This should be compared with the BAU scenario shown earlier (Figure 1.8). In the context of the ENV-Linkages model, the upward pressures on GHG emissions from the substantial rise in GDP per capita over the period 2005-2050 (especially in developing countries) is more than offset by gains in energy efficiency and, to a lesser extent, a switch to less carbon intensive sources of energy. For instance, a look at electricity generation by sources of energy (Figure 1.15) shows that in Scenario A the share of fossil fuels in overall electricity production falls from 67% in 2005 to 30% in 2050 to the advantage of various sources of renewable energies. The total amount of energy consumed in 2050 under this scenario is much lower than in the BAU baseline, which again underscores the major contribution from higher energy efficiency in emission reductions. As regards the emission intensity of energy, it should be stressed that GHG emissions are not necessarily all linked to energy production. Therefore, the contribution from the emission intensity of energy to the reduction in GHG per capita observed in Figure 1.14 may also reflect a change in the structure of the economy towards sectors that produce fewer greenhouse gases, and not only a switch to less carbon intensive sources of energy.

Figure 1.14. Source of growth in GHG emissions per capita by country/region[1]

Scenario A, % change over the period 2005-2050

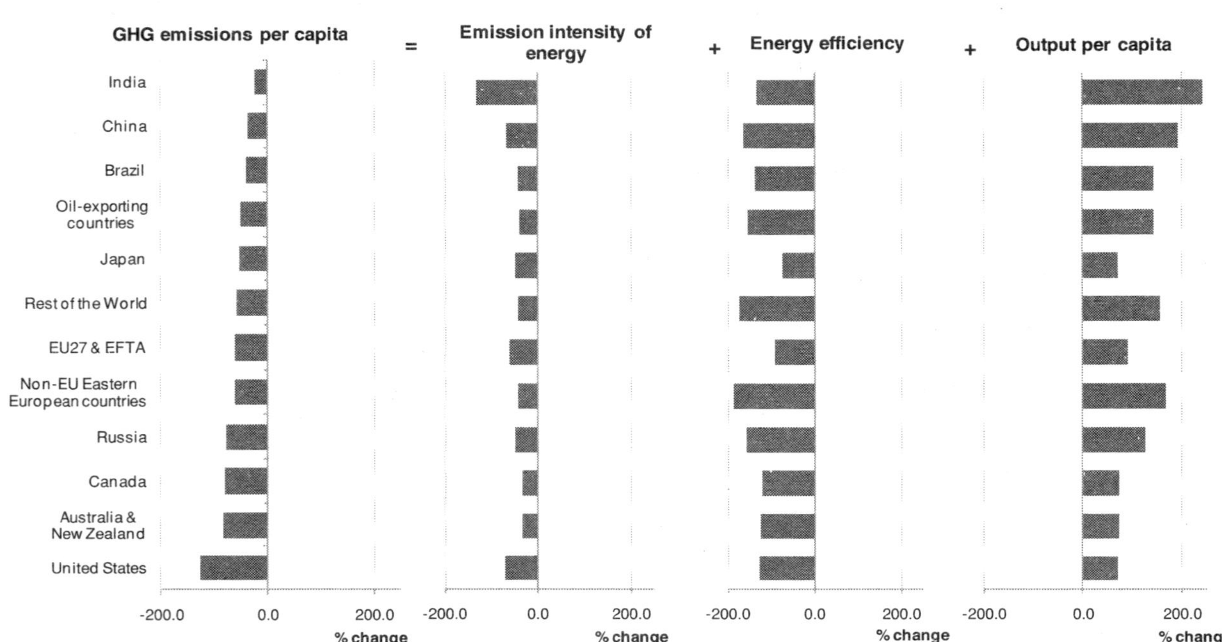

1. Note that not all emissions are linked to the production of energy used to generate output. Hence, a change in the structure of the economy could lead to changes in GHG/energy that are not necessarily linked to a switch to lower-emission technologies or source of energy.

Source: OECD, ENV-Linkages model.

1.5.2. The cost of stabilising the climate

Scenario A is estimated to lower world GDP by 3.9% in 2050 compared to the BAU scenario (Table 1.2, "550 ppm-base" Scenario A). Only small costs are incurred as long as emission cuts remain modest, *i.e.* before 2025 in practice (Figure 1.16). However, GDP costs are projected to rise exponentially over time, reflecting the combination of higher emission reductions and rising marginal abatement costs as low cost abatement opportunities are exhausted. A higher degree of overshooting would reduce costs by postponing more of the emission cuts required until after 2050 (Table 1.2, Scenario B). However, this would come at the price of higher emission cuts and thereby higher costs after 2050, and the projected temperature increase would be both larger and faster, with increased risks of irreversible events.[17] By contrast, avoiding overshooting would reduce environmental risks but would raise the cost of action. For example, a 50% emission cut by 2050 from 2005 levels (Scenario C) is found to reduce world GDP by about 7% in 2050, lowering average annual world GDP growth projected over 2012-2050 from about 3.5% in the absence of mitigation policies to 3.3% when policies are implemented.

Figure 1.15. Electricity generation by source of energy

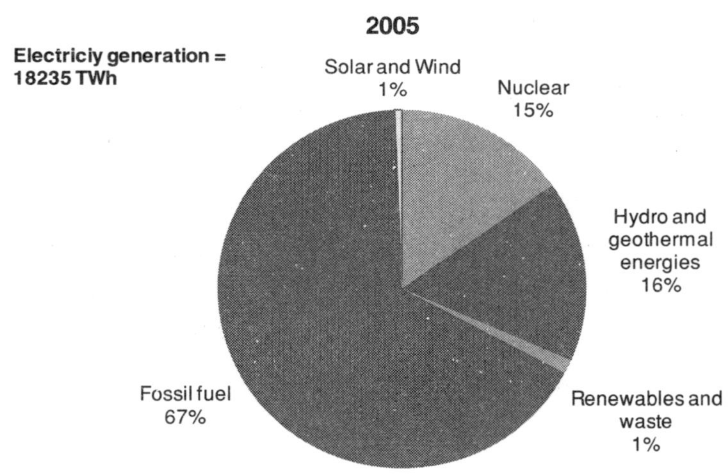

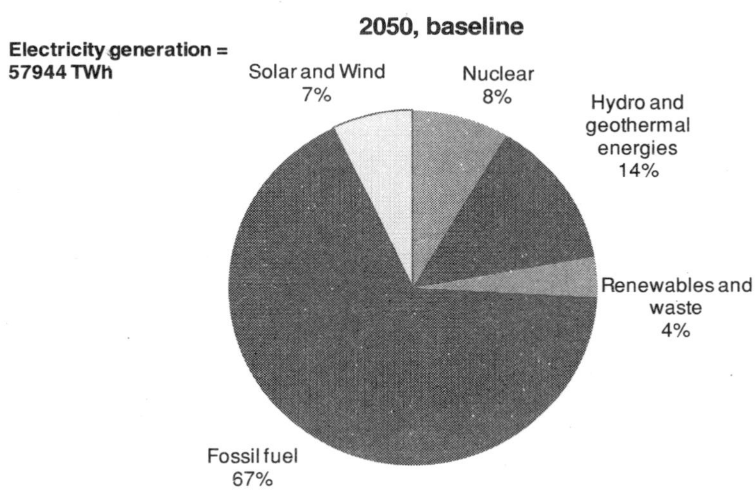

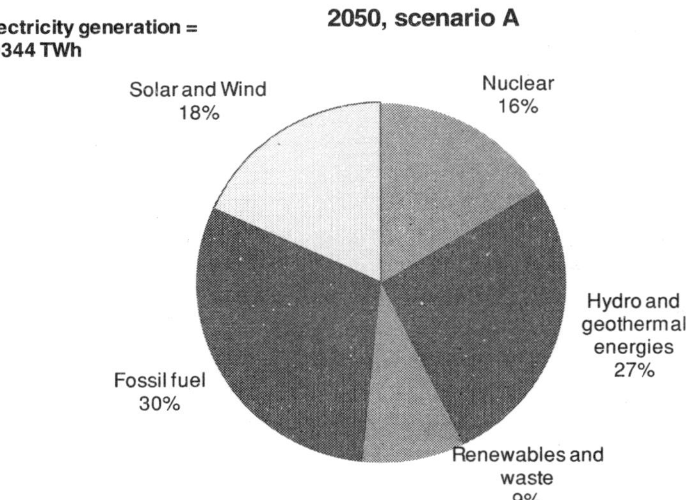

Source: OECD, ENV-Linkages model.

Table 1.2. Economic costs and environmental impacts of alternative cost-effective policy scenarios

Scenario	Peaking year	Change in total emissions in 2050 relative to 2005[1]		Economic costs				Maximum CO_2 concentration over 2012-2150	
	Year	All greenhouse gases	CO_2	Marginal abatement costs in 2050 (2005 USD per ton of CO_2)	GDP loss in 2050 (%)	Average GDP loss 2012-2050 (%)	Average annual GDP growth rate loss 2012-2050 (percentage points)	Year	Level (ppm)
A) 550ppm-base: Stabilisation of CO_2 concentration at 450ppm, and of overall GHG concentration at about 550ppm CO_2 eq, with modest overshooting	2020	-34%	-36%	282	-3.9	-1.7	-0.11	2065	461
B) 550ppm-high: Stabilisation of CO_2 concentration at 450ppm, and of overall GHG concentration at about 550ppm CO_2 eq, with high overshooting	2030	-9%	-6%	145	-1.7	-0.5	-0.05	2060	495
C) 50 rel. to 2005: Less 50% in 2050 relative to 2005	2020	-50%	-52%	531	-6.9	-3.2	-0.19	2050	447
D) 650ppm: Stabilisation of CO_2 concentration at 550ppm, and of overall GHG concentration at about 650ppm CO_2 eq, without overshooting	2030	17%	22%	40	-0.6	-0.2	-0.02	2130	548

1. Including emissions from Land Use, Land-Use Change and Forestry. These are exogenous and similar across all policy scenarios, as they are not yet incorporated in the OECD ENV-Linkages model.

Source: OECD, ENV-Linkages model.

Figure 1.16. Time profile of economic costs and GHG emissions price under the '550ppm-base' GHG concentration scenario (Scenario A)

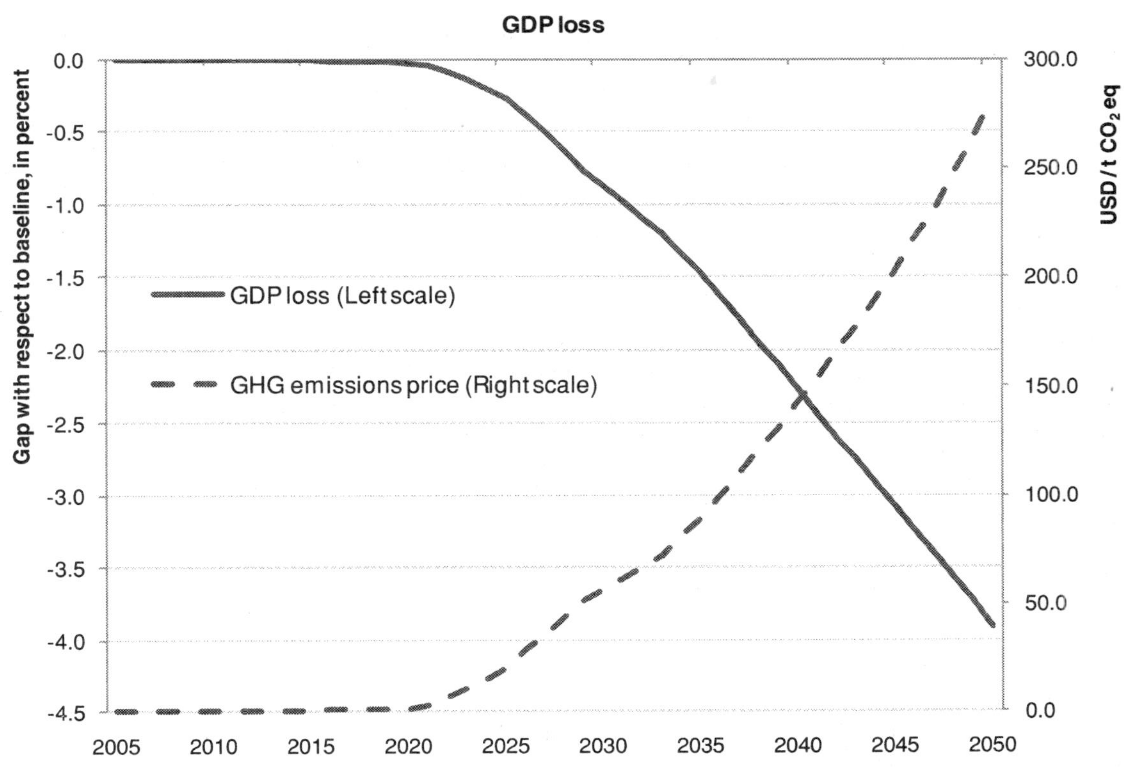

Source: OECD, ENV-Linkages model.

Emission reduction costs are also estimated to vary disproportionately with the stringency of the target. Relatively modest mitigation objectives can be achieved at a low economic cost by taking advantage of the flexibility provided by substitutions across GHGs, fuels and industries. For instance, the cost of stabilising CO_2 concentration at 550 ppm, and overall GHG concentration at about 650 ppm CO_2eq, without overshooting, is estimated to be just 0.6 % of GDP in 2050 (Table 1.2, Scenario D). However, the obvious counterpart of the lower cost of less stringent targets is the risk of higher environmental damage. These cost estimates are broadly in line with other studies (Box 1.2).

The estimates also include the potential cost savings from recycling revenues from pricing carbon emissions. Depending on the policy instrument used these revenues originate either from carbon taxes or the auctioning of permits for carbon emissions (see Chapter 2). Large fiscal revenues are expected in the more stringent emission reduction scenarios, reaching for instance 3% of GDP for the OECD and 6% of GDP for the world as a whole in 2050 in Scenario A. If these revenues were used to lower taxes whose negative effects on the supply of labour and/or capital *are greater* than those from GHG taxes or permit sales,[18] mitigation costs could fall below these estimates. By contrast, if permits were allocated free of charge instead of being auctioned, mitigation costs could exceed the estimates reported here because they do not factor in the possible detrimental effects on labour supply of the higher consumption prices that firms would charge to recoup abatement costs (which would be equivalent to the effects of a consumption tax hike).[19] These considerations underline the importance of using policy instruments which raise revenues when addressing climate change.

Box 1.2. Comparison of ENV-Linkages mitigation cost estimates with other recent studies

Of the key parameter values and modelling assumptions that drive mitigation cost estimates, emissions growth in the BAU scenario is critical. For instance, achieving a 50% cut in all GHG emissions in 2050 from 2005 levels is in fact equivalent to a reduction relative to the BAU baseline 2050 levels by over 70% (Figure 1.13). Such a large cut puts the world economy on the steeper part of the "global" marginal abatement cost curve, thereby raising costs. Due to a number of recent developments, as well as changes in the modeling framework and assumptions, some of the cost estimates of the more stringent mitigation scenarios reported in this chapter are higher than those noted in the *OECD Environmental Outlook to 2030* (OECD, 2008b). This reflects a variety of factors, including higher projected world GDP and thereby higher underlying energy demand growth, upward revisions of fossil fuel price assumptions, and delayed action, assumed to start in 2013 instead of 2008. Overall, however, these cost estimates fall approximately in the middle of the range of recent estimates. A comparison of 21 models of long-term 550 ppm CO_2 only concentration stabilisation scenarios yields average world GDP costs and marginal abatement costs (*i.e.* carbon prices) in 2050 of about 1.4% and USD 43 per ton of CO_2 (in 2000 USD), respectively (de la Chesnaye and Weyant, 2006). This is roughly in line with the 0.6% of GDP and USD 40 (in 2005 USD) reported in Table 1.2 for Scenario D. Furthermore, a comparison of the responsiveness of emissions to carbon prices points to slightly stronger sensitivity in ENV-Linkages than in other models, implying slightly lower marginal abatement costs (Hoogwijk *et al.* 2008). Finally, estimates of the cost of bringing world emissions down to their 2005 level by 2040 are in line with recent International Monetary Fund simulations of such a scenario (IMF, 2008).

The costs from mitigation policies are expected to be unevenly distributed across countries. With a global carbon tax – or equivalently full auctioning of emission permits – and for any given concentration target set in a global emission mitigation agreement, countries that use carbon intensively and/or export fossil fuel (see Figure 1.5), such as Russia and the Middle East, would face the largest GDP costs (Figure 1.17).[20] In general, despite their cheaper emission abatement opportunities, non-OECD countries are affected much more than OECD countries because the level and growth of their output is more intensive in fossil fuels.

The estimated mitigation costs reported in this section in terms of GDP losses relative to the BAU scenario should be taken as a lower bound, assuming that the coverage of carbon pricing is broad and efficient. However, the conditions and instruments for such cost-effective actions may not be in place for many years to come. While the next chapter reviews the range of climate change mitigation policy instruments and their potential role in a desirable policy mix, some of the implications of this incomplete coverage – in terms of countries, sectors and/or emission sources – are examined in Chapter 3. On the other hand, a number of factors not taken into account in the simulation analysis reported above could help to reduce mitigation costs. These include: *i)* the possible removal of energy subsidies; *ii)* the eventual emergence of major new low-carbon (so-called "backstop") technologies in the future, such as carbon capture and storage on a large scale; and *iii)* the existence of forestry mitigation options. Each of these factors is examined in other parts of this book, notably in Chapter 3 (forestry), Chapter 4 (energy subsidies) and Chapter 5 (new technologies).

THE ECONOMICS OF CLIMATE CHANGE MITIGATION – ISBN: 978-92-64-05606-0 – © OECD 2009

Figure 1.17. Costs from stabilising long-run GHG concentration at 550 ppm vary across regions[1]

(% deviation from BAU baseline GDP)

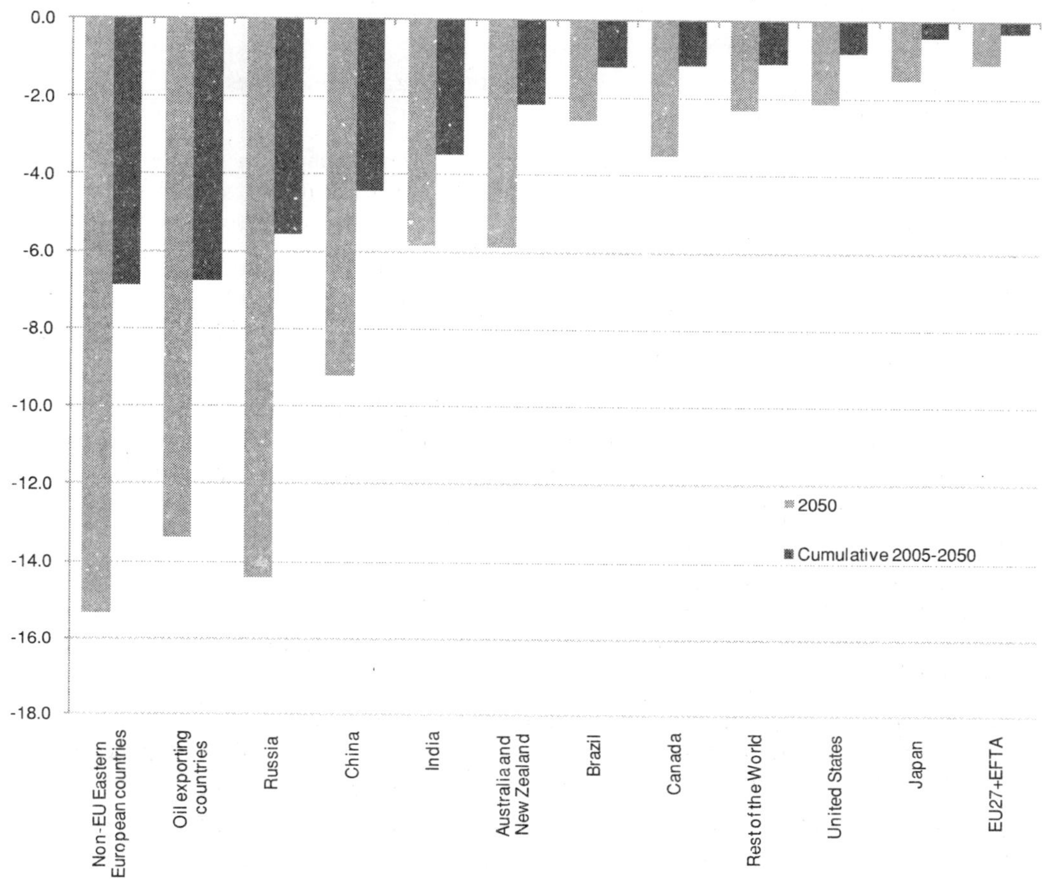

2050
Cumulative 2005-2050

0.0
-2.0
-4.0
-6.0
-8.0
-10.0
-12.0
-14.0
-16.0
-18.0

Non-EU Eastern European countries
Oil exporting countries
Russia
China
India
Australia and New Zealand
Brazil
Canada
Rest of the World
United States
Japan
EU27+EFTA

1. Scenario "550ppm-base" (Scenario A), see table 1.2. " 2050" denotes the cost as a per cent of GDP in 2050 relative to BAU baseline. "Cumulated 2005-2050" denotes the cumulated costs over 2005-2050 and represents the gap (in per cent) between the (undiscounted) sum of annual GDPs over 2005-2050 in the "550ppm-base" scenario and the corresponding sum in the BAU scenario.

Source: OECD ENV-Linkages.

Notes

1. This culminated in a temporary stabilisation in the early 1990s as GDP fell in transition economies.
2. Between 1990 and 2005, GHG emissions rose by around 15% in Japan, 18% in the United States, 26% in Canada, 29% in Australia and over 40% in the fast growing developing economies of Brazil, Russia, India, and China (BRICs).
3. The greater energy efficiency would result in a sharp slowdown in annual world emissions growth to about 0.8% over 2030-2050, down 1.7 percentage point from the 1995-2005 average.

4. The projected temperature increases mentioned in this section represent instantaneous effects at a given date. Long-term equilibrium temperature increases are larger, due to the inertia of the earth's system.

5. The 66% confidence intervals for global mean temperature increases are 1.3-3°C and 2.2-5.8°C in 2050 and 2100, respectively.

6 More recent studies also consider socio-economic development in parallel with climate change. This could be expected to limit health damage, as development should lower vulnerability to climate change by increasing provision and access to health services (see Tol and Dowlatabadi, 2001; and Tol, 2005a).

7. Reilly *et al.* (2007) find that a mean temperature increase below 3°C relative to 2000 levels would have a positive effect on agricultural production through this channel (although the negative impact of ozone on production is not considered).

8. The respective contributions of labour and capital to future economic growth are another related influence on projected emissions. If capital and energy were complements rather than substitutes in the production process, a larger contribution of capital would boost the growth of energy-intensive sectors and thereby increase emissions, all other things being equal.

9. This is because the exhaustion of these reserves is expected, *ceteris paribus*, to induce a shift towards more carbon-intensive coal. However, crude oil and natural gas reserves are not yet explicitly modelled in the current version of the ENV-Linkages model. A reserve constraint is approximated through exogenous assumptions about crude oil supply in the oil-exporting region of the model.

10. See *e.g.* the recent controversy surrounding the Stern Review, where the social discount rate used was lower than in many other studies (Dasgupta, 2007; Nordhaus, 2007; Stern, 2007). Some explain this choice as an attempt to capture extreme events indirectly (Weitzman, 2007a).

11. Climate irreversibilities and their uncertainty justify early action and stringent targets, so as to retain the possibility to cope with future climate change and its consequences (Arrow and Fisher, 1974; Henry, 1974). The unknown probability of "extreme" events further reinforces this "catastrophe insurance" motive for strong early action (Weitzman, 2007b). On the other hand, abatement costs are also widely uncertain, especially over longer horizons, and many of the investments made also entail irreversibilities. This would argue for postponing action so as to retain the option to take better informed and cheaper measures in the future (see Pindyck, 2007).

12. Innovation could also help reduce the cost of adaptation.

13. These scenarios are not entirely cost-effective since they do not include a removal of energy subsidies, the use of R&D policy instruments, or policies to reduce emissions from land use changes, all of which should be part of a cost-effective policy mix. Furthermore, given that the current version of ENV-Linkages does not incorporate GHG emissions from land-use changes, this mitigation option is omitted in all policy scenarios.

14. In all CO_2 concentration scenarios, the percentage reduction in CO_2 emissions compared to a BAU baseline is also assumed to apply to non-CO_2 gases, expressed in CO_2 equivalent (CO_2eq) based on their global warming potential (GWP) over 100 years. Nonetheless, CO_2 and non-CO_2 gas concentrations are reported separately here, partly because of the methodological issues surrounding the GWP of each gas, which can differ significantly depending on the length of the period considered.

15. The emission pathway associated with a target is expressed in terms of future concentrations, which may vary in terms of the peak year of emissions, the degree of temporary overshooting (if any)

 THE ECONOMICS OF CLIMATE CHANGE MITIGATION – ISBN: 978-92-64-05606-0 – © OECD 2009

allowed relative to the concentration target, and the year and level at which concentrations are stabilised. Therefore, a concentration target gives more leeway to choose a pathway of emission reductions that softens the disruptive impact of mitigation on the economy. However, it may introduce some confusion in the international policy debate since the link between emissions and concentrations is uncertain.

16. Stabilising concentrations around this level beyond 2050 would mean reducing emissions by about 1% a year after 2050.

17. According to simulations using the MAGICC climate module, global temperature would rise by 1.9°C by 2070 in the "high" overshooting Scenario B, *versus* 1.6°C in the "modest" overshooting Scenario A.

18. In ENV-Linkages simulations, revenues are assumed to be redistributed to households through lump-sum transfers, although they could in fact be used to reduce other distortive taxes on labour or capital. These effects cannot thoroughly be simulated because, for instance, labour supply is fixed in ENV-Linkages. For attempts to estimate these effects, see however De Mooij (1999), Goulder (1995), Goulder *et al.* (1999), Pezzy and Park (1998). Nonetheless, it might be argued that major tax distortions could still be at least partly eliminated independently from carbon tax revenues, *e.g.* by changing the tax structure (see Johansson *et al.* 2008).

19. In fact, based on recent OECD analysis of the employment effects of tax wedges (Bassanini and Duval, 2006), and assuming that carbon pricing would affect labour supply just like any other component of the labour tax wedge, a back-of-envelope calculation suggests the additional cost of carbon pricing in terms of reduced labour supply (not captured here) could reach as much as 1 percentage point of GDP for OECD countries in 2050. Raising and recycling revenues from carbon pricing could bring this cost down to zero or even – if accompanied by an appropriate change in the tax structure – turn it into a gain.

20. Countries with large emissions from deforestation could also face high costs if these emissions were covered by a mitigation policy, but this is not reflected in this simulation.

ISBN: 978-92-64-05606-0
The Economics of Climate Change Mitigation
Policies and Options for Global Action beyond 2012

Chapter 2

The Cost-Effectiveness of Climate Change Mitigation Policy Instruments

This chapter presents analysis of the various national and international policy instruments for tackling climate change, their respective pros and cons, and how they can best be integrated into a coherent policy framework. It assesses carbon taxes, emissions trading schemes (including cap-and-trade), standards, and technology-support policies (R&D and clean technology deployment) according to three broad cost-effectiveness criteria: i) Static efficiency, i.e. *does the instrument help fully exploit existing low-cost abatement opportunities, ii) Dynamic efficiency,* i.e. *does it encourage innovation in order to lower future abatement costs? iii) Ability to cope effectively with climate and economic uncertainties. The chapter concludes with a discussion of potential complementarities and overlap across policy instruments.*

Key Messages

- *No single policy instrument will be sufficient to tackle the wide range of sources and sectors emitting GHG and to achieve ambitious mitigation objectives at a reasonable cost. A broad policy mix is needed, potentially including emissions trading or cap-and-trade schemes, carbon taxes, standards, and technology support policies* (e.g. *support to R&D and clean technology deployment).*
- *A cost-effective policy mix will need to meet three criteria: static efficiency, dynamic efficiency, and an ability to cope effectively with climate and economic uncertainties. Meeting these criteria requires overcoming many market imperfections and political obstacles. In this regard, carbon taxes or emissions trading schemes turn out to be more effective and comprehensive than other policy tools. However, their cost-effectiveness could be enhanced by complementing them with other instruments to create a mixed climate policy package.*
- *The core of a cost-effective policy package is putting a price on GHG emissions through carbon taxes, emissions trading schemes* (e.g. *cap-and-trade systems), or a hybrid system combining features of both. This encourages emitters to look for and implement the cheapest abatement options.*
- *As appropriate, these should be complemented by regulations or standards* (e.g. *building codes, electrical appliance standards, diffusion of best practices) and information instruments* (e.g. *eco-labelling) to encourage changes in behaviour.*
- *Encouraging R&D and technology adoption is important to overcome barriers to innovation and diffusion of emissions-reducing technologies. While R&D funding could help to develop new technologies, such as carbon capture and storage, it is unlikely that these technologies will be aggressively deployed without complementary policies that place a sufficiently high price on carbon.*
- *The overall cost-effectiveness of a climate policy package can also be enhanced by reforming other policies that encourage GHG emissions (such as energy or agricultural subsidies) or that raise the cost of mitigation (such as regulatory barriers to foreign trade and investment).*
- *Although multiple policy instruments are needed to mitigate climate change, there are also risks that poorly-designed policy mixes result in undesirable overlaps, which would undermine cost-effectiveness and, in some cases, environmental integrity. As a general rule, therefore, different instruments should address different market imperfections and/or cover different emission sources.*

Introduction

The political acceptability of any post-2012 international climate policy framework will ultimately hinge, to a large extent, on its overall cost-effectiveness and the way costs and benefits are spread across emitters. In turn, cost effectiveness both across and within countries will be determined by the choice and design of the policy instruments that will be selected to achieve any particular climate objective. It is, therefore, of key importance to policymakers to be fully aware of the pros and cons of each available instrument, as well as how these can best be integrated into a coherent framework. Moreover, in order to address climate change at least cost, instruments will have to be applied as widely as possible across emission sources. Thus, the purpose of this chapter is to provide an overview of the various instruments available at both international and national levels, and the interactions among them. The overview is set within a theoretical framework for thinking about climate policy design that explicitly incorporates political economy considerations.

Climate policy will need to focus not only on mitigation but also on adaptation.[1] Generally there is broad support for increased adaptation and the need to scale-up financing for this, However, the focus here lies mainly on instruments for reducing GHG emissions because distributing the burden of reducing greenhouse gas (GHG) emissions across countries is a major focus of the international negotiations for a post-2012 agreement. The chapter only briefly touches upon existing policies that encourage emissions or make mitigation difficult, such as energy subsidies (Chapter 4), barriers to international trade in emissions-reducing technologies, or emissions from deforestation (Chapter 3). Also, the chapter takes as given the climate mitigation objective itself. The emphasis is thus more on the cost-effectiveness of alternative climate policy options than on the efficiency, since the latter would imply optimising across *both* the GHG emissions path *and* the instruments required to achieve it. Still, it should be borne in mind that policy choices may need to reflect not only cost-effectiveness considerations but also the ambition, nature and horizon of climate mitigation objectives themselves. For instance, available research suggests that only a narrow range of policy combinations may allow the most ambitious targets to be met (*e.g.* Gupta *et al.* 2007).

The remainder of this chapter is structured as follows. Section 2.1 sets up a simple framework for thinking about climate mitigation policy design, emphasising a number of criteria any cost-effective instrument (or set of instruments) should meet. Section 2.2 explores the extent to which the main instruments for reducing GHG emissions meet these criteria in practice. The instruments include taxes, emissions trading (including trading at the sectoral level in the context of sectoral agreements), information instruments and command-and-control approaches, technology-support policies and voluntary agreements. Section 2.3 highlights possible interactions among mitigation instruments – including both complementarities to address different objectives and potential overlaps – as well interactions among mitigation instruments and existing policies in other areas.

2.1. A simple framework for thinking about climate mitigation policy instruments

A crucial requirement for an international climate policy framework is to minimise the overall economic cost of achieving any *given* climate mitigation objective. As already mentioned in the previous chapter, an ideal set of instruments should therefore be cost-effective *per se*, and applied as widely as possible across countries, sectors and GHGs. This condition can only be met if sufficient political incentives exist for adoption of and compliance to the instrument(s).

Next, it should stimulate innovation and diffusion of GHG emissions-reducing technologies in order to lower *future* marginal abatement costs. Furthermore, it should be responsive to changes in the risks and uncertainties surrounding climate change impacts and mitigation costs. Given the very long time horizon and potentially huge mitigation costs, these two criteria are particularly important for an efficient climate policy.

In order to meet these three criteria, a wide range of market imperfections needs to be overcome (Table 2.1). A number of these are likely to prevent the equalisation of marginal abatement costs across emission sources:

- *The global public good nature of climate.* As GHGs are uniformly mixing in the atmosphere, the benefits from reducing emissions are spread over the world, and it is impossible to exclude countries from the benefits of an improved climate. This "public good" nature of the climate system results in perhaps the most obvious market imperfection. Since a country benefits as much from emission reductions by others as from domestic emission reductions that they have to pay for, all countries have an incentive to let most of the reductions be carried out by others. This "free rider" problem makes it inherently difficult for any environmentally-effective policy framework to cover all emitters (Chapter 6).
- *Monitoring and enforcement costs.* These can be large for certain emission sources, including deforestation and methane emissions resulting from pipeline leakage.
- *Information problems.* Poorly-informed households and firms may act inefficiently even if faced with adequate incentives. For example, it may be costly for households to monitor and, therefore, to optimise energy consumption by electrical appliances. In addition, the energy efficiency of buildings may be undermined if information and incentives to act differ between landlords and tenants.
- *Malfunctioning of financial markets.* This may, for instance, affect the ability of households and small firms to finance investments in profitable energy-saving equipment that has high "upfront" costs but low running costs.

Table 2.1. A simple framework for assessing policy options to reduce GHG emissions

Final policy objective	Intermediate policy objectives	Lower-level policy assessment criteria	Market imperfections to be addressed
Set up a cost-effective international climate policy framework, *i.e.* minimise the overall economic cost of achieving a given climate mitigation objective	Tend towards equal marginal abatement costs across all existing GHG emission sources	Cost-effectiveness of the instrument or set of instrument(s) Country and activity coverage, *i.e.* adoption and compliance incentives for all emitters both across and within countries	The global public good nature of climate creates a free-rider problem Monitoring and enforcement costs can be large for some emission sources Information problems may prevent some cheap abatement opportunities from being exploited Emitters' power in their output market (*e.g.* in the energy sector) and pre-existing policies (*e.g.* fuel taxes and subsidies) can distort the incentive effects of climate mitigation instruments
	Foster innovation and diffusion of GHG emissions-reducing technologies	Strength of R&D incentives Strength of technology diffusion incentives	Inventors are unable to capture the full social benefits of their innovation Adoption of existing technologies entails positive externalities through learning-by-doing effects Lack of credible commitment devices mean that innovation and adoption incentives are politically uncertain and even time-inconsistent. Capital market imperfections may act as adoption barriers, *e.g.* deterring households and small firms from investing in energy-savings equipment
	Cope effectively with risks and uncertainties surrounding both climate change and abatement costs	Responsiveness to risks and uncertainties surrounding climate change Responsiveness to risks and uncertainties surrounding abatement costs	Incomplete information on climate change damage and abatement costs

 THE ECONOMICS OF CLIMATE CHANGE MITIGATION – ISBN: 978-92-64-05606-0 – © OECD 2009

Other market distortions, while not necessarily preventing the equalisation of marginal abatement costs across emission sources, may still undermine the cost effectiveness of climate mitigation policy. This is the case for instance when large emitters can influence prices in their output markets, not least in the energy sector. The presence of pre-existing policies whose side effects are to encourage carbon emissions (*e.g.* fuel taxes and subsidies) may also undermine the effectiveness of climate policy instruments. Because it is often politically difficult to reform such pre-existing policies, the choice and/or design of climate policy instruments may have to take this into account.

Market mechanisms (*e.g.* taxes, subsidy reform, and emissions trading schemes) alone may be unable to deliver an adequate level of innovation and diffusion of GHG emission-reducing technologies. First, market failures affect innovation and diffusion in general. In particular, the limited ability to capture the returns from new ideas due to the diffusion of knowledge through various channels (a phenomenon known as "knowledge spillovers") is likely to induce firms to invest less in R&D than would be desirable for society. While intellectual property rights (IPRs) can help address this issue, they are often imperfect in practice, meaning that private inventors are not always able to capture the full social benefits from their innovation. Second, firms are also often unable to capture all the social returns from technology adoption. For instance because the benefits of a new technology spread out as individuals learn to use it (learning-by-doing) or because such benefits increase as the number of individuals using it gets larger, as often is the case in infrastructure networks ("network externalities"). Since such benefits cannot be fully captured by investors, the speed of diffusion of new technologies can be slowed down (Chapter 5). Finally, information differences between the firm and potential investors about the future returns from R&D and/or adoption of existing technologies may hamper a firm's ability to raise capital for such activities.

Market failures affecting innovation and technology diffusion may be magnified in the area of climate change mitigation. In particular:

- The gap between social and private expected benefits from R&D and adoption of existing technologies may be amplified by the political uncertainty surrounding the characteristics, and even the existence, of future climate policy. This, in turn, fundamentally reflects the lack of credible ways through which current governments can commit future ones.[2] The commitment issue is often less acute in other public policy areas, either because their time scale is shorter or because policies are better established. Climate policy is not only uncertain but may even be "time-inconsistent", in that governments may be under pressure to ease the policy at a later date, once irreversible investments in R&D and new equipment have been made.[3]
- The country and/or sector coverage of price-based instruments is unlikely to be comprehensive, at least over the medium run. Thus the innovation and diffusion of some clean technologies may be stimulated in the sectors or countries where these price-based instruments or other policies are applied, but not in others. This further raises the gap between social and private returns, and provides an "imperfect" setting for R&D policies.
- Given the potentially large welfare consequences of any major breakthrough in climate-friendly technological innovation (*e.g.* in the area of electricity production), IPR protection may be insufficiently strong for private investors, who may fear that governments will deprive them of any major innovation profits at a later date, *e.g.* to facilitate the diffusion of the new breakthrough technology[4].
- Specific market failures and policy distortions in the electricity sector may explain the low levels of R&D compared with other industries (Chapter 5). In particular, already installed infrastructure may be a barrier to the adoption of new technologies (network effect), thereby discouraging research. For instance, most national grids are not suited for receiving electricity

from many small renewable electricity sources, while large-scale suppliers of renewable sources may also encounter problems if located too far from existing grids.[5] Finally, low market competition and distortions such as fossil fuel subsidies may also keep R&D spending low in the electricity sector.

Finally, in order to cope effectively with risks and uncertainties surrounding both climate change and abatement costs, the incompleteness of available information needs to be addressed. There is uncertainty surrounding future economic growth, the links between economic growth and GHG emissions, the climate effects of GHG emissions and the damage caused by climate change. Furthermore, there is a probability of large and irreversible consequences from climate change.[6] This raises a major challenge for policy, in a context where there are long lags between action and its mitigating impact on climate change.

2.2. Instruments to mitigate climate change

It is unlikely that cost-effective climate mitigation can be achieved through a single policy instrument. This is because different instruments are needed to overcome different obstacles to mitigation in different areas or sectors and to provide the right incentives to households and firms. This section reviews how each of the most commonly available instruments performs against the assessment criteria developed above. It also discusses possible options which have been proposed to remedy, at least in part, some of the weaknesses of these instruments.

2.2.1. GHG emission taxes

Intrinsic cost-effectiveness

A GHG emission tax is a relatively straightforward instrument for achieving cost-effective climate mitigation. The tax provides a way to set a price on the negative side effects of certain economic activities on the global climate, effects that are otherwise "invisible" to individual market participants.[7] In the absence of any other market failure, a global tax on GHG emissions – or, equally, fully harmonised domestic GHG emission taxes – should persuade emitters to adopt all cheap abatement options that are available (depending on the level of the tax). From this perspective, a tax instrument is intrinsically cost-effective (sometimes called the "static efficiency" property of the tax).[8]

In practice, administration and compliance costs also shape the cost-effectiveness of the tax. Such costs are usually lower under a tax than under most other instruments, at least if carbon taxation is applied "upstream" to the wholesale use of fossil fuels.[9] Nevertheless, based on a variety of country case studies on industrial air pollution control, Blackman and Harrington (2000) argue that lower-income countries may lack the institutional capacity to enforce an emissions tax, especially given the indirect and intermittent methods that are typically used to monitor GHG emissions. In addition, the way in which the revenues from the tax are recycled is important. In theory, the more revenues are used to reduce other taxes that have negative side effects on economic activity, the greater the cost effectiveness of the scheme. This is the so-called double-dividend of corrective taxes on pollution.[10] In practice, as discussed below, this principle may conflict with the need to build up local political support for the tax, which is also needed to ensure wide coverage and may call for a different allocation of the tax proceeds.

More fundamentally, the fact that a GHG emissions tax does not address all market imperfections also undermines its cost effectiveness:[11]

- The high costs of monitoring certain emission sources either raise tax collection costs or, if the emissions concerned go untaxed, prevent potentially cheap abatement options from being exploited.
- Emissions caused by inadequate or asymmetric information sharing among economic agents are not addressed by a GHG emissions tax, and this may undermine its full effectiveness.
- The monopolistic power of emitters in their output markets, especially the energy sector, reduces the welfare gain from the GHG emissions tax. Indeed, emitters that have market power will respond to the emissions tax by adjusting product prices to maximize their profits (Buchanan, 1969; Cropper and Oates, 1992).
- The effectiveness of the tax can also be reduced by its interaction with other policies that affect the incentives firms may have to use less carbon-intensive processes, including fiscal incentives to energy production/use and agricultural subsidies.[12]
- Public or quasi-public enterprises may not have strong incentives to respond adequately to the tax, partly because they have objectives other than profit maximisation, and laxer budget constraints than firms in the private sector.

Adoption and compliance incentives

Perhaps the most important precondition for a global GHG emissions tax to be cost-effective is that it covers the largest possible share of global GHG emissions.[13] It is, therefore, of prime importance to assess the political incentives for governments to adopt such a tax and to enforce it domestically.

A global GHG emissions tax has at least two attractive political features. First, it can be implemented through national legal systems and institutions, without any strong need for international harmonisation of the institutional setting or the creation of a new international institution. Second, partly as a result of this legal simplicity, it is flexible. A country can quickly join (or withdraw) without any need for a round of international negotiations, as it just needs to create a new national tax set equal to the global carbon tax rate. Likewise, two countries or groups of countries can harmonise their distinct carbon tax schemes simply by equalising the tax rates.[14]

Nevertheless, these political advantages are more than offset by several drawbacks, which explain why a global tax does not rank high on policymakers' agenda. For example, at the international level, the immediate economic impact of the tax would, in general, be greater on developing countries, reflecting the higher carbon-intensity of their economies. This deters developing countries from adopting the tax, and may also be seen to be unfair. An international agreement specifying lump-sum payments – or alternatively transfers of a share of future international tax revenues – from developed to developing countries could address this issue. However, it is unclear whether electorates in developed countries would support the large, transparent payments that are likely to be involved. Also, such transfers might raise governance issues in recipient countries.

Another problem is that the costs from a GHG emissions tax are highly transparent, occur immediately and are concentrated on relatively well-organised groups. By contrast, its benefits are widely dispersed and will only be reaped far in the future. Furthermore, unlike other instruments, a GHG emissions tax does not build up any political constituency with a strong interest in maintaining the tax. Thus, affected groups may be able to lobby successfully against the tax (*e.g.* Olson, 1965) or for offsetting measures (*e.g.* taxes on substitutes for carbon or subsidies for complements to carbon), thereby undermining any international tax harmonisation agreement (Stavins, 1997). Another political obstacle to implementation is that a carbon tax raises genuine national income distribution concerns – in other words it might tax the poor disproportionately, *e.g.* to the extent that a larger share of their incomes is spent on carbon intensive goods or services (such as energy or fuel). While this issue can, at least in principle, be addressed via the tax-benefit system, this option is not always available in lower-income countries with weaker social policy settings. In principle, domestic support for a GHG emissions tax can be built by partially redistributing the tax revenues to affected industries and/or household groups. Nevertheless, apart from reducing cost-effectiveness (OECD, 2007a), revenue-recycling may be seen as insufficiently credible in practice. In contrast with the tax, compensatory schemes may be perceived as transitory, as governments cannot easily commit to maintaining them beyond the current budget horizon. From this perspective, a single, large, lump-sum payment upon implementation might ease the adoption of the tax.

R&D and technology diffusion incentives

A GHG emissions tax gives emitters a continuing incentive to develop and/or adopt new emissions-reducing technologies. This is the "dynamic efficiency" of taxes and market-based mechanisms in general. Furthermore, at least in principle, a tax provides a stable price signal to investors since the only source of carbon price volatility should come from unforeseen political adjustments to the tax rate. This is important in view of the long investment horizons needed for climate mitigation problems; even a small amount of uncertainty can severely reduce expected returns from investment in such a context.

However, a carbon tax addresses only one of the many market imperfections undermining R&D and technology diffusion. And the fact that a carbon tax may also be perceived to have an uncertain political future and be subject to change, also undermines incentives for R&D. While suggestions have been made to fix this problem, none seems to have gained broad political support. One option would be to earmark the tax revenues to finance investments in R&D (Marsiliani and Renström, 2000).[15] However, this argument should be weighed against the additional constraint on fiscal policy implied by earmarking, which generally makes Finance Ministries very reluctant to engage in earmarking. Alternatively, time inconsistency of the tax rate could be avoided by giving the power to set the GHG emissions' tax rate to an independent climate policy authority, akin to a "conservative" central banker (Helm *et al.* 2004; Helm, 2005). However, ensuring that such an institution retains full independence may be easier in a national, rather than in an international, context.

Ability to cope effectively with risk and uncertainty

In the short run, by setting the marginal cost of reducing GHG emissions, a tax gives some certainty about overall abatement costs, but it does not address uncertainty about the total emissions that will result at this cost, and thus the environmental effectiveness of the policy approach. An unanticipated shock, for instance in economic growth, energy supply or technology, after the tax rate has been set, may lead to a change in the level of emissions. In contrast, in an emissions trading scheme the level of emissions will certain as it is established by the overall cap, and a shock will instead lead to a change in the price of permits (*i.e.* price uncertainty). Thus, when the social costs of getting the price wrong is higher than the social costs of getting the emission level wrong, taxes are preferable over emissions trading (Weitzman, 1974). This situation holds when the marginal (climate) damage curve is "flatter" than the marginal cost curve. This condition is likely to be met in the case of climate change, because the marginal damage from higher-than-expected emissions is relatively constant in the short run, since only cumulative – not current – emissions matter for the climate impacts. This is true at least in the current situation where GHG concentration levels remain significantly below the thresholds that might trigger extreme and irreversible events, such as for instance the melting of the Greenland and West Antarctic ice sheets. Marginal abatement costs on the other hand tend to increase exponentially with emissions. Recent research suggests that this flexibility gain from taxes could be large in practice (Hoel and Karp, 2001; Newell and Pizer, 2003; Pizer, 2002).

Over the longer term, the uncertainty problem that policy needs to address becomes somewhat different. In order to achieve any mitigation target, a tax would need to be revised regularly depending on its environmental impact. The mitigation target itself may also need to change. A tax which is being adjusted would, however, provide no certainty about longer-term abatement costs and could undermine R&D and technology adoption incentives. Therefore, a key challenge is to design the tax so that future changes in response to environmental outcomes and mitigation costs are sufficiently predictable. Built-in rules guiding adjustment might help to address this trade-off between policy flexibility and predictability.

2.2.2. Emissions trading schemes

Intrinsic cost-effectiveness

While experiences with GHG emissions taxes remain limited (*e.g.* Sweden), the international community has made some progress towards implementing emissions trading schemes (Section 2.4).

A system of tradable emission permits (emissions trading) is an administrative approach used to control emissions by providing economic incentives for achieving reductions. The most popular form is cap-and-trade. A central authority (usually a government or a supranational body) sets a limit or cap on the amount that can be emitted. Companies or other groups are required to obtain an equivalent number of allowances (or credits) which represent the right to emit a specific amount of GHG (emission permits). The total amount of permits cannot exceed the cap, limiting total emissions to that level. Companies that need to increase their emission allowances must buy permits from those who pollute less than the amount of permits they hold. The transfer of allowances is referred to as emissions trading. In effect, the buyer is paying a charge for emitting, while the seller is being rewarded for having reduced emissions below the allowed amount. Firms will sell permits as long as their market price exceeds their marginal abatement costs; conversely, they will buy permits as long as their market price falls short of their marginal abatement costs. If the permit market is competitive, the price of permits will eventually ensure that no more profitable trade opportunities exist. Thus, in theory, those who can reduce emissions most cheaply will do so, achieving the reduction at the lowest possible cost to society.

In principle, in a perfectly competitive permit market and in the absence of uncertainty, both a emissions trading scheme and a tax are cost-effective, and they are in fact equivalent. Also, as long as permits are fully auctioned, both instruments have similar potential to generate revenue for the government, which can be used to lower other taxes potentially harmful for economic activity (yielding a double-dividend from mitigation policies). However, it is generally thought that transaction costs in GHG emission permit markets are larger than those from a tax, although there is little empirical data available (OECD, 2007a). This is especially the case for downstream schemes, under which multiple small emission sources may only be covered at a significant cost (or even be exempted), thereby hampering the overall cost-effectiveness of the system. Downstream schemes also raise practical implementation problems when there is no reliable initial data on emissions. Also, pricing emissions from diffuse sources – *e.g.* from agriculture, where many small emitters operate – may be harder to achieve through emissions trading than through taxes. Setting up an emissions trading scheme may be even more challenging for developing countries than collecting an emissions tax (because tax collection institutions are already in place), and may also be more vulnerable to lobbying (Blackman and Harrington, 2000). Many of the transaction costs associated with permit markets also reflect insufficient market liquidity. Therefore, moving towards a truly integrated international emissions trading scheme would be expected to improve cost-effectiveness,[16] although this gain should be weighed against the cost of enforcing a policy that crosses national jurisdictions.

Market power in the permit market can also undermine cost-effectiveness. A monopolistic permit seller would drive a wedge between the permit price and its own marginal abatement cost, thereby forcing permit buyers to buy more expensive permits or abate more at a higher cost. Such concerns matter only if permits can be stored for future use – *e.g.* in the context of multiphase programmes – and if trading only takes place between countries. Even large firms would be unlikely to have enough power to affect prices in an international permit market. [17]

Adoption and compliance incentives

An emissions trading scheme faces many of the same political challenges as a tax, namely the difficulty to overcome fundamental lack of adoption and enforcement incentives both across and within countries. However, an emissions trading scheme has its own strengths and weaknesses. A basic strength is that a number of national and regional schemes already exist. Another advantage is the existence of "flexibility mechanisms" – such as the Clean Development Mechanism of the Kyoto Protocol – that enable emission reduction commitments under the emissions trading schemes to be met by undertaking project-based emission reductions in other geographical areas. There is, therefore, some basis for developing linkages between existing schemes and scaling-up and improving the use of flexibility mechanisms (Chapter 4).

Yet, emissions trading raises a number of political challenges. Unlike a tax, a truly international scheme cannot easily be implemented through existing legal frameworks and institutions. In practice, the rules of existing national and regional schemes are all fairly different, thus hindering possible future integration (*e.g.* Capoor and Ambrosi, 2006; Ellis and Tirpak, 2006). The system therefore lacks the flexibility to incorporate new participating countries quickly. It may also be somewhat more vulnerable to lax monitoring and enforcement in some participating countries.[18]

In practice, however, these weaknesses of emissions trading may be more than offset by a number of politically attractive features at both international and domestic levels. At the international level, any income transfers required to encourage large developing countries to join in may be more acceptable to the electorates of developed countries if they take place indirectly, through permit allocation, rather than through direct income transfers. At a domestic level, emissions trading has the following advantages over a tax:

- It creates a well-identified domestic constituency (permit holders) with a strong financial interest in enforcing the policy in the future, at least if permits have a sufficiently long life.
- It also provides direct flexibility to build political support for the scheme through permit allocation rules. This largely explains the popularity of "grandfathering" (*i.e.* giving the permits for free to existing emitters) in practice (*e.g.* OECD, 2007a). Some limited grandfathering may also be justified as a way to compensate holders of existing assets for the costs (*e.g.* due to the depreciation of part of their polluting capital stock) they incur with the implementation of the scheme (Johnston, 2006). However, grandfathering of permits compromises the cost-effectiveness of the scheme in the longer term, including by distorting industry dynamics, *i.e.* entry and exit incentives. It also raises equity concerns, since it provides "windfall profits" to emitters financed by consumers. There is, therefore, a strong case for limiting "grandfathering" both in scope and time.

- Permit allocation rules can also be used to address international competitiveness and/or national income distribution concerns. For instance, emissions trading has been put forward as a primary tool to address competitiveness concerns associated with government-led international sectoral agreements (Chapter 4).
- Finally, unlike a tax, international emissions trading enables some degree of subsidiarity to be maintained in implementation at the country level. An international emissions trading agreement between governments may indeed allow a variety of policy arrangements to meet emission objectives *within* each country. For instance, governments may have the freedom to choose between grandfathering and auctioning the permits allocated to the country.

R&D and technology diffusion incentives

Emissions trading has the same basic strengths and weaknesses as a tax when it comes to providing adequate incentives for R&D and technology diffusion. While neither a tax nor an emissions trading scheme address the full range of market failures undermining innovation and diffusion of climate-friendly technologies, both give emitters continuing incentives to search for cheaper abatement options through both existing and new technologies. Lack of certainty about the future carbon price and potential policy changes may undermine these incentives to some extent.

However, taxes and emissions trading can differ in several respects:

- Innovation and diffusion incentives may be lower under emissions trading than under a tax. First, carbon price volatility is likely to be higher under a simple quantity instrument such as emissions trading than under a tax. Because R&D and the adoption of new technologies involve sunk costs, price volatility could further delay firms' decisions to invest in emissions-reducing activities (Dixit and Pindyck, 1994 and sub-section below). However, including both a price cap and a price floor would help stabilise prices and boost R&D incentives (Burtraw *et al.* 2006). Second, because the diffusion of new technologies is expected to lower the equilibrium price of emissions under emissions trading, individual adoption incentives may be lower than under a tax (Box 2.1).
- Both schemes would need to be revised over time, reflecting changes in desired stringency requirements and technological developments. Whether adjustable taxes yield greater innovation incentives than adjustable trading schemes is likely to depend on the predictability of the revisions. But once markets are established and permits are allocated, the risk of arbitrary policy changes may be lower under emissions trading than under a tax.[19] However, once a tax is established, firms have lower incentives to lobby against policy adjustments, thereby making policy changes more predictable. This is because the optimal response of policymakers to cost-reducing technological change is to lower the tax rate, *i.e.* to reduce the costs imposed on firms. By contrast, the optimal response under emissions trading is to tighten the emissions cap, and thereby increase the permit price and the costs incurred by firms (as explained in detail in Box 2.1).

Box 2.1 R&D and technology adoption incentives under GHG emission taxes *versus* simple emissions trading schemes

While emission taxes and emissions trading schemes (cap-and-trade) have the same basic strengths and weaknesses in terms of providing adequate R&D and technology adoption incentives, existing literature points to some differences. These depend on whether and how both policies are expected to be revised in the future.

A fixed tax is likely to provide greater incentives than a fixed cap-and-trade scheme, because of the so-called abatement cost effect (Denicolò, 1999; Keohane, 1999).[1] For any individual firm, the fact that other firms are expected to adopt the new technology reduces the expected permit price and, therefore, the expected cost savings from adopting the technology. By contrast, under a tax, the individual firm's incentive to adopt a new technology depends only on the level of the tax and not on other firms' behaviour. Parry (1998) finds that in practice, this superiority of taxes over cap-and-trade is only significant for major innovations. In a more general theoretical framework, Fischer *et al.* (2003) find the welfare gains from taxes to always be larger than those from cap-and-trade, provided marginal environmental benefits from emission reductions are relatively flat (as is the case in the area of climate change) and there is no possibility for firms to imitate the patented technology.

Previous literature had argued that auctioned permits provided larger adoption incentives than taxes and free (grandfathered) permits (Milliman and Prince, 1989; Jung *et al.* 1996). This result reflected an "emissions payment effect": firms that have to pay for permits can expect to gain from a fall in the permit price. This effect is absent under free permits as the gains and losses to net buyers and sellers of permits cancel out. However, Keohane (1999) argues that in a competitive permit market, each firm enjoys the fall in the permit price regardless of whether it adopts the new technology. Because the gains from the fall in price are induced by *aggregate* adoption decisions, they do not affect *individual* adoption incentives.

Assuming that both schemes are likely to be revised over time, it becomes less clear whether taxes provide greater innovation incentives than cap-and-trade. One advantage of cap-and-trade may be the lower perceived political risk of arbitrary policy adjustments, once permit markets are established and permits are allocated. One advantage of taxes is that firms will not have an incentive to lobby against policy adjustments, so they are more predictable (Milliman and Prince, 1989; Biglaiser *et al.* 1995). This is illustrated in Figure 2.1.

For a given time period, the optimal policy is to balance the marginal damage (MD) from emissions and the marginal cost (MC) of a reduction in emissions. The optimal policy is to emit Qa tonnes of carbon at price Pa. This can be achieved either by a carbon tax (Pa), or through an emissions trading scheme that sets an emissions cap (Qa). In both cases, the equilibrium is (Qa, Pa) before innovation takes place. Innovation would be typically expected to shift the marginal cost curve MC downwards. In the absence of revision to the policy, the new equilibrium would be (Qc, Pa) under a tax and (Qa, Pb) under emissions trading. However, none of these equilibria would be optimal, since marginal damages and marginal costs would differ. Therefore the policymaker would have an incentive to revise the policy to achieve the new optimum (Qd, Pd). Under a tax system, this would imply a reduction in the tax, from which firms would benefit. Under emissions trading, this would imply a tightening of the cap and an increase in the emissions price, from which firms would lose, and which they are, therefore, likely to oppose. Because the outcome of such lobbying may be uncertain, policy revisions may be less predictable under emissions trading than under a tax.

Box 2.1. continued on next page.

Box 2.1 R&D and technology adoption incentives under GHG emission taxes *versus* simple emissions trading schemes

(continued)

Figure 2.1. Innovation will impact optimal policy for taxes less than for emissions trading

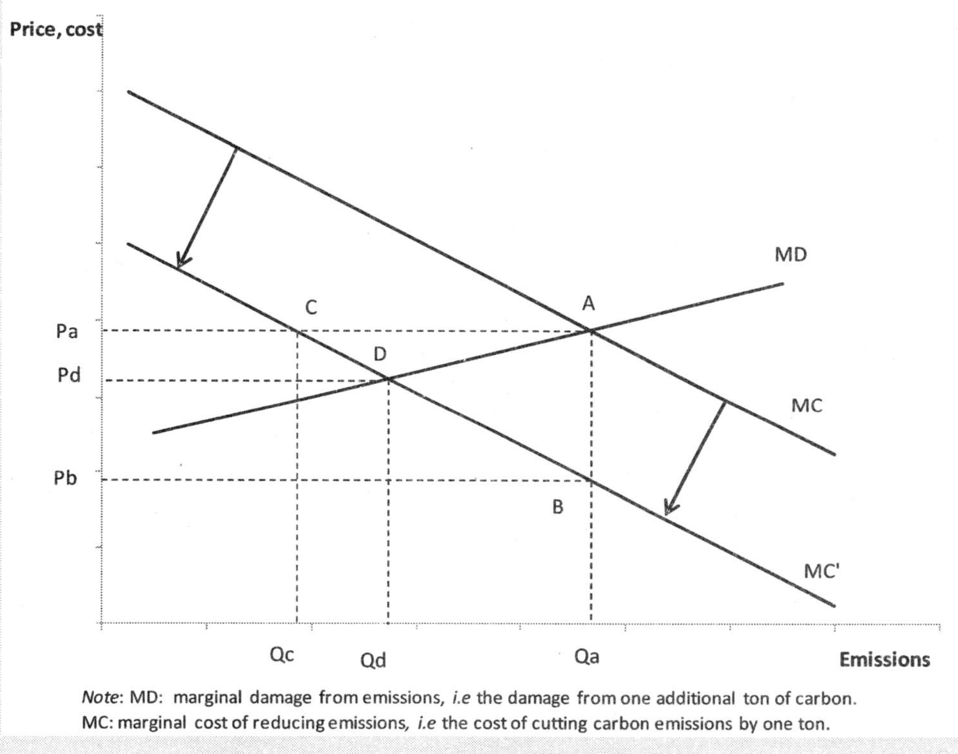

Note: MD: marginal damage from emissions, *i.e* the damage from one additional ton of carbon.
MC: marginal cost of reducing emissions, *i.e* the cost of cutting carbon emissions by one ton.

Ability to cope effectively with risk and uncertainty

Compared with a tax, an emissions trading system yields more certain environmental outcomes but has more uncertain economic costs. As already noted, this is not an efficient way of dealing with short-run uncertainty in the case of climate change, because the welfare consequences of unexpectedly high abatement costs are likely to be higher than those from unexpectedly high emissions.[20] For example, under an emissions trading scheme with a set of fixed sectoral targets, changes in participation (*e.g.* exemption of a major emitting sector) would induce large fluctuations in the carbon price and impose large costs on the participating sectors (under unchanged national emission objectives). OECD simulations of a calibrated microeconomic model of firms' investment decisions under price uncertainty and investment irreversibility point to large detrimental effects of energy price volatility on investment (Box 2.2).[21] For instance, the carbon price volatility that has occurred since the creation of the EU-ETS might reduce firms' energy-efficient investments by as much as a quarter, compared to a stable carbon price scenario.[22]

Box 2.2 The impact of uncertainty on firms' irreversible investments

When investment is reversible, the impact of carbon price uncertainty on firms' decisions to invest in emission-reducing equipment is determined by the relationship between investment cash flows and the carbon price. For emission-reducing equipment, it is likely that the higher the carbon price uncertainty, the higher the expected cash flow and the higher the size of the investment (*i.e.* this cash flow function is convex, Figure 2.2). In practice, however, most investments in clean technologies are at least partially irreversible and thus the extent to which firms can adjust their capital stock to fluctuations in carbon and energy prices is limited. This also affects investment decisions.

A stylised, calibrated model can help to assess the impact of carbon and energy price uncertainty on irreversible investment in emission-reducing equipment. A firm is assumed to produce a good with two inputs: capital[1] and fossil fuel energy. While energy purchases entail no sunk costs (*i.e.* they can be resold at no cost), capital is assumed to be irreversible, *i.e.* once installed it cannot be resold. In this context, the firm can be seen as holding a "real option" that gives it the right to invest in the emission-reducing equipment in order to receive uncertain future cash flows that fluctuate with time, depending on carbon prices. It is then profitable for the firm to exercise this option when the expected return on investment exceeds the sum of its cost *and* the loss of the option to invest later with additional information. Higher carbon price uncertainty increases the value of that option, thereby delaying and reducing the size of the investment (Dixit and Pindyck, 1994; IEA, 2007a[2]).

With a convex cash flow function, the "convexity" and "irreversibility" channels through which uncertainty affects the investment decision act in opposite directions, so that the impact of uncertainty on investment is ambiguous. However, for reasonable values of the main parameters, it can be shown that the irreversibility effect prevails over the convexity effect (Jamet, 2009). The higher the uncertainty, the higher the value of the investment option, the more investment is delayed, and the lower the optimal capital stock at the time of investment. For instance, model simulations suggest that carbon price uncertainty, such as that observed during the second phase of EU-ETS, could lower the capital stock by as much as 25%, compared to a stable carbon price scenario (Figure 2.3). The lower carbon price fluctuations that prevailed under the first phase of the scheme would be consistent with a 5% reduction in the capital stock.[3]

Figure 2.2. Convexity implies that higher uncertainty leads to higher expected cash flow

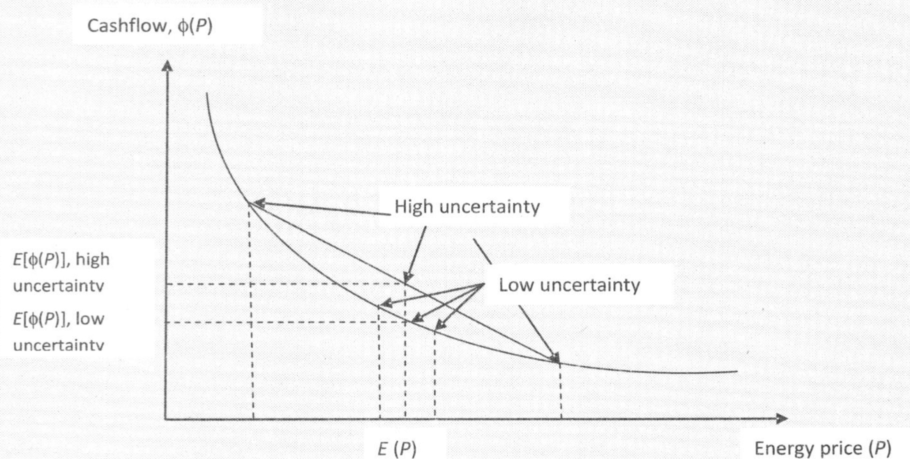

Note: E(.) denotes the expectation operator. Two distributions of the energy price with the same expected price are considered, one with low uncertainty and one with high uncertainty. With a convex cashflow function, the higher the uncertainty, the higher the expected cashflow.

Box 2.2. continued on next page.

Box 2.2 The impact of uncertainty on firms' irreversible investments

Figure 2.3. Uncertainty will reduce the capital stock

Ratio of the capital stock with and without uncertainty at the time of investment

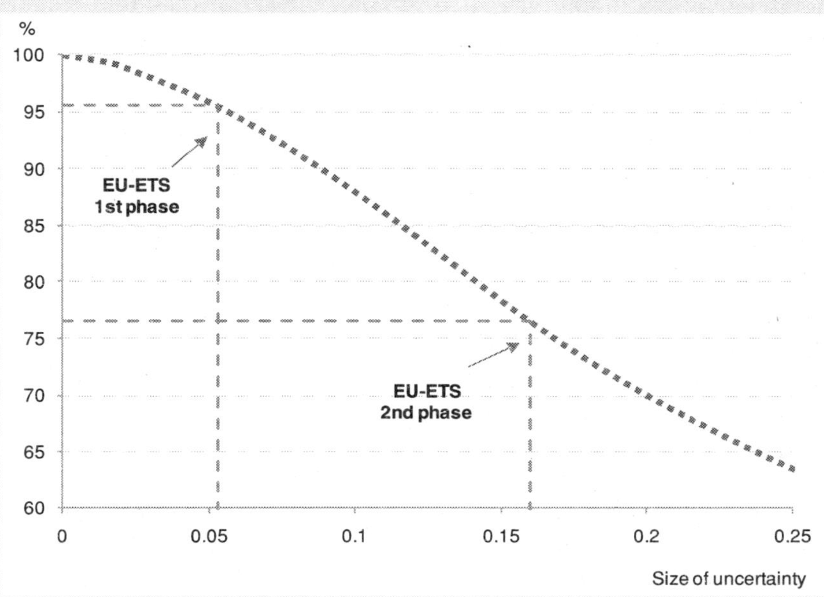

1. Capital is a broad aggregate that includes all the technologies that allow a firm to produce a good without paying the energy price. It includes for instance renewable energy technologies.
2. Using a model for the electricity sector, IEA (2007a) finds that extending a policy from 5 to 10 years would strongly reduce the delaying impact of uncertainty on investments. The model does not capture the impact of uncertainty on the size of investments.
3. In a global carbon market, carbon price uncertainty would be partly offset by less volatile fossil fuel energy prices, as higher than expected carbon prices would coincide with lower than expected world fossil fuel energy prices (and *vice versa*). However, given the limited coverage of the EU-ETS, this effect is assumed to be small.

This difference between taxes and emissions trading may be less clear-cut over the longer term, however, if both instruments adjust regularly to environmental or economic impacts. In both cases, the key long-term challenge would be to set up a policy that responds to new information, but in a predictable enough way to preserve R&D and technology adoption incentives. From this perspective, trading schemes may be more responsive than taxes. This is because any change in the expected path of policy – *e.g.* a larger than expected tightening of the emission reduction objective in the future, following a larger than expected rise in temperature – would affect current permit prices,[23] while under a tax prices would remain fixed until policymakers decided to reset them.

A number of options have been suggested for enhancing the resilience of emissions trading schemes to short-term cost uncertainty:

- Set a price floor in order to prevent the price of emissions from falling too low, *i.e.* too far below the marginal damage from emissions in the presence of short-term shocks.[24] This would reduce the risk of large price fluctuations (especially large price falls) and thus would provide some of the advantages of a tax. A price floor may be particularly useful if emission caps are felt to be unresponsive to (unexpected) good news about abatement costs – *i.e.* when the emissions cap is not tightened when it could be due to lower than expected marginal abatement costs– possibly as a result of political lobbying (Box 2.1).[25]

- Allow flexibility in the timing of emission reductions, *e.g.* through banking provisions which allow permits to be stored for future use in multi-phase programmes. Banking is also likely to reduce the risk of large price fluctuations under general circumstances.[26] It also makes sense from an environmental standpoint, since the precise timing of emissions has in general little impact on the ultimate damage. Furthermore, by allowing permits to be established over a sufficiently long horizon, banking may facilitate the emergence of forward markets. However, unlike a price floor, banking would not provide full certainty about the minimum price of emissions. Banking can be effective only when individual emitters expect (discounted) future prices to be higher than the current price.

- Include a price cap or "safety valve" in emissions trading schemes, *i.e.* a fixed maximum price at which the regulator commits to selling any excess number of permits demanded by participants. Roberts and Spence (1976) have shown such hybrid quantity-price instruments to be preferable to simple quantity instruments when abatement costs are uncertain,[27] and more recent research has confirmed this finding in the context of climate change (Pizer, 2002).[28] McKibbin and Wilcoxen (2002; 2007) suggest that an internationally-co-ordinated system of hybrid national policies, each consisting of a fixed supply of long-term permits and a more flexible supply of short-term permits, would combine some of the strengths of price and quantity instruments: i) like a tax, it would reduce short-term cost uncertainty, could be implemented readily through existing national institutions, and would allow straightforward linking across countries through short-term permit price harmonisation; and ii) like a trading scheme, it would build up a clear constituency with a strong interest in maintaining the policy over the long-run.

- Set intensity targets (*e.g.* emissions per unit of output) rather than absolute targets (Chapter 4, Box 4.1). One advantage of intensity targets is that they can enable the *automatic* adjustment of emission objectives to unexpected changes in economic growth. Such changes, along with genuine shocks to marginal abatement costs, represent one of the two main sources of uncertainty surrounding the overall cost of meeting an absolute emissions cap.

- Link domestic schemes and facilitate the development of hedging instruments. This would be expected to mitigate the impact of shocks and thereby to reduce price volatility, even though shocks could become more frequent as the system is no longer immune to developments in other areas (Chapter 4). For instance, the carbon price effect of unexpectedly high short-term economic growth in one country would be lower under linked trading schemes than under a smaller domestic system, especially as the country considered is small compared with the overall area covered through linking.

2.2.3. Command-and-control (CAC) approaches

Command-and-control (CAC) approaches are regulatory instruments that dictate abatement decisions. They fall into two broad categories: *i)* technology standards, which require emitters to use specific abatement technologies; and *ii)* performance standards, which set specific environmental targets that must be met (*e.g.* a certain amount of emissions per unit of output), but without requiring particular technologies.

Intrinsic cost-effectiveness

By forcing all firms to undertake specific emission reduction efforts regardless of their individual abatement costs, CAC instruments do not, in general, achieve marginal abatement cost equalisation and, thus, do not minimise overall abatement costs because they impose the same constraints to firms that have ample or few cheap abatement options (*e.g.* Bohm and Russell, 1985). Also, technology standards are usually more costly than performance standards, as the latter give firms greater flexibility in selecting the abatement option that is most adapted to their individual situation.[29] For a CAC instrument to be as cost-effective as a market-based incentive, firms' marginal abatement costs should be similar, or the regulator should have full information about individual cost structures and set regulations accordingly. However, these conditions are unlikely to be met in practice. Finally, unlike price-based instruments, standards lack the potential for delivering a "double dividend" since they do not raise fiscal revenues.[30]

However, if carefully designed, CAC instruments can help deal with a number of market imperfections that are not dealt with by market-based incentives:

- When emissions cannot be perfectly observed (*e.g.* fugitive emissions from pipelines, methane from agriculture), market-based incentives no longer minimise abatement costs because such emissions are not properly monitored. In principle, cost-effectiveness can then be enhanced through the use of technology standards – although performance standards are useless in this context since their implementation also requires adequate emissions monitoring. When monitoring problems are large and when abatement costs are relatively homogenous across agents, technology standards have been shown to be more cost-effective than market-based incentives (Montero, 2005). Their performance can be further enhanced by combining them with market incentives whose effects can be measured, when these are available.[31]
- When information is not equally available to two contracting parties with opposite goals, adverse selection and/or moral hazard problems may arise. In this situation, well-designed CAC instruments may also perform better than market incentives. Examples of such market failures have especially been identified in energy service markets (Sorrell *et al.,* 2000; IEA, 2007b). For instance, in the housing market, landlords have better information than tenants but have little incentive to install the most energy-efficient equipment because they do not pay the energy bill. Likewise, asymmetric information between buyers and sellers may also prevent house prices from fully reflecting the discounted value of energy-efficiency investments. The invisible energy-efficiency performance of electrical appliances and light bulbs may also prevent households from optimising energy consumption. In such cases, policy can address directly this problem through information instruments like public disclosure requirements or eco-labelling. However, when information instruments are costly or insufficient, standards are justified and have been found to yield sizeable welfare gains.[32]
- CAC instruments can be preferable to market-based incentives when agents are irresponsive to price signals. For instance, lack of institutional – including monitoring – capability may prevent market-based incentives from working properly in lower-income countries, while technology standards may be easier to implement and track (Blackman and Harrington, 2000; Russell and Vaughan, 2003). Standards may also help increase emissions abatement efforts in state enterprises with market power to levels that would be undertaken if such firms operated under private governance in competitive markets (Sterner, 2003).

The theoretical case for CAC instruments should, however, be qualified on three grounds:

- Policymakers should make sure that the use of standards addresses genuine market failures, rather than merely high transaction costs. Hidden transaction costs may explain why apparently efficient investment decisions – *e.g.* in energy-efficient equipment – are often not made by households and firms. For example, transaction costs rather than market imperfections may partly explain why landlords and tenants do not sign the type of shared-savings contracts that would seem to benefit both parties in theory. More broadly, economists have often been skeptical about the existence of profitable ("negative cost") abatement opportunities.[33] When hidden transaction costs are at fault rather than market failures, it is less clear that standards would have any net social benefits; direct policies to reduce the transaction costs would be more effective.
- Some of the market failures and/or transaction costs that are put forward to justify the use of CAC instruments may in fact not be fully independent of the existence of a carbon price. For example, in terms of information asymmetry, the higher the price of GHG emissions and energy bills, the stronger the incentives for tenants and buyers to find out about the energy efficiency of alternative equipment, and for landlords and sellers to reveal this information. A similar argument could be made for contract incompleteness. For instance, consumers currently have little or no choice over the energy efficiency of the services provided by television set-top boxes (IEA, 2007b). If the carbon price was high enough, however, there would be greater incentives for buyers and sellers to separate the choice of the television set-top boxes and the services.
- Finally, the theoretical case for policy intervention should be weighed against the risk of policy failure. There are two main risks of policy failure: a) as just noted, the magnitude of the market imperfection(s) to be addressed is hard to pin down in practice; and b) in the absence of detailed information about individual abatement costs, it is challenging for the regulator to determine how stringent the standard should be. This underlines the need for serious cost-benefit analysis before setting up standards.

Adoption and compliance incentives

CAC instruments have a number of political features that encourage their adoption. They are already the most common form of environmental regulation, can be easily enforced through existing national institutions, and, unlike price instruments, their costs are not immediately visible to voters. It has also been argued that international negotiations to set technology standards for key emitting industries could bring large emitters from developing countries on board, if accompanied by technology transfers (Barrett, 2007a).

However, CAC instruments offer little scope for addressing the free-rider problem affecting international climate policy negotiations. As a result, if large reductions in worldwide GHGs were to be secured through the use of standards, adoption incentives could be weak. Unlike emissions trading schemes, burden-sharing rules cannot be built into CAC instruments and would therefore have to be negotiated separately. Information problems would affect such negotiations, reflecting the difficulty of assessing the costs of implementing standards. Finally, it is unclear whether international standards would actually be desirable. While expanding the international coverage of price instruments always reduces the overall cost of reducing global GHG emissions, mandating uniform standards across all countries may not.

R&D and technology diffusion incentives

Unlike price instruments, standards do not give emitters incentives to exploit cheap abatement options beyond what they need to comply with the standards. In other words, they create lower innovation and adoption incentives (Jaffe *et al.* 2003; Downing and White, 1986; Jung *et al.* 1996; Keohane, 2001; Milliman and Prince, 1989; Zerbe, 1970).[34] Technology standards, especially, give firms no incentive to develop alternative, potentially more effective technologies than those mandated by the regulation. Innovation incentives are stronger under performance standards, but are limited by the fact that emitters do not gain from reducing emissions below the levels demanded by the regulation. Research in regulated firms may also be reduced by the knowledge that standards would be further tightened once a new technology was found (the "regulatory ratchet", *e.g.* Hahn and Stavins, 1991).[35] More broadly, uncertainty about future regulation and, therefore, about the future (implicit or "shadow") price of emissions undermines research incentives. Finally, while ambitious technology and performance standards can in principle be set to "force" innovation, it is difficult for the regulator to determine the appropriate standards required in advance, with the risk that innovation incentives will be either too weak or too strong.

Ability to cope effectively with risk and uncertainty

CAC instruments are not well suited for coping with the uncertainty surrounding both the damage from climate change and the costs of reducing GHG emissions. They do not provide certainty about GHG emissions or about abatement costs. Furthermore, they do not accommodate change – whether in emission targets, economic conditions or abatement technologies – as easily as price instruments. For instance, under taxes or emissions trading, an individual emitter's response to new technologies is spontaneous and decentralised. By contrast, under a CAC approach, firms have little control over specific abatement decisions, and when faced with a change, the regulator must re-specify all the standards affecting the many different types of emitters.

2.2.4. Technology-support policies

Technology-support policies provide R&D and/or technology adoption incentives (Chapter 5). On the R&D side, they range from basic public research to direct government funding of private R&D and tax incentives, and can also strengthen intellectual property rights (IPRs). On the technology adoption side, they may include subsidies, public purchases, and legal obligations (*e.g.* for electricity providers to purchase a certain share of their electricity from renewable sources, which may be best achieved through market mechanisms such as "green certificates").

For a global problem like climate change, the question is whether (and how) such incentives should be co-ordinated across countries. International co-ordination sends consistent signals to investors worldwide, spreads risks and avoids duplication, but it involves higher transaction costs. This section discusses the rationale for using technology-support policies to address climate change, but do not discuss the pros and cons of each possible instrument or institutional arrangement.[36]

Intrinsic cost-effectiveness

R&D and/or technology adoption instruments *alone* are not a cost-effective way of achieving a given GHG emissions reduction objective, for three main reasons (see in particular Fischer and Newell, 2007; Schneider and Goulder, 1997):

- Most importantly, unlike taxes or emissions trading, they do not directly address the negative externality from GHG emissions. As a result, they do not change demand patterns. For instance, they do not provide incentives to reduce energy intensity (through an increase in energy prices) or to reduce the emissions intensity of fossil fuels (*e.g.* by shifting from coal-fired to gas-fired power plants).
- When these policies take the form of subsidies they need to be financed, thereby creating distortions in the economy. Such distortions are of particular concern if large R&D and/or technology adoption incentives are required to offset the absence of a carbon price to achieve a given emissions reduction objective (Fischer and Newell, 2007).
- Finally, in the case of R&D policies, cost-effective early abatement opportunities are foregone, and all emission reductions must be achieved at a later stage by making new technologies less expensive than "carbon-intensive" technologies, in the absence of carbon pricing. This may require very large initial R&D spending.[37]

Adoption and compliance incentives

Technology-support policies have a number of attractive political features:

- The perceived trade-off between economic growth and mitigation policies is lower with such policies, for two main reasons. First, because technology-support policies help address innovation failures, they may actually boost economic growth.38 Second, they postpone actual emission cuts until new technologies become available in the future. As a result, they are usually seen as less costly to the current generation than other available options. Certain R&D policies, such as advanced commitments, can even be "free" in the short run.
- From a standard political economy perspective, their costs are usually spread widely across the population, while their benefits are more concentrated on potential innovators. This increases the likelihood that they will be adopted.
- They offer a possible burden-sharing mechanism, and as such may be used to facilitate wide adoption of a post-2012 agreement. For instance, it has been suggested that developed countries could finance most of the research into new technologies and subsidise their transfer to developing countries, *e.g.* by buying out IPRs and transferring the technologies at below-market price.

R&D and technology diffusion incentives

R&D policies and technology adoption incentives are better suited than price and CAC instruments for correcting specific innovation and technology diffusion failures that undermine the creation and diffusion of emissions-reducing technologies. The case for R&D support seems most convincing for major innovations whose rents are most difficult to capture (mainly if IPRs cannot be protected strongly enough). And in order to be most effective, R&D policies should target emissions-reducing technologies as much as possible. For instance, R&D in energy efficiency may be less effective than R&D focused on reducing the carbon intensity of energy. This is because improvements in energy efficiency have a direct negative impact on the demand for fossil fuels, but an indirect positive effect via the associated fall in fossil fuel prices.

The case for technology-adoption incentives, *e.g.* in the form of subsidies to renewable energy or biofuels, can be justified by the presence of learning-by-doing and/or using effects, because of the positive spillovers that adoption brings to other potential adopters. However, the potential benefits from policy intervention need to be weighed against its economic and environmental costs (especially for biofuels). Furthermore, public support for technology diffusion can be a double-edged sword; poor policy choices and lobbying by interest groups run the risk of "locking-in" the wrong technologies, especially if there are increasing returns to adoption.[39]

As already mentioned, in the absence of any price on GHG emissions, technology-support is not a cost-effective way to stimulate sufficient innovation and technology diffusion (Fischer and Newell, 2007 and Chapter 5).[40] It is, therefore, most effective as a *complement* to carbon pricing. However, technology-support policies are also potentially time-inconsistent in that what is optimal now may not be optimal later. To address this concern, it has been suggested that a global fund could commit in advance to reward any major innovation through a legally enforceable and, therefore, credible contract (Box 5.2, Chapter 5). However, given that firms are likely to be better informed than governments about costs and potential returns from R&D, setting the appropriate level of the reward – *i.e.* one that encourages innovation today without providing excessive profits to future innovators – would be challenging.[41]

Ability to cope effectively with risk and uncertainty

Technology-support policies provide no certainty about environmental outcomes, even in the long run. This reflects the uncertainty surrounding the time lags before R&D yields a benefit. As a result of this slow response, technology-support policies would be vulnerable to worse-than-expected climate trends. Neither would such policies provide certainty about abatement costs in the long run, if used *alone* to achieve a specific emissions reduction target.

2.2.5. Voluntary agreements

Voluntary agreements (VAs) between governments and private parties to limit GHG emissions are another possible climate mitigation instrument. VAs have long been used in a number of environmental areas in some OECD countries and have received growing attention for climate change in recent years. By contributing to information gathering and diffusion of best-practice, they can help address information problems in a way that is similar to information instruments. Furthermore, they raise awareness and understanding of mitigating options for firms and sectors, rely on consensus building and are easy to implement. All of this makes their adoption easier than for more stringent instruments. Because of this, VAs may also pave the way for the adoption of more stringent policies at a later stage, although they also run the risk of regulatory capture.

However, implementation is key for reaping these potential benefits. Indeed, VAs can vary widely in terms of stringency, monitoring and enforcement. Agreements that are likely to be most effective include measurable emission targets below a well-defined baseline scenario, monitoring and reporting requirements by an independent party, and compliance incentives, such as penalties (Hanks, 2002; OECD, 2003). In any event, the impact of VAs on emissions and their cost-effectiveness is hard to assess, given potential selection bias (*e.g.* more energy-efficient firms have larger incentives to enter into VAs) and the difficulty to determine the impacts (*i.e.* the deviation from emission trends in the absence of the VA).

VAs should best be seen as domestic complements to national or international policy frameworks including more cost-effective policies, not least price instruments. Indeed, on their own, VAs do not meet the main criteria against which to assess the overall cost-effectiveness of alternative policies, namely:

- They are not intrinsically cost-effective. There is no reason to expect any impacts on emissions to be achieved by exploiting the cheapest abatement opportunities – if only because of partial coverage.
- They do not provide appropriate innovation incentives on a broad scale, although they may facilitate the diffusion of existing emissions-reducing technologies within the industries covered. At best, they are likely to face the same limits as standards, *i.e.* emitters do not have continuing incentives to find cheap abatement options beyond what is agreed within the context of the VA.
- Finally, they cannot cope effectively with risk and uncertainty. They provide certainty neither about GHG emissions nor about abatement costs, and unlike price instruments they do not accommodate change spontaneously.

2.3. Interactions across policy instruments

The wide range of available GHG emissions-reducing policies and possible interactions among them raises the issue of whether and how they can be integrated into a coherent framework. While multiple market failures arguably call for multiple policy instruments, poorly-designed policy mixes can result in undesirable overlaps, which would undermine cost-effectiveness and, in some cases, environmental integrity. There are basically three main possible types of interaction among policy instruments (Sorrell, 2002; Sorrell and Sijm, 2003):

- Direct interaction: when the target groups directly affected by two policies overlap in some way. For example, some or all of the participants in a emissions trading scheme may at the same time be subject to a carbon or fuel tax.
- Indirect interaction: when a target group that is directly – or sometimes indirectly – affected by one policy is also indirectly affected by another policy. For example, there is an indirect interaction between a "downstream" emissions trading scheme (one that includes the electricity generators) and an electricity tax on consumers. This is because consumers are directly affected by the electricity tax and indirectly affected – through higher electricity prices – by the emissions trading scheme. Likewise, there is an indirect interaction between a downstream emissions trading scheme and any obligation upon electricity suppliers to purchase – possibly in the form of tradable credits – renewable electricity, as both ultimately lead to higher consumer prices.
- A trading interaction: where two policies interact with one another through the exchange of an environmental trading commodity, such as a GHG emissions allowance. For instance, allowances from one emissions trading system may be exchangeable for allowances from another scheme, under specific rules. The Clean Development Mechanism (CDM) of the Kyoto Protocol, or any linking between two different emissions trading schemes, are good examples. Likewise, there may be trading interactions between GHG emission permits and tradable credits for renewable electricity, if allowances from the latter can be used for compliance with the former. Trading interaction may be seen as a special case of indirect interaction, where the target group directly affected by one scheme is indirectly affected by the other through allowances trading.

Whether these interactions are desirable on the grounds of cost-effectiveness – and, in some cases, environmental integrity – depends on whether the instruments address different market imperfections and/or affect different target groups (*e.g.* OECD, 2007b). If so, they are complementary and their combination will enhance cost-effectiveness more than when only a single instrument is used. If not, they overlap and overall mitigation costs increase for two main reasons: i) double regulation usually entails some loss of flexibility on the part of firms in picking-up least-cost abatement options; and, ii) administrative costs are unnecessarily increased. The rest of this section highlights a number of important examples of policy complementarities and overlaps that are likely to be encountered in practice.

2.3.1. Policy complementarities

Complementarities across climate policy instruments

As the previous section has shown, none of the instruments commonly available to policymakers can simultaneously address the multiple market imperfections involved in achieving cost-effective GHG emission reductions. Therefore, overall mitigation costs may be lowered by combining policy instruments according to their comparative advantage in addressing each market imperfection.[42] In light of the previous discussion, the various market imperfections could be addressed by combining all of the following:

- Putting a price on GHG emissions, either through taxes or emissions trading.
- Using R&D and technology adoption instruments to address innovation and diffusion failures that are specific to emissions-reducing technologies. These instruments would be over and above policies that deal with general innovation and diffusion failures.
- Using information and CAC instruments to overcome information failures (asymmetric information, imperfect monitoring).

Furthermore, carbon pricing is unlikely to cover all world emission sources in practice, at least over in the medium term. This leaves a number of cheap abatement opportunities unexploited and further widens the gap between social and private returns from emissions-reducing technologies. Against this background, there may be an argument for using CAC instruments and technology-support policies to curb unpriced emissions and boost innovation and technology adoption incentives, respectively. These can be justified in the following cases:

- CAC instruments will work best if their target groups differ from those covered by taxes or emissions trading schemes. Their implicit (shadow) price should not exceed the carbon price. As well, their use should not encourage vested interests that would oppose the adoption of price instruments at a later stage.
- Technology-support policies could involve an international trading system which would give credit (through permit allocation rules) to participants for their R&D investments. This might increase both participation and R&D incentives, thereby dealing with the public good nature of both climate and innovation. However, this would need to be done in a way that does not undermine the environmental integrity of the trading scheme, and does not give excessive rewards to R&D efforts, since carbon pricing would already provide some R&D incentives.

Complementarities between climate mitigation instruments and policies in other areas

The overall cost-effectiveness of a climate policy package can also be enhanced by reforming a number of policies that either: (i) increase GHG emissions; or (ii) distort the incentives and therefore raise the cost of mitigation instruments. These include:

- *Energy policies:* Fuel tax rebates and energy price regulations are still being used as social policy devices in many developing and middle-income countries, including China, India, Russia, and parts of Eastern Europe (Chapter 4). They reduce incentives for energy efficiency, and thereby distort the incentive effects of mitigation instruments and resource allocation throughout the economy more broadly. In addition, energy markets – electricity production and distribution in particular – remain highly regulated in many countries. Greater competition would increase the welfare gains from emission taxes or trading schemes.

- *Trade policies:* Tariff and non-tariff barriers to imports of emission-reducing goods and services are an unnecessarily obstacle to effective abatement policies. Applied most-favoured nation (MFN) tariffs on bioethanol exceed 20% on an *ad valorem* basis (*i.e.* based on value rather than quantity) in many OECD economies, including Australia, the European Union and the United States (Table 2.2).[43] As a result, only about 10% of the world's ethanol consumption is currently met through international trade (Walter *et al.* 2007), even though biofuels produced in tropical regions from sugarcane and palm oil have a considerable comparative advantage over those derived from agricultural crops in temperate zones, owing both to their intensity in cheaper labour and much higher physical yields (Girard and Fallot, 2006). Existing barriers to imports of energy-efficient electrical appliances (*e.g.* low-energy light-bulbs, refrigerators, air conditioners, clothes washers, water heaters, computer etc.) and renewable-energy products and technologies (*e.g.* solar photovoltaic systems, wind turbines and pumps etc.) are other examples of trade protection hampering the cost-effectiveness of mitigation policy and/or leading to increased emissions. Applied tariffs on such goods are typically low across the OECD but are at or above 15% on an *ad valorem* basis in many developing countries, with bound tariffs sometimes reaching much higher levels (Steenblik, 2005; Steenblik *et al.* 2006).[44] Overall, there seems to be room both for lower tariffs in many non-OECD countries and for lower non-tariff barriers in their OECD counterparts – at least via greater harmonisation of criteria and tests for energy-efficiency requirements.[45]

- *Agricultural policies:* Agricultural support policies in developed countries – not least in the European Union (EU), the United States (US) and Japan – distort relative prices, although the resulting impact on world GHG emissions is not straightforward. On the one hand, they raise emissions directly through encouraging higher agricultural outputs (*e.g.* methane emissions from rice and livestock), and indirectly through the overuse of pesticides and fertilisers. On the other hand, their removal would shift agricultural output towards producers from developing countries that may be more GHG-intensive, and would partly reallocate resources towards non-agricultural industries that may emit more GHG.

- *Legal frameworks:* Lack of legal frameworks and effective and enforced property rights encourages widespread deforestation in some parts of South America, South-East Asia and Africa. Unsustainable land use practices are even more widespread, including in OECD countries as well as developing regions. Establishing stronger legal frameworks for land use management, emissions monitoring and property rights, along with specific burden-sharing arrangements, may be needed to stimulate cheap emission reductions in this area.

Table 2.2. Subsidies to ethanol and biodiesel per ton of CO_2 equivalent avoided are high in many OECD countries

(USD per ton of CO_2eq)

	Ethanol	Biodiesel
United States	300	250
European Union	700	250
Australia	400	150
Canada	250	250
Switzerland	300	250

Source: Steenblik (2007).

2.3.2. Policy overlaps

Policies overlap if they address similar market failures and affect the same target groups directly or indirectly. Two prominent illustrations of such double regulation are the following:

- Similar emission sources that are directly or indirectly covered by both emissions trading and a carbon tax. Under an emissions trading system, overall emission levels are set by the cap. By increasing emitters' abatement efforts, a carbon tax frees up emission permits and puts downward pressure on their price (*e.g.* OECD, 2007a, 2007b). Ultimately, the carbon tax is fully offset by a fall in the permit price, leaving total emissions unchanged but unduly raising administrative costs. A carbon tax is, therefore, redundant, unless it is set at a level high enough to bring the permit price down to zero, in which case it is the emissions trading system that becomes redundant. Furthermore, if the target groups of both instruments overlap partly rather than fully, different emitters face different incentives to cut emissions, thereby raising mitigation costs. This is because emissions are then priced once or twice, or unpriced depending on whether emitters are covered by one instrument, both or none. As a result, some emitters end up reducing emissions too much and others too little compared with the (marginal) cost of doing so.[46]
- Similar emission sources that are covered both by an economy-wide (national or international) trading scheme and by a potential international cap-and-trade scheme at the sectoral level (*i.e.* a binding sectoral agreement). This is another example where the target groups of two instruments partly overlap, with emissions being priced once or twice depending on whether emitters are covered by one or both schemes. In such cases, the possibility to exchange permits between schemes, along with double crediting of emission reductions for those emitters that are covered twice, would ensure that all emitters face similar emission prices, thereby ensuring economic efficiency.

A similar source of policy overlap arises if carbon pricing – whether through taxes or emissions trading – is supplemented with other instruments to address *only* the environmental problem of GHG emissions (the environmental externality). Such instruments may include transport fuel taxes, energy efficiency standards, or requirements for electricity suppliers to purchase renewable energy ("green") certificates, etc. Under emissions trading, any of these additional policies could reduce the permit price but would leave overall emissions unchanged, unless the policy is so stringent that the permit price falls to zero. Under a carbon tax, the additional policy reduces overall emissions, but raising the carbon tax rate would achieve the same result at a lower cost. The bottom line is that in the presence of a carbon price, there is little or no role for other policies in addressing the environmental externality. For instance, keeping a transport fuel tax can be justified only for raising general tax revenues and/or for addressing *other* externalities such as congestion and local pollution. Likewise, renewable energy regulations should reflect adoption spillovers and/or energy security considerations.

Trading interactions across different schemes also need to be taken into account in order to avoid overlaps and preserve overall environmental integrity. For instance, if a firm is covered by two different emissions trading schemes, there can be a risk of counting the same emissions ("double coverage") or the same emission reductions ("double crediting") twice (Sorrell and Sijm, 2003). Double coverage is usually offset by double crediting, in which case the environmental integrity of either scheme is not threatened. However, this is not always the case. For example, if firms covered by a trading scheme can earn credits through particular energy-efficiency improvements or renewable energy projects they could have undertaken anyway to meet their emission commitments, there will be double crediting without any compensating double coverage, and the emissions cap will be breached.

Notes

1. Climate policy might even focus on so-called "geo-engineering", or "solar radiation management", which may be loosely defined as any attempt to inject into the atmosphere substances (*e.g.* sulphur) to offset the global warming effects of GHGs. It has been argued that adaptation and geo-engineering, along with mitigation, could be part of an international climate policy agreement, given the theoretical case for equalising marginal costs across each of these alternative options to address climate change (*e.g.* Barrett, 2007a; Schelling, 2007).
2. It should be stressed that unlike such political uncertainty, economic uncertainty does not in general represent a market failure.
3. Kennedy and Laplante (1999).
4. Such concerns have been put forward as an explanation for low private research on vaccines against major worldwide diseases such as malaria, tuberculosis or HIV (Kremer, 2001a, 2001b).
5. Network effects also exist in road transport, where high penetration of low-carbon technologies (*e.g.* electricity and hydrogen-fuel-cell vehicles, biofuels) would likely require new infrastructure.
6. The implications of such a "structural" uncertainty for the economic analysis of low-probability high-impact events are discussed in Weitzman (2007b).
7. Economists call these effects "negative externalities" on the "public good" represented by climate stability.
8. The notion of a corrective tax on pollution, or more broadly any negative externality, dates back at least to Pigou (1920). It should be noted that a carbon tax *per se* is not a perfect proxy for a tax on GHG emissions, since only the latter provides incentives to reduce GHG emissions through ways other than reducing the use of carbon-based inputs. Discussions of a global GHG emissions tax often assume that some tax credits would be provided to activities that remove GHGs from the atmosphere, such as afforestation or carbon capture and storage.

9. However, one potential drawback of pricing carbon upstream is that it provides no incentive for carbon capture downstream.

10. De Mooij (1999), Goulder (1995), Goulder *et al.* (1999), Pezzy and Park (1998). However, one limit to the argument is that major tax distortions could still be eliminated independently from carbon tax revenues, *e.g.* by changing the tax structure. Also, eliminating harmful side effects of other taxes may not be the best possible way to use the financial room for manoeuvre provided by carbon tax revenues. Subsidising R&D in emissions-reducing technologies may actually be better policy.

11. There are also concerns that because fossil fuel reserves are exhaustible, producers may react to the expected path of the tax – and that of any policy that reduces fossil fuel demand – in such a way that undermines the environmental and/or cost effectiveness of the tax. For example, an expected gradual increase in the tax rate (the so-called climate policy ramp advocated by most economists in the field) may induce fossil fuel producers to speed up extraction so as to benefit from higher revenues while fossil fuel demand and prices are still high (Sinn, 2007). This would increase emissions and/or force governments to opt for a higher initial tax rate than initially desired.

12. Policies that discourage GHG emissions (*e.g.* fuel or electricity consumption taxes) will also usually undermine the cost-effectiveness of a GHG emissions tax. Interactions across different emissions-reducing policies are studied in detail in the next section of this chapter.

13. The loss of cost-effectiveness and/or environmental integrity associated with incomplete coverage depends on the magnitude of emissions "leakage". Leakage occurs when there is an increase in GHG emissions in one country (or industry or firm) as a result of an emissions reduction by a second country with a strict climate policy (Chapter 3).

14. In practice, two issues may complicate somewhat the harmonisation of carbon taxes across countries. First, tax exemptions for certain industries may be granted in some countries but not in others. Second, different countries may levy the tax at different stages of the carbon supply chain, with the risk that some emissions may be priced twice or, on the contrary, could avoid taxation. For instance, in order to avoid double taxation, a country with a tax on fossil fuel suppliers would have to exempt from the tax all fuels exported to countries that apply a similar tax rate downstream, on fossil fuel users.

15. Tax earmarking, or hypothecation, is when tax revenues are allocated to a specific end use.

16. In particular, the costs of searching for information about permit prices, finding trading partners and negotiating with them can be expected to decline strongly with market size. Kerr and Maré (1998), for some taxonomy of transaction costs affecting permit markets. These authors estimated that transaction costs led to an over 10% efficiency loss from trading in the US market for lead permits during the lead phase down from 1982 to 1987.

17. However, the market power issue arose in the context of the Kyoto Protocol, with several papers showing that a cartel formed by transition countries – in particular, Russia and Ukraine – would lower the gains from the international trade mechanism (Maeda, 2003; OECD, 1999).

18. Lax monitoring by one country may raise bigger concerns under a permit scheme than under a tax. Under cap-and-trade, laxity in one (large) country reduces emission prices, thereby undermining emission reduction incentives in all other countries. By contrast, under a set of harmonised taxes, laxity in one country does not affect emission prices and reduction incentives in other countries. Furthermore, because a permit trading scheme is more difficult to monitor and enforce than a tax in developing countries, developed countries may be more concerned about linking permit systems than about harmonising emission taxes.

19. Still, political uncertainty about the future price path of carbon may be higher *ex ante* under a system of fragmented domestic emissions trading schemes (with different prices to be harmonised in the future) than under a true international emissions trading system. This suggests that speeding up the linking of existing schemes may help to improve both static and dynamic efficiency.

20. However, Montero (2005) shows that this weakness of quantity-based instruments diminishes and may even be reversed under imperfect emissions control. This is essentially because imperfect enforcement "softens" the quantity instrument, with some firms choosing not to comply when abatement costs prove to be higher than expected.

21. The analysis focuses on the impact of carbon price uncertainty coming from exogenous changes (shocks), such as changes in the design of the scheme or the disclosure of new information (*e.g.* on actual emissions, as happened during the first phase of the EU ETS). However, it ignores uncertainty about the abatement costs of the emergence of a breakthrough technology, which would be endogenous to investment decisions. Zhao (2003) incorporated the latter form of uncertainty into a stylised model and found that, for some model specifications, firms' investment incentives decrease more under a carbon tax than under an emissions trading scheme.

22. While the investment effect of uncertainty is unambiguously negative in the short run, it is less clear-cut in the long-run (Jamet, 2009). Higher uncertainty induces firms to delay their investments, but it also increases the incentive to invest when conditions are favourable, *i.e.* when energy prices are high. When large sunk costs and low capital stock depreciation are involved, capital stock remains high even if conditions become less favourable. This effect tends to increase the steady-state capital stock.

23. This would be the case at least if some flexibility is allowed in the timing of emissions, *e.g.* when permits can be stored for future use (so-called "banking" of permits).

24. One straightforward way to set a price floor would be for governments to auction a sizeable portion of the allowances, and to withhold as many allowances from the auction as needed to maintain that price. Also, in multi-phase schemes, future allocations could be reduced when current prices are deemed too low, which would raise current prices, provided banking is allowed. This latter option was used in the United States within the context of the 2005 Clean Air Interstate Rule on SO_2 and NO_X emissions.

25. Burtraw *et al.* (2006) argue that in the case of the US SO_2 cap-and-trade scheme, lack of policy responsiveness to lower-than-expected abatement costs generated significant welfare losses in the 1990s. This could have been avoided had a price floor been in place.

26. For example, lack of banking provisions seems to have amplified the large drop in the EU ETS permit price which occurred in early 2006, following the release of lower-than-expected CO_2 emission figures for the year 2005. Indeed, while the future price fell from over EUR 30 per tonne of CO_2 to about EUR 15 between early 2006 and early 2007, the spot price dropped from over EUR 30 to under EUR 1. By allowing participants to store permits for the second phase of the programme, banking would have supported the spot price (although it would have also reduced the environmental effectiveness of the EU ETS during the second phase).

27. The authors find that when abatement costs are uncertain, standard emissions trading is inferior to a hybrid system in which firms have the option to pay a fee (an "escape" or "safety" valve) instead of buying permits when costs happen to be higher than expected.

28. Borrowing provisions – *i.e.* the possibility for an emitter to borrow permits – could also help avoid large price spikes. However, unlike a price cap, they would only be effective if emitters expect future prices to be lower than the current price (*e.g.* Congressional Budget Office, 2008). They may

also provide excessive incentives for emitters to defer emission reductions to the future, when the stringency and even the existence of future climate policy may be uncertain.

29. One exception is when emissions are difficult and/or costly to monitor, in which case performance standards are ineffective and technology standards provide a better option.

30. However, when fiscal revenues from market instruments are used to compensate for the losses incurred by industries directly affected by mitigation policies, the relative performance of standards improves, and might even turn into an absolute advantage under extreme conditions where industry-compensation requirements are high and distortive, and producers' abatement costs are homogenous and known by the regulator (Bovenberg *et al.* 2008).

31. For instance, in a study of local car pollution, Fullerton and West (2000) found that where emissions monitoring is imperfect and where there are differences in abatement costs across producers, over two-thirds of the potential welfare gain not captured by standards could be recovered by complementing standards with a set of taxes and subsidies based on vehicle age and size.

32. For instance, Levine *et al.* (1994) and Eto *et al.* (1994) found large net private benefits (without even factoring in the environmental gains) from US appliance standards and US lighting programmes, respectively.

33. For instance, Enqvist (2007) argues that a significant amount of GHG emissions could be reduced globally at a net financial benefit. For some theoretical support for the view that regulation can help (non-optimising) firms reap costless pollution abatement opportunities, Porter and van der Linde (1995). For a sceptical economist view, Palmer *et al.* (1995).

34. For empirical evidence that permit trading gives larger technology adoption incentives than binding performance standards, Kerr and Newel (2004) and Keohane (2001). They looked at historical experiences in the United States with the phase-out of lead in gasoline, and the reduction in sulphur dioxide emissions, respectively. In theory, the stronger innovation incentives under market-based instruments may not always hold under oligopolistic competition. Montero (2002) finds that a stringent emissions standard may have a larger innovation impact than a tradable permit scheme under quantity-based (Cournot) competition, but not under price-based (Bertrand) competition. This is because firms spontaneously under-invest in R&D under quantity-based competition, since the change in rival firms' output as a result of R&D spillovers would reduce the innovating firm's profits.

35. A parallel could be drawn here with the so-called "RPI-X" price cap regulation of monopolies. RPI-X regulation aims to mimic the incentives for cost efficiency found in competitive markets by setting a pre-determined price cap. In principle, this provides strong incentives for monopolistic firms to cut costs in order to increase profitability. In practice, however, under RPI-X regulation the regulator has an incentive to revise the price cap downwards at a later date, if cost reductions and the associated monopoly rents turn out to be higher than expected.

36. For some recent OECD comparative analysis of R&D incentives, and empirical evidence of their effects on R&D and innovation, Jaumotte and Pain (2005); and Guellec and van Pottelsberghe (2004).

37. For this reason, based on a calibration of their theoretical model to the US electricity sector, Fischer and Newell (2007) found R&D subsidies to be the costliest policy option for reducing emissions from electricity production, followed by renewable energy adoption incentives, emissions performance standards and emissions pricing.

38. One potential mitigating factor is that large increases in R&D in carbon-free technologies may come at the expense of R&D in the rest of the economy (Schmalensee, 1994; Goulder and Schneider, 1999).

39. See the discussion in Jaffe *et al.* (2003).

40. However, two empirical studies (Jaffe and Stavins, 1995 and Hassett and Metcalf, 1995) find larger impacts on energy efficiency improvements in US homes from technology cost subsidies than from energy taxes. Possible explanations for these findings include uncertainty over the future price of energy and capital market failures (Jaffe *et al.* 2003)

41. Kremer (2001b) discussion of markets for vaccines. The author suggests that the reward offered by the global fund could start relatively low and then pick up gradually if the pace of innovation is not fast enough. This process would mimic an auction, which often offers an efficient procurement method when costs are unknown. However, such an iterative procedure may be difficult to apply to climate mitigation technologies, because the lag between the policy decision and a perceptible impact on innovation is likely to be long (*e.g.* for electricity production).

42. In particular, there is burgeoning theoretical and empirical evidence that a policy package combining carbon pricing and technology-support policies could significantly reduce mitigation costs. For instance, based on a theoretical model calibrated on US electricity sector data, Fischer and Newell (2007) suggest that optimal R&D and renewable subsidies could lower by over a third the CO_2 emissions price needed to achieve a 5% cut in US electricity sector emissions, and could bring down the overall cost of the policy package to zero, due to the positive spillovers generated by the technology-support policies.

43. Tariffs on biodiesel are much lower, varying roughly between 0% and 7%, but can be high in developing countries (Steenblik, 2006).

44. In the case of electrical appliances, standards are also applied in virtually all OECD countries, and increasingly so in non-OECD ones. While these may be partly justified to address market imperfections that limit the adoption of energy-efficient technologies, they can act as non-tariff trade barriers, all the more so as energy-performance metrics and testing criteria vary widely across countries (Steenblik *et al.* 2006). For recent analysis of existing trade barriers in the areas of electricity supply, buildings and industry, OECD (2007b).

45. An opportunity to achieve this at the multilateral level is the negotiating mandate given to members of the World Trade Organization (WTO) in Doha in November 2001, which explicitly covers "the reduction or, as appropriate, elimination of tariff and non-tariff barriers to environmental goods and services".

46. For instance, the co-existence of comprehensive carbon taxation with the participation of electricity generators in a permit-trading system distorts the incentives to substitute between electricity (covered twice) and other emission sources (covered once).

ISBN: 978-92-64-05606-0
The Economics of Climate Change Mitigation
Policies and Options for Global Action beyond 2012

Chapter 3

Mitigating Climate Change in the Context of Incomplete Carbon Pricing Coverage: Issues and Policy Options

This chapter identifies a number of issues that arise when carbon pricing coverage is incomplete. These include unexploited cheap options for GHG emissions reduction, carbon leakage and competitiveness concerns. A number of policies that have been suggested to address these issues, such as countervailing duties on imports or border tax adjustments and free allocation of permits ('grandfathering'), are closely examined. The chapter also assesses the role that Reducing Emissions from Deforestation and forest Degradation (REDD) can play, and discusses the main implementation issues and options for financing mechanisms for REDD.

Key Messages

- *An incomplete coverage of carbon pricing mechanisms in terms of countries, industries, emission sources and gases has negative implications for the cost and effectiveness of mitigation action, while raising issues of competitiveness.*
- *Incomplete coverage reduces the range of low-cost abatement options, which increases the overall cost of achieving world emission reduction targets, and makes stringent emission or concentration targets virtually out of reach. For instance, achieving GHG emissions targets through CO_2 emission cuts alone would raise costs significantly, illustrating the large low-cost mitigation potential of non-CO_2 gases.*
- *Incomplete coverage also leads to "carbon leakages",* i.e. *an increase in carbon dioxide emissions in one country as a result of an emissions reduction by another country (or region) with a stricter climate policy. Partial coverage therefore undermines the environmental and cost-effectiveness of carbon pricing, and also leads to competitiveness losses for energy-intensive industries. Model-based estimates suggest that leakage rates would fall rapidly if the coalition of acting countries were to increase in size. For example, if the European Union cut emissions unilaterally by 50% in 2050 (over 2005 emission levels), 11.5% of this abatement effort would be wasted through carbon leakage. However, if a similar emission reduction is spread across all Annex I countries, less than 2% of the reduction would be lost.*
- *Some countries have proposed tackling carbon leakage by imposing countervailing duties on imports from non-participating countries based on their carbon content, possibly through a generalised system of predictable, permanently applied environmental tariffs. While this would contribute to "level the playing field" in the goods and services markets and reduce the extent of carbon leakage, it may fail to reduce the output losses incurred by energy-intensive industries in participating countries. Furthermore, countervailing duties on imports from non-participating countries are estimated to entail costs to both those countries that apply them and to other countries with which they trade. They could also involve potentially large administrative costs, and run the risk of trade retaliation.*
- *One way to address international competitiveness concerns is through the free allocation of permits to energy-intensive industries exposed to international competition. The drawbacks include the high financing costs that this would entail as well as a reduction in recipients' incentives to lower their own emissions. To limit the latter, policymakers should in such a case announce in advance that grandfathering will be gradually phased out, as has been the practice under the EU-ETS.*
- *The coverage of emission sources could be significantly broadened by incorporating forestry into a global agreement. Emissions from deforestation account for up to 17% of total GHG emissions. Reducing Emissions from Deforestation and forest Degradation (REDD) can be achieved relatively cheaply, and could potentially reduce the cost of global action by 40% (although there could be an impact on land and food prices). In order to tap this potential, however, important challenges need to be overcome, including the development of a consistent and comparable monitoring, reporting and verification system; as well as ensuring sufficient and sustainable financing, perhaps through a global fund or the creation of a REDD credit trading market.*

Introduction

It was earlier suggested that standard model simulations may overestimate the costs of mitigation policies because they do not include deforestation and carbon capture and storage (Section 1.4 in Chapter 1). On the other hand, post-2012 policies could also turn out to be much costlier, as the coverage of carbon pricing is likely to be much less complete, at least initially, than cost-effective stabilisation strategies presented in Chapter 1 assume.

This chapter discusses the implications of an incomplete coverage of carbon pricing. Leaving some countries, sectors or emission sources outside the scope of a global policy to reduce GHG emissions would increase its cost and could make it impossible to reach ambitious concentration targets (Section 3.1). In addition, the effectiveness of unilateral action by one group of countries may be partly undermined by the existence of carbon leakages, an issue that is partly related to the loss of competitiveness of energy intensive industries on international markets (Section 3.2). The chapter shows that the importance given to this issue far exceeds its economic significance and that most policy options to address this issue may well raise the cost of mitigation while doing little to reduce the loss of competitiveness incurred by energy intensive industries (Section 3.3). Finally, while Reductions in Emissions from Deforestation and forest Degradation (REDD) could be achieved at a relatively low cost, integrating these emission reductions into a carbon markets approach is expected to be difficult in the short-run (Section 3.4). The importance of reducing emissions from deforestation and forest degradation for lowering mitigation costs, but also the mechanisms needed for implementing such a policy in the context of global mitigation action are discussed.

3.1. Implications of incomplete coverage for the costs and effectiveness of mitigation action

The losses resulting from incomplete country carbon pricing coverage can be illustrated through two simple exercises. First, it is clear that even moderately stringent concentration targets will be impossible to meet if only Annex I countries were to take action. For instance, stabilising overall GHG concentrations at about 650 ppm CO_2eq would require a reduction in world GHG emissions by over 23 Gt by 2050. Such a reduction could not be achieved by Annex I countries alone, since their emissions would have to become negative. Second, even GHG concentration targets below 750 ppm CO_2eq – though technically feasible – are virtually out of reach if Annex I countries act alone, as they would imply a carbon price spiralling up to very high levels by mid-century. In this context, only a lax 800 ppm CO_2eq target, corresponding to an increase in temperatures by more than 4°C relative to pre-industrial levels in the long-run, could be met by Annex I countries acting alone; this would cost about 1.3% of their combined GDP in 2050.

Likewise, reaching a target by restricting emission reductions to CO_2 only (without including other greenhouse gases), or exempting energy-intensive industries from policy action, would raise costs further than in the all-encompassing, cost-effective scenarios presented above. For instance, reducing GHG emissions (in CO_2eq terms) by the same amount as in the "550 ppm-base" scenario (Scenario A in Chapter 1) through CO_2 emission cuts only, rather than all greenhouse gases, would raise costs in 2050 from 4% to 7% of world GDP (Table 3.1). This illustrates the large low-cost mitigation potential of non-CO_2 gases, especially when seeking to achieve less stringent mitigation targets.[1] Similarly, achieving a target by exempting energy-intensive industries (chemicals, metallurgic, other metal, iron and steel industry, paper, and mining products) would increase the cost of the "550 ppm-base" scenario from 4% to 6% of world GDP.

Table 3.1. An incomplete coverage of industries or GHGs would raise the economic costs of stabilising overall GHG concentration below 550ppm

Scenario	Marginal abatement cost in 2050 (2005 $US per t CO_2eq)	Average cost 2012-2050 (% of real GDP)	Cost in 2050 (% of real GDP)
550ppm-base (Scenario A)[1]	282	-1.7	-3.9
550ppm-base with CO_2 only	836	-3.2	-7.4
550ppm-base without energy-intensive industries	592	-2.5	-5.8

1. Stabilisation of CO_2 concentration at 450ppm, and of overall GHG concentration at about 550ppm CO_2eq, with modest overshooting.

Source: OECD, ENV-Linkages model.

3.2. Implications for carbon leakage and competitiveness

Smaller country coalitions entail larger mitigation costs in part because they are ineffective from an environmental perspective; their emission cuts may be partly offset by increases elsewhere. This phenomenon is often referred to as "carbon leakage". Carbon leakage may arise through two main channels: *i)* the competitiveness channel, as carbon-intensive industries in participating countries lose market shares to their foreign competitors and/or relocate capital in non-participating countries; and *ii)* the fossil fuel price channel, as emission reduction efforts in participating countries lower world demand for fossil fuels, thereby inducing a price decline that triggers greater fossil fuel use and higher GHG emissions in non-participating countries.

Simulation analysis to illustrate the issue related to leakage is undertaken by means of examples where, in many cases, the European Union is acting alone. This choice was purely for illustrative purposes. The intention was not to judge the merits of individual action *per se*. In one scenario, in which the European Union cuts emissions unilaterally by 50% in 2050 (relative to 2005 emission levels), leakage was found to amount to almost 11.5% of the reduction the European Union achieved in 2050 (Table 3.2).[2] However, if a similar emission reduction (2.8 Gt, or about 3.9% of projected 2050 world emissions) is spread across all Annex I countries, carbon leakage becomes negligible, falling to less than 2%. This reflects both the larger country coverage and the fall in marginal abatement costs in participating countries. Moreover, it is not only the magnitude but also the nature of leakage that changes with the size of the coalition. The wider the country coverage, the smaller the market share losses for energy-intensive industries in participating countries (the first leakage channel), but the larger the impact of policy action on international fossil fuel prices (the second leakage channel). Finally, the leakage rate also declines substantially when non-CO_2 gases are covered. For instance, if the European Union were to cut only CO_2 rather than all GHG emissions by 50% in 2050, the leakage rate is estimated to rise from about 11.5% to 16%.[3] This reflects the lower marginal abatement costs when all GHGs are included, and the fact that incorporating non-CO_2 gases shifts some of the burden of emission reductions onto sectors, such as agriculture, that have only marginal influence on world fossil fuels markets.

 THE ECONOMICS OF CLIMATE CHANGE MITIGATION – ISBN: 978-92-64-05606-0 – © OECD 2009

Table 3.2. Carbon leakage rates fall when countries and GHGs coverage is increased

Leakage rates implied by an emission reduction of 2.7 Gt in 2050 with respect to 2005 levels[1]

Leakage rates (%)		2020	2050
EU acting alone:	CO_2 only	13.0%	16.0%
	All GHG	6.3%	11.5%
Region acting (across all GHGs):	EU	6.3%	11.5%
	Annex I	0.7%	1.7%
	Annex I and Brazil, India and China	0.2%	0.2%

1. The size of this emission cut is equivalent to a 50% cut in EU emissions in 2050 relative to 2005 levels.

Source: OECD, ENV-Linkages model.

The magnitude of carbon leakage is driven by a number of factors, not least the degree of competition between energy-intensive goods produced by different countries and, even more importantly, the responsiveness of fossil fuel supply to fossil fuel prices at the world level (Burniaux and Oliveira Martins, 2000). Intuitively, the less responsive is the supply of fossil fuel, the more difficult it is to reduce emissions, and the larger the amount of leakage resulting from unilateral action. This is because the less fossil fuel producers lower their supply in response to lower demand from the coalition, the more fossil fuel prices would decrease and the more demand will increase outside the coalition. The relative values of supply elasticities for different fossil fuels also matter, as they imply different price response to a carbon constraint, which may either amplify or mitigate leakage.[4] Thus the behaviour of fossil fuel producers at the world level is critical in determining the amount of leakage.

While carbon leakage may become very small in a large coalition, the impact of carbon pricing on the output of energy-intensive industries in domestic and international markets may still be large, reflecting a shift in economic structure away from carbon-intensive production. For instance, under a global carbon price scenario where world emissions are reduced by 50% by 2050 relative to 2005, the global output of energy-intensive industries is projected to drop by 13%, even though there is no leakage (Table 3.3, Panel A).This world output loss would be unequally distributed across regions. For example, the output of European energy-intensive industries would increase slightly, reflecting competitiveness gains relative to their less energy-efficient foreign competitors, not least from developing countries. The overall size and unequal regional distribution of the output loss of energy-intensive industries suggest that including them in a wide international agreement could meet political obstacles.

Table 3.3. Impact of alternative policy scenarios on the output of energy-intensive industries[1] in 2050

Scenario	Region	Production
		% deviation in reference to baseline
Panel A. Sectoral output effects		
Scenario – 50% rel. to 2005 (Global action)		
	World	-13
	Western Europe	2
	Rest of the world	-16
Scenario "leakages" (EU action only)		
	World	-0.4
	Western Europe	-4
	Rest of the world	0.2
Panel B. Sectoral output effects of imposing countervailing duties		
Scenario "countervailing tariff" (EU action only)		
	World	-1
	Western Europe	-5
	Rest of the world	0.1

1. Energy-intensive industries include chemicals, metallurgic, other metal, iron and steel, industry, paper and mining products.

Source: OECD, ENV-Linkages model.

3.3. Pros and cons of policy alternatives to address leakage and competitiveness issues

A number of possible policy responses are currently being considered to address carbon leakage and loss of competitiveness in the context of incomplete country coverage. The responses analysed in this section include free allocation of permits to energy-intensive industries and countervailing duties. Another response is discussed in Chapter 4: a sectoral approach to expand mitigation actions to developing countries.

3.3.1. Domestic permit allocation rules

Permit allocation rules have already been used to address international competitiveness concerns, *e.g.* by grandfathering permits[5] to energy-intensive industries exposed to international competition in the context of the EU-ETS. However, this approach does little to alleviate deterioration in international price competitiveness, since some of the costs of abating emissions to meet the cap in these industries are ultimately passed onto consumers – at least in reasonably competitive markets – irrespective of permit allocation rules. Nonetheless, if firms have to maintain their activity in order to be eligible for free permits, grandfathering may still soften the output and employment effects of mitigation policies by implicitly subsidising the continuation of otherwise unprofitable activities. However, this comes at a cost to society, due both to the financing of the implicit output subsidy itself, and the fact that larger and costlier cuts then have to be imposed on other parts of the economy for the emissions target to be met. Finally, expectations that permits will continue to be grandfathered in the future might undermine recipients' incentives to lower their own emissions to avoid reducing their future expected entitlements.

At a minimum, this suggests that policymakers should announce in advance that grandfathering will be gradually phased out, as has been the case for instance under the EU-ETS.

3.3.2. Countervailing duties

One policy response to leakage that is receiving growing attention is to impose countervailing tariffs on imports from non-participating countries based on their carbon content (*e.g.* Stiglitz, 2006[6]). In principle, countries that are taking action against climate change could apply a border-tax adjustment equal to the local carbon price to each tonne of carbon used in the production of imported goods (ideally both directly and indirectly via inputs). This would "level the playing field" in their goods and services markets. Model simulations suggest that such countervailing tariffs would reduce the risk of carbon leakage for very small coalitions of acting countries. For instance, they are estimated to reduce leakage significantly in a scenario where the European Union unilaterally cuts GHG emissions by 50% (Table 3.4).[7] This confirms the importance of the competitiveness channel for leakage when only a few of the main emitters take action. While addressing leakage, countervailing tariffs may not curb the output losses incurred by energy-intensive industries located in the European Union, which are found here to slightly increase (relative to the baseline scenario) from 4% to 5% after the introduction of tariffs (Table 3.3, Panel B). Several factors contribute to offset the positive effects of the market share gains created by countervailing tariffs on the output of these industries. These include the impact of costlier (energy-intensive) imported inputs on the production costs of EU energy-intensive industries (which is somewhat larger than for other sectors), a slight increase in the carbon price required to meet the EU emission target, and the fact that energy-intensive industries still face some competitiveness losses as a result of the indirect impact of the European carbon price on the price of their non-energy inputs.

The role and the effectiveness of countervailing duties decline rapidly as the coalition size increases, because leakage rates are much lower and tariffs address a smaller share of remaining leakage. For instance, when mitigation action and tariffs are applied across Annex I countries, the leakage rate falls from 7% to 4% (Table 3.4), assuming a targeted reduction in their emissions by 50% in 2050 (about 14 Gt, or 19% of projected 2050 world emissions). This reflects the greater importance of the fossil fuel price channel – which countervailing duties do not address – when country participation is larger.

Despite some effectiveness when applied to small coalitions, countervailing import tariffs raise a number of important concerns. They raise the costs of mitigation in participating countries, but they also entail economic losses for non-participating countries. For instance, in a scenario where Annex I countries cut their emissions unilaterally by 50% by 2050, a countervailing duty helps reduce world emissions by about 0.4 Gt (or about 0.6% of projected 2050 world emissions) but the cost to world GDP in 2050 would increase from 0.5% to 1.2% (Table 3.4). Partly reflecting the losses incurred by affected trade partners, countervailing tariffs might also trigger retaliation rather than increase participation in mitigation action. Also, it is not certain that the current World Trade Organisation (WTO) legal framework provides grounds for such measures (OECD, 2006b; Perez, 2007). In order to partly meet some of these concerns, a generalised system of predictable, permanently applied environmental tariffs has been advocated (Perez, 2007). However, while such a system might prevent some escalation of trade barriers, it would still entail significant economic and administrative costs to both participating and non-participating countries. Indeed, the practical difficulties of calculating a tariff based on the carbon content of imports from different origins would likely entail large administrative costs. It certainly seems unlikely that the indirect carbon content of imported goods could be taken into account. Finally, and perhaps most importantly, while they may address competitiveness concerns, they do little to address the carbon leakage that occurs through the fall in world fossil fuel prices – which in turn results from lower demand for carbon-intensive fuels in participating countries.

Table 3.4. Effects of countervailing import tariffs on carbon leakage and mitigation costs

	Reduction of 50% in EU countries in 2050		Reduction of 50% in Annex I countries in 2050	
	Without a countervailing tariff	With a countervailing tariff	Without a countervailing tariff	With a countervailing tariff
Leakage rates in 2050	11.5%	2.9%	7.1%	4.0%
Average GDP effect 2012-2050				
(% deviation in reference to baseline)				
In participating countries	-0.9%	-1.1%	-1.2%	-1.2%
In non-participating countries	0.0%	-0.1%	-0.1%	-0.3%
World	-0.2%	-0.3%	-0.7%	-0.9%
GDP effect in 2050				
(% deviation in reference to baseline)				
In participating countries	-1.5%	-1.8%	-1.9%	-2.0%
In non-participating countries	0.0%	-0.1%	-0.1%	-0.4%
World	-0.3%	-0.4%	-0.5%	-1.2%

Source: OECD, ENV-Linkages model.

3.4. Incorporating a deforestation and forest degradation into an international mitigation action plan

As noted in previous work (*e.g.* Karousakis and Corfee-Morlot, 2007), a least-cost post-2012 climate policy framework would likely have to include specific mechanisms to Reduce Emissions from Deforestation and forest Degradation (REDD) in developing countries, and to enhance forest carbon sinks more broadly. Emissions from land use, land use change and forestry, including agricultural emissions, may account for about 31% of total GHG emissions, with emissions from deforestation alone accounting for up to 17% (IPCC, 2007).[8] Studies suggest that REDD could potentially reduce the economic cost of stabilising GHG concentrations in the atmosphere. However, there are wide uncertainties associated with both emission levels and potential cost savings and technical and methodological issues need to be addressed before the long-term goal of integrating REDD in the existing carbon market can be achieved. There are therefore alternative approaches to deal with REDD emissions during the transition towards a unified carbon market. The following sections discuss the importance of REDD for lowering mitigation costs, but also the mechanisms needed for implementing such a policy in the context of global mitigation action.

3.4.1. Emissions from deforestation and forest degradation: past, present and future

There are large uncertainties around estimates of global CO_2 emissions from deforestation. For the 1990s, some studies agree on annual emissions of about 7.3 $GtCO_2$, or about 18% of world GHG emissions (Fearnside, 2000; Malhi and Grace, 2000; Houghton, 1999, 2003). Others report substantially lower estimates of just 3.5 $GtCO_2$ (DeFries *et al.*, 2002; Achard *et al.*, 2004) or as low as 2.1 $GtCO_2$ per year (DeFries *et al.*, 2002). The IPCC reports a central estimate of 5.9 $GtCO_2$ within a very wide range (from 2.9 to 8.8). Most recent estimates for the post-2000 period put annual CO_2 emissions at about 5 to 6 $GtCO_2$ (4.8 in Sohngen *et al.*, 2008, and 5.8 in Houghton, 2008).

Overall, total GHG emissions from land-use changes (including deforestation) increased by about 1% per year on average between 1980 and 2000, although some stabilisation seems to have occurred during the 1990s (Figure 3.1). Asia and South America together accounted for almost 80% of these emissions in 2000. Likewise, the bulk of emissions are in fact concentrated in a relatively small number of countries, including Indonesia, Brazil, Bolivia, Cameroon, Malaysia, the Democratic Republic of Congo, Ghana, and Papua New Guinea (Eliasch, 2008).

Figure 3.1. GHG emissions from land-use changes and forestry by region

(1980-2000, in $GtCO_2eq$)

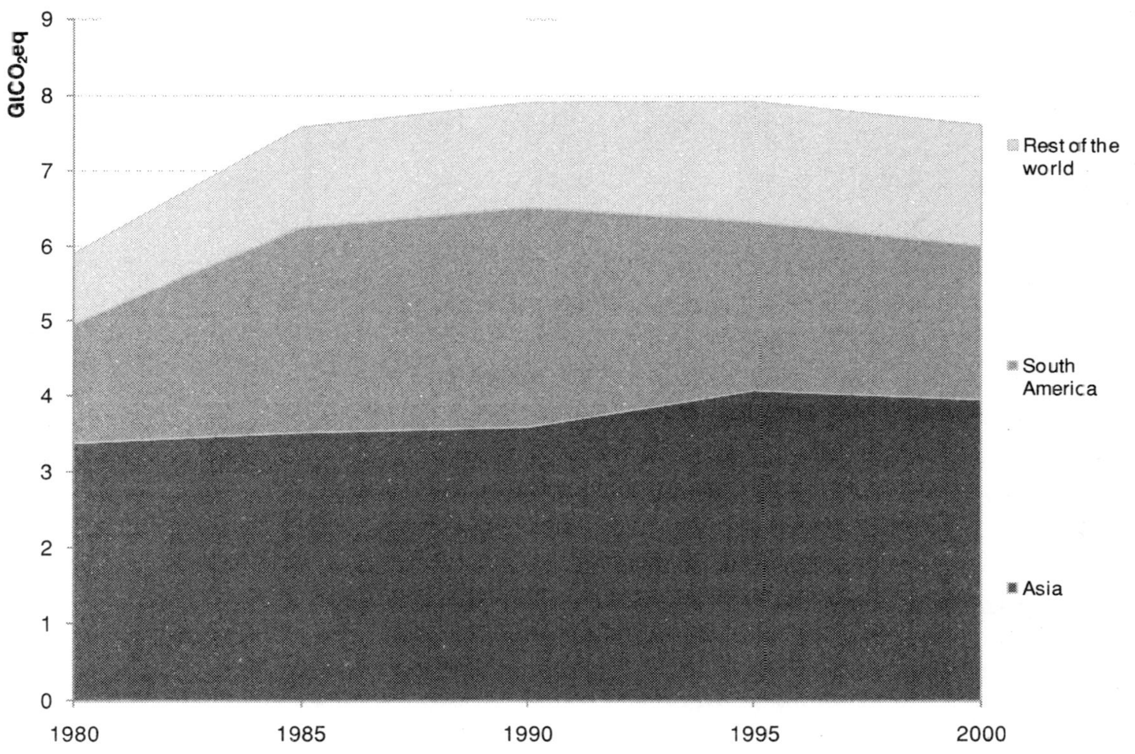

Source: World Resources Institute (WRI), 2009.

There is clear consensus across available projections that deforestation rates are declining and that emissions from land-use changes (including deforestation) will fade out progressively over the coming decades, disappearing completely during the second half of the century even in the absence of any policy to halt deforestation (Figure 3.2). However, the cumulative amount of carbon from deforestation released in the atmosphere under such a business as usual (BAU) scenario would still be very large, amounting to about three times 2005 world GHG emissions over the period 2000-2050. Avoiding these emissions by taking advantage of the large mitigation potential of forestry is therefore important.

Figure 3.2. CO_2 emissions from deforestation are projected to decrease in the business-as-usual scenario

(2000-2100)

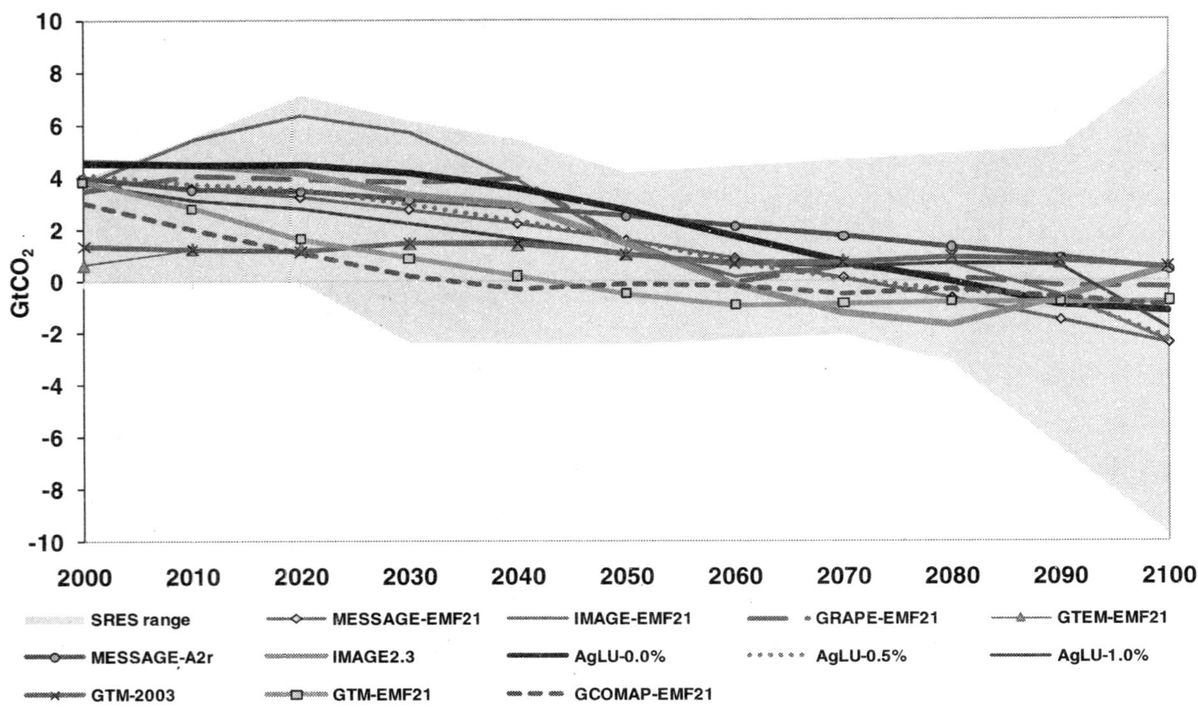

Notes: MESSAGE-EMF21 = Rao and Riahi (2006) scenario from EMF-21 Study; GTEM-EMF21 = Jakeman and Fisher (2006) scenario from EMF-21 Study; MESSAGE-A2r = Riahi *et al.* (2006) scenario with revised SRES-A2 baseline; IMAGE 2.3 = van Vuuren *et al.* (2007) scenario; The IMAGE 2.3 LUCF baseline scenario also emits non-CO_2 emissions (CH_4 and N_2O) of 0.26, 0.30, 0.16 $GtCO_2$ eq in 2030, 2050 and 2100 respectively.

Source: Fisher *et al.* 2007.

3.4.2. The abatement potential of preventing deforestation

Existing studies suggest that REDD is a low-cost mitigation option in comparison to other abatement alternatives, although the measurement of this cost-saving potential is still in its infancy and remains subject to a large degree of uncertainty. Various methodologies have been used to estimate this cost-saving potential, ranging from partial forestry to full general equilibrium models. Although results vary widely depending on the methodology used, there is evidence that afforestation/reforestation options could provide sizeable low-cost abatement potential, especially in the short run (Box 3.1).

Box 3.1 Estimating the abatement potential of avoiding deforestation

Regional and area-based estimates conclude that halting deforestation could be achieved at a cost of no more than a few USD per tonne of CO_2 (Nepstad *et al.* 2007; Grieg-Gran, 2006 and 2008). Strassburg *et al.* (2009) include a larger set of countries and suggest that more than 90% of global deforestation could be stopped at a price of USD 8 per tonne of CO_2. The global GHG abatement cost curves estimated by McKinsey (McKinsey & Company, 2009) also suggest substantial mitigation potential at a cost of below USD 8 per tonne of CO_2eq. However, these estimates are probably on the low side, because they do not include transaction and capacity building costs or, more fundamentally, the economic costs of the carbon price policies needed to make these options profitable.

Existing global forestry models[1] yield much higher cost estimates, in part because their coverage is more complete, allowing more spill-over effects to be captured (such as the impact of avoiding deforestation on the supply of agricultural land). According to these models, half of the emissions from deforestation projected in the baseline, or 1.5 to 2.7 $GtCO_2$ per year, could be avoided at a cost ranging between USD 8 and 19 per tonne of CO_2. This points to a mitigation potential in 2010 of around 3.8 $GtCO_2$ per year (around 7% of projected world emissions) at a cost of USD 50 per tonne of CO_2 (with a range from 3 to almost 5 Gt CO_2 per year). This mitigation potential declines over time, falling to 3 $GtCO_2$ per year in 2030, in line with the expected decline in emissions from deforestation in the baseline scenario. Based on a survey of different studies, IPCC (2007) suggests a somewhat lower mitigation potential of around 1.9 $GtCO_2$ per year at a price of USD 50 per tonne of CO_2.

These estimates suggest that incorporating REDD in a global abatement programme could substantially reduce costs.[2] For instance, based on a partial equilibrium approach, one study finds that allowing the full use of forestry credits within the CDM market could reduce the CDM carbon price in 2020 by 40%, from EUR 20 to EUR 12 per tonne of CO_2eq (New Carbon Finance, 2009). Piris-Cabezas and Keohane (2008) report much more moderate cost reductions, with REDD credits estimated to reduce the permit price by approximately 13%. The Eliasch Review (2008) suggests that by including REDD and afforestation/reforestation options, global mitigation costs at the world level could be lowered by 25-50% and 20-40% in 2030 and 2050, respectively. Dixon *et al.* (2008) expect reductions in mitigation costs of around 50% with unrestricted REDD credits, most of which would be reaped in the short term. Tavoni *et al.* (2007) report a reduction in the carbon price of 40% in 2050 when REDD and afforestation/reforestation mitigation options are included in the WITCH model. Using the same model, but with a modified approach which included only REDD, overall mitigation costs drop by 25% (Bosetti *et al.* 2009*a*).

1. The Global Timber Model (GTM) (Sohngen and Mendelsohn, 2003; Sohngen *et al.*, 1999), the Generalized Comprehensive Mitigation Assessment Process Model (GCOMAP) (Sathaye *et al.* 2006) and the Dynamic Integrated Model of Forestry and Alternative Land Use (DIMA) (Kindermann *et al.*, 2006, and Kindermann *et al.*, 2008).

2. Furthermore, if designed appropriately, REDD can help protect biodiversity, provide benefits to indigenous, forest-dependent communities, and alleviate some regional problems such as water scarcity, soil degradation and desertification. These co-benefits may offer important incentives for countries to participate in a REDD mechanism.

To investigate this further, two aggregate marginal abatement cost curves for 2020 are compared: *i)* a cost curve from the ENV-Linkages model, which *excludes* forestry and other land use, land use changes and forestation options; and *ii)* an average of the aggregate curves from three global models[9] which *incorporates* emissions from deforestation. This comparison suggests that in order to reduce global emissions by 19 $GtCO_2$ per year (about one-third of projected global GHG emissions for 2020), incorporating emissions from deforestation could reduce the marginal abatement cost by up to 40%, from 90 to 55 USD per tonne of CO_2 (Figure 3.3). However, this partial approach ignores the likely effects of a large land use change at the world level on land and food prices. Techniques to quantify average cost savings from land use, land use changes and forestation in a general equilibrium framework are currently in their infancy.[10]

Figure 3.3. Incorporating emissions from deforestation would lower the marginal abatement curves from the ENV-Linkages model

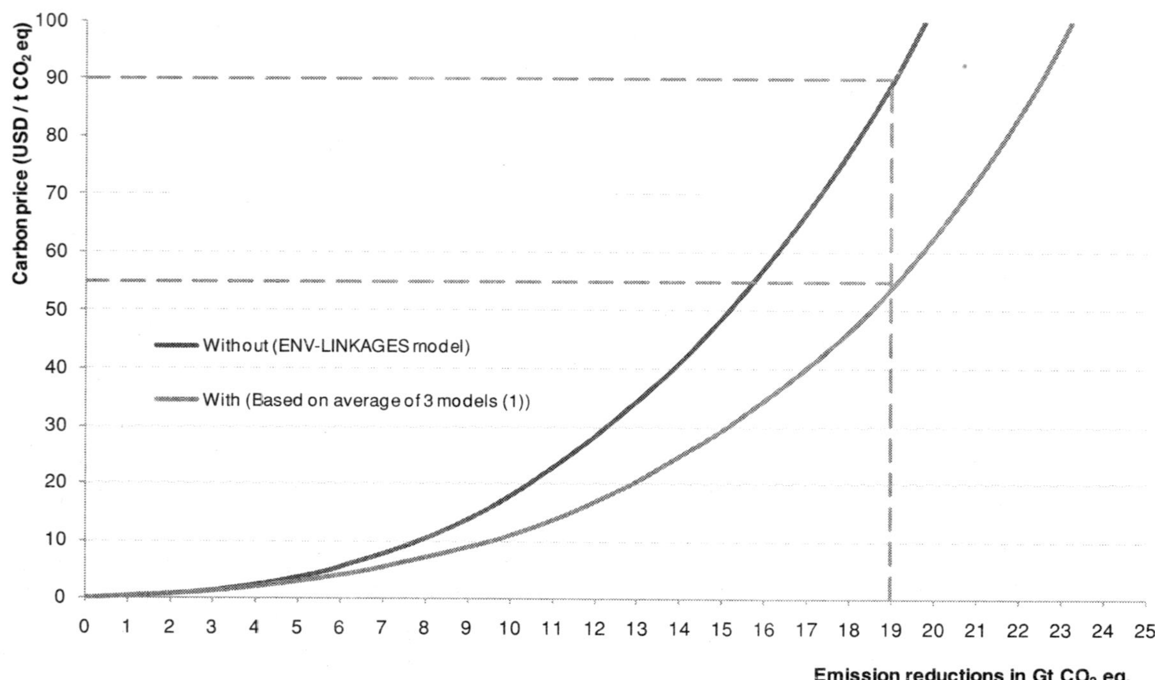

1. The three models are: DIMA, GTM and GCOMAP (Kindermann *et al.*, 2008).

Source: OECD ENV-Linkages model.

3.4.3. Incorporating REDD into a global carbon agreement: implementation issues

The previous discussion indicates that, although subject to large uncertainties, REDD can potentially reduce the economic costs of stabilising GHGs concentration in the atmosphere substantially. However, in order to exploit this potential, a number of technical and methodological steps will need to be taken that may also shape the choice of ways in which a REDD mechanism could be financed:

- *Ensure consistent and comparable monitoring, reporting and verification*: Emission reductions need to meet specified monitoring, reporting and verification standards. Monitoring REDD requires two sets of data: *i)* data on the size and type of changes in land uses (for instance, from forestry land to pastures); and *ii)* data on the corresponding change in the carbon stock.[11] "Bottom-up" methods (on-the-ground sampling, land-use surveys, and their statistical processing) must be combined with "top-down" methods involving a combination of satellite images, aerial photographs, and remote sensing data. Technical capabilities have advanced since the 1990s and operational forest monitoring systems at the national level are now a feasible goal for many developing countries (Mollicone *et al.* 2003; DeFries *et al.* 2005). The quality of data on forestry-related emissions also varies across countries. Brazil and India tend to have more reliable data than most other developing countries, but substantial efforts are currently being made to improve data quality. The pre-2012 period provides an opportunity to improve developing countries' capacity to monitor emissions from deforestation and forest degradation, among other things by developing national inventories of land use changes, with capacity building assistance from developed countries.

- *Design appropriate baselines.* A baseline is needed against which to assess emission reductions. Baselines could be established at the project level, as in the current CDM, or at the sectoral level (Chapter 4).[12] One way to address the large uncertainties associated with monitoring emission reductions and to ensure the environmental integrity of a REDD mechanism would be to develop conservative baselines, although this may come at the cost of some potential low-cost abatement opportunities being lost.
- *Avoid creating perverse incentives for speeding up deforestation.* A baseline based on most recent trends may encourage countries to accelerate deforestation before the base year begins, to make it easier to make emission reductions against that baseline. To avoid this, the baseline could be negotiated in advance based on historical data and, possibly, business-as-usual projections. Once decided, this baseline could not be modified until the next negotiation round. This approach would avoid making the possibly erroneous assumptions that future trends will resemble past trends. It would also reduce the potential for introducing perverse incentives and allow equity issues to be addressed through the negotiation process. A prerequisite for establishing any baseline is to have time-series data for forest areas and corresponding carbon stocks.
- *Avoid intranational and international carbon leakage.* If the accounting coverage is not wide enough, emission leakage can occur as deforestation and forest degradation shifts from covered to non-covered areas. National baselines are therefore better able to address intranational leakage than project-by-project baselines (Plantinga and Richards, 2008). Broad international participation in a REDD mechanism would help alleviate international leakage.
- *Ensure permanence.* It is important to ensure that emission reductions are permanent and do not merely reflect delayed deforestation. A REDD mechanism should be designed to address this risk, for instance by issuing temporary credits, insurance mechanisms and/or reserves with debits from future credits (Karousakis and Corfee Morlot, 2007).

3.4.4. Financing mechanisms for REDD

An appropriate financing mechanism should include the following performance criteria: *i)* the ability to achieve effective reductions of emissions from deforestation within the 2013-2030 timeframe; *ii)* the ability to achieve these reductions in a way that improves the cost-effectiveness of global GHG emission mitigation; *iii)* the provision of sufficient and sustainable financing for REDD; and, *iv)* fair access to and distribution of this financing to all countries with a high potential for REDD. Two key options have been proposed for financing REDD: a market-based crediting approach and a (non-market) fund-based approach. Other "hybrid" proposals combine some elements of both approaches.

The market-based crediting approach

In principle, a market-based REDD mechanism could be introduced either via a sectoral cap-and-trade scheme or via a crediting mechanism. One advantage of the cap-and-trade approach is that it ensures compliance with the cap, and thus also provides a greater degree of certainty about the emission reductions that would be achieved. However, unlike a crediting mechanism, a cap-and-trade would imply a mitigation commitment from developing countries. At this stage, only crediting mechanisms are being considered in current REDD negotiations for the post-2012 commitment period.

The market-based crediting approach would allow developing countries that reduce their emissions from deforestation and forest degradation below a pre-specified baseline to generate carbon credits which they could sell in carbon markets. In principle, these REDD credits would be equivalent to other credits such as those generated through the CDM or the allowances from Annex I ETS and could be traded on the same carbon markets. This approach would then lead to a cost-effective allocation between REDD and other GHG emission reductions, and would generate sustainable and long-term finances to compensate developing countries for REDD below the baseline.

A commonly-raised concern with the market-based approach is that the environmental integrity, and ultimately the credibility, of the international carbon market could be undermined if it were to be flooded with low-quality REDD credits. One option to limit this risk is to control the supply of REDD credits through a price floor (Weitzman, 1974; Baumol and Oates, 1988), or by imposing maximum limits on supply. The supply limit could be adjusted upward if the carbon market price becomes too high – in which case REDD credits would become "offset safety valves" – or when the REDD market becomes safer and more mature. Therefore, although a global cap-and-trade system including REDD credits should be aimed for as a medium-term objective, adequate monitoring capabilities and capacity building are prerequisites for its implementation. Until these capabilities are in place, allowing REDD credits to be traded with other carbon credits without any limit should be avoided. On the other hand, once a country meets pre-defined eligibility criteria,[13] linking to the international carbon market could be allowed, possibly subject to a transition period over which supply restrictions would be gradually phased out.

Another way to prevent low-quality REDD credits from undermining the environmental integrity of international carbon markets is to keep REDD and other carbon markets separate (Ogonowski *et al.* 2007). Under this proposal, a new market for REDD credits only would be created, with no link to other international carbon markets. Each Annex I country would commit to meet a given share of its own reduction target by purchasing GHG reductions for REDD actions in developing countries, subject to a maximum established by the Conference of Parties. In order to be effective, this commitment would be a firm pledge. Commitments could not be modified before the next commitment period. REDD credits would be tradable but could not be exchanged against CDM credits or permits.[14] As with the market-based approach, such restrictions on the tradability of credits could be lifted gradually as countries meet pre-defined environmental integrity criteria. Although this approach has a number of advantages, it does not altogether eliminate outstanding uncertainties associated with REDD actions (such as, difficulty of proving additionality, and problems of leakages and permanence). Furthermore, whether this approach guarantees a complete segmentation of the REDD and carbon markets depends on how it is implemented in practice.

The fund-based approach

A non-market-based alternative would be to create a fund, to be distributed to governments based on REDD performance, *i.e.* emission reductions below a pre-determined baseline. The fund would rely on voluntary or institutionalised payments from developed country governments and other sources. A number of funding sources have been proposed, including official development assistance (ODA), international financial institutions, and earmarking of revenues from permit auctions under ETSs. Performance-based payments to governments would give them incentives to address the domestic causes of deforestation and forest degradation. Governments could also provide payments directly to individual landowners and communities to compensate them for the lost opportunity costs of conserving forest rather than converting it (*e.g.* similar to Payments for Ecosystem Services schemes). Fund-based and market-based schemes could be combined over time in a phased approach, with a first phase primarily fund-based to ensure capacity building, with REDD credits then gradually integrated into a carbon market under appropriate conditions.

The major advantage of the fund-based approach is that it would be even better than a segmented-market approach at avoiding contaminating a well-performing carbon market. Therefore, it may not require as high monitoring, reporting and verification standards as market-based approaches. It also provides a framework for directly financing capacity building, as well as protecting existing forests. However, basing it on voluntary contributions might mean inadequate incentives for contributing to the fund(s), and funding levels might therefore prove to be insufficient and unsustainable. This therefore runs the risk of leaving cheap abatement opportunities unexploited and, if not appropriately designed, could reduce the potential role of the private sector. If funding were sufficient, the cost-effectiveness of this approach could be improved by linking the amount of transfers to international carbon prices (Chapter 4).

Notes

1. With current technology, the marginal abatement costs of non-CO_2 gases are initially lower than those of CO_2, but their marginal abatement cost curve ultimately becomes steeper. As a result, their mitigation potential is exhausted more rapidly, and the bulk of any further emission reductions is achieved by cutting CO_2 emissions.

2. This means that for each Gt cut by the European Union in this illustrative scenario, emissions in the rest of the world rise by around 0.1 Gt, so that the net decline in world emissions is slightly less than 0.9 Gt.

3. This actually understates the "true" increase in leakage, since a 50% CO_2 emission cut scenario is in fact less stringent than a 50% GHG emission cut scenario.

4. For instance, if the supply of coal were to be more responsive to prices than that of crude oil, coal would become relatively more expensive in world international markets if a carbon constraint is imposed. This would induce non-participating countries to substitute other material for more carbon-intensive coal, leading to a decline in emissions that would amount to negative carbon leakage.

5. Grandfathering consists in allocating permits for free based on historical emissions.

6. In 2006, Joseph Stiglitz proposed that US trade partners ask the World Trade Organisation for authority to impose countervailing duties on exports of US steel and other energy-intensive products that benefit from the refusal to join the Kyoto Protocol.

7. Model simulations in Table 3.4 assume countervailing tariffs apply fully to the direct carbon content of imports, but only partly to the indirect content – *i.e.* to the electricity input only.

8. WRI (2009) estimate very similar numbers (32% and 18%, respectively).

9. The models are DIMA, GTM and GCOMAP (Kinderman *et al.* 2008).

10. At the time of writing this chapter, very few general equilibrium models incorporated GHG emissions from deforestation in a consistent way or were used to quantify the cost saving potential of abating these emissions (Hertel *et al.* 2008; Tavoni *et al.* 2007).

11. The most widely used database on land uses is from the United Nation's Food and Agriculture Organization (FAO). A database on land uses specific to general equilibrium models (the Agro Ecological Zones database) has been compiled by the Global Trade Analysis Project (GTAP). It uses data collected by the FAO and the International Institute for Applied Systems Analysis

(IIASA). The IPCC has compiled "good practice" methods for determining carbon stock changes associated with national inventories of GHG emissions from land uses, land use changes and forestry. In general, there are three sorts of databases: i) traditional forest inventories; ii) forest inventories including additional data on canopy cover based on high resolution remote sensing; and iii) the FAO database. Inventories based on remote sensing data are more accurate but tend to cover mainly productive forests.

12. In the REDD terminology used in the UNFCCC, the sectoral baseline here refers to "national" approaches/baselines.

13. Eligibility requirements for the participation of developing countries in a REDD market mechanism have yet to be established.

14. However, some indirect linking would still be possible, for instance if many Annex I countries use the carbon market to offset shortfalls in their REDD commitments.

ISBN: 978-92-64-05606-0
The Economics of Climate Change Mitigation
Policies and Options for Global Action beyond 2012

Chapter 4

Towards Global Carbon Pricing

This chapter examines ways in which a global carbon price can be built up gradually to achieve broad-based international pricing of carbon. Important steps include removal of environmentally harmful fossil fuel energy subsidies and increasing the use of emissions trading schemes while linking them together. The chapter investigates the global and regional gains from linking regional emissions trading schemes, and the harmonisation issues that need to be addressed in the case of direct linking. It examines indirect linking, for instance through the Clean Development Mechanism (CDM) or possible sectoral crediting approaches. It concludes with a discussion of market regulatory issues and the role of financial markets.

Key Messages

- *The use of domestic/regional emission trading schemes (ETSs) is spreading rapidly internationally. Together with international crediting mechanisms, these are important elements in the gradual build-up of a global carbon price. Global carbon pricing could help to reduce mitigation costs overall, and might also potentially reduce carbon leakage and limit competiveness concerns.*

- *Removing environmentally harmful fossil fuel energy subsidies, especially in non-OECD countries is an important first step. This would reduce greenhouse gas (GHG) emissions drastically in the subsidised countries, in some cases by over 30% relative to business-as-usual (BAU) levels by 2050 and it would also raise GDP per capita in most of the countries concerned. A multilateral removal of energy subsidies would cut GHG emissions globally by 10% by 2050 relative to BAU and this cut could be increased if developed countries adopt binding emission caps. The removal of energy subsidies would lower the cost of achieving a given mitigation target.*

- *Directly linking domestic or regional ETSs could form a key building block of a global carbon market by helping a single international carbon price to emerge. Linking reduces the cost of achieving the joint target and increases carbon markets liquidity. However, linking also raises a number of concerns including i) the uneven distribution of the gains from linking across countries, ii) the spreading of some design features of a particular scheme to others and iii) the risk of a dilution of the environmental integrity of the linked system. The distributional effects of linking can be mitigated through permit allocation rules and possibly by allocating commitments across countries conditionally on expected growth or by the use of an intensity target. While the other two concerns could be addressed by imposing some limits on linking, a more cost-effective approach would be to reach an agreement on the harmonisation of key ETS design features prior to linking. Such harmonisation would also increase the liquidity of carbon markets, which would foster the development of derivative markets, thereby lowering the cost of insurance against carbon price uncertainty.*

- *Linking domestic or regional ETSs indirectly through a common crediting mechanism like the CDM would help build up an integrated world carbon market and lower mitigation costs. Modelling analysis suggests that allowing Annex I (industrialised) regions to meet 20% of their commitments through emissions reductions in non-Annex I (developing) countries would nearly halve their mitigation costs. Raising the cap from 20% to 50% would bring further benefits, especially for those Annex I regions with high marginal abatement costs and which are most carbon-intensive. However, in order for these potential gains to be reaped, the current CDM would have to be carefully reformed.*

- *Even very large emission reductions in developed countries would not, on their own, suffice to halt climate change. Sectoral approaches can help to broaden participation to developing countries. The most effective approach would be to focus on the largest emitting sectors, such as energy intensive industries and the power sector, and/or key countries. Sectoral approaches would expand the potential for lower-cost emission reductions and could reduce leakage and competiveness issues, but they would need to be based on ambitious sectoral baselines or to include emission caps in order to ensure net additional emissions reductions.*

- *Negotiation and consensus building should be placed at the core of the development of the carbon market. Inter-governmental institutions that support implementation of the UNFCCC, the Kyoto Protocol, and others could help provide a framework in which participating governments can harmonise and co-ordinate their targets and the design features of emission trading schemes prior to linking. Compliance mechanisms at the national, regional or international level will also be needed. A working group of regulators could facilitate exchange of information about regulations and risks associated with the development of spot and but also derivative carbon markets.*

 THE ECONOMICS OF CLIMATE CHANGE MITIGATION – ISBN: 978-92-64-05606-0 – © OECD 2009

Introduction

Stabilising GHG concentrations at an ambitious level will be difficult to achieve immediately. It will require international action by all the main emitters, driven by a cost-effective set of policy instruments (including a global international carbon price, R&D policies and targeted regulations and standards). This chapter therefore examines how to achieve broad-based international carbon pricing gradually in practice. A range of policy instruments is considered:

- Removing environmentally harmful fossil fuel energy subsidies – as these amount to a negative carbon price. This would be a first step towards broad-based international carbon pricing and would free up budgetary resources to target more directly the social objectives supported by the subsidies. The first Section of this chapter analyses the potential environmental and economic effects of removing energy subsidies in non-OECD countries.
- The direct linking together of domestic/regional emissions trading schemes. With domestic/regional ETSs spreading internationally, albeit with a large heterogeneity in terms of both targets and design features, a global carbon market may gradually build up as domestic/regional ETSs become linked together. The conditions and implications of this direct linking of ETSs are explored in Section 4.2.
- Linking domestic/regional ETSs indirectly through the use of a common crediting mechanism. This is another way to gradually build up an integrated world carbon market and to lower mitigation costs. This is analysed in Section 4.3.
- The use of sectoral approaches, which can broaden participation to developing countries. This will be necessary because even very large emission reductions in developed countries alone would not be enough to halt climate change. Section 4.4 explores ways of designing sectoral agreements in order to move towards a global carbon price and to limit carbon leakage and competitiveness concerns.[1]
- The institutions and rules needed to foster the development of carbon markets and to address likely risks within a linked system of multiple independent and heterogeneous emission trading schemes. The final Section explores this.

4.1. Removing environmentally-harmful energy subsidies[2]

In many non-OECD countries there are currently large subsidies to the consumption of fossil fuels which keep fossil fuel use, and hence GHGs emissions, at high levels. Furthermore, as they imply some decoupling of domestic energy prices from world prices, they prevent the price signals of world energy markets from affecting domestic markets. Removing these subsidies would be an obvious initial step in pricing carbon worldwide. In addition to environmental benefits, it would yield economic gains because of a more efficient allocation of resources in the countries which remove these subsidies. Thus this step is one of the few "no regret" options for contributing to climate stabilisation.

Very few studies have attempted to quantify the impact of removing these subsidies in non-OECD countries. In its 1999 *World Energy Outlook,* the International Energy Agency (IEA) estimates the impact of removing energy subsidies in eight non-OECD countries (IEA, 1999, using a partial equilibrium approach). For this sample of countries, CO_2 emissions were estimated to fall by 16% on average, translating into a reduction of 5% in world emissions. Corresponding gains accruing to these countries were estimated to amount to 0.7% of their GDP on average, reaching approximately 2% in some cases. Using the general equilibrium model GREEN, Burniaux *et. al.* (1992) estimated that removing all existing distortions on primary fossil fuels would reduce world CO_2 emissions by 18% relative to the baseline in 2050 while generating an average discounted real income increase at the world level by 0.7% over the period 1990-2050. Again using a general equilibrium approach, the OECD (1999) found that removing energy subsidies in Annex I countries would reduce the costs of achieving the Kyoto Protocol, albeit only by a modest amount. Taken together, Annex I countries would benefit from such subsidy cuts, and the efficiency gains achieved in those that remove their subsidies (Russia and Eastern European countries) would benefit the others (mainly the United States and the EU), as these efficiency gains are entirely "exported" through the Annex I-wide ETS assumed in the OECD analysis.

This Section assesses the potential environmental and economic benefits of removing energy subsidies using the OECD model ENV-Linkages and a recent dataset assembled and provided by the IEA.

4.1.1. The size of environmentally-harmful energy subsidies

Energy subsidies take many different forms and can involve both direct and indirect subsidies, with the latter being more difficult to measure. Some subsidies aim at increasing fossil fuel consumption, while others aim to support domestic production. A common way to subsidise energy consumption is by exempting some energy consumptions from normal taxation (IEA, 1999). While each of these forms of subsidies should ideally be modelled explicitly in order to quantify their impact, this approach was not feasible in this analysis due to lack of data. Instead, it is assumed that different forms of subsidies result in a lower domestic energy price relative to a reference price. Accordingly, the energy goods are assumed to be relatively similar, and various forms of subsidies are summarised by a single statistic, the observed price gap between the energy domestic price and the reference price, differentiated across different types of end-use consumers (households, power generation, manufactures and services) when data were available. Although this approach has a number of well-known limitations[3] it is the only one possible given the information currently available on these subsidies in non-OECD countries.

The IEA has estimated price gaps corresponding to energy subsidies for 2005 and 2007 in 20 non-OECD countries, accounting for about 40% of world energy consumption (IEA, 2009). These gaps were estimated after adjustments were made to take into account market exchange rates, transportation margins and domestic taxes (including VAT). For fossil fuels, the reference price is the corresponding international price. As electricity is rarely traded, the reference price corresponds to an estimation of the production cost in the country considered (expressed in local currency).

The price gaps estimated for 2007 by energy sources and by countries/regions are significant in a number of cases (Table 4.1). As the influence of international energy prices on domestic markets is incomplete,[4] these gaps are likely to have changed following the 2008 oil price spike and then again when oil prices fell. The first column of the table shows the average gaps for all energy demands that are *effectively* subsidised in each country/region, thereby illustrating the magnitude of the gaps (the larger the number in absolute terms, the greater the subsidy). The second column reports the average gap across *all* demands, so that the difference between both columns depends on whether subsidies, for each fossil fuel, concern some specific demands or are broadly used across all types of demand. Countries not covered in the IEA database are included in regional aggregates (for instance, the "rest of the world" region) for which gaps of zero have been assumed. This assumption is fairly conservative as it is likely that some of these countries do also subsidise part of their energy consumption. The table shows how energy gaps differ across energy sources and countries/regions. Energy tends to be subsidised more heavily in Russia (especially natural gas), India and non-EU Eastern European countries. By contrast, the subsidy rates estimated by the IEA for China are rather moderate. The subsidy rates in oil-exporting countries and the

 THE ECONOMICS OF CLIMATE CHANGE MITIGATION – ISBN: 978-92-64-05606-0 – © OECD 2009

rest of the world regional aggregates appear to be relatively low, but they are understated due to the incomplete country coverage in the IEA estimates.

Table 4.1. Energy price gaps are found to be significant in a number of non-OECD countries

Energy price gaps in non-OECD countries,[1] 2007

		% deviation of domestic relative to world prices	
Country	Energy	Average subsidy rate over the demands that are effectively subsidised for each type of fuel	Average subsidy rate over the total demand for each type of fuel
China	Coal	-18.1	-0.5
	Gas	-27.0	-2.8
	Refined oil	-7.1	-2.0
	Electricity	-22.3	-3.2
India	Coal	0.0	0.0
	Gas	-53.6	-28.3
	Refined oil	-51.8	-10.1
	Electricity	-19.6	-9.1
Brazil	Coal	-40.4	-8.5
	Gas	0.0	0.0
	Refined oil	-14.4	-2.2
	Electricity	0.0	0.0
Russia	Coal	-51.6	-1.2
	Gas	-84.7	-26.8
	Refined oil	-23.6	-3.3
	Electricity	-48.9	-35.0
Oil-exporting countries	Coal	0.0	0.0
	Gas	-18.9	-5.9
	Refined oil	-29.2	-22.3
	Electricity	-21.9	-20.4
Non-EU Eastern European countries	Coal	-30.0	-4.9
	Gas	-39.6	-20.4
	Refined oil	-5.4	-1.8
	Electricity	-37.4	-20.7
Rest of the world	Coal	-2.1	-0.5
	Gas	-25.6	-7.7
	Refined oil	-8.5	-3.4
	Electricity	-6.7	-5.[illegible]

1. Energy subsidies are approximated by the difference in the domestic energy price and world prices.

Source: IEA (2008a).

4.1.2. The impact on GHG emissions and mitigation costs of removing environmentally-harmful energy subsidies

To measure this impact two scenarios are analysed:

i) The impact on GHG emissions and income of removing existing energy subsidies gradually in non-OECD countries between 2013 and 2020 assuming that no other mitigation action is implemented. Two cases are considered: 1a) a unilateral removal of energy subsidies in each non-OECD country/region (*i.e.* each country takes the action alone); and 1b) a multilateral removal of energy subsidies in all non-OECD countries/regions (*i.e.* all countries act simultaneously).

ii) The impact on the mitigation cost of removing energy subsidies in the context of a GHG mitigation policy. Again, two cases are considered: 2a) a reduction in GHG emissions (of 20% and 50% respectively in 2020 and 2050 compared to 1990 levels), combined with removing energy subsidies, with both actions taken in Annex I countries only; and 2b) the implementation of a world carbon tax designed to reduce global emissions to stabilise overall GHG concentrations below 550 ppm CO_2 equivalent ("550 ppm-base scenario"), combined with the multilateral removal of energy subsidies in all non-OECD countries.

The gradual multilateral removal of existing energy subsidies in non-OECD countries (Scenario 1b) would lead to quite a substantial drop of GHG emissions from fossil fuel combustion by 2050 in some countries/regions, amounting to around 30% or more in non-EU Eastern European countries, Russia and the Middle East (Figure 4.1).[5] However, while GHG emissions from fossil fuel combustion would fall by 14% in non-Annex countries in 2050, they barely decline in Annex I countries. This is because reductions in Russia and non-EU Eastern European countries are offset by increases in those Annex I countries that do not subsidise their energy demand, encouraged by falling world energy prices induced by the multilateral removal of subsidies. Of the 8.8 $GtCO_2$-eq emission reduction achieved by removing energy subsidies in non-OECD countries in 2050 (corresponding to a reduction of their emissions by 16% relative to the baseline), around 16% would be offset by an increase of emissions in OECD countries. As a result, global GHG emissions would be reduced by 10% in 2050 through this subsidy removal compared with business as usual.[6] With binding emission caps in OECD countries, the "leakages" would be contained, and the environmental benefits of subsidy removal would be even larger. For purposes of comparison, if each non-OECD country/region were to remove existing subsidies in isolation (unilateral removal, Scenario 1a), emission reductions would be lower than for a multilateral removal (Figure 4.2).[7]

All countries/regions (with the exception of non-EU Eastern European countries[8]) would benefit from a unilateral removal of energy subsidies and real income gains would range from 0.1% in Brazil to over 2% in India and Russia in 2050 (Table 4.2).[9] However, these gains would differ in the case of a multilateral simultaneous removal of energy subsidies in all non-OECD countries. Some of the non-OECD countries – especially Russia, the Middle East and non-EU Eastern European countries – that remove their subsidies would no longer enjoy real income gains. This is because the efficiency gains from improved resource allocation would be more than offset by the terms-of-trade losses associated with the sharp fall in world energy prices that a multilateral removal of subsidies would induce. However, energy-importing OECD countries, especially the European Union and Japan, would enjoy significant terms-of-trade and income gains. Overall, GDP and real income gains at the world level would be small, amounting to just 0.1% relative to BAU in 2050. This primarily reflects the fact that demand for energy goods is not very sensitive to price, so that the distortive impact of energy subsidies and the gain from their removal are limited.[10]

 THE ECONOMICS OF CLIMATE CHANGE MITIGATION – ISBN: 978-92-64-05606-0 – © OECD 2009

Table 4.2. Most countries would benefit from unilateral and multilateral removals of energy subsidies

(Household equivalent real income,[1] % deviation relative to the BAU)

Regions	Impact of unilateral removal of energy subsidies		Impact of multilateral removal of energy subsidies	
	2020	2050	2020	2050
Australia & New Zealand	0.0	0.0	0.0	-0.6
Brazil	0.0	0.1	0.0	0.1
Canada	0.0	0.0	-0.4	-1.5
China	0.0	0.3	0.1	0.7
EU27 & EFTA	0.0	0.0	0.4	0.9
India	1.1	2.2	1.4	2.5
Japan	0.0	0.0	0.4	0.9
Oil-exporting countries	-1.1	1.0	-2.1	-4.5
Non-EU Eastern European countries	0.5	-1.8	-2.0	-15.2
Rest of the world	0.0	0.2	-0.1	0.0
Russia	1.3	2.2	0.1	-3.7
United States	0.0	0.0	0.1	0.1
Annex I			0.2	0.1
Non-Annex I			-0.2	0.0
World			**0.1**	**0.0**

1. Hicksian "equivalent real income variation"defined as the change in real income (in percentage) necessary to ensure the same level of utility to consumers as in the baseline projection.

Source: OECD, ENV-Linkages model.

Figure 4.1. A multilateral removal of energy subsidies would lower GHG emissions in non-OECD countries

(% deviation in GHG emissions relative to BAU)

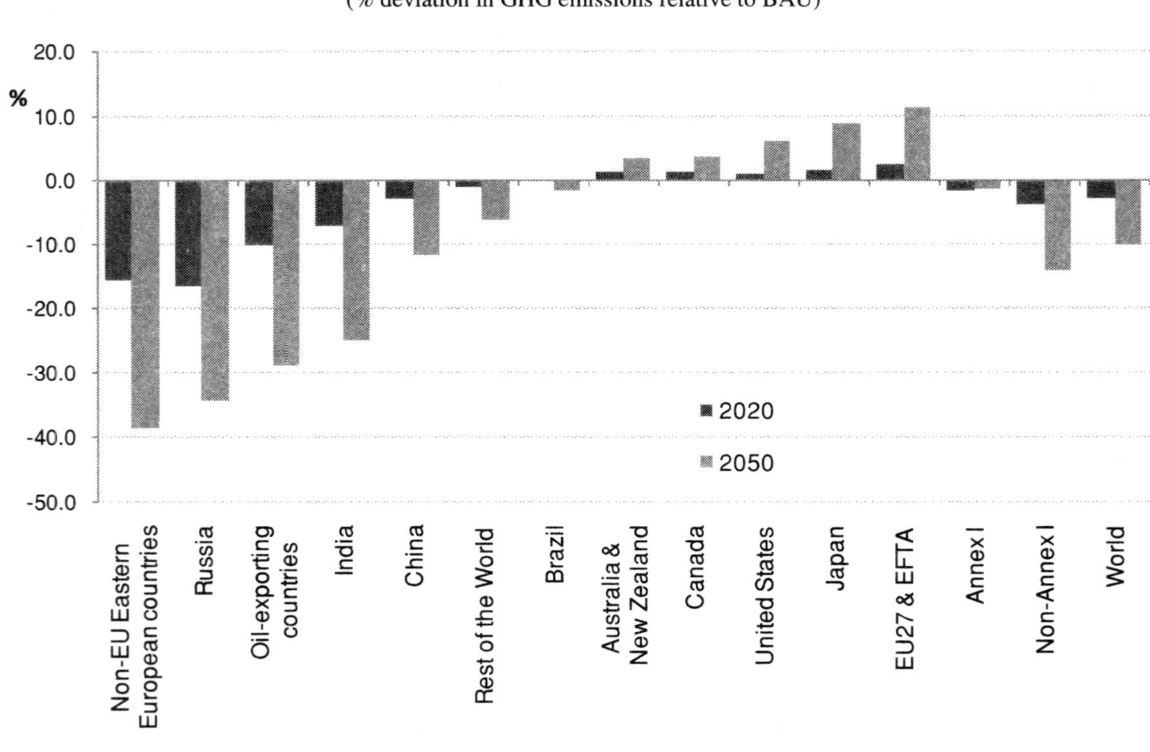

Source: OECD, ENV-Linkages model.

In the context of efforts to reduce their emissions as part of a post-2012 agreement, Annex I countries might also aim to remove their energy consumption subsidies. The cost savings associated with this action are estimated to be small, in line with the results reported in OECD (1999). Figure 4.3 reports the estimated economic costs of Annex I countries cutting their emissions by 20% and 50% by 2020 and 2050 respectively (relative to 1990 levels), with and without a removal of their energy subsidies (scenario 2a as described above). Overall, the cost savings are concentrated in Russia and the European Union, reflecting some efficiency gains and a terms-of-trade improvement, respectively.

Table 4.3. The treatment of energy subsidies in the business-as-usual and policy scenarios matters for the global GDP cost of a 550 ppm CO_2eq concentration stabilisation

Scenarios	World GDP loss in 2050 (% difference from BAU)
"550 ppm-base" scenario with energy subsidies in place	-3.4
"550 ppm-base" scenario with complete removal of energy subsidies in non-OECD countries	-3.2

Source: OECD, ENV-Linkages model.

The impact of removing energy subsidies is then assessed in the presence of a world carbon tax policy to stabilise overall GHG concentration below 550 ppm CO_2eq ("550 ppm-base" scenario[11] or scenario 2b as described above). Assuming that energy subsidies are kept in place, the stabilisation effort is estimated to reduce world GDP by 3.4% in 2050, compared with the business as usual scenario (Table 4.3).[12] The removal of energy subsidies generates a slight GDP gain and reduces emissions, making the stabilisation target easier to achieve. As a result, there is a lower world GDP loss in 2050 from mitigation action when energy subsidies are also removed (-3.2% as opposed to -3.4% when subsidies are in place). India and, to a lesser extent, China and OECD countries, benefit from the subsidy removal, while mitigation costs increase in energy-exporting countries (Figure 4.4). Cost savings at the world level are relatively small mainly because the economic distortion from energy subsidies is limited.[13]

In conclusion, removing existing energy subsidies in non-OECD countries would help to reduce world emissions, and lead to GDP gains in these countries. But part (almost one-fifth) of the environmental benefit of this reform would be lost unless emissions are capped in OECD countries. As theory suggests, removing these subsidies would generate real income gains in the countries where this reform is applied, as well as in OECD countries. As a result, incorporating the removal of energy subsidies into a global mitigation action will reduce the economic costs of this action.

Another important step in developing a global carbon market is then analysed – the linking together of emission trading schemes.

Figure 4.2. Unilateral removal of energy subsidies in non-OECD countries would lower GHG emissions but to a lesser extent than in the case of a multilateral removal

(% deviation in GHG emissions relative to BAU)

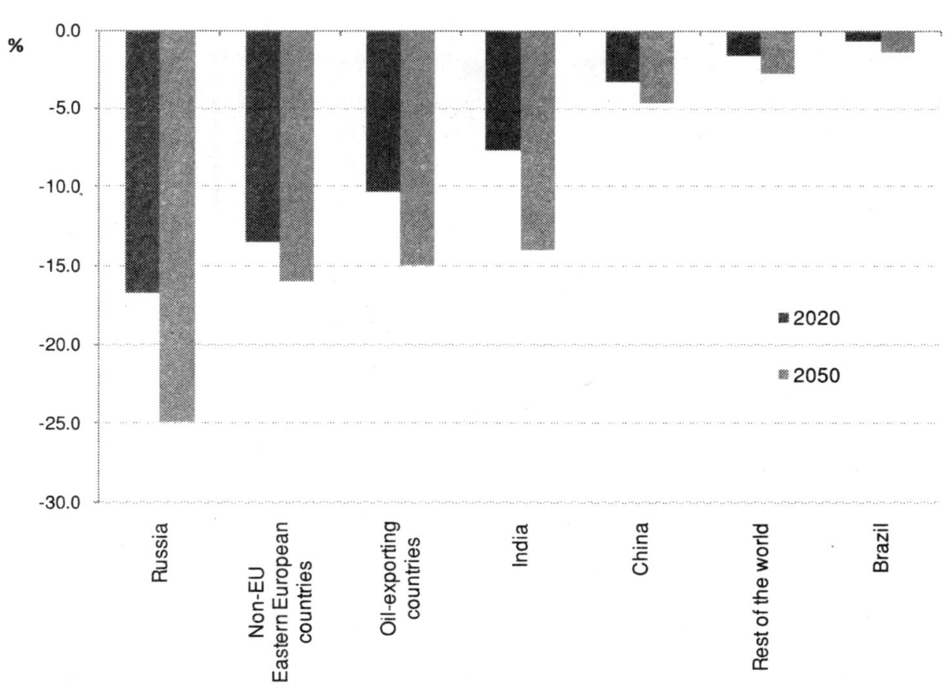

Source: OECD, ENV-Linkages model.

Figure 4.3. Removing energy subsidies in Annex I countries would slightly lower mitigation costs in these countries

Mitigation costs under a 20% cut by 2020 and a 50% cut by 2050 relative to 1990 levels in each Annex I region, household equivalent real income[1], % deviation relative to BAU

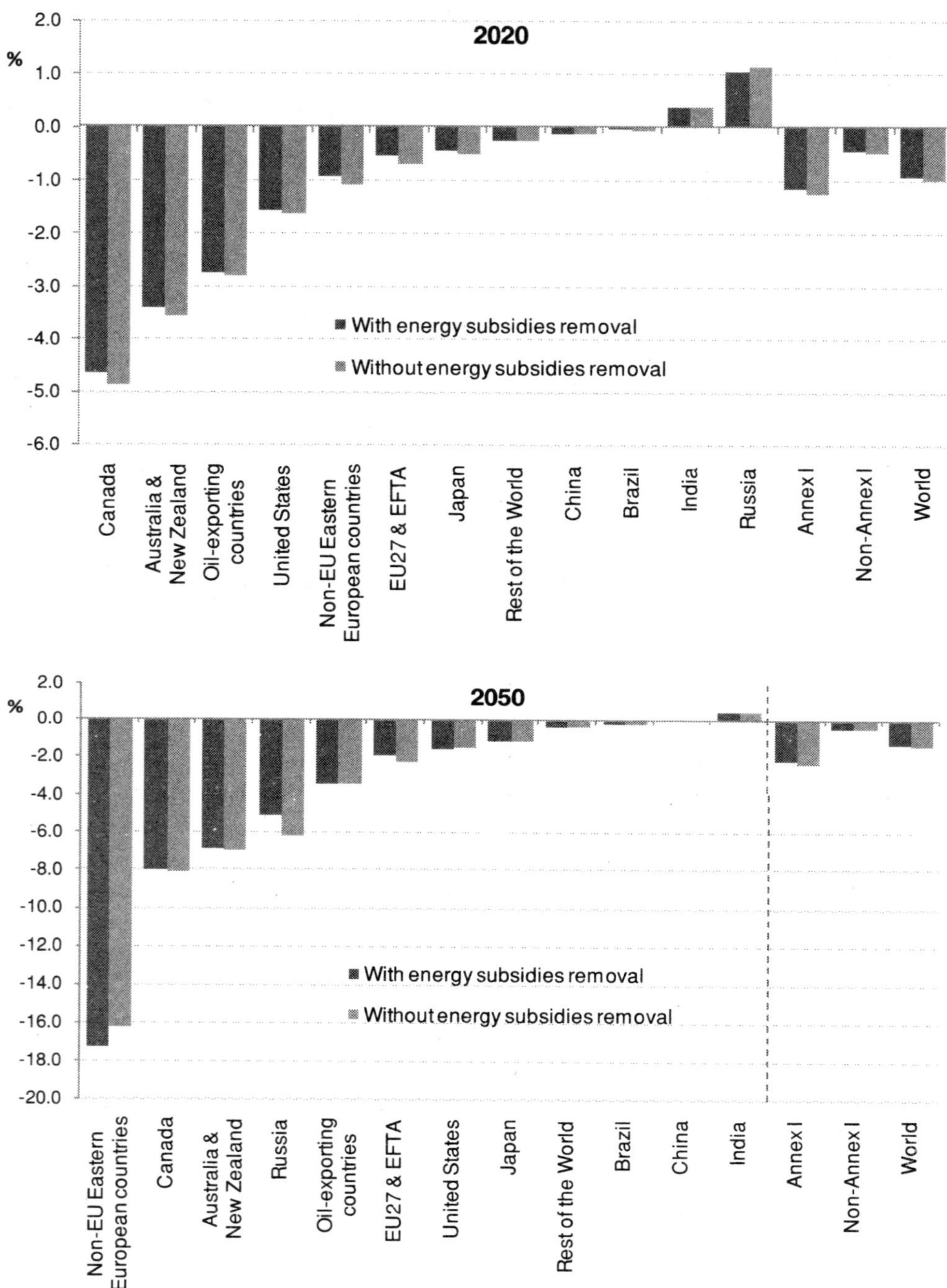

1. Hicksian "equivalent real income variation" defined as the change in real income (in percentage) necessary to ensure the same level of utility to consumers as in the baseline projection.

Source: OECD, ENV-Linkages model.

Figure 4.4. A multilateral removal of energy subsidies would lower the global mitigation costs of stabilising GHG concentration at 550 ppm CO_2eq

Mitigation costs under the "550ppm-base" scenario[1], household equivalent real income[2], % deviation relative to BAU

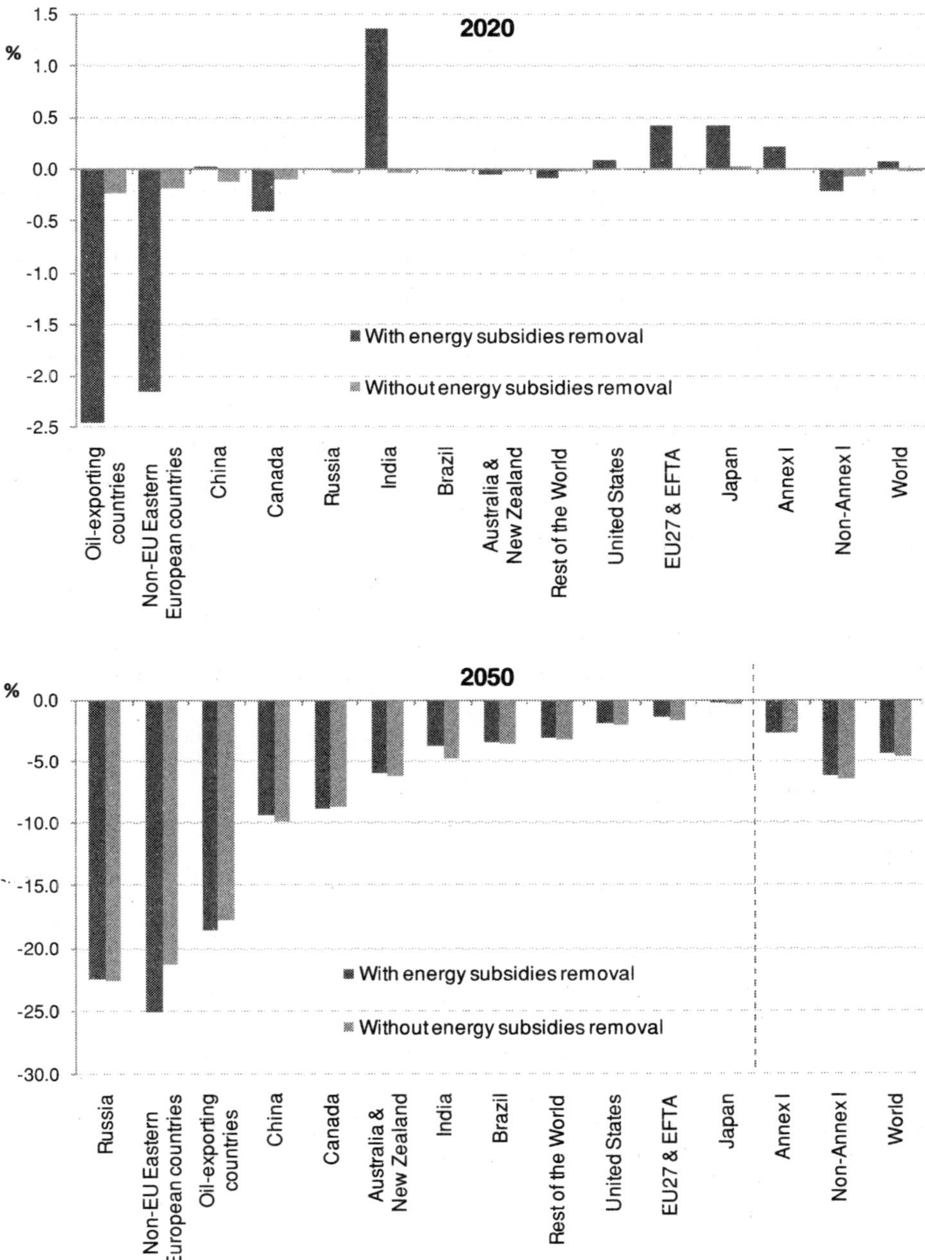

1. The pathway of emissions corresponds to a stabilisation below 550ppm (all gases) identical to the "550 ppm-base" case described in Chapter 1, Table 1.2.
2. Hicksian "equivalent real income variation" defined as the change in real income (in percentage) necessary to ensure the same level of utility to consumers as in the baseline projection.

Source: OECD, ENV-Linkages model.

4.2. The direct linking of emission trading schemes

Several domestic/regional GHG emission trading or cap-and-trade schemes (ETSs) are already in place or are emerging. These place a cap on GHG emissions from a number of sectors and allocate rights to emit amongst the firms in these sectors. The total amount of emission rights or permits cannot exceed the cap, limiting total emissions to that level. The participating firms are then allowed to buy or sell emission rights amongst themselves. Firms with opportunities for relatively cheap emissions reductions implement these and sell their emission rights to those for which emission reductions would be more expensive. The ETSs in place or emerging all vary significantly in terms of their target, size, and other design features. At present there are virtually no direct links between them, other than the link between the EU and Norwegian ETSs. Yet, as more ETSs are expected to emerge in the future, direct linking is likely to gain prominence and could form a key building block of a global carbon market and thus reduce global mitigation policy costs. However, it does raise a number of concerns that will have to be addressed to ensure environmental effectiveness (Section 4.2.3). Different ETSs can be linked either directly, or indirectly through access to a common crediting mechanism that allows for emission reductions to take place in countries not covered by an ETS. This Section focuses on direct linking, while the indirect link through crediting mechanisms is discussed in Section 4.3.

The effects of linking different domestic ETSs are mainly illustrated here using the OECD model ENV-Linkages to run a "benchmark" scenario. Under this scenario, each Annex I region is assumed to use an ETS to cut its GHG emissions unilaterally below 1990 levels by 20% by 2020 and by 50% by 2050. On its own, this commitment would be insufficient to achieve ambitious climate objectives. World emissions would still rise by about 20% and 50% by 2020 and 2050 respectively, *versus* about 85% by 2050 in a baseline scenario with no further mitigation policy action. It would, therefore, need to be fairly rapidly tightened and/or supplemented with further action, including in non-Annex I countries. Nevertheless, the illustrative benchmark scenario raises a number of lessons about the cost-effectiveness and competiveness impacts of linking.

4.2.1. The benefits of linking

Improving cost-effectiveness

Direct linking occurs if the tradable permit system's authority allows regulated entities to use emission allowances from another ETS to meet their domestic compliance obligations. Direct linking can be "two way" if each system recognises the others' allowances, or "one way" if one system recognises the other system's allowances but the other does not reciprocate. Linking ETSs directly tends to lower the overall cost of meeting their joint targets by allowing higher-cost emission reductions in one ETS to be replaced by lower-cost emission reductions in the other. Once ETSs are linked, this cost-effectiveness is achieved regardless of the magnitude of the initial emission reduction commitment across countries or regions; the distribution of emission reductions is determined through market mechanisms. The potential gains from linking are greater the larger the initial difference in carbon prices – and thereby in the marginal costs of reducing emissions – across individual ETSs.

Figure 4.5. Linking regional Annex I emission trading schemes would affect where emission reductions take place

(Under a 20% cut by 2020 and a 50% cut by 2050 relative to 1990 levels in each Annex I region)

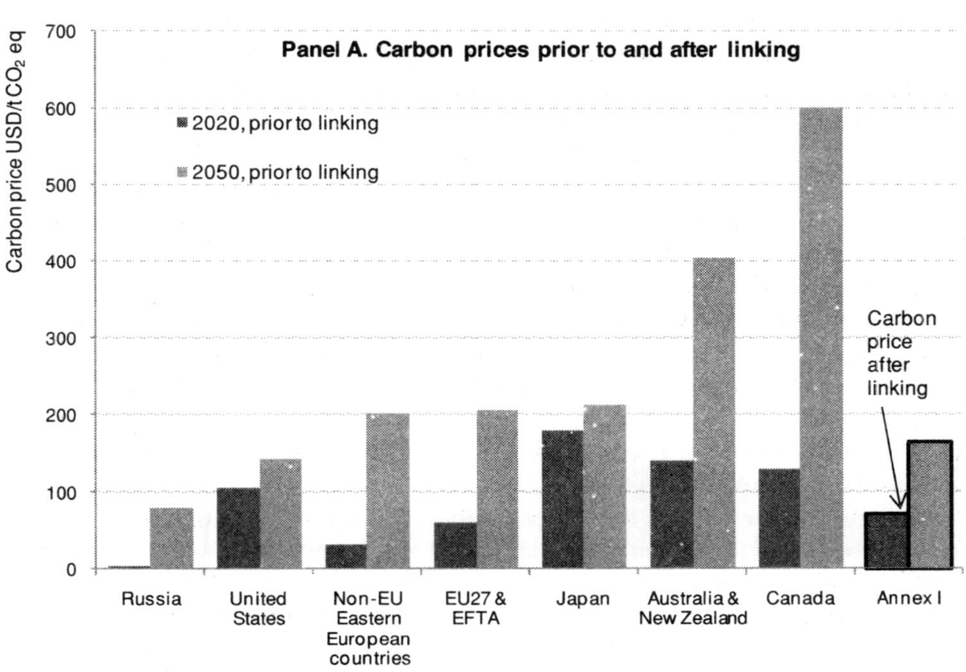

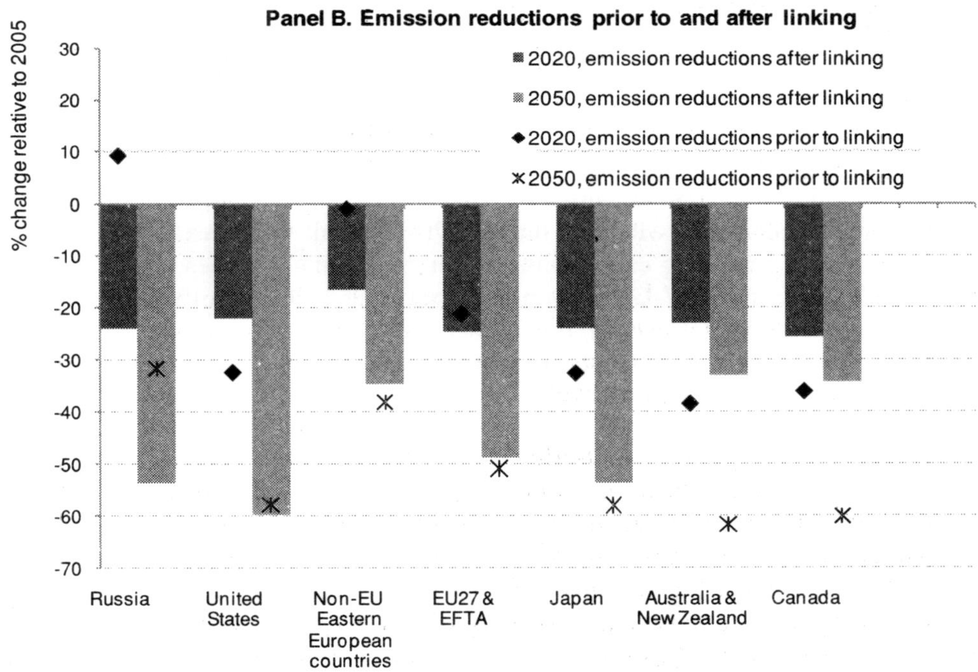

1. There is no crediting mechanism in these simulations, *i.e.* all emission reductions must be achieved in Annex I regions only.

Source: OECD, ENV-Linkages model.

As an illustration, the gains from linking together the domestic ETSs of Annex I regions are assessed in the benchmark scenario above. This is done by considering another scenario in which the same GHG emission reduction at the Annex I level is achieved through a linked system of ETSs. Concretely, an Annex I-wide ETS is assumed to be established, under which each participating region is allocated emission rights corresponding to a -50% individual emission reduction target by 2050 (compared to 1990 levels), as in the benchmark scenario. In the benchmark scenario, meeting their domestic caps alone was found to cost Annex I regions about 1.5% and 2.8% of their income on average by 2020 and 2050, respectively. Linking is found to enhance emission reductions in those schemes which had lower marginal abatement costs before linking (especially Russia, Figure 4.5 Panel B), but to weaken emission reductions in the others (Figure 4.5 Panel B). However, the associated reduction in overall mitigation costs for Annex I countries is just under 10%, or about 0.2 percentage points of income by 2050 (Figure 4.6, Panel B). This reduction in mitigation costs if fairly limited in part because in the illustrative benchmark scenario, carbon price differences prior to linking are estimated to be relatively small across the larger Annex I economies who account for the bulk of Annex I GDP (Figure 4.5 Panel A). Larger gains from linking would be found under more heterogeneous emission reduction commitments by Annex I countries than considered here.

In addition to improving the overall cost-effectiveness of the linked ETS system, linking is expected to benefit each participating region (*e.g.* Jaffe and Stavins, 2007 and Figure 4.6). The larger the change in the carbon price after linking, the larger the income gain, other things being equal. In turn, the carbon price level prior to linking depends on the size of the country's commitment, as well as on the availability of cheap abatement opportunities. In the illustrative scenario considered here, countries with lower pre-linking carbon prices (mainly Russia) gain because the equilibrium price of the linked system exceeds their marginal abatement costs, enabling them to abate more and sell the saved permits with a surplus while countries with higher pre-linking carbon prices (Australia and New Zealand, Canada, Japan) benefit from the lower carbon price (Figure 4.7). [14]

While basic economic theory suggests that permit trading among Annex I regions should benefit all participants, modelling does not always produce this result in practice. This reflects the so-called Dutch disease effects in the presence of various market imperfections. Because of this, non-EU Eastern European countries – which together form the "Rest of Annex I" region of the ENV-Linkages model – are found to lose from linking by 2050 (Figure 4.6). This is because their large permit export flows lead to a real exchange rate appreciation, which in turn results in a fall in the exports and output of their manufacturing sector, where scrapping capital entails costs. Nevertheless, these "Dutch disease" effects should be discounted because the ENV-Linkages model exacerbates them, partly due to a lack of explicit modelling of the international capital market. For instance, the real exchange rate appreciation could be smoothed in practice if some of the revenues from permit sales were recycled in international capital markets and if linking were to occur progressively.[15]

Linking schemes can also improve cost-effectiveness by increasing the size and liquidity of carbon markets. In the scenario presented above, *i.e.* when Annex I ETSs are linked, the size of the market is projected to reach 2.5% of Annex I GDP in 2020. As idiosyncratic shocks are shared across regions under linking, a larger market size tends to dampen the impact of such shocks, thereby lowering overall carbon price volatility and enhancing incentives for firms to make emission reduction investments.[16] Furthermore, transaction costs are expected to be smaller in a larger, more liquid market, especially if some regional schemes are too small to foster the development of institutions for reducing such costs. Larger market size also reduces problems that may arise if some sellers or buyers have market power (Hahn, 1984). Finally, market liquidity can lower the cost of insuring against uncertainty by fostering the development of derivative markets (Section 4.5).

 THE ECONOMICS OF CLIMATE CHANGE MITIGATION – ISBN: 978-92-64-05606-0 – © OECD 2009

Figure 4.6. Linking regional Annex I emission trading schemes would affect the distribution of mitigation policy costs across countries for a 50% emission cut in Annex I

(Under a 20% cut by 2020 and a 50% cut by 2050 relative to 1990 levels in each Annex I region)

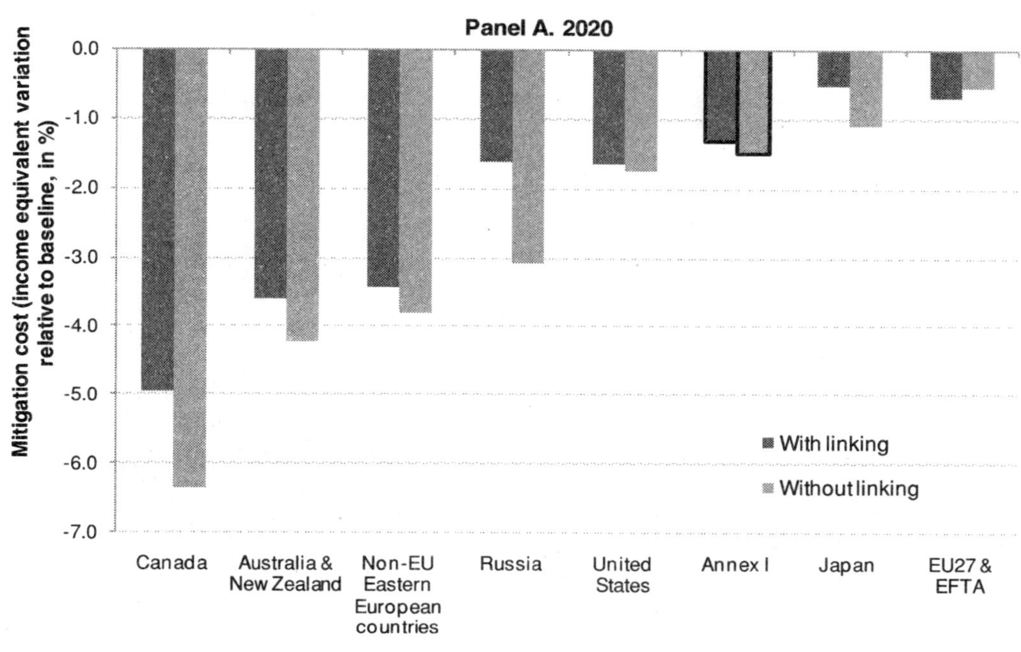

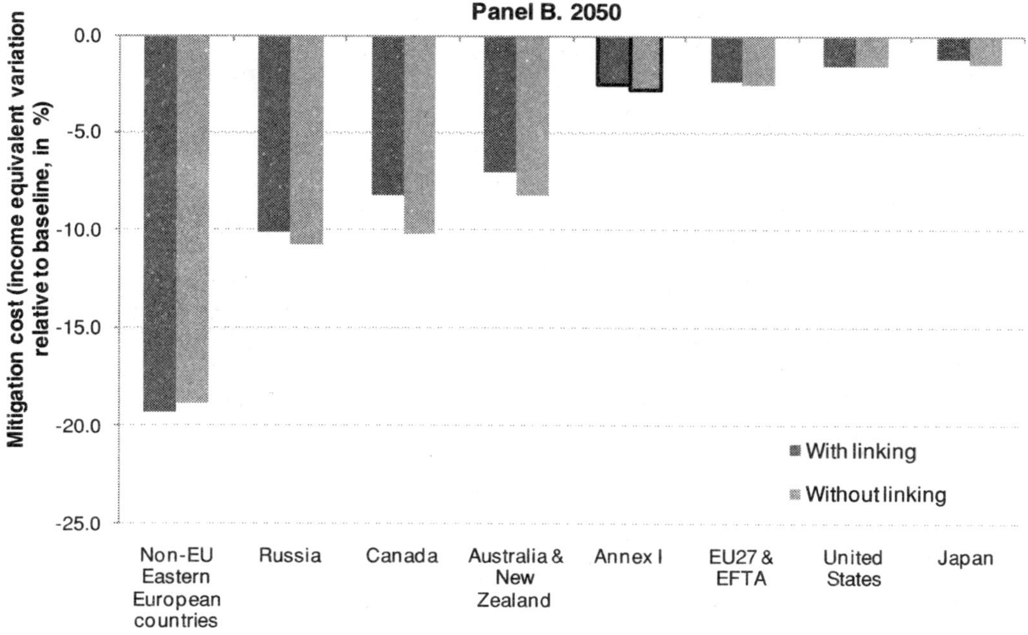

Source: OECD, ENV-Linkages model.

Figure 4.7. Projected geographical distribution of permit buyers and sellers under a 50% emission cut in Annex I[1]

(Under a 20% cut by 2020 and a 50% cut by 2050 relative to 1990 levels in each Annex I region)

Panel A. 2020

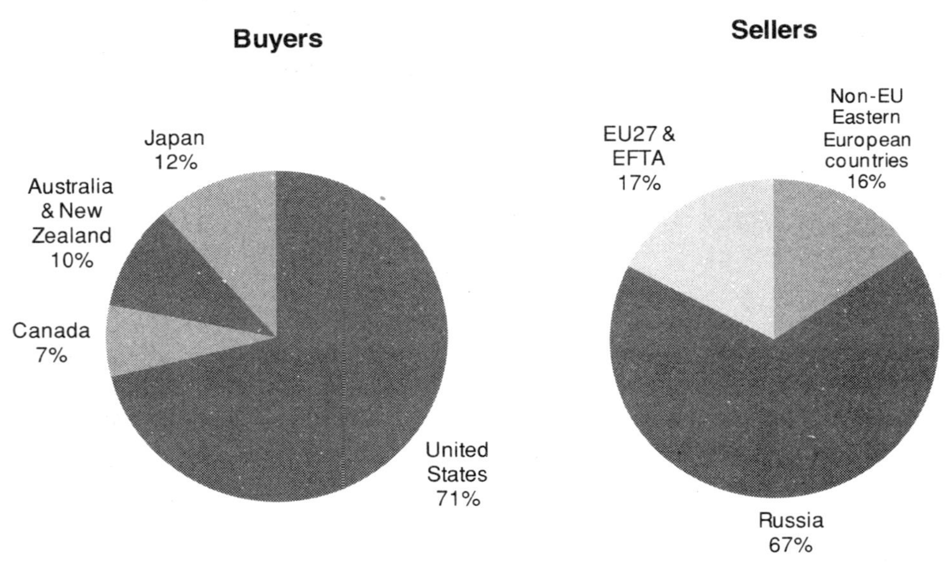

Panel B. 2050

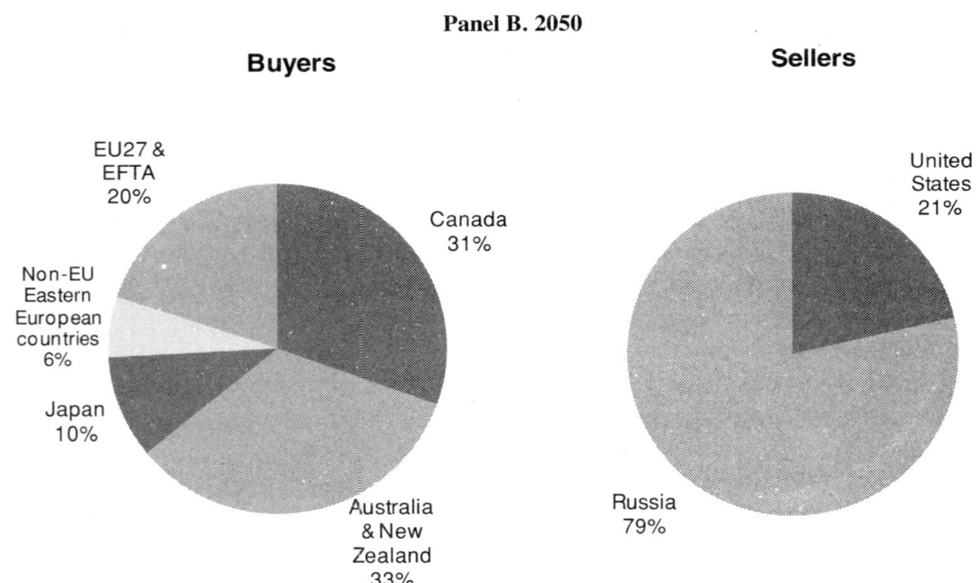

1. This simulation assumes there is no crediting mechanism, *i.e.* all emission reductions are achieved in Annex I regions only.

Source: OECD, ENV-Linkages model.

THE ECONOMICS OF CLIMATE CHANGE MITIGATION – ISBN: 978-92-64-05606-0 – © OECD 2009

Mitigating competitiveness concerns

Another advantage of linking is its ability to reduce competitiveness concerns in regions with higher pre-linking carbon prices, by allowing carbon prices to converge across linked schemes. Full convergence in prices will be achieved provided the recognition of allowances is mutual and there are no limits on trading. One-way linking (when system A recognises system B's allowances but the latter does not) ensures that the price in system A never exceeds the price in system B, and hence, would only limit competitiveness concerns for firms belonging to system A.[17] However, although competitiveness problems are reduced through linking, the losses in output of energy intensive industries would still be unevenly distributed across countries with countries with the lowest marginal abatement costs (Russia and non EU Eastern European countries, Figure 4.5, Panel A) facing the largest losses (Figure 4.8, Panel A). Furthermore, competitiveness problems would remain for regions in which GHG emissions are not priced or curbed by other means.

In the absence of strategic behaviour, linking across two ETSs does not affect the total emissions of the linked schemes since the number of permits is simply the sum of those issued under each system. However, it can still affect the overall environmental effectiveness of the scheme indirectly through its effect on carbon leakages towards uncapped countries, which occurs when emission reductions in one set of countries are partly offset by increases in countries elsewhere. If linking lowers the carbon price in the region that faces the highest leakage rate, then leakage towards uncapped countries is reduced. By the same token, if linking raises the carbon price in the region that faces the lowest leakage rate, then leakage towards uncapped countries is increased. In the illustrative benchmark scenario examined here, model simulations suggest that overall, linking among Annex I regions slightly reduces leakage (Figure 4.8, Panel B).

Applying the principle of "common but differentiated responsibilities and respective capabilities"

Compared with a global emissions trading system, it has been argued that a linked system of regional ETSs may be an easier way to reflect "common but differentiated responsibilities and respective capabilities" across regions, and thereby to extend participation to developing countries (Jaffe and Stavins, 2007). Permit allocation rules make it possible to differentiate across regional commitments and costs under a top-down approach. However, such differentiation can also be achieved through regions' own assessment of their responsibilities and reflecting their specific national circumstances – *as revealed de facto by* their target choice -- under a bottom-up approach. The gains from linking Annex I ETSs to potential non-Annex I country ETSs would be larger than those achieved through linking within Annex I only, if the heterogeneity in pre-linking carbon prices (and hence in commitments or actions) between Annex I and non-Annex I is higher than within Annex I.

Figure 4.8. Linking Annex I regional emission trading schemes would affect the distribution of energy-intensive industries output losses across regions and would lower carbon leakage rates in 2020

(Under a 20% cut by 2020 and a 50% cut by 2050 relative to 1990 levels in each Annex I region)

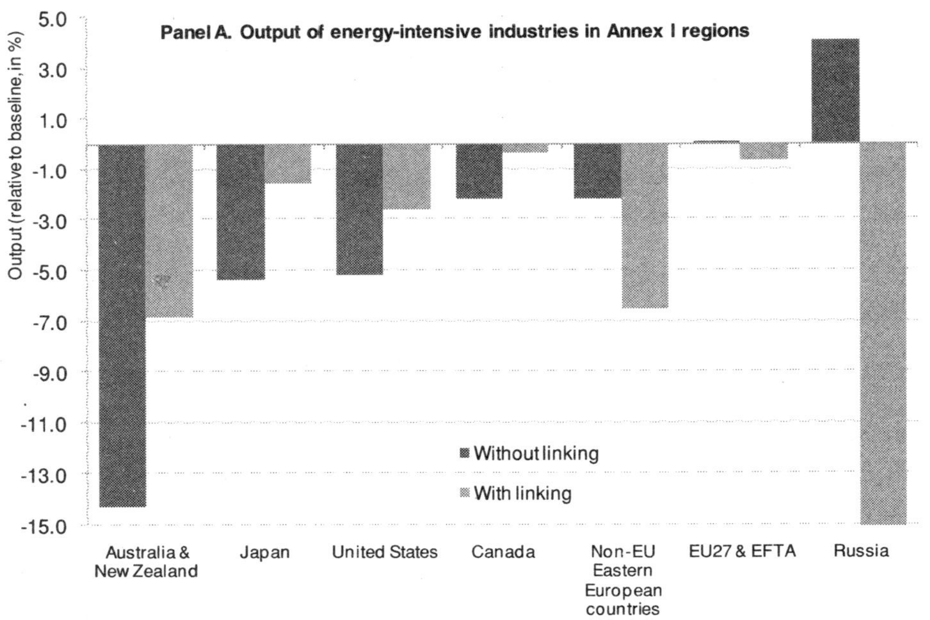

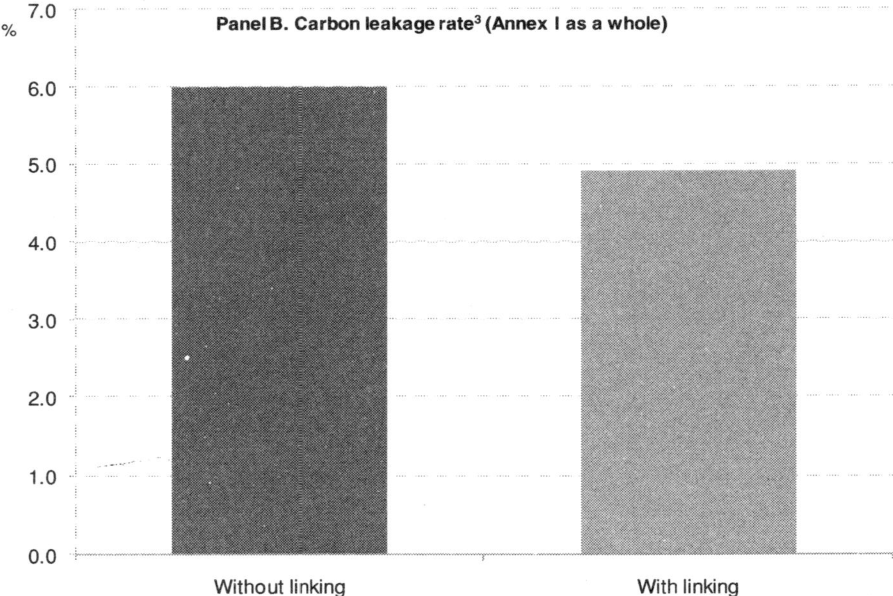

1. Energy intensive industries include chemicals, metallurgic, other metal, iron and steel industry, paper and mineral products.
2. There is no crediting mechanism in these simulations, *i.e* all emission reductions must be achieved in Annex I regions only.
3. The carbon leakage rate is calculated as: [1-(world emission reduction in $GtCO_2eq$)/(Annex I emission reduction objective in $GtCO_2eq$)]. It is expressed in per cent. When the emission reduction achieved at the world level (in $GtCO_2eq$) is equal to the emission reduction objective set by Annex I (in $GTCO_2eq$), there is no leakage overall, and the leakage rate is 0.

Source: OECD, ENV-Linkages model.

4.2.2. Potential risks of linking

Though linking ETSs yields a number of benefits, it also raises environmental and income distribution concerns.[18] These mainly arise from differences in the design features of ETSs prior to linking. Their impact on the gains from linking are reviewed below and summarised in Table 4.4 (Sterk *et al.* 2006; Baron and Bygrave, 2007; Flachsland, *et al.* 2008a, 2008b; Haites and Mullins, 2001). These issues would need to be addressed in order to reap the full gains from linking, and to avoid potential risks.

The distributional impacts of linking and the implications of differences in allocation rules

Although linking ETSs tends in general to lower the mitigation cost of each of the participating regions, it affects the distribution of costs, both across and within schemes. After linking, the shared carbon price settles somewhere between the pre-linking levels in the two regions considered (Figure 4.5). The larger the gap between the pre- and post-linking carbon price levels, the larger the gain to one region and the smaller to its foreign counterpart, other things being equal. Furthermore, within the region where linking leads to a carbon price increase, permit sellers gain while permit buyers lose, (and *vice versa* within the regions where linking results in a carbon price decline). The magnitude of these distributional effects depends on the extent to which domestic carbon prices are affected by linking, which in turn is determined by several factors, including the respective sizes of the permit markets, the difference in pre-linking targets and the steepness of the supply and demand curves for permits. In particular, the larger the difference between regions in the stringency of targets prior to linking, the stronger the distributional impacts, other things being equal. Likewise, the larger the relative size of the market to which the domestic ETS links, the larger the distributional effects are expected to be.

However, these distributional effects are similar in nature to those of international trade. Some of their political economy problems can be reduced through permit allocation rules if necessary; for instance through allowing transitory grandfathering[19] upon linking in the region with the lower pre-linking carbon price. While differences in allocation rules across linked schemes sometimes raise competitiveness concerns (Jaffe and Stavins, 2007), these effects would typically have existed before the schemes were linked and, therefore, would not be exacerbated by linking.[20] Furthermore, in reasonably competitive goods and services markets, the opportunity cost of free permits is reflected in firms' output prices, and therefore allocation rules have no effect on output and competitiveness.

The spread of cost-containment measures and the risks for environmental effectiveness

Linking would automatically lead to the spreading across regions of some design features specific to one particular scheme. As a result, governments in the linked regions would lose control over several features of their existing ETS. In particular, provisions to contain the cost of mitigation (cost-containment measures), such as carbon price caps ("safety valves"), or provisions for credits to be banked for or borrowed from future commitment periods, would be spread through linking (Ellis and Tirpak, 2006; Jaffe and Stavins, 2007; Flachland *et al.* 2008a, 2008b; Table 4.5).

The spread of cost-containment measures can undermine the environmental effectiveness of the overall system. For example, the spread of the safety valve implies that the overall target is relaxed once the safety valve is reached. Likewise, linking to an offset credit system whose environmental integrity is weaker than that of an ETS could also raise environmental concerns in countries that have more restrictive policies for the use of offsets. Partly for these reasons, the EU directive on linkage currently forbids linking to a scheme featuring a safety valve.

Table 4.4. Different design features in pre-linked emission trading schemes would affect the performance of the linked system

	Impact of linking on:					
ETS design feature differences in:	**Technically feasible?**	**Cost-effectiveness**	**Environmental effectiveness**	**Competitive distortion**	**Distribution of costs and gains within each scheme**	**Suggested solution**
Emission target	Yes	Improved if the regions with less stringent targets prior to linking are those with the lowest abatement costs	Possibly affected because of leakage, strategic behaviour and the "hot air" issue[2] but the overall effect is undetermined	No effect	Depends on the gap between pre- and post-linking carbon price levels	Common cap or at least a procedure to set the cap
Link with another scheme	Yes, but the link with the scheme also applies to other schemes	Improved if marginal abatement cost is lower in the offset scheme	Possibly reduced if the environmental integrity of the offset scheme is weak	No effect	Affected	Find agreement on decisions to link to another scheme and define procedures to decide future linking.
Allowance allocation rule	Yes	No effect unless permits are grandfathered on a regular basis	No effect	No effect unless permits are grandfathered on a regular basis	Determines who will be the winners and the losers within each scheme	Specific allocation rules can be used to avoid the resistance of some sectors, firms, households to linking
Absolute *versus* intensity target	Yes, but an intensity target makes little sense and is difficult to achieve within a linked system	No effect	Affected, and can be reduced if the allocation rule is adjusted to growth	No effect	No effect	Harmonisation is desirable. If one scheme has an intensity target, the allocation rule should preferably be made prior to linking rather than being frequently updated
Safety valve *(i.e.* carbon price cap) in one of the schemes	Yes, but the safety valve[1] to other schemes will be spread	No effect	Reduced	Reduced since all firms have access to the safety valve under the linked system	No effect	Harmonisation is desirable
Banking and borrowing	Yes, but borrowing and banking will also apply to the other schemes	Improved	No effect, unless there is a "hot air" problem	Reduced since all firms have access to these provisions	No effect	None
Heterogeneity in sector and/or gas coverage, downstream versus upstream schemes	Yes	Improved	No effect	No effect	No effect	Need to adopt a common measure in terms of CO_2 equivalent if gas coverage differs

Table 4.4. continued on next page.

Table 4.4. Different design features in pre-linked emission trading schemes would affect the performance of the linked system

(continued)

		Impact of linking on:				
ETS design feature differences in:	**Technically feasible?**	**Cost-effectiveness**	**Environmental effectiveness**	**Competitive distortion**	**Distribution of costs and gains within each scheme**	**Suggested solution**
Lifetime of permits	Yes	Can be undermined through a decrease in market liquidity	No effect	No effect	No effect	Harmonisation is desirable
Compliance period	Yes	Can be undermined through a decrease in market liquidity	No effect	No effect	No effect	Harmonisation is desirable. Avoid attaching permits to compliance periods
Monitoring, reporting, enforcement provision	Yes	Can be undermined	Can be undermined	No effect	No effect	Harmonisation is desirable. Use a common centralised institution to verify offsets

Notes: This table shows the implications of differences in design feature on the overall performance of the system after linking. It does not show impacts that would occur anyway without linking. For instance, two schemes with different sectoral coverage would raise some competitive distortion concerns even if the two systems are not linked.

1. Provisions to contain the cost of mitigation, such as carbon price caps.
2. A "hot air issue" can occur if the aggregate emissions cap in one of the schemes exceeds its business-as-usual emissions. In the absence of linking, and if this scheme does not allow banking, the surplus allowances would be lost after the trading period. However, in a linked scheme, the surplus is sold to relax the cap of the scheme with the binding target, thereby allowing increased emissions from the overall system.

Table 4.5. Most cost-containment measures would be spread through linking

Type of cost-containment measure				
Cap level	**Safety-valve**	**Offsets**	**Banking**	**Intensity targets**
Cap relaxed to lower the allowance price	Buy-out provisions to cap allowance prices	Import credits from non-capped sources	Allowances carried over for compliance in future periods	Define obligations in terms of emissions per unit output
Implications for the newly linked-in system without cost containment provisions				
The allowance price declines but the country/region gains from exporting credits	Allowance price decreases to ceiling	Imported credits implicitly accepted	Banking indirectly available	No implication if allowance allocation is set beforehand. Possible increase in price stability if allowance allocation is updated with output

Source: EPRI (2007) and OECD.

Creating a link between an ETS and a carbon tax

To some extent, similar concerns would be raised by creating a link between a domestic ETS price and a foreign carbon tax. This would imply allowing domestic firms to pay the foreign carbon tax rather than purchase a domestic permit. The effect would be to introduce a safety valve equal to the foreign carbon tax, or even allow a switching to the foreign carbon tax if it is lower than the domestic permit price.[21] The region with the carbon tax might find it easier to allow firms to switch from the carbon tax to ETS permits, although fiscal revenues would be lost in that firms that buy (cheaper) foreign permits are exempted from the tax. Under this one-way linking, the region with the carbon tax would gain if its tax was higher than the foreign permit price. The region with the ETS would benefit from permit sales to foreign firms, which would more than offset the higher mitigation costs arising from permit prices rising towards the foreign carbon tax level.

A one-way link between a carbon tax system and an ETS could also emerge if a government took on binding commitments to reduce emissions, set a carbon tax to achieve these reductions, and then bought permits at the end of the compliance period if the emission reductions turned out to be insufficient to reach its commitment (or is allowed to sell permits if emission reductions were going to be higher). Such a link would benefit each participant and enhance the cost effectiveness of the global system. In theory, the overall gain would be maximised if the carbon tax were set at a level that would prevail if the country had instead opted for an ETS that was linked to the foreign ETS. This would mimic a full linking of two ETSs, but may have little practical feasibility or relevance.

Linking absolute level and intensity target schemes

Another way to contain costs is to adopt "intensity targets", which are expressed in terms of emissions per unit of output as opposed to absolute targets, which are expressed in terms of emissions (Box 4.1). Such targets may be seen as an insurance policy against the risk of high costs in case of higher-than-expected GDP growth. The impact of linking an ETS with intensity targets to an ETS with absolute targets depends on the permit allocation rules. If the cap on emissions in the system with the intensity target is set *ex ante* on the basis of projected GDP growth, then that scheme is *de facto* equivalent to an ETS with an absolute cap, and linking does not affect overall emissions.[22] By contrast, if the permit authority of the intensity target scheme regularly adjusts the supply of permits in order to meet its intensity target, overall emissions will fluctuate. Within a linked system, such adjustments need to be more frequent and larger than within an independent one because emissions from any particular region are determined endogenously by market forces, and depend on all shocks to the system – including those specific to other regions (*e.g.* a cold winter in a large participating region). Furthermore, the impact of permit supply adjustments on domestic emission intensity will depend in part on the extent to which some of the newly emitted permits are bought by foreign firms.

THE ECONOMICS OF CLIMATE CHANGE MITIGATION – ISBN: 978-92-64-05606-0 – © OECD 2009

Box 4.1 Intensity targets and their implications for linking

Why intensity targets?

Uncertainty about future economic growth can be an obstacle to adopting emission caps because it means greater uncertainty about compliance costs. Intensity targets, under which permit allocations would be linked to future GDP, and would automatically adjust to unexpected growth shocks, have been proposed to reduce carbon price and mitigation cost uncertainty (Marcu and Pizer, 2003; Kolstad, 2006; Gupta *et al.* 2007; Jotzo and Pezzey, 2007). They may be more acceptable than absolute caps for developing countries that are experiencing strong but nevertheless uncertain long-term economic growth prospects (Fischer and Morgenstern, 2008). This is the case even though intensity targets increase mitigation costs when GDP is unexpectedly low and lower mitigation costs when GDP is unexpectedly high, which might be seen as an undesirable insurance property. Also, ways would need to be found to make such targets compatible with the need for fast-growing emerging economies to take on more (rather than less) stringent mitigation action as they catch up with developed countries.

Intensity targets would deal with uncertainty about future GDP, but not with uncertainty about future emission intensity or about structural abatement costs (Jotzo and Pezzey, 2007, Marschinski and Lecocq, 2006). Furthermore, the extent to which intensity target can limit mitigation cost uncertainty depends on the share of GHG emissions that are linked to GDP. Intensity targets are likely to be an effective insurance device in countries where emissions mainly come from fossil fuel combustion, and so are strongly correlated with GDP. They would be less effective for countries where a significant proportion of emissions come from land-use and land use changes. It has been shown that there is an optimal degree of indexation of emission targets to GDP, which depends positively on the share of emissions linked to GDP and on the stringency of the target.

Under intensity targets, uncertainty is shifted to some extent away from costs onto emissions levels, since the overall amount of emission reductions is not fixed (Dudek and Golub 2003). However, the overall environmental performance of an intensity target scheme may not necessarily be weaker than under an absolute cap, for three reasons (Jotzo and Pezzey, 2007). First, because they lower mitigation costs, intensity targets can induce countries to take on more stringent commitments. Second, the impact on long-term emissions depends on the nature of shocks. Prevalence of unexpected positive (negative) growth shocks would increase (lower) emissions *ceteris paribus*, but insofar as such shocks are uniformly distributed around an average, they would be expected to at least partly offset each other over a long time period. Finally, if a limited number of emitters is involved in the scheme, temporarily relaxing the target as a result of medium-term indexation of emissions to GDP would only have a small effect on the stock of GHGs in the atmosphere.

Ways of implementing intensity targets

There are basically two ways of implementing an intensity target: An *ex ante* permit allocation rule, under which the amount of emission credits is set once and for all in order to meet an intensity target, conditional on a pre-specified projected GDP path; and an *updating* allocation rule, under which the amount of emission credits is adjusted over time based on the actual GDP path, in order to meet the intensity target *ex post*. While the former rule is ultimately equivalent to an absolute target, the latter is not since the cap is adjusted upward in order to allow firms to emit more when GDP is higher than projected. In practice, there would necessarily be some delay between GDP growth developments and the adjustment of emission credits under the latter rule, making it difficult to meet the intensity target strictly.

Box 4.1 continued on next page.

Box 4.1 Intensity targets and their implications for linking

(continued)

Implications for linking

From a technical perspective, linking a scheme with an absolute cap to another with an intensity target is feasible under both types of allocation rule since in both cases governments will have to translate the target into a fixed quantity of assigned units in order to allow emission trading (Philibert, 2005).[1] From an environmental perspective, the impact of having one system with an intensity target depends on the allocation rule. Insofar as the intensity target scheme has an *ex ante* rule, linking to other schemes with absolute targets should not affect total emissions. The only risk would be that, if GDP growth turns to be lower than projected, the emission quota may turn out to exceed business as usual emissions, in which case the surplus would be sold to absolute target schemes, thereby increasing total emissions. However, this problem is in fact similar to a "hot air issue", and could also be encountered with an absolute target.

If the amount of emission credits is updated with GDP growth so as to meet an intensity target within a linked system, governments would have to intervene frequently in order to adjust the supply of permits. This is because once systems are linked, the distribution of emissions reductions across participating regions is endogenously determined and is affected by any shocks to the system (*e.g.* a cold winter in a large participating region). In the case of a positive growth shock, a larger number of permits will have to be emitted under a linked system than under a system in which ETSs are not linked, since some of the newly-emitted permits would be bought by foreign firms. This would tend to stabilise the carbon price in the linked system at the cost of more uncertain emissions. One way to ensure the predictability of total emissions within the linked system would be for participating regions with absolute targets to agree to adjust their caps so as to offset changes in the supply of allowances from regions with intensity targets. Under such an arrangement, the latter regions would in effect transfer some of the risk of unexpected changes in their mitigation costs to the former regions, which would then lose the carbon price stabilisation gains from linking to an intensity target scheme.

When applied at the firm – or even possibly at the sector, but probably not at the national – level, and under grandfathering, intensity targets may yield perverse incentives for firms to increase their output and thus, their emissions, in order to obtain more credits. This incentive is reinforced by linking, since firms then have the possibility to export these permits. One possible answer to such concerns is to introduce a "gateway" in order to limit the net permit sales from the intensity rate-based programme, as is the case in the UK system, although such restrictions also impose economic costs on the overall system.

1. With an absolute target, the number of credits is determined directly by the cap. With an intensity target, the government must set the intensity target, derive the corresponding emissions on the basis of a GDP projection, and compute the amount of credits accordingly.

Permit supply adjustments by one region to meet its intensity target would increase carbon price stability within the linked system, at the cost of greater uncertainty about overall emissions. Overall environmental performance does not have to be undermined if emissions merely fluctuate around the level that would prevail under absolute caps, but it could be affected if positive growth shocks prevail, or if the intensity target system creates an incentive to increase production and emissions in order to obtain additional credits. One way to ensure the predictability of total emissions within a linked system would be for participating regions with absolute targets to agree to adjust their caps so as to offset changes in the supply of allowances from regions with intensity targets. Under such an arrangement, the latter regions would in effect transfer some of the risk of unexpected changes in their mitigation costs to the former regions, which might otherwise lose the carbon price stabilisation gains from linking to an intensity target scheme.

Linking may raise some environmental concerns that would need to be addressed by appropriate institutions and regulations (Section 4.5):

- The region with the lower carbon price *ex ante* has a further incentive to relax its cap in order to generate additional revenue from exporting allowances – and a larger gain from linking more broadly once systems are linked (Helm, 2003; Rehdanz and Tol, 2005). In order to alleviate this, the region with the higher carbon price may also relax its target, thereby triggering a "race to the bottom". This problem may be most acute for countries that face only limited damages from climate change (Helm, 2003).[23]
- Another source of environmental concern associated with linking is the "hot air" issue. It arises if the aggregate emissions cap in one of the schemes exceeds its business as usual emissions. In the absence of linking, and if this scheme does not allow banking, the surplus of allowances would be lost after the trading period. By contrast, with linking, the surplus is sold to relax the cap in the scheme with the binding target, thereby increasing the emissions of the overall system.

Addressing differences in sectoral, gas and time coverage

Differences in sectoral, gas and time coverage across linked schemes increase the complexity of the overall system, but are no cause for concern in general:

- Different rules for a given sector could raise competitiveness concerns; firms covered by a more stringent scheme might compete with firms that are exempt from binding commitments in the other. However, this problem already exists regardless of linking. The same holds for the risk of double taxation associated with linking a scheme in which the carbon price is applied at an "upstream" level of the energy supply chain to one in which the carbon price is applied at a downstream level. However, this can be addressed by exempting fossil fuel imports from the upstream ETS from carbon pricing in downstream ETSs.
- Differences in the lifetime of permits (the period during which they can be used for compliance) would be expected to be reflected in price differentials; the market is likely to put a higher price on credits with a longer lifetime, especially as future permit issuances are expected to be low and uncertainty is high.
- Differences in the compliance period are unlikely to be a source of institutional incompatibility, but if permits cannot be banked between compliance periods, they may unnecessarily multiply permit vintages (that can be used for different compliance periods), lower market liquidity and thereby increase price volatility (Section 4.5).

4.2.3. Addressing the concerns about environmental integrity and the spread of design features

There are some instrumental approaches that have been put forward to prevent linking from weakening the environmental integrity of the overall system and to prevent one particular scheme's design features from spreading to the others (Box 4.2). However, major drawbacks of such limits to trading between schemes are that they hinder the full convergence in carbon prices and lower the cost-effectiveness of linking. Both countries lose: the "protectionist" country because it has to achieve more of its emission reduction domestically at a higher price; and the other country because permit export revenues fall. Moreover, these instruments would lower market liquidity and increase its complexity. They would also only contain, but may not fully prevent, the importation of the foreign scheme's design features. The only way to do so would be one-way linking, under which trade with one of the domestic schemes is not allowed, but again this would limit the cost-effectiveness gains from linking. Finally, limits to international trading may run the risk of triggering retaliation by affected countries.

Box 4.2 Some instruments for maintaining environmental integrity in linked schemes

Three main strategies have been put forward to prevent linking from weakening the environmental integrity of the overall system and to prevent the spreading of one particular scheme's design features to the others (Rehdanz and Tol, 2005):

- Discounting permit imports from the less restrictive schemes, meaning that an imported emission credit normally worth one unit of CO_2 counts for less than that in the purchasing country.
- Setting permit import quotas, *i.e.* requiring that a certain amount or percentage of emission reduction must be achieved domestically.
- Applying tariffs on permit imports; unlike quotas, these would bring fiscal revenues into the importing country.

By limiting trading, these instruments have the potential to reduce the exposure to shocks in other schemes, and they can also limit the spreading of specific foreign scheme design features, such as safety valves or links to offset credit systems. Other instruments to maintain the environmental integrity of the linked schemes, such as a system of buyer liability, are discussed in Section 4.5.

In light of these drawbacks, the instruments in Box 4.2 may best be seen as emergency measures rather than as permanent provisions. A more cost-effective approach to addressing concerns about environmental integrity and the spread of design features would be for regions to agree on key issues prior to linking, notably:

- The level of, or the procedures for, setting emission caps in future compliance periods. This would remove governments' incentives to adjust future domestic caps in a way that maximises domestic gains from linking, improve the environmental integrity of the overall scheme, and provide greater certainty and incentives for clean investment by market participants.
- Whether to include a safety valve, given the spreading of this feature.
- The type of overall target (absolute *versus* intensity) and the allocation rule. In the long run, as fast-growing emerging economies catch up with developed countries in terms of income levels, they may switch from intensity to absolute targets as the latter would have lower environmental uncertainty. In the context of a global emissions trading scheme based on absolute targets, one way to reflect economic development concerns would be to allocate commitments across countries conditional on expected economic growth rates, and to adjust them over time.
- Procedures for assessing the future expansion of linking (to emission trading and offset systems). Given the potentially large distributional and environmental impacts of an expansion of the linked system, the rules applying to future linking of one participating region to other, non-participating schemes should if possible be set in advance.

4.3. The role of emission crediting mechanisms and related challenges

Linking can also occur "indirectly" when an ETS allows part of a region's emission reductions to be achieved in countries outside the ETS, for example through a common crediting mechanism such as the Clean Development Mechanism (CDM), which is one of the flexibility mechanisms of the Kyoto Protocol.

4.3.1. The potential gains from well-functioning crediting mechanisms

The CDM allows emission reduction projects in non-Annex I countries – *i.e.* developing countries, which have no GHG emission constraints – to earn certified emission reduction (CER) credits, each equivalent to one tonne of CO_2eq. These CERs can be purchased and used by Annex I countries to meet part of their emission reduction commitments. In principle, assuming that developing country emitters do not take on binding emission commitments in the near future, well-functioning crediting mechanisms could play four important roles: i) improve the cost-effectiveness of GHG mitigation policies in developed countries, both directly and indirectly through partial linking of their ETS; ii) reduce carbon leakage and competitiveness concerns by lowering the carbon price in developed countries; iii) boost clean technology transfers to developing countries; and (iv) facilitate the implementation of explicit carbon pricing policies in developing countries at a later stage by putting an opportunity cost on their GHG emissions.

Well-functioning crediting mechanisms appear to have very large potential for saving costs, reflecting the vast low-cost abatement potential existing in a number of developing countries, particularly China. To illustrate this, the same hypothetical "benchmark" scenario as in the previous Section is considered. Under this scenario, each Annex I region of the ENV-Linkages model is assumed to establish a regional ETS that caps GHG emissions at 20% and 50% below 1990 levels by 2020 and 2050, respectively. As stressed earlier, this scenario is purely illustrative and, at best, based on a transitory arrangement that is not in itself compatible with meeting ambitious climate change mitigation targets. Compared with that benchmark scenario, allowing Annex I regions to meet 20% of their commitments through reductions in non-Annex I countries is estimated to nearly halve their mitigation costs (Figure 4.9). Raising the cap on offsets allowed from 20% to 50% would bring further benefits. Cost savings are found to be largest for those Annex I regions that otherwise face the highest marginal abatement costs – and, therefore, the highest carbon price levels (Figure 4.10) – and/or are most carbon-intensive. Australia, New Zealand, and Canada fall into both categories, while Russia falls into the latter. Non-Annex I regions would enjoy a slight income gain from exploiting cheap abatement opportunities and selling them profitably in the form of offset credits. In this illustrative scenario, China would be by far the largest seller and the United States the largest buyer in the offset credit market, accounting for about half of worldwide sales and purchases by 2020, respectively (Figure 4.11).

Figure 4.9. Mitigation policy costs under a 50% emission cut in each Annex I region can be cut by allowing access to a well-functioning crediting mechanism

(Under a 20% cut by 2020 and a 50% cut by 2050 relative to 1990 levels in each Annex I region)

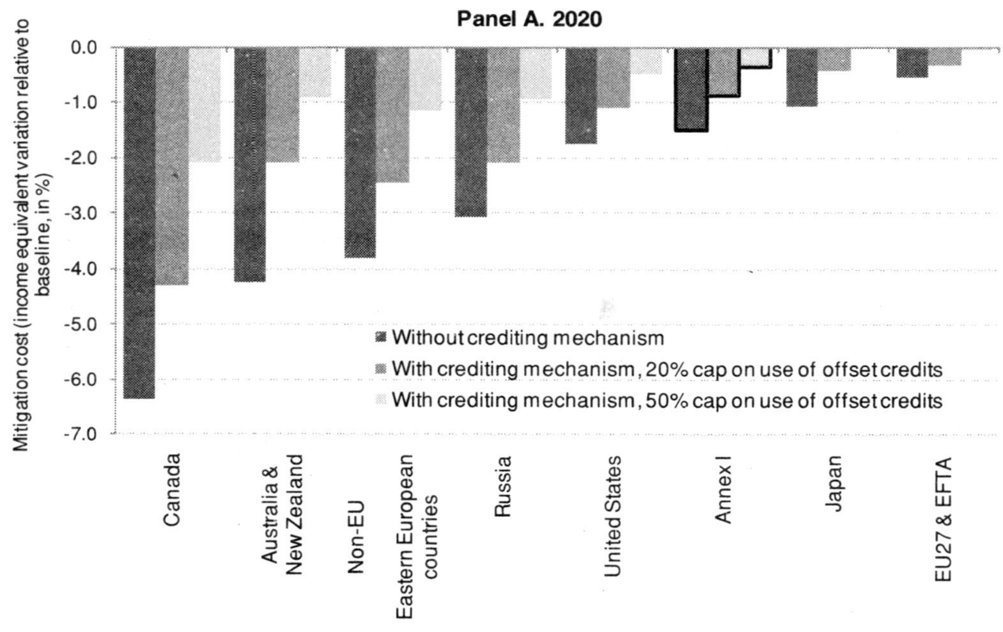

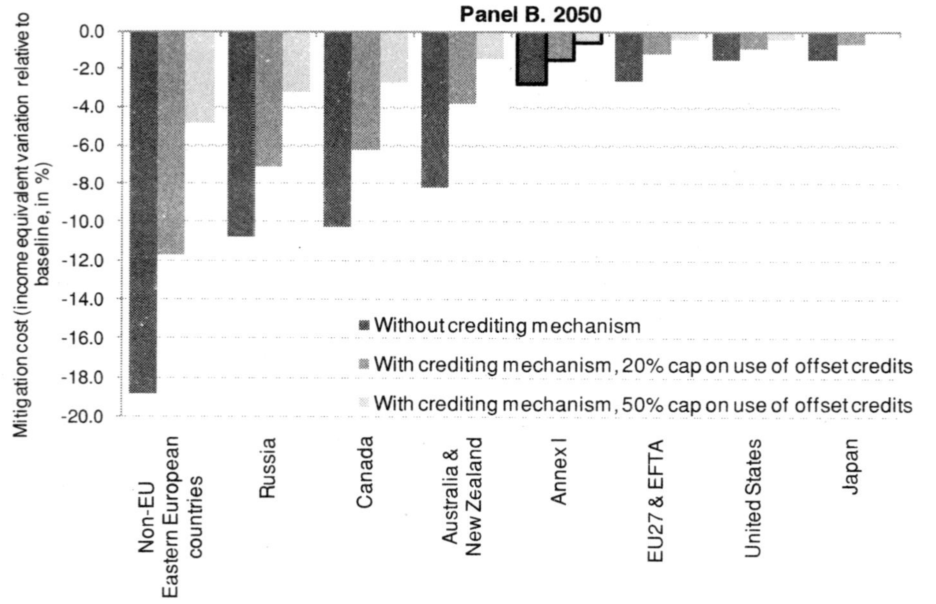

Source: OECD, ENV-Linkages model.

Figure 4.10. A well-functioning crediting mechanism would lead to a convergence in carbon prices

Carbon prices under a 50% emission cut by 2050 relative to 1990 levels in each Annex I region separately, with and without crediting mechanisms

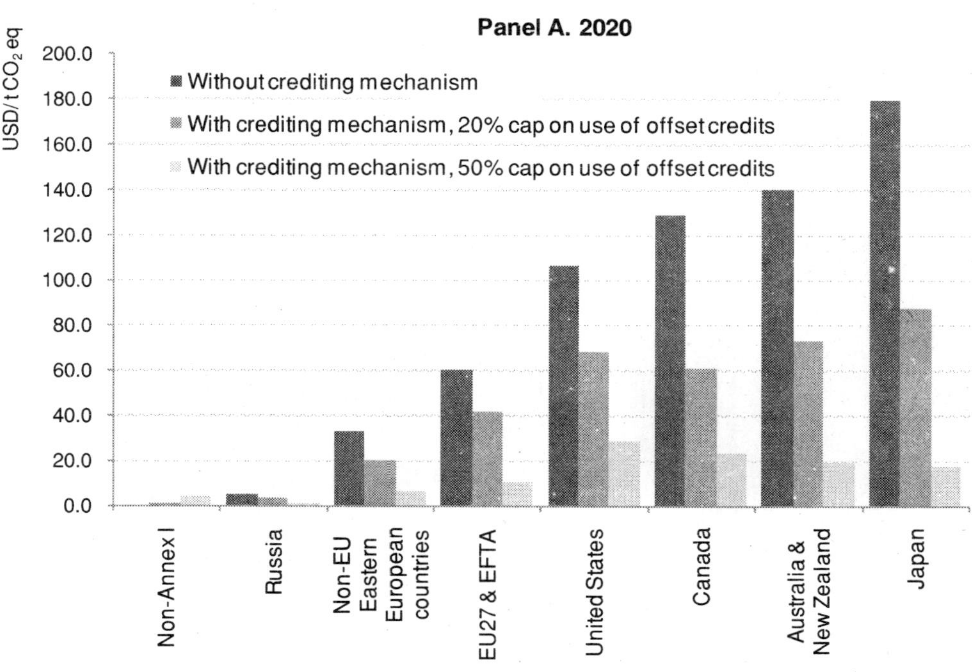

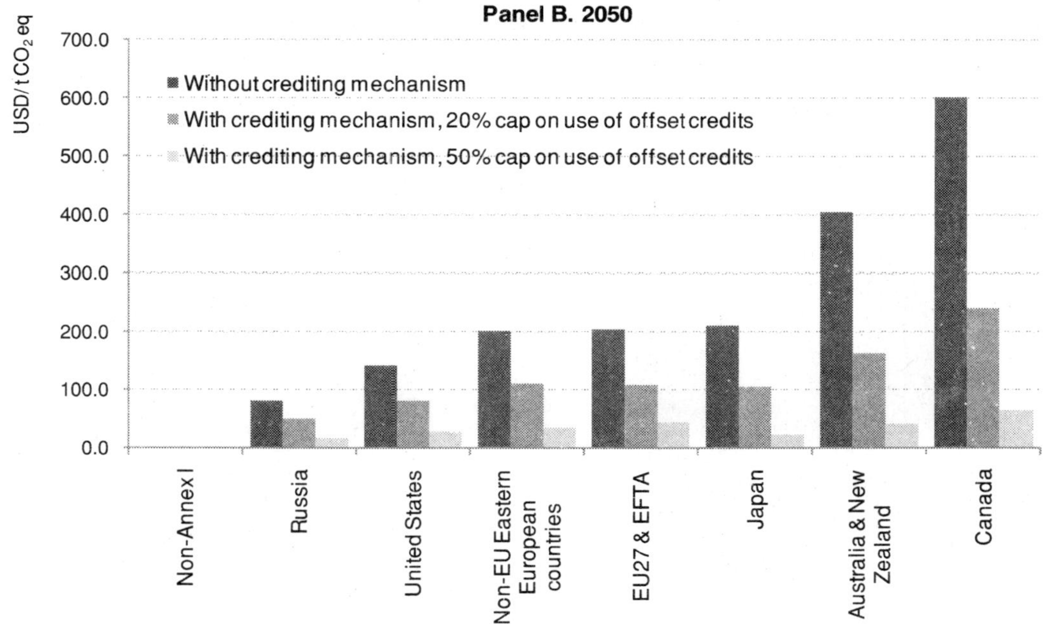

Source: OECD, ENV-Linkages model.

Figure 4.11. Geographical distribution of offset credit buyers and sellers by 2020 under a 50% emission cut in each Annex I region separately

Panel A. With a 20% cap on use of offset credits in Annex I countries

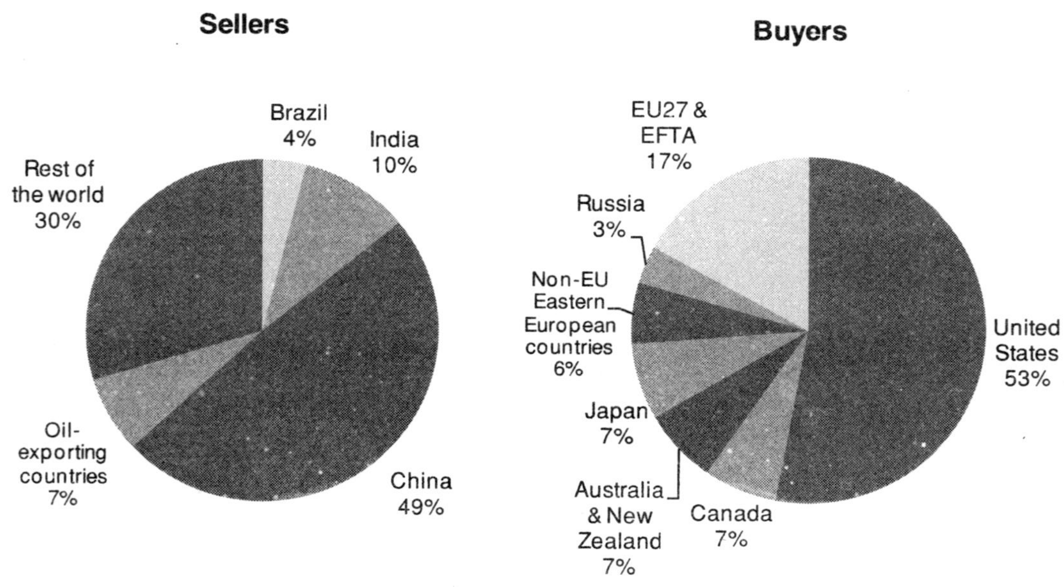

Panel B. With a 50% cap on use of offset credits in Annex I countries

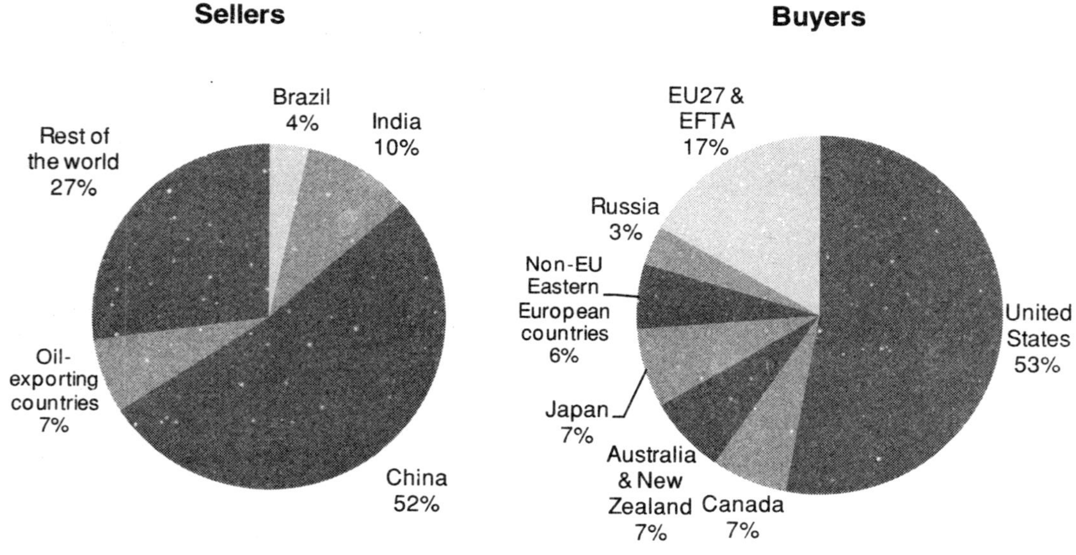

Source: OECD, ENV-Linkages model.

Box 4.3 CDM baselines, credits and carbon leakage

In order to receive credits under the current CDM, several steps must be undertaken in the project registration and issuance process. This is designed to ensure that approved CDM projects generate "real, measurable and verifiable emission reductions" compared to a baseline, which UNFCCC (2005) defines as "the scenario that reasonably represents the emissions by sources of GHGs that would occur in the absence of the proposed project activity". The Marrakech Accords consider three types of baseline, based on either actual or historical emissions, technology type or emissions from previous, similar project activities.

The choice of the baseline against which certified emission rights (CERs) are granted does not only have an impact on the volume of credits generated, but also matters for carbon leakage. This is because an emissions baseline established *before* the project is implemented depends on the assumptions made about policies and projects in other sectors and regions, and their effect on output and emissions within the project boundary. Three approaches can be identified in setting a baseline:

1. *Accounting* for the impact of all other CDM projects on the project's expected emissions. If these other projects lower the international carbon price and thus reduce leakage from countries covered by binding emission caps within the project boundary, they should lower the project's emission baseline. This would be the "theoretically correct" baseline under current UNFCCC guidelines. However, implementing this approach is complex and costly, and would likely remain so even under a scaled-up CDM.
2. *Excluding* the impact of all other projects on the project's expected emissions. Because of the complexity and cost of the first approach, the CDM Executive Board and our model take as the baseline the project's emission level under a scenario where some countries – currently most of the Annex I countries – have emission commitments while the rest of the world does not. This therefore does not account for the effect of other projects on the output from, and therefore credit generated by, the CDM project. Implicitly, this assumes that all individual CDM projects have a marginal effect on the world economy.
3. Setting the baseline as the BAU emission level in a hypothetical "no world action" scenario where no country has binding emission commitments. In this case, CDM projects would receive fewer credits than under approach 1, as they would be required to more than offset any leakage within the project boundary resulting from action in other sectors and regions. However, this approach would imply a lower credit volume than the approach in current UNFCCC guidelines, and indeed it does not appear to fit current practice whereby "market leakage" is not taken into account in CDM baselines. For example, the CDM Executive Board does not quantify the impact of the EU-ETS on emissions in non-Annex I countries.

Under all three approaches, Kallbeken (2007b) find that the CDM would lower the carbon price differential between countries that face binding emissions caps and other countries, and would thereby reduce leakage (all other factors being equal). However, these leakage reductions are typically smaller under the second, and perhaps most plausible, approach above. This is because the approach does not account for the fact that implementing all *other* CDM projects together reduces international carbon prices, leakage and thereby the projected emissions of any other project considered. Consequently, the volume of credits that would be granted for each project is higher than both in the "theoretically correct" approach and – to an even greater extent – in the "no world action" approach. As a result, "too many" CERs are granted, and the more so the higher the number of projects that are implemented, *i.e.* the larger the share of recipient countries' emissions that benefits from CERs.[1] In the absence of any constraint on the use of CERs in Annex I countries, the effect of the CDM under such a baseline would be simply to reallocate emissions between Annex I and non-Annex I countries, without addressing the fact that actions in Annex I boosted the emissions of non-Annex I countries before implementation of the CDM.

In practice, the effects of these alternative approaches have been found to be limited under moderate mitigation action scenarios – and, therefore, fairly low carbon prices and leakage – and limited CDM use (Kallbeken 2007b).[2] There are some remaining questions which call for further research. Firstly, is this still true given the current boom in CDM projects? Secondly, would this still be true under more stringent commitments and a scaled up CDM, especially if fairly lax caps are put on CDM use in countries covered by binding emission commitments?

1. Alternatively, if the total volume of credits is fixed (*e.g.* because of demand constraints), this will imply that fewer projects can be undertaken.
2. Vöhringer *et al.* (2006) stress the difference between the marginal impact of an individual project and the combined effect of all projects together, which can lead to significant leakage. They propose attributing leakage proportionally to individual projects.

Figure 4.12. The gains from direct linking across Annex I emission trading schemes when they are already linked through a crediting mechanism would be limited

(Under a 50% emission cut in each Annex I region separately by 2050 relative to 1990 levels, with a 50% cap on use of offset credits)

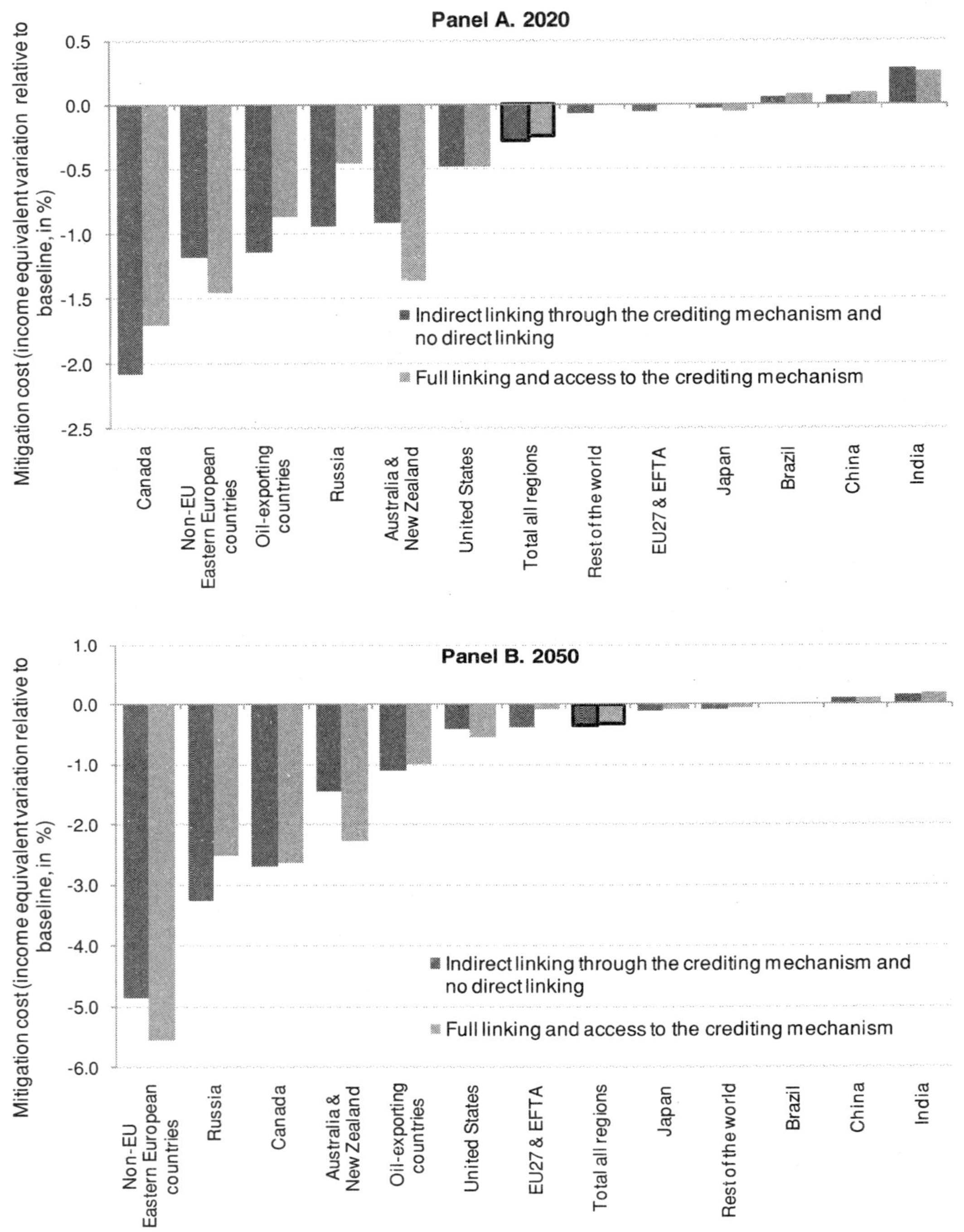

Source: OECD, ENV-Linkages model.

THE ECONOMICS OF CLIMATE CHANGE MITIGATION – ISBN: 978-92-64-05606-0 – © OECD 2009

Figure 4.13. A well-functioning crediting mechanism would have a limited effect on carbon leakage rate but would lower output losses of energy-intensive industries in Annex I countries

50% emission cut by 2050 relative to 1990 levels in each Annex I region separately, with and without crediting mechanisms, 2020

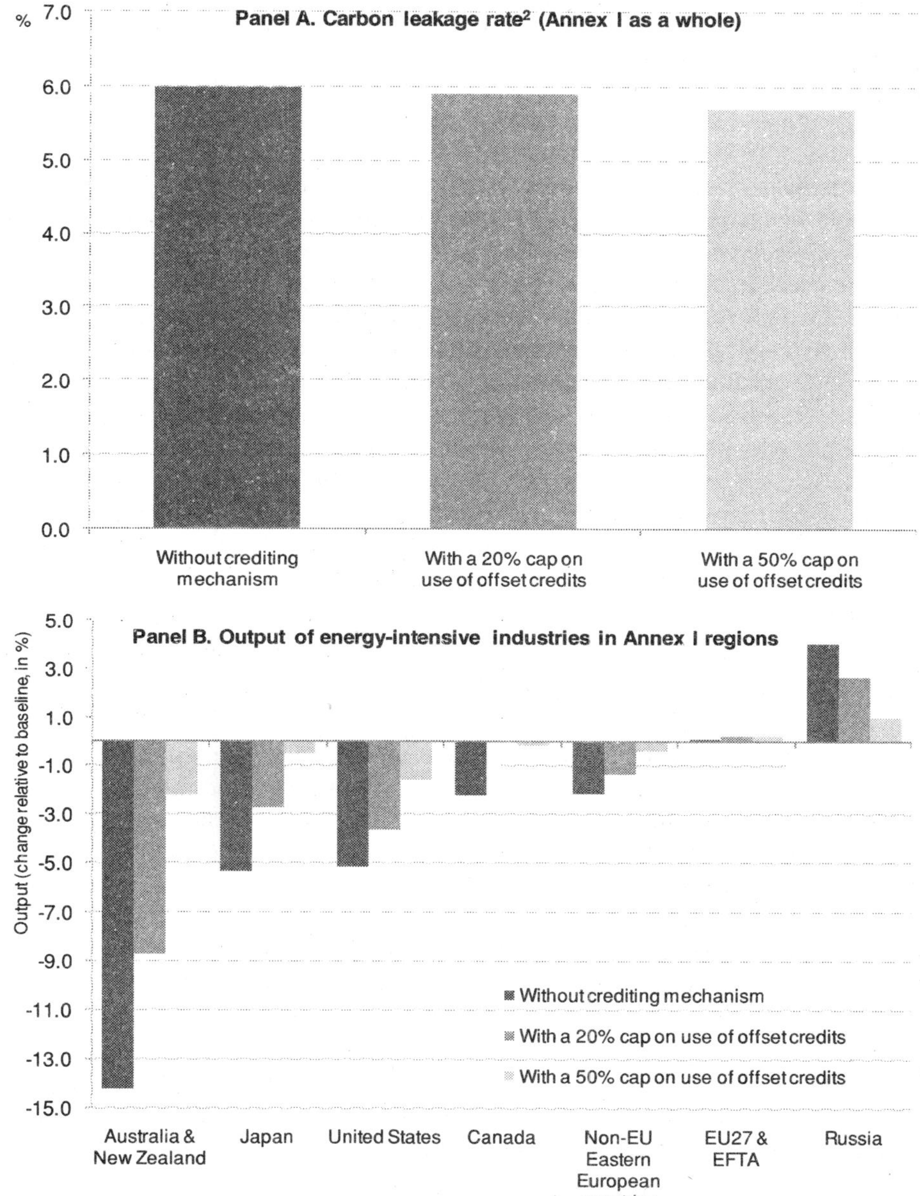

1. Energy intensive industries include chemicals, metallurgic, other metal, iron and steel industry, paper and mineral products.
2. The carbon leakage rate is calculated as: [1-(world emission reduction in $GtCO_2eq$)/(Annex I emission reduction objective in $GtCO_2eq$)]. It is expressed in per cent. When the emission reduction achieved at the world level (in $GtCO_2eq$) is equal to the emission reduction objective set by Annex I (in $GTCO_2eq$), there is no leakage overall, and the leakage rate is 0.

Source: OECD, ENV-Linkages model.

However, these cost saving and trade flow estimates should be seen as upper bounds, because they assume a crediting mechanism with no transaction costs and no uncertainty on delivery, as is apparent from the very low projected offset prices in these simulations (Figure 4.10). In practice, there are numerous market imperfections and policy distortions which may prevent some of the non-Annex I abatement potential from being fully reaped. These include transaction costs and bottlenecks, information barriers, credit market constraints, and institutional and regulatory barriers to investment in host countries (Chapter 6).[24] This well-functioning crediting mechanism that is modelled here is largely equivalent to an international (asymmetric) ETS covering all non-Annex I countries, in which each of them is assigned a target equal to their baseline emissions.

Crediting mechanisms also indirectly link the ETSs of countries covered by binding emission caps if credits from a single mechanism (*e.g.* the CDM) are accepted in several different ETSs. Indeed, they result in partial convergence of carbon prices and marginal abatement costs across the different ETSs, which improves their cost-effectiveness as a whole. In the illustrative scenario run here, the variance in carbon prices across Annex I regions is found to decline dramatically as the cap on the use of offsets is relaxed, becoming fairly small for instance under a 50% cap (Figure 4.10). As a result, once schemes are indirectly linked through crediting mechanisms, the additional gains from direct linking are smaller than discussed in Section 4.2. They depend on the degree of carbon price convergence already achieved through indirect linking, which in turn depends in part on limits to the use of offset credits. The looser the constraints on the use of credits, the stronger the indirect linkage between systems, and the smaller the additional gains from explicit linking. For instance, ENV-Linkages simulations suggest that if Annex I regions are allowed to meet up to 50% of their domestic commitments through the use of offsets, the overall additional gain from direct linking would be close to zero, although some countries would still benefit significantly (Figure 4.12).[25]

4.3.2. Challenges with crediting mechanisms generally, and the current CDM specifically

In theory, crediting mechanisms may also reduce carbon leakage and mitigate competitiveness concerns. Compared with a situation where countries covered by binding caps cut their emissions unilaterally, the availability of credits lowers the differences between carbon prices in participating and non-participating countries. These differences are an important driver of leakage. However, whether leakage is actually reduced partly hinges, in practice, on the definition of the baseline against which credits are granted (Kallbekken *et al.* 2007a). The baseline used in the modelling work for this chapter already incorporates some leakage, *i.e.* it is "too high" (Box 4.3). This baseline corresponds to the BAU level in non-Annex I countries under emission reduction action in Annex I – an approach close to that followed by the CDM up to now. As a result, the reduction in leakage from emission crediting could turn out to be small, or even non-existent (Box 4.3, and Kallbekken 2007b).[26] For instance, in the illustrative 50% Annex I emission cut scenario above, while simulated carbon price levels in Annex I countries fall drastically when emitters are allowed to meet part of their commitments through offsets, the leakage rate[27] barely declines (Figure 4.13, Panel A) – although leakage is estimated to be small to start with, in line with most other existing models.[28] Under this baseline definition, crediting mechanisms primarily reallocate emissions between Annex I and non-Annex I countries, without addressing the fact that leakage boosted the baseline emissions of non-Annex I countries in the first place. Nevertheless, by lowering the carbon price in most Annex I countries, crediting is found to be an effective way to mitigate the competitiveness and output losses of their energy-intensive industries (EIIs) (Figure 4.13, Panel B).[29]

THE ECONOMICS OF CLIMATE CHANGE MITIGATION – ISBN: 978-92-64-05606-0 – © OECD 2009

More importantly, in its current form the CDM raises a number of issues which, if not addressed, will undermine its ability to deliver the expected benefits:

- *Additionality, transaction costs and bottlenecks.* The so-called additionality criterion is key to ensuring the environmental integrity of the CDM. Under this, only emission reductions that can be attributed to the carbon project give rise to certified emission rights or carbon credits (CERs). Otherwise, CERs would amount to a mere income transfer to recipient countries without reducing GHG emissions. However, the transaction costs and bottlenecks associated with ensuring that CERs are indeed "real, additional and verifiable" are large and well documented (Capoor and Ambrosi, 2008; Ellis and Kamel, 2007). They have increased as the CDM has become a victim of its own success, with more than 4 000 projects currently in the pipeline. Despite these costs, it has been argued that a large share of CDM projects do not bring about actual reductions in emissions (ICCP, 2007; Schneider, 2007; Wara and Victor, 2008). These strains on the system have emerged even though the supply of CERs remains lower than it would under future increasingly stringent emission targets in Annex I countries. For instance, the annual volume of CERs issued was about 0.25 Gt of CO_2eq in 2008. Based on the number of projects currently in the pipeline and planned, it is expected to reach about 1.4 Gt of CO_2eq in 2012 (Figure 4.14). Under the illustrative scenario presented above, of a 50% emission cut in each Annex I region by 2050, the simulated supply is estimated to reach over 3 Gt of CO_2eq in 2020 if up to 50% of domestic commitments can be made through the use of offset credits.
- *Perverse incentives to raise emissions.* The CDM is asymmetric in that it rewards emission reductions but does not penalise increases. As such, the CDM comes close to an emission reduction subsidy. This makes it subject to the "dynamic inefficiency issue" (Baumol and Oates, 1988). By reducing firms' total expected investment costs, the CDM can create perverse incentives to raise initial investment and output in carbon-intensive equipment, so as to get emission credits for reducing emissions later, depending on expectations about how future baselines will be set.[30] The larger the gap between the market price of CERs and the abatement cost, the greater such perverse incentives would be. This may be seen as a form of "intertemporal leakage", whereby expected action tomorrow increases emissions today.
- *Reduced incentives for non-Annex I countries to take ambitious mitigation action.* Another incentive problem is that the large financial inflows from which developing countries may benefit under a future CDM could undermine their willingness to take on binding emission commitments at a later stage. This is because most of them would earn more under a well-functioning crediting mechanism than they would under most rules for allocating emission rights in a world ETS, except for the most favourable rules. For example, non-Annex I countries as a whole gain more in the illustrative benchmark scenario (50% emission reduction in Annex I, with Annex I countries allowed up to 50% of offsets to meet their commitments), than in a scenario where the same world emission reduction (in Gt CO_2eq) is achieved by granting every human being the same amount of allowance (global ETS with per capita allocation rule). China in particular would lose from moving to a world ETS like this (Figure 4.15).

Figure 4.14. CERs issued under the CDM: trends and breakdown by type of project to 2012

Panel A. Volume of CERs

Million CERs: 1600, 1400, 1200, 1000, 800, 600, 400, 200, 0

Already issued

Projected

31-12-2004 31-12-2006 31-12-2008 31-12-2010 31-12-2012

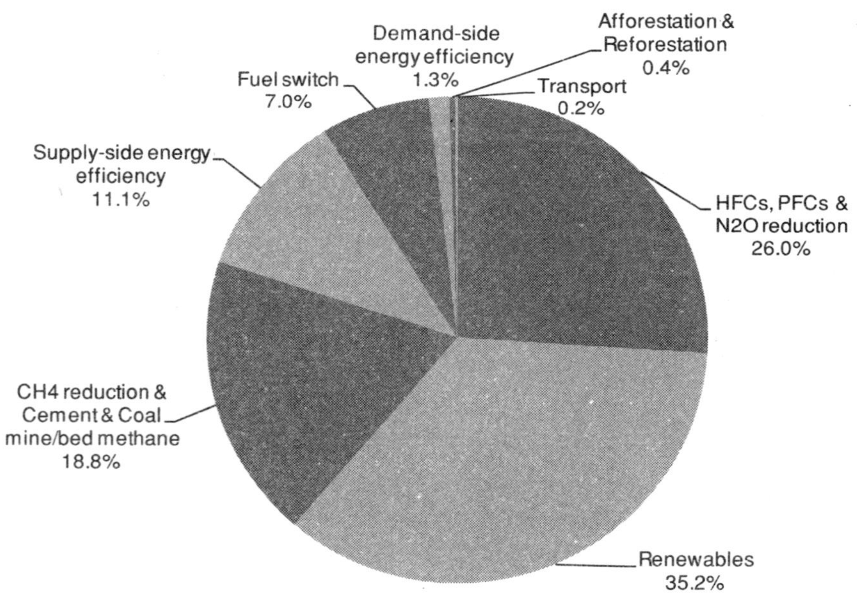

Note: A project has to go through four stages before the associated CERs can be issued: validation, verification, registration and issuance. The future volume of CERs is projected based on assumptions over the 2009-2012 period regarding the number of projects that will be submitted to validation, the share of projects currently at the validation stage that will be validated, the share of projects that will successfully go through the registration stage, and the amount of CERs registered projects will effectively generate (issuance success).

Source: UNEP RISØ Center.

Figure 4.15. A crediting mechanism may lower the incentive for non Annex I countries to join a world ETS

Mitigation policy costs under a world ETS and equivalent Annex I mitigation action with a crediting mechanism

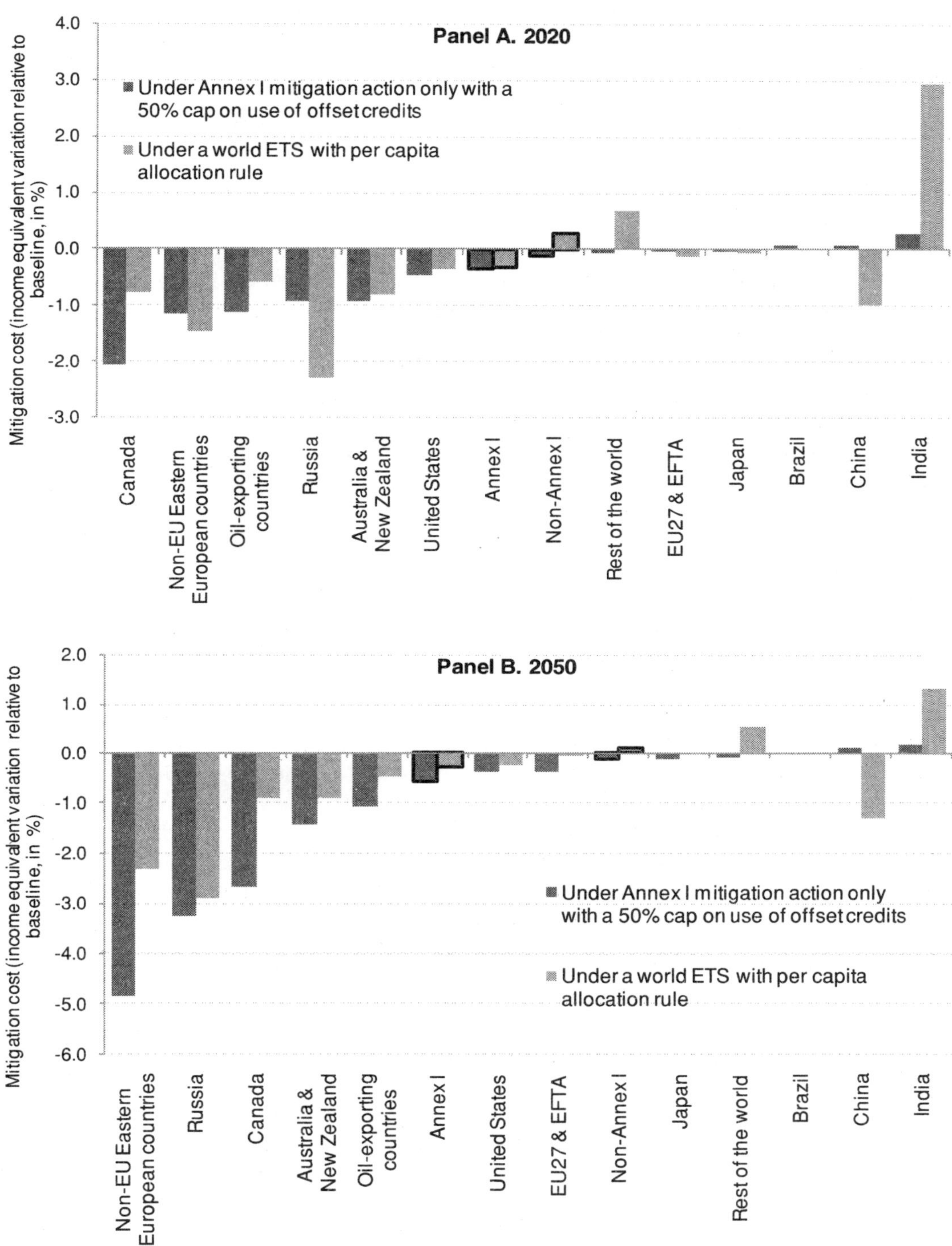

Source: OECD, ENV-Linkages model.

- *The permanence problem.* Some types of carbon projects might not involve permanent emissions reductions. In other words, CERs may be issued for emission reductions made initially, but these might be offset by increases in the more distant future. This issue could be significant if sequestration projects such as carbon capture and storage or avoided deforestation become eligible for the CDM.[31] For instance, carbon storage capacities might not be maintained,[32] and deforestation might be simply delayed rather than permanently avoided. This problem could be compounded by the difficulty for firms to commit, and for insurance companies to cover the risk of non-compliance, over very long periods.

4.3.3. CDM reform options

Despite these drawbacks, crediting mechanisms have the potential to significantly lower the future mitigation costs incurred by regions covered by emission caps. Therefore, in the absence of a global permit trading architecture involving all the main emitters, the CDM should be scaled up. This would require a move from a project-by-project to a wholesale approach in order to reduce transaction costs and bottlenecks drastically (*e.g.* Bosi and Ellis, 2005). A number of proposals have been made for how to do that. These approaches are not mutually exclusive, although potential overlap – in particular risks of double counting – would need to be carefully addressed. They may also complement, rather than replace the project-by-project approach, which may have to continue in sectors with dispersed emission sources (*e.g.* agriculture), or where emission reductions are clearly additional (*e.g.* CCS, or some non-CO_2 projects such as N_2O destruction activities, whose only revenues would be the CERs). The three main CDM scaling-up options are:

- *Bundling and "programmes of activities".* These two forms of scaling up have been eligible under the CDM since a 2005 decision (4/CMP.1) at the Meeting of the Parties to the Kyoto Protocol (COP/MOP1) on "further guidance to the CDM".[33] Bundling involves bringing together several small-scale CDM project activities to form a single CDM project activity or portfolio without losing the distinctive characteristics of each project. Credits are obtained for bundled projects. Under the "programme of activities" approach, credits may be granted for a range of projects that differ in timing or geographical location (*e.g.* Hinostroza *et al.* 2007). This may be especially useful in the area of energy efficiency, where the CDM is currently under-developed.[34] Bundling together small dispersed projects which alone would have prohibitively high transaction costs could ultimately lead to large emission reductions. It may also help expand CDM use to geographic regions where it is currently negligible partly due to the relatively small scale of potential projects, such as in Africa.
- *Sectoral crediting mechanisms* would further scale up the CDM by allowing emission reductions at the sector level to yield credits after validation against a pre-defined baseline (*e.g.* Baron and Ellis, 2006). This "sectoral CDM" would require setting up sectoral baselines for selected industries in each potential recipient country. This would raise a number of methodological issues. In particular, using a standardised baseline for an industry across countries may not be appropriate. There are good economic reasons for cross-country differences in emission levels and intensity within a given industry (*e.g.* differences in goods and/or production processes, factor prices, or natural resource endowments), including EIIs and the power sector to some extent (Baron and Ellis, 2006).[35] Intensity baselines (emissions per output) are often considered to be easier to establish than absolute baselines. However, they would be more complex to monitor and enforce as they would require measures of both output and emissions. This approach is also discussed below in the broader context of sectoral approaches (Section 4.4).

THE ECONOMICS OF CLIMATE CHANGE MITIGATION – ISBN: 978-92-64-05606-0 – © OECD 2009

- *Policy CDM* would allow specific government policies to deliver CERs (*e.g.* Aldy and Stavins, 2008). Eligible policies could be sectoral, in which case they would be equivalent to sectoral crediting mechanisms. Or they could be cross-sectoral, and might include for instance renewable energy standards (*e.g.* a policy of installing energy-efficient light bulbs), building codes or even possibly the implementation of carbon taxes or a removal of energy subsidies. One advantage of a policy CDM is that additionality may be easier to check for. However, this approach would share the drawbacks of technology standards, *i.e.* it would run the risk of mandating the use of specific technologies that could eventually turn out to be costlier than alternatives, and might also undermine innovation incentives. Furthermore, setting a baseline at a "policy" level and, especially, monitoring and verifying the emission reductions achieved from a policy could raise major methodological difficulties and affect the environmental integrity of the scheme. Also open to question is whether electorates in developed countries would support the large, transparent payments to developing countries that would likely be involved if that option were to be used extensively.

While these options could achieve drastic cuts in transaction costs and thereby vastly increase the volume of credits issued, they would not specifically address the deeper problems of additionality, leakage and perverse incentives. One way to reduce these concerns might be to negotiate baselines today for the largest possible number of sectors for a sufficiently long time period (*e.g.* a decade), and to set these baselines below BAU emission levels expected without further world mitigation action efforts. Establishing long-term baselines would address the perverse incentive issue by ruling out the possibility that any future increase in emissions might, if offset by subsequent reductions, deliver CERs. It would also minimise the risk of leakage, especially as the number of countries and sectors covered would be large. Setting baselines below BAU levels might be seen as an insurance against the risk of over-estimating baseline emissions and the excess supply of CERs, but it may mean that some potential low-cost abatement opportunities are lost. The main weakness of this approach is that estimating and negotiating baselines simultaneously across a wide range of countries and sectors would mean overcoming significant methodological and political obstacles.

An international agreement on CDM reform could also incorporate built-in "graduation mechanisms". This would encourage developing countries to take on increasing GHG mitigation actions or commitments over time as their income levels converge with those of developed countries, and/or to stop hosting crediting projects under certain conditions or after a given period of time. Even if the latter is not agreed internationally, it is likely that developed countries will unilaterally limit CDM offsets to projects in only some partner countries (*e.g.* lower income developing countries) and/or some sectors. Such graduation measures would: i) address environmental integrity concerns; ii) reduce the disincentive for recipient countries to take on binding commitments once scaled-up CDMs are in place; and iii) help put world emissions on a path towards meeting ambitious long-run global targets. For instance, the sectoral and/or country baselines negotiated in the context of a scaled-up CDM might be gradually tightened, along with some relaxation of restrictions on offset use in countries covered by ETSs, where additionality would be less of a concern. This would induce some convergence between "hard" permit and credit prices, albeit at some cost to developed countries. Over the longer run, the tighter baselines might in turn be converted into binding emission caps, which could then be gradually lowered (Section 4.4).

As a radical alternative, some have suggested moving away from a strict accounting, "tonne-for-tonne" emission reduction logic towards direct support to actions that create progress toward mitigation in developing countries (Keeler and Thompson, 2008). However, relaxing the additionality criterion may only make it harder to gather political support in developed countries for the large and transparent international financial transfers that would be associated with a policy CDM.

4.4. The potential and limitations of sectoral approaches

On their own, even large emission reductions in Annex I countries cannot stop climate change (Section 3.1). Sectoral approaches are being proposed as a way to broaden participation to developing countries, and therefore to expand the potential for emission reductions and/or lower their cost. They are also expected to mitigate leakage and competiveness issues.

4.4.1. Forms of sectoral approaches

A range of sector-based mitigation policies has been discussed in the policy debate and the literature (Baron *et al.* 2009). They can be classified into three main groups, depending on the level of commitment they impose on countries:

- *Binding sectoral targets.* Quantitative emission targets would be negotiated at a national or international level for specific sectors.[36] A cost-effective way to achieve them would then be to set up national or international sectoral emission trading systems, under which allowances would be allocated to firms on the basis of the usual rules (*e.g.* auctioning or grandfathering).[37] Allowances might be traded *within* one or several sectoral markets, and possibly *between* them and some economy-wide ETSs. The system would involve a cap-setting process, as well as monitoring, reporting and verifying (MRV) procedures. Binding sectoral targets could also be achieved through the development and transfer of technologies.
- *Sectoral crediting mechanisms.* Another option is to establish sectoral emission baselines (*e.g.* for EIIs) at a national or international level; sectors which reduced their emissions below this baseline would generate credits that could be sold in international carbon markets. This option would involve a baseline-setting process, MRV procedures, and a crediting mechanism for verified emission reductions.
- *Non-binding technology-oriented approaches.* The focus here would be on voluntary agreements to promote more efficient or cleaner technologies, with no reward from the international community for emission cuts achieved. However, unlike the previous two options, this approach would put neither a price nor an opportunity cost on carbon. As a result, it would be unlikely to provide emission reduction incentives to firms in the sectors covered, and for this reason it is not considered further in our analysis.

While sectoral approaches could, in principle, be applied across a wide range of sectors and countries, special emphasis might be placed in practice on the largest emitting sectors and, within those, possibly on key country players. The argument is that a narrowly-focused agreement covering firms that share some characteristics and compete among themselves may be easier to achieve than broader agreements. Indeed, a relatively small number of sectors account for a large share of world emissions. In particular, EIIs and the power sector account for almost half of current world GHG emissions (excluding emissions from land use, land use change and forestry), over half of which are in non-Annex I countries (Figure 4.16). A sectoral approach could also be useful in the international shipping and air transport sectors due to their significant contribution to world emissions and their transnational character.[38]

Figure 4.16. Energy-intensive industries and the power sector are responsible for a significant share of world GHG emissions

Contribution of energy intensive industries[1] and the power sector to world GHG emissions[2], 2005

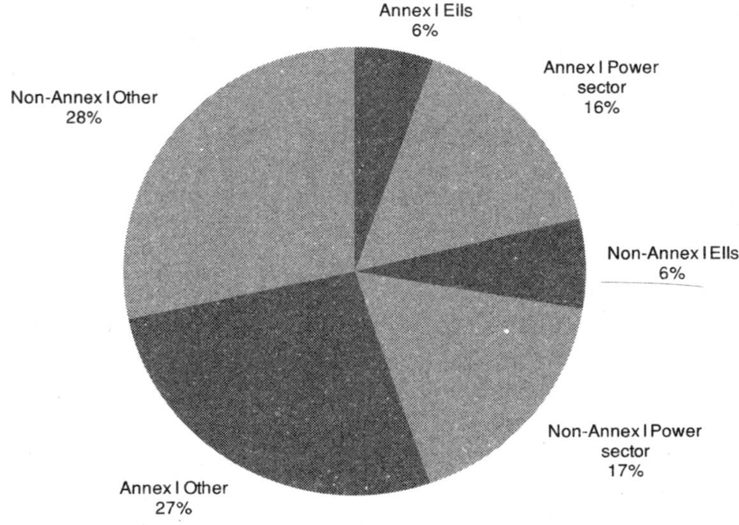

1. Energy-intensive industries include chemicals, metallurgic, other metal, iron and steel industry, paper, mineral products.
2. Excluding emissions from Land Use, Land-Use Change and Forestry.

Source: OECD, ENV-Linkages model.

4.4.2. Increasing emission reductions and lowering mitigation costs through sectoral approaches

The OECD model ENV-Linkages is used to illustrate the impact on overall mitigation costs and emission reduction potential of sectoral approaches covering developing countries. Two main types of scenarios are explored:

- *Scenario 1. Binding sectoral cap with different linking scenarios.* A 50% emission cut in each Annex I region by 2050 from 1990 levels, with full linking across their ETSs (Section 4.2), is now assumed to be supplemented with a binding sectoral cap in EIIs and the power sector in non-Annex I countries. Under this, emissions are reduced just under 10% in 2020 and 20% in 2050 relative to 2005 levels.[39] Three versions of this scenario are considered: Scenario 1(a): no linking, *i.e.* each non-Annex I country has to achieve its sectoral target alone; Scenario 1(b): direct linking across non-Annex I regions, *i.e.* international sectoral permit trading is allowed within the non-Annex I area; and Scenario 1(c): full linking, *i.e.* permit trading is allowed within the non-Annex I area as well as between non-Annex I and Annex I countries (a single ETS).
- *Scenario 2. Sectoral crediting mechanism.* Here a sectoral crediting mechanism for EIIs and the power sector is assumed to be introduced in non-Annex I countries. Credits are granted for emissions reductions against a baseline corresponding to the BAU level in a scenario where only Annex I countries cut their emissions (by 50% in 2050 relative to 1990). Annex I countries are allowed to achieve up to 20% of their emission target by buying these credits.

Scenario 1 results: binding sectoral cap and linking options

A binding sectoral cap covering EIIs and the power sector in non-Annex I countries could substantially reduce emissions worldwide.[40] Owing to the fast emission growth expected in non-Annex I countries, a 20% emissions cut in these sectors in non-Annex I countries would achieve a larger reduction in world emissions (compared to a scenario under which the world took no action) than a 50% cut in Annex I countries by 2050. The emission reductions under the former scenario would be 24% and 30% higher in 2020 and 2050 respectively than under the 50% cut in Annex I countries. Nevertheless, world emissions would barely decline by 2020 relative to 2005 levels, and would rise slightly beyond 2020. This indicates that in order to achieve more ambitious global emission reductions, either targets would need to be more ambitious or an agreement would need to include more sectors, which would be a far cheaper option (Figure 4.17, Panel A).[41]

Binding sectoral caps would entail costs which would vary across non-Annex I countries. The costs involved would depend on the level of emission reductions demanded by the cap, the availability of cheap abatement options (the shape of the marginal abatement cost curve), the carbon intensity of output, and whether international permit trading was allowed. For instance, in the illustrative scenario considered here (Scenario 1 above), India is found to incur larger mitigation costs than China (Figure 4.18), mainly due to its faster projected BAU emission growth. However, that gap would be reduced substantially if international permit trading (internal linking) was allowed across non-Annex I regions (compare the scenarios "with no linking'' and "with direct linking within non-Annex I" in Figure 4.18). Despite facing a smaller emission reduction relative to BAU than Annex I countries (-25% *versus* -30% by 2020 and -40% *versus* -60% by 2050) and benefiting from their larger potential to reduce emissions more cheaply, non-Annex I countries would incur larger costs (more than 3% of their joint income in 2020, compared to less than 1.5% for Annex I countries), reflecting their higher carbon intensity, particularly by 2020.

Linking sectoral ETSs in non-Annex I countries to economy-wide ETSs in Annex I countries could also generate aggregate gains by exploiting the wide heterogeneity of (marginal) abatement costs between the two areas, as long as carbon prices differ sufficiently prior to linking. At the same time, such linking could have significant redistributive effects across countries. Therefore, allocation rules may need to be adjusted upon linking to ensure that the gains from linking are shared widely across participating countries. However, in the scenario considered here (Scenario 1c "full linking"), there is virtually no aggregate gain. This is because the initial difference in carbon prices across the schemes happens to be low (2005 USD 75 per tonne of CO_2eq in Annex I countries, *versus* USD 98 in non-Annex I countries in 2020) because they are both quite similar in their stringency. The general rule – that permit sellers in the market with the lower pre-linking carbon price gain, while permit buyers lose (and *vice versa*) – applies here for countries when two region-wide ETSs are linked, rather than for firms. Non-Annex I countries (India, oil-exporting countries) which bought permits from China before linking with Annex I, lose from the increase in the permit price after linking. On the other hand, Annex I countries (the United States, Russia) which sold permits to the rest of Annex I lose from the price decline induced by competition with China.

Figure 4.17. The impact of sectoral approaches in non-Annex I regions on world emission reductions and mitigation costs

Panel A. 50% emission cut in Annex I by 2050 and binding sectoral cap (20% cut by 2050) in non-Annex I covering EIIs and the power sector

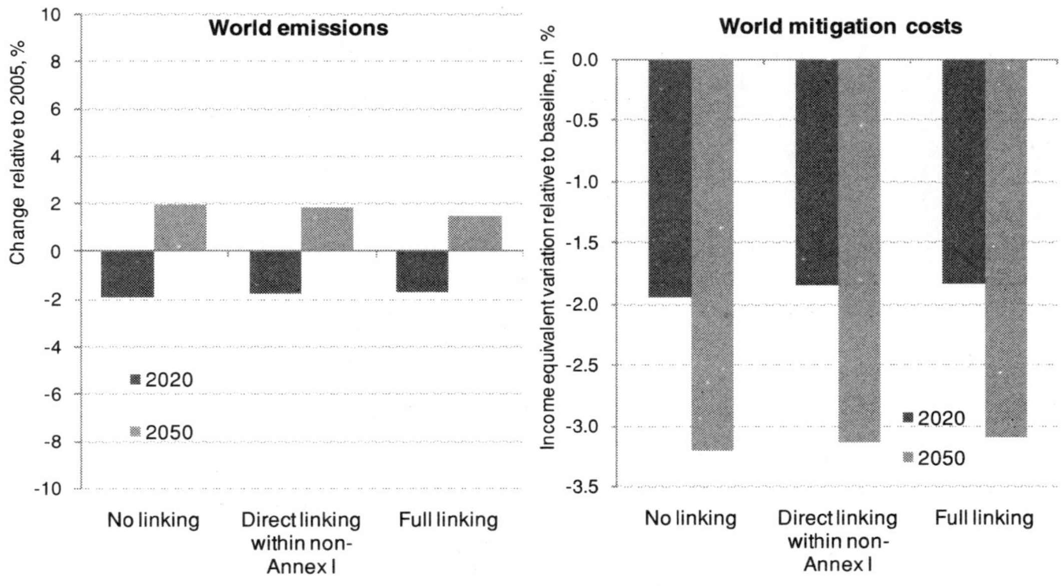

Panel B. 50% emission cut in Annex I by 2050 and sectoral crediting mechanism covering EIIs and the power sector[1]

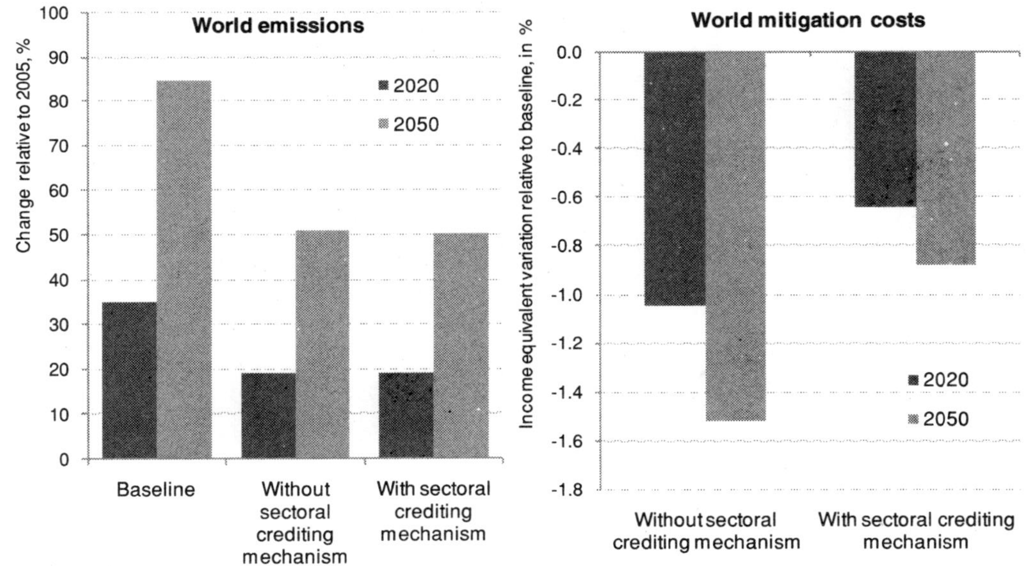

1. With a 20% cap on use of offset credits.

Source: OECD, ENV-Linkages model.

Figure 4.18. Mitigation costs under an international ETS in Annex I and binding sectoral caps in non-Annex I regions

50% cut in Annex I regions and 20% cut in EEIs and power sector in non-Annex I regions by 2050

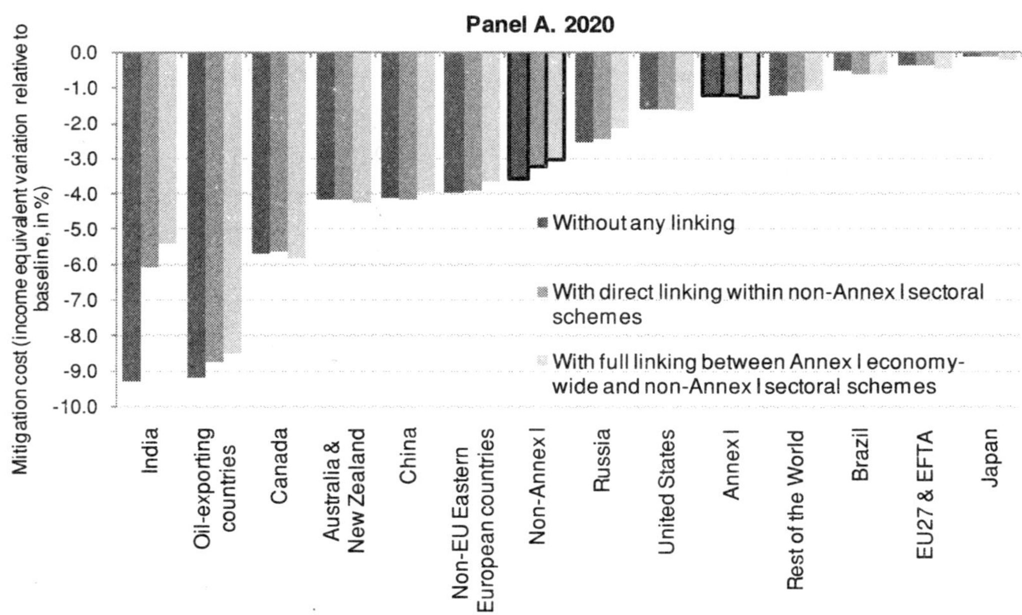

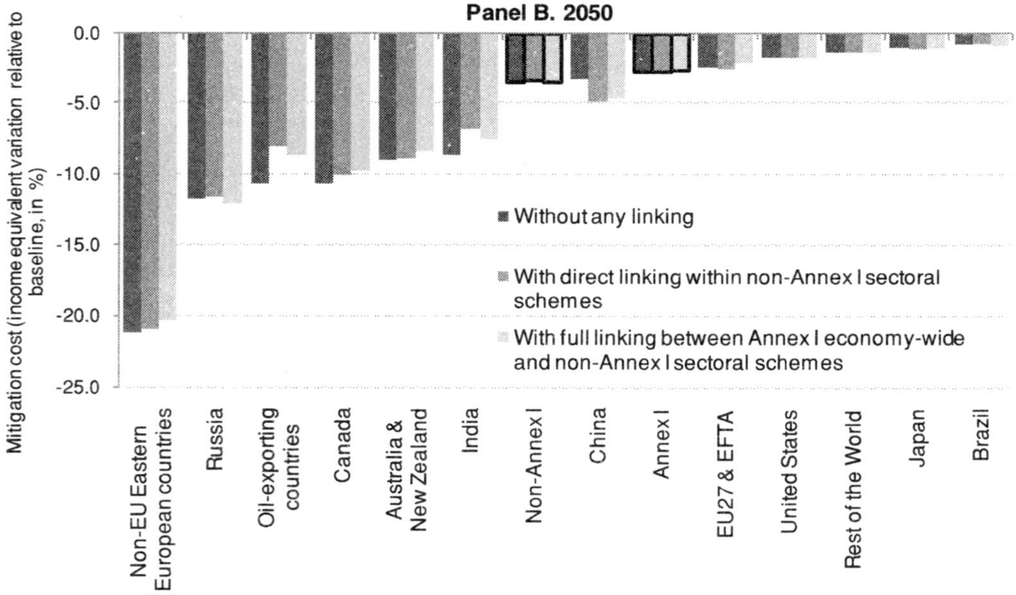

Note: All scenarios combine a 50% emission cut in Annex I (relative to 1990 levels) and a 20% cut in EIIs and the power sector in non-Annex I (relative to 2005 levels) by 2050.

Source: OECD, ENV-Linkages model.

Figure 4.19. The impact of sectoral crediting on mitigation costs in Annex I and non-Annex I regions

(Under a 20% cut by 2020 and a 50% cut by 2050 relative to 1990 levels in each Annex I region)

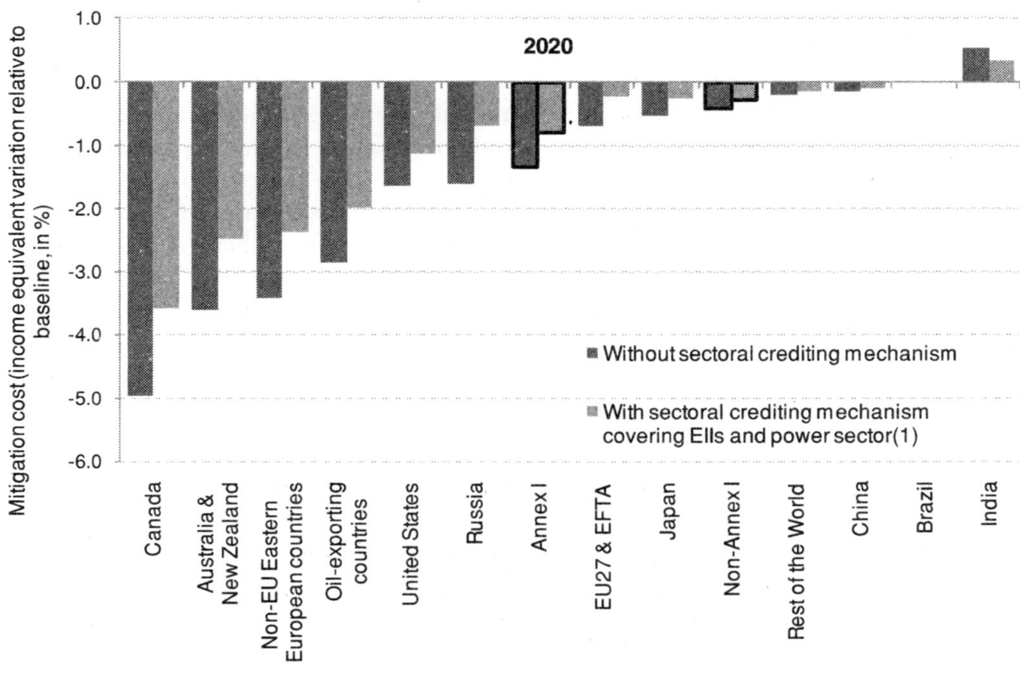

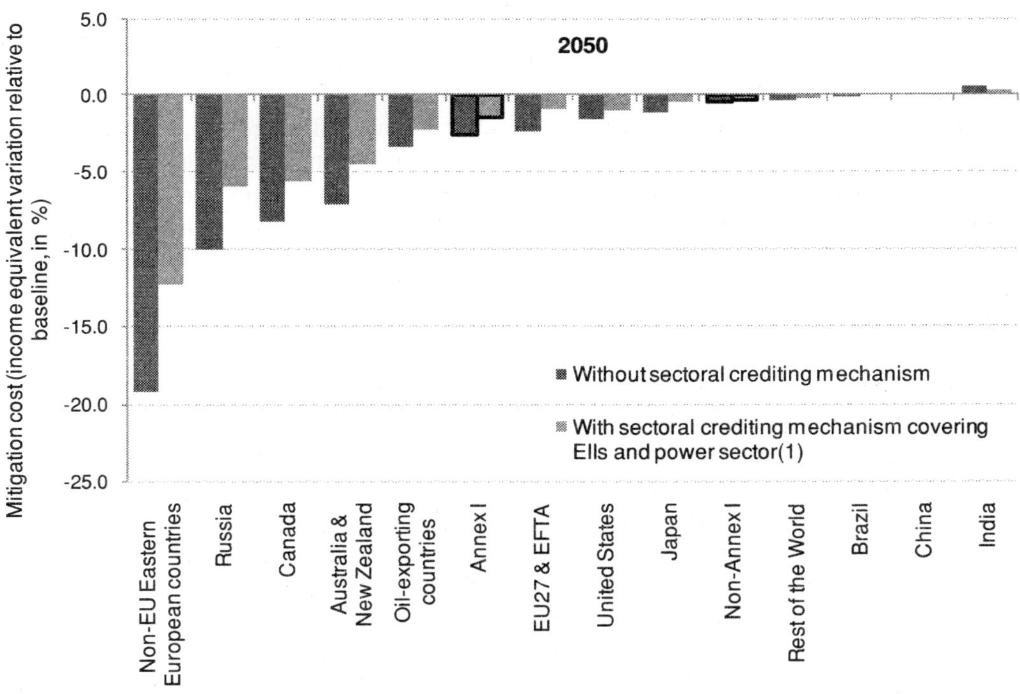

1. With a 20% cap on use of offset credits.

Source: OECD, ENV-Linkages model.

Scenario 2 results: sectoral crediting mechanism

The second scenario, the sectoral crediting mechanism, would affect emissions only through a small decrease in carbon leakage. Thus, it has a limited effect on world emissions, which are found to rise sharply relative to 2005 (Figure 4.17, Panel B).[42] Like any other crediting mechanism, however, sectoral crediting in developing countries can lower the cost of achieving an emission reduction target in developed countries (Section 4.3). Because it lowers mitigation costs, sectoral crediting might still indirectly help achieve more ambitious targets by encouraging Annex I countries to adopt more stringent objectives. It would also be expected to reduce considerably the transaction costs and bottlenecks experienced in the current CDM, since credits would be granted on the basis of a sector-wide baseline rather than on a project-by-project basis.[43] Compared with a scenario where Annex I meets its 50% emission reduction objective alone, and despite the fairly restrictive 20% limit on offset use, a well-functioning sectoral crediting mechanism appears to lower Annex I mitigation costs (in income-equivalent terms) from 1.3% to 0.8% in 2020, and from 2.6% to 1.5% in 2050 (Figure 4.19). A model simulation (not reported) in which this crediting mechanism is expanded to all sectors of non-Annex I economies finds costs to decline only marginally further.

4.4.3. Impact of sectoral approaches on carbon leakage and competitiveness concerns[44]

Binding sectoral targets and – to a lesser extent, depending on their design – sectoral crediting mechanisms have the potential to reduce carbon leakage. Since leakage fundamentally results from incomplete coverage of binding mitigation action, sectoral targets for EIIs and the power sector address it automatically. Leakage would then only be likely to occur in non-covered sectors in developing countries or to a more limited extent in sectors with very lax targets. In Scenario 2, sectoral crediting in EIIs and the power sector is found to lower carbon prices in Annex I countries, thereby also reducing leakage to other (non-covered) sectors in non-Annex I countries, and overall leakage rates (Figure 4.20). In practice, the extent to which sectoral crediting reduces leakage depends in part on the baseline against which credits are granted (Section 4.3). In particular, if firms ultimately receive the proceeds from credit sales, they would benefit from a surplus that could lower output prices and, therefore, increase local demand, output and emissions.[45] This would apply to industries sheltered from international competition, such as the power sector in many developing countries. If agreed sectoral baselines are set in a way that does acknowledge this effect, they might be "too high", in which case sectoral crediting could increase rather than reduce leakage (Bollen *et al.* 1999, 2005). No such problem arises in the above scenarios, as baselines are assumed to be set before the start of the whole compliance period, *i.e.* before sectoral crediting is implemented.

Sectoral approaches may also help to reduce competitiveness concerns in developed countries by "levelling the playing field" in internationally competitive industries (*e.g.* Sawa, 2008). A binding sectoral cap in EIIs in major developing countries can be expected to curb and, depending on its stringency, even possibly reverse the market share and output losses of firms in Annex I countries by pricing the emissions of their non-Annex I competitors. For instance, in the illustrative 50% Annex I emission reduction scenario explored previously, the output loss of EIIs in Annex I countries appears to be significantly reduced when a sectoral cap is put on EIIs and the power sector in non-Annex I countries (Figure 4.21). This is especially the case if Annex I and non-Annex I markets are linked and carbon prices fully converge. By reducing the carbon price, sectoral crediting is also found to limit the output losses of EIIs in Annex I countries. Whether sectoral crediting is more effective than a sectoral cap in addressing competitiveness problems depends in part on which approach achieves the strongest degree of convergence in carbon prices between developed and developing countries. While linking economy-wide ETSs in developed countries to sectoral ETSs in developing countries can achieve full convergence, sectoral crediting cannot – at least while there are constraints on offset credit use. As simulated here, sectoral crediting puts a relatively low opportunity cost on carbon in non-Annex I countries, and thereby has smaller effects on the output of EIIs in Annex I countries than a sectoral cap approach. However, the two simulations cannot be readily compared as they achieve different world emission reductions.

Figure 4.20. Sectoral crediting would lower carbon leakage rates

Carbon leakage rate for Annex I as a whole, under a scenario where emissions in Annex I regions are cut by 20% by 2020 and 50% by 2050 relative to 1990 levels

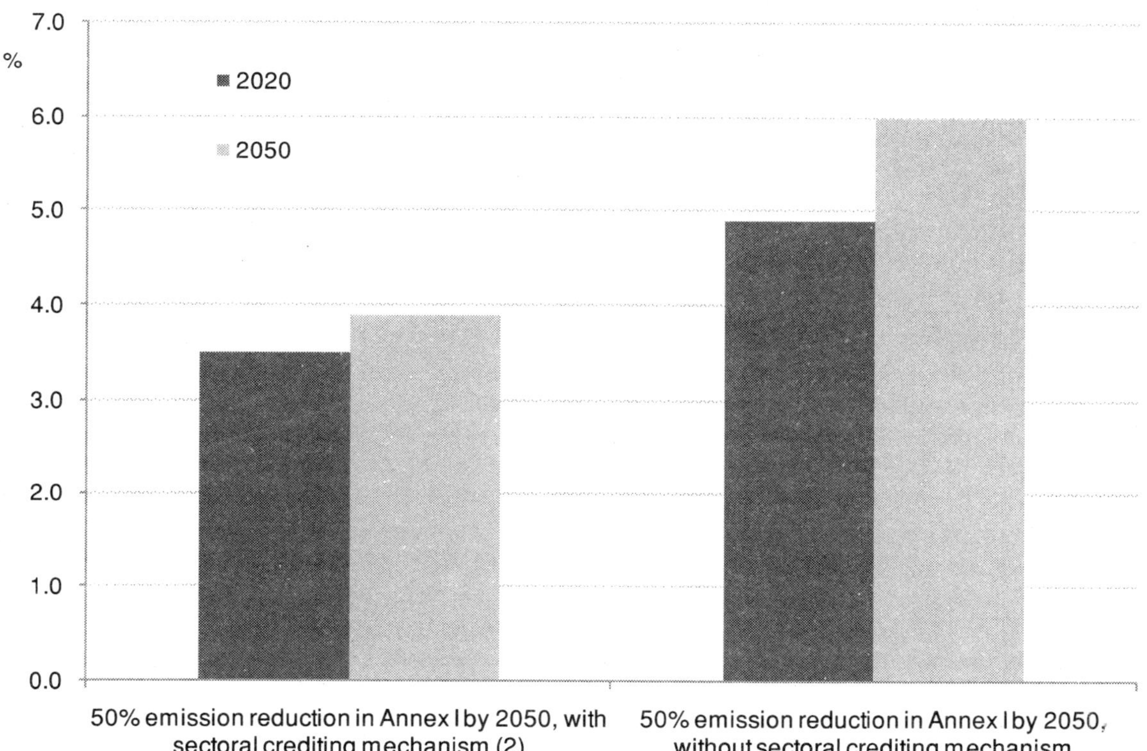

1. The carbon leakage rate is calculated as: [1-(world emission reduction in $GtCO_2eq$)/(Annex I emission reduction objective in $GtCO_2eq$)]. It is expressed in per cent. When the emission reduction achieved at the world level (in $GtCO_2eq$) is equal to the emission reduction objective set by Annex I (in $GTCO_2eq$), there is no leakage overall, and the leakage rate is 0.
2. With a 20% cap on use of offset credits.

Source: OECD, ENV-Linkages model.

Figure 4.21. Impact of sectoral approaches on the output of energy-intensive industries

(% deviation relative to baseline)

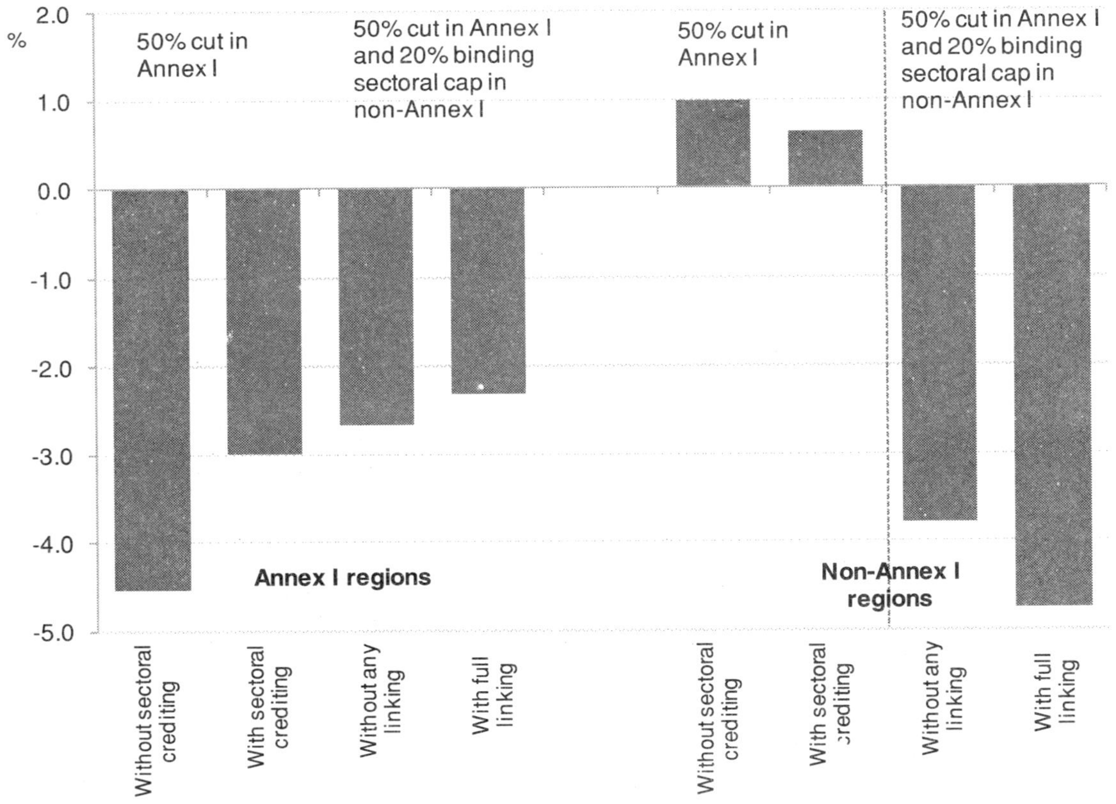

1. Energy-intensive industries include chemicals, metallurgic, other metal, iron and steel industry, paper, mineral products.
2. The scenario "50% cut in Annex I" and "50% cut in Annex I and 20% binding sectoral cap in non-Annex I" are not directly comparable as they do not acheive the same emissions reductions, with the latter one being more stringent than the former one.

Source: OECD, ENV-Linkages model.

4.4.4. Limits of sectoral approaches and options for the future

While sectoral crediting would reduce transaction costs and bottlenecks, it may not necessarily address major concerns over the current CDM regarding additionality, perverse incentives to raise emissions, and, to some extent, leakage (Section 4.3). A sectoral crediting mechanism would also raise the question of how to transfer the carbon price signal to firms (Baron *et al.* 2009). In practice, under this system, it is generally expected that governments in developing countries would receive the credits generated from below-baseline sectoral emissions in their countries, and would then need to find ways to induce firms to effectively reduce their emissions. In principle, this could be achieved by: i) setting up a domestic carbon tax; or ii) a firm-level crediting mechanism under which local firms in the sector would be assigned baselines (reflecting the overall sectoral baseline) and would receive credits for emission cuts below those baselines. This might prove difficult in practice, however, especially for countries with weak institutions. A weaker price signal for firms would reduce emission reduction incentives and sectoral crediting would achieve lower cuts than expected. The simulations discussed above implicitly assume that the price signal is fully transmitted to firms.

In any event, sectoral crediting is likely to have to evolve eventually into more binding arrangements such as sectoral caps, which raise smaller environmental integrity problems, but potentially allow larger world targets to be adopted. While, in principle, both sectoral crediting and absolute sectoral emission caps can be designed to achieve similar emission cuts, they imply very different distributions of mitigation costs across countries. Given the fast rate at which emissions are projected to rise in most developing countries under a BAU scenario, meeting ambitious world targets through sectoral crediting alone would mean that developed countries would need to have negative emission level objectives (or to store more CO_2 than they are emitting) by 2030-2040 (Chapter 6). There would also have to be either lax or no constraints on offset credit use so that these targets could be met. This would impose large economic costs on developed countries, while developing countries would gain from this world mitigation framework. Assuming that this arrangement is implausible, a sectoral crediting approach would therefore have to evolve into binding caps, at least for key developing country emitters. Simulation results suggest that even relatively moderately stringent caps on EIIs and the power sector have the potential to generate large emission reductions relative to the baseline. Over the lifetime of the sectoral crediting scheme, baselines could be progressively tightened – *i.e.* set further below BAU emission levels – from one commitment period to the next.

One option that has sometimes been put forward in the policy debate would be to start with sectoral intensity targets – in which the allowable amount of emissions is a function of future output – rather than absolute targets. At the sectoral level, emission intensity tends to be driven by technology choices and energy efficiency, rather than by output. This makes it easier to identify the changes in advance, and thereby the costs needed to meet an intensity target, while the costs of absolute targets are more uncertain as they depend on future output (Bradley *et al.* 2007). However, one of the challenges for emission trading is to transform the intensity target into an absolute amount of emission rights that can be traded (Section 4.2). This would require an initial allocation of permits based on a projected output path, followed by regular adjustments of permit supply to reflect (unexpected) output growth developments. If permits can be traded between sectors, achieving the intensity target in a given sector would not be straightforward, in part because newly emitted permits could be bought by firms from another sector (Box 4.3 above). An alternative option is to assign permits for a sufficiently long time period based on a projected sectoral output path, without adjusting permit supply before the next commitment period. In this case, the intensity target ultimately boils down to a particular rule for allocating permits under an absolute cap, and sectoral schemes could be easily linked to other sectoral or economy-wide systems. However, this approach does not provide insurance against the risk of mitigation cost increases that would result from higher-than-expected output growth.

4.5. Regulatory issues and the role of financial markets

Carbon markets will naturally develop as more and more countries undertake mitigation actions. These carbon markets are expected to become large. They are likely to reach 1% of world GDP by 2050 if Annex I countries alone reduce their emissions by 50% (relative to 1990 levels), and 5% of world GDP under a global carbon price scenario that stabilises overall GHG concentration below 550 ppm CO_2eq.[46] Institutions and rules will be needed to foster their development and to address risks that are expected to emerge within a linked system of multiple independent and heterogeneous emission trading schemes. This Section discusses these risks and outline the institutions needed to overcome them.

4.5.1. The risks associated with the development of carbon markets

The development of carbon markets raises four main risks (Table 4.6):

- *An environmental risk,* which may be the major risk associated with a linked system of several independent and heterogeneous ETS and crediting mechanisms (Sections 4.2 and 4.3).
- *Lack of market liquidity.* Liquid primary markets foster the emergence of derivative instruments (futures, forwards, options, and swaps) that would lower the cost for firms to insure against future carbon price uncertainty.[47] Liquid markets would also reduce the opportunities for market manipulation. Markets can fail to become liquid for several reasons. If the treatment of two types of allowances differs across two systems – *e.g.* due to limits on the use of the other system's allowances, or the use of a discount rate for allowances whose environmental quality is perceived to be low – the allowances would be imperfect substitutes and traded at different prices in spot markets, thereby leading to market fragmentation. Likewise, if some credits entail specific risks, as is the case under the current CDM, they will be traded at different prices to those of other units in the primary market.[48] For instance, the price difference between future EU permits (EU allowances, EUA) and high-quality – *i.e.* those with the higher price – forward CER contracts on the primary market was around EUR 10 in 2008 (World Bank, 2008). These differences disappear in secondary markets after the CER has been traded once. Differences in permit design features in terms of lifetime or banking possibilities would also reduce the liquidity of markets. Such differences would also affect futures and other derivatives in carbon markets. Investors might hold different expectations for possible programme changes in the various emission trading systems, thereby making allowance futures imperfect substitutes and fragmenting the derivatives market. Nonetheless, market liquidity concerns could be reduced in the future as the size of carbon markets increases with broader country participation and more stringent objectives.
- *Risk associated with the development of derivative markets.* Speculative trading is expected to play an important role in the development of carbon derivative markets. This is because, unlike in other commodity markets, if permits are mainly auctioned, most regulated firms will tend to hedge the cost of their compliance obligation by buying allowance futures and financial traders will have to take most of the opposite position, selling allowance futures, thereby taking part of the net risk.[49] The role of speculative trading is expected to be reflected in futures prices in the form of financial traders' risk premia.[50]
- *A counterparty risk.* With 70% of carbon trading in Europe being conducted through bilateral negotiations between participants – the "over-the-counter" (OTC) markets – and with most of this trading being for deferred delivery (Point Carbon, 2007), the counterparty risk, the risk to each party of a contract that the counterparty will not live up to its contractual obligations, is significant in current carbon markets and could lead to market dysfunction and reduced cost-effectiveness. As markets develop and if transactions continue to operate mainly through OTC markets, this risk could increase. However, it could be reduced if organised exchanges expand, for example through the intermediation of clearinghouses that verify trade orders and net out offsetting contracts by the same clearing member.

4.5.2. Institutions and regulations to address carbon market risks

Policies aiming at environmental integrity

Given the various incentives for countries to free ride and to increase their emissions, it has sometimes been suggested that an independent international institution acting as a central bank could help achieve mitigation targets at least cost, while preserving environmental integrity and anchoring carbon price expectations (*e.g.* Grubb and Neuhoff, 2006; Yohe, 2007 and Edenhofer *et al.* 2007). Indeed, the comparison between emission credits and money has often been made. In practice, however, countries are unlikely to accept such a transfer of their power, and attempting to create a new global institution would run the risk of further delaying mitigation action (Mc Kibbin, 2007). Therefore, the following discussion tries, as far as possible, to build on existing institutions and rules.

Table 4.6. Regulations to address carbon market risks

Carbon market risks	Consequences	Provisions/recommendations
Environmental risk	The system (international or emerging from regional initiatives) does not achieve its emission target	Agree within a centralised institution (*e.g.* UNFCCC body) on emission targets, emission trading schemes design features, cost-containment measures, links to other systems, and MRV procedures Use complementary compliance mechanism, such as a system of performance bonds
Market liquidity risk	Lack of liquidity would imply: • Larger carbon price volatility • Higher transaction costs • Risk of market power problems • Higher cost of derivatives	Allow regular spot sales of short-term permits Allow banking Ensure credible commitments on future mitigation policies (to foster the development of derivative markets)
Derivative markets risk	Could make financial markets unstable	Harmonise regulations on position limits for financial traders Eventually introduce limits on banking for financial traders Identify financial market authorities responsible for carbon markets
Counterparty risk	Market dysfunction, reduced cost-effectiveness	Extend the access to clearinghouses or introduce penalties for performance failure in contracts Ensure credible commitments to future mitigation policies (to limit the risk of imbalances between allowances supply and demand)

Given the difficulty of enforcing international rules in sovereign states, negotiations and consensus building must be at the core of the development of the carbon market. In order to facilitate future linking and to maximise its market liquidity benefits, participating governments should seek to agree on their targets and the emission trading schemes design features that will need to be harmonised prior to linking, including cost containment measures (Section 4.2), decisions to link to another system, and how to co-ordinate monitoring, reporting and verification efforts (Haites and Wang, 2006). However, this has not happened so far in practice, as existing ETSs have very different rules on allocation methodologies, non-compliance provisions, and allowable offsets (*e.g.* Ellis and Tirpak, 2006; Reinaud and

Philibert 2007). Centralised institutions that support implementation of the UNFCCC, the Kyoto Protocol, and any future protocol could help by providing a framework to discuss issues of linking national and regional ETSs. Already, a centralised permit registry has been created under the UNFCCC, and the Kyoto Protocol's project-based mechanisms (CDM and Joint Implementation) are managed centrally.

A number of options exist to reduce the risks of non-compliance and to relax the target in future compliance periods once systems are linked. However, none of them would fully address the issue of enforcing international commitments by sovereign governments, which will ultimately require adequate participation incentives to be provided (Chapter 6). As a general principle, longer-term agreements on well-defined emission caps would help limit the need and room for frequent re-negotiations. One possible complementary compliance mechanism could be the emission of performance bonds. Under this approach, governments would put some of their own bonds before the start of a compliance period into the hands of a compliance committee (*e.g.* a UNFCCC body), which would then have the right to either sell those bonds in the open market if the country fails to meet its commitment, or return them to governments if they do. International agreement on such a system may be hard to reach. Nevertheless, it could be an improvement over the penalty system embedded in the Kyoto protocol (which involves making up excess emissions in the next period plus a 30% penalty), which has proved to be weak in the absence of a long-term framework. A reserve, such as the existing "commitment period reserve" under the Kyoto protocol, which requires governments to keep a certain percentage (90%) of their assigned units in a fund, would also limit the risk of "overselling" by participants that do not meet their targets. However, this could come at the cost of imposing limits on trading and weakening the cost-effectiveness of the scheme (OECD, 2001). Yet another alternative would be to use trade sanctions, but these have been found to be costly and might trigger trade retaliation, rather than greater country co-operation (Chapter 3).

An alternative to explicit enforcement mechanisms would be to give governments incentives to comply, *e.g.* through a system of buyer liability, under which buyers would be liable for the poor quality, in terms of environmental performance, of the permits or offsets they hold (Baron, 2000; Victor, 2001; Keohane and Raustiala, 2008).[51] The validity of permits or offsets emitted by a given country would be assessed on a regular basis, and if some permits of the country are found to be of a poor quality, all of them would then be discounted on a national basis. Under this system, (net) selling countries would be induced to improve the quality of their permits so as to increase export revenues, while buyers would have similar incentives to gather information *in advance,* and possibly buy low-quality permits at a discount price, as on the international sovereign bond market. One major weakness of this proposal, however, is that quality checks would probably have to be performed by an independent agency,[52] which may thus face the same problems as the current CDM executive board. Furthermore, improved environmental integrity would come at the cost of reduced market liquidity, because permits would have different prices according to their quality and country of issuance. Also, the system ultimately rests on the willingness of (net) buying countries to enforce penalties on their domestic emitters. If buyers were reluctant to endorse such an approach, they could instead apply a penalty later, in the form of discounts on all permit imports from the selling country concerned (Box 4.2).

Reaching agreement on standards and procedures for validating and verifying the domestic and/or international offset credits accepted within ETSs is also essential, since the use of such offsets has effects across linked systems, even if only one of these formally recognises them (Sections 4.2 and 4.3). The easiest way to achieve agreement would be through the use of a common centralised institution to manage the offset verification programme, as happens for the CDM. An alternative would be to share full information about standards and procedures so that mutual confidence is built in offsets' environmental integrity. Reforming the CDM to reduce the additionality issue (Section 4.3) and lower

 THE ECONOMICS OF CLIMATE CHANGE MITIGATION – ISBN: 978-92-64-05606-0 – © OECD 2009

transaction costs and bottlenecks would help to make allowances from ETS and CERs closer substitutes, thereby also increasing market liquidity.

Policies to improve market functioning

Some permit design features can foster the development of derivative markets and lower the cost of hedging. Permits are usually valid for only one single tonne of carbon ("short-term" permits), and the lifetime during which they can be used is either fixed (a particular year or compliance period), or undefined if permits can be banked. Liquid spot markets (through regular spot sales of short-term permits), banking and credible commitments on future mitigation policies may be the most effective way to foster the development of least cost derivatives. Some imperfect substitutes for futures contracts have also been proposed to help the formation of future prices, such as the emission of future vintages of allowances (if permits cannot be banked), or of long-term permits that grant the holder the right to emit one tonne of carbon annually (*e.g.* McKibbin and Wilcoxen, 2006).[53] However, each of these instruments has its own characteristics, risks and price. If different types of instruments are allowed to multiply for future delivery, this can also fragment the market and possibly reduce liquidity in particular instruments. This could occur for instance if credits cannot be banked between compliance periods and multiple vintages are traded in spot markets alongside derivative contracts. For these reasons, short-term permits that can be banked between compliance periods seem preferable. Long-term permits can be considered to show governments' commitment and to create a constituency (permit holders) that supports mitigation policies, but they also run the risk of fragmenting the market. Therefore they may be primarily considered in cases where the credibility of the scheme could be weak otherwise, or once carbon markets are sufficiently large.

Carbon market regulation will need to strike the right balance between environmental integrity, stability and liquidity objectives. In particular, one open issue is whether position limits on financial traders in spot and derivative commodity markets should also be set in permit markets in order to limit the risk of sudden or unwarranted carbon price fluctuations. One option might be to impose limits on banking for financial traders, to prevent them from possibly banking large amounts of allowances in response to changes in expectations and thereby being able to manipulate and cause large fluctuations in spot markets. Such restrictions would have to be weighed against the fact that financial traders will provide liquidity and firms will need derivative markets to hedge against price uncertainty. Since within a linked system, limits on the positions of financial traders in derivatives markets would spread across schemes, national and/or regional regulators would also have to co-ordinate and possibly harmonise regulatory frameworks. The supervision of carbon markets will typically fall under existing financial market authorities, but for countries with multiple financial market authorities, those responsible for carbon markets will have to be clearly identified. Broad regulations that already exist or will be developed in response to the recent financial crisis will also apply, and thus should incorporate the carbon market dimension.

In the short run, it will remain a major challenge to devise regulations that generate confidence among participants and that protect against sources of future market fragility, while not impeding innovation and market development. Given the wide variety of possible permit design and regulatory features in emission trading schemes, best practice may emerge only gradually and harmonisation is likely to take time. During that transitory period, in order to avoid the risk of significant market disruptions caused by linking, limits to trading between schemes could be set up that would then be gradually phased out as knowledge about best practice builds up and scheme design features are harmonised. The creation of a carbon market working group made up of international regulators, perhaps as part of the Financial Stability Board, could facilitate exchange of information about regulations, risks and harmonisation needs.

Finally, there are several ways to address the counterparty risk that arises from the fact that a large proportion of transactions take place in over-the-counter markets. Contracts could specify penalties for performance failures and allow the seller or buyer to complete the transaction with another party after a specified short number of days. It is also possible to let participants access a clearinghouse even though transactions are over-the-counter – as is the case under the EU ETS for small players – or to require transactions above a certain size to be passed through clearinghouses (Point Carbon, 2007). If there is concern that delivery failures may occur because the number of allowances is smaller than the demand coming from financial traders with short futures positions, limits on futures positions could be tightened, although this may also increase the cost of hedging. Limiting the uncertainty on long-term emission reduction commitments – and the associated amount of allowances – as well as extending ETSs to other countries will also be crucial to address the counterparty risk.

Notes

1. The issue of carbon leakage and competiveness concerns of climate change mitigation policies is also analysed in Chapter 3.

2. This Section focuses on subsidies affecting the demand for fossil fuels – including indirectly through electricity subsidies – in non-OECD countries only. Though OECD countries do provide subsidies to energy production and consumption, these are generally indirect and often not transparent, which makes it very difficult to estimate their magnitude. Direct subsidies to fossil fuel consumptions in OECD countries are small in comparison to non-OECD countries. Subsidies targeted to renewable energy sources in OECD countries are not covered in the analysis here.

3. In particular, the estimated gap may reflect market imperfections other than subsidies, such as differences in quality or uses, imperfectly competitive behaviour or a lack of representativeness of the chosen reference price. Although this approach treats all subsidies as if they were consumer subsidies, removing a producer subsidy will have, in practice, a different impact from removing a consumer subsidy, even if both types of subsidies ultimately contribute to lower the price and increase the consumption of the corresponding energy source. IEA (1999) – discussion of the pros and cons of the "price gap" approach.

4. This is the case for instance when energy prices are set administratively.

5. This analysis assumes that the subsidy wedges remain constant in the business as usual (BAU) scenario. Alternatively, assuming some decoupling of domestic energy prices relative to world energy prices would lead to an increase in subsidy wedges over time, given the projected rise in world energy prices in the BAU scenario. The impact of subsidy removal on emissions would therefore be larger under that alternative assumption.

6. These reductions are comparable with those reported in IEA (1999), taking into account that the sample of countries for which subsidy data have been collected here covers a much larger share of world energy demand.

7. In the case of a multilateral removal of energy subsidies, oil and gas prices fall by more than coal prices, mainly because coal is generally less heavily subsidised. This change in relative prices would induce a substitution from coal to oil and gas, which are less polluting, and would therefore reduce GHG emissions. This effect would not occur in the case of a unilateral removal, since no country acting alone has a sufficiently large impact on world relative prices of coal, oil or gas.

8. This regional aggregate consists of very different economies (Armenia, Azerbaijan, Belarus, Croatia, Georgia, Kazakhstan, Kyrgyzstan, Moldova, Tajikistan, Turkmenistan, Ukraine, Uzbekistan), where the removal of the subsidies induces a dramatic shift in the economic structure

towards low-productivity sectors. The resulting overall productivity loss more than offsets the welfare gains from the subsidy removal.

9. It is often argued that subsidies are justified on equity grounds, for instance to alleviate poverty. In this simulation, the budgetary saving obtained from the subsidy removal is entirely refunded to households through a lump-sum (non-distorting) way. This implies that subsidies for the consumption of fossil fuel are replaced by a direct and larger transfer to households. Alternatively, this transfer could be used to reduce other distorting taxes, which would increase the real income gain from subsidy removal, or to reduce poverty in a more targeted and efficient way than through a uniform subsidy to fossil fuel consumption.

10. An additional explanation for the small magnitude of world real income gains is that the fall in world fossil fuel prices induces producers to reduce their supply, leaving more of their reserves in the ground. This leads to a GDP loss, all other things being equal.

11. Chapter 1, Table 1.2 – emission path corresponding to the "550 ppm-base" scenario.

12. This world GDP cost estimate is lower, by 0.4%, than the one presented in Chapter 1. This is because, here, energy subsidies are explicitly incorporated in the BAU scenario, which lowers the mitigation cost because of so-called "second-best effect", Burniaux *et al.* (2009), Box 2.

13. Another reason is that he "second best" GDP gain coming from the reduction of the share of sectors that are subject to distortion because of energy subsidies is then lost, Burniaux *et al.* (2009), Section 3.

14. For regions with lower pre-linking carbon prices, the gains from exporting permits more than offset the additional economic costs from the increase in carbon prices, in the absence of market imperfections. Likewise, for regions with higher pre-linking carbon prices, the reduction in mitigation costs associated with the decline in carbon prices more than offsets the cost of importing permits.

15. More broadly, the OECD ENV-Linkages model incorporates many market imperfections and distortions and, therefore, the impact of permit trading on each participating region has to be interpreted in a second-best context. As countries sell permits abroad, imports must rise and/or other exports must decline in order to satisfy the exogenous balance-of-payments constraint (see Annex 2). Restoring the external balance requires an appreciation of the real exchange rate, which triggers costly reallocation of capital across sectors, reduces aggregate output and, in some cases, lowers income and welfare. These model features tend to exacerbate Dutch disease effects.

16. Carbon price volatility may still increase in one of the two schemes if the other is subject to larger and/or more frequent shocks, and is large enough to have significant influence on the overall carbon price after linking.

17. However, under one-way credits to firms in system linking, firms in system A would be penalised by not being allowed to sell B.

18. By changing the distribution of emission reductions, linking will affect the co-benefits of mitigation policies in terms of reduced local air pollutant emission. This calls for pricing of local air pollution benefits separately through local, targeted (*e.g.* transport and electricity) taxes.

19. Grand-fathering consists in allocating permits for free on the basis of historical emissions.

20. One exception may be if firms – especially those in the region with the higher initial carbon price – expect permits to continue to be grandfathered in the future. This would undermine their incentives to reduce emissions compared with one-off grandfathering which generates only windfall gains.

21. It should be noted that under a system that combines a carbon tax and an ETS, regardless of whether systems are linked or not, the overall amount of emissions is not fixed, unless the cap of the ETS and/or the carbon tax are adjusted in order to achieve a given joint target.

22. Linking may still increase emissions if the cap is set on the basis of a strongly overestimated GDP and turns not to be binding ex post, as extra permits could then be sold to other schemes upon linking. This problem is a "hot air" issue.

23. Once schemes are linked, there is also an incentive for net permit seller countries to issue more permits. However, this can be addressed through an appropriate regulatory framework (Section 4.5).

24. For instance, under a USD 20 carbon price in Annex I countries, Bakker *et al.* (2007) tentatively estimate that the amount of emissions abated through crediting projects in non-Annex I countries might be reduced by a factor of up to two if these barriers were taken into account.

25. Full linking between ETSs implies that the 50% cap on offsets applies to the Annex I region as a whole rather than to each country individually. Full linking in addition to indirect linking through the CDM generates a marginal gain for regions taken as a whole. However, some countries would lose, notably Australia and New Zealand, because they benefit from a smaller amount of offset when the cap on offset is set at the Annex I level as a whole and allocated across countries in a cost-effective manner.

26. At a more basic level, the CDM may increase leakage if changes in the whole supply chain of the project considered are not fully taken into account when granting the emission credits. For example, although a company might use a more efficient technology, it might be built from materials that are produced in a highly energy-intensive way. In this case the net impact of the project on emissions is less than the gross impact. For a discussion of such leakage effects and a methodology to account for them, Geres and Michaelowa (2002).

27. With the CDM, the computation of carbon leakage rates needs to account for the fact that the CDM substitutes emission reductions in non-Annex I countries for increases in their Annex I counterparts. Therefore the carbon leakage rate is calculated here as: [1-(world emission reduction in GtCO2eq)/(Annex I emission reduction objective in GtCO2eq)]. When the emission reduction achieved at the world level is equal to the emission reduction objective set by Annex I (in GtCO2eq), the leakage rate is zero.

28. Hourcade and Shukla (2001), or Kallbekken (2007b). One exception is Babiker (2005), who finds large leakage rates when assuming increasing (rather than constant) returns to scale in energy-intensive industries and homogenous (rather than heterogenous) goods.

29. EIIs exposed to international trade competition include here non-ferrous metals, iron and steel, chemicals, fabricated metal products (excluding machinery and equipment), paper and paper products, and non-metallic minerals (including cement). See Annex 2 for details.

30. As an extreme example, Schwank (2004) estimates that producers of chlorodifluoromethane (HCFC-22) in non-Annex I countries could expand output indefinitely, give that output away, and still make a profit simply by implementing process changes to reduce emissions of trifluoromethane (HFC-23) – a very potent GHG and a by-product of HCFC-22 manufacture – and selling the CERs for that greenhouse gas.

31. Reforestation/afforestation projects are eligible under the CDM, but avoided deforestation is not.

32. For discussion of the permanence and liability issues associated with incorporating CCS in the CDM, and how these could be addressed, Philibert *et al.* (2007). While additionality would not be an issue in general, one possible exception is enhanced oil recovery projects.

THE ECONOMICS OF CLIMATE CHANGE MITIGATION – ISBN: 978-92-64-05606-0 – © OECD 2009

33. For some discussion of differences and possible overlap between bundling and "programmes of activities", Ellis (2006).

34. For evidence of this under-development, *e.g.* Arquit Niederberger and Fecher (2006). For details on how to set up programmatic CDMs to enhance energy efficiency, Figueres and Philips (2007).

35. One additional problem is the existence of linkages across different activities. For instance, in industries where the emission-intensive component of the production process can be outsourced (*e.g.* cement), the whole supply chain may have to be considered in order to avoid leakage.

36. International caps might be easier to negotiate in more concentrated sectors, such as aluminum.

37. Another cost-effective way to achieve binding sectoral targets would be through a carbon tax, but this option has not gained much interest in practice.

38. For instance, air transport is planned to be included in the EU ETS by 2011.

39. The base year for sectoral emission reductions in non-Annex I countries is assumed to be 2005 rather than 1990 partly due to existing uncertainties around 1990 emission levels in a number of developing countries, particularly for non-CO_2 emissions.

40. This is true under the three alternative linking scenarios.

41. Chapter 1 underlines the gains from broadening the sectoral coverage of mitigation action beyond EIIs and the power sector. While a 9% cut in world emission levels relative to 2005 was found to cost 1.7% of world GDP (compared to the baseline) in 2050 (Chapter 1, Table 1.2), here a 2% rise in emissions appears to lower world GDP by over 3% in 2050, (Figure 4.18).

42. As with the CDM, the cap on Annex I countries is unchanged with sectoral crediting (-50% by 2050 relative to 1990 levels in the simulations considered here), but part of the emission reductions are bought and achieved in non-Annex I countries.

43. As all general equilibrium models used to assess the economic effects of alternative climate policies are either economy-wide or – like ENV-Linkages – sectoral models, they cannot assess the implications of moving from a project-by-project to a sectoral approach. As simulated here, sectoral crediting replaces rather than complements the current CDM, which might imply a reduction in the sectoral coverage of emission crediting mechanisms, and thereby a more limited access to cheap abatement opportunities. However, restriction to EIIs and the power industry does not appear to be binding in practice, because these sectors encompass a sizeable share of low-cost abatement opportunities in non-Annex I countries.

44. See Chapter 3 for estimates of the magnitude of carbon leakages and competiveness concerns.

45. For each tonne of CO_2 abated, the surplus would equal the difference between the credit price and the abatement cost. It arises because the price paid for credits in a reasonably competitive world market would be determined by the abatement cost of the marginal project which, due to the convexity of the abatement cost curve, exceeds the abatement costs of all other (cheaper) projects.

46. By comparison, for instance, in 2007 the US sub-prime mortgage market (total outstanding amount of sub-prime loans) amounted to about 9.5% of US GDP, or about 3% of world GDP at current exchange rates (OECD, 2007c).

47. In particular, carbon price uncertainty discourages investment (Jamet, 2009).

48. These risks include registration risks, risks coming from the financial situation of the project leader and its access to credits, and several host country risks (Point Carbon, 2007).

49. The sellers of allowances (governments) have no interest in hedging and therefore, hedging is expected to be one-sided in the carbon market. In most other commodity markets, hedging is two-sided (producers of the commodity hedge by selling futures while processing firms hedge by buying futures), hedging demands are at least partly offsetting and speculative trading is less needed for the development of derivative markets. If permits are allocated for free, the market will be more two-sided, since firms undertaking investment to reduce emissions would hedge against the risk of a decrease in the future carbon price.

50 Other types of hedging costs (fees, bid-ask spreads, and the costs of maintaining margin) should be comparatively small.

51. Under this system, buyers would be liable to make up the difference between invalid permits that do not represent the full amount of carbon reduction their face value implies, and valid ones. In the case of offsets, the additionality would have to be assessed. In the case of allowances, the validity could be assessed on a broader range of criteria including the validity of monitoring, reporting and verification (MRV) procedures and the stringency of the country's allocation of permits during the compliance period.

52. In the international bond market, the quality of sovereign bonds is priced by markets. No independent international agency is needed to rate bonds because buyers have a clear financial incentive to assess the risk of default in advance. By contrast, in the international permit/credit market, neither buyers nor sellers would have a financial incentive to assess the environmental quality of permits or credits in advance, unless an independent authority has the power to enforce a penalty at the end of a project if there have been environmental integrity problems.

53. Compared with a future contract, future vintages of allowances or long term allowances have the advantage of being more flexible, as they can be used to meet compliance obligations if needed, before the future contract maturity date.

 THE ECONOMICS OF CLIMATE CHANGE MITIGATION – ISBN: 978-92-64-05606-0 – © OECD 2009

ISBN: 978-92-64-05606-0
The Economics of Climate Change Mitigation
Policies and Options for Global Action beyond 2012

Chapter 5

Technology and R&D Policies

This chapter explores the impact of various policy instruments to stimulate R&D and technology deployment, using a model that incorporates the process of technological change and innovation, i.e. *induced technological change. It starts with a review of spending trends in energy-related R&D, followed by an assessment of the impact of R&D policies and spending on innovation and technology deployment. The chapter continues with an analysis of the effects of carbon pricing and technology policies on the costs of mitigating climate change. Finally, it addresses the question of whether technology policies will work in the absence of carbon pricing.*

Key Messages

- *Speeding up the emergence and deployment of low-carbon technologies will ultimately require more reallocation of financial resources in energy-related R&D. Technological progress will need to achieve two goals: to bring down the cost of available or emerging emission-reducing technologies and to expand the pool of available technologies and increase their mitigation potential. However, average public energy-related R&D expenditure has declined dramatically across the OECD since it peaked in the early 1980s.*
- *Pricing GHG emissions – including removing implicit emission subsidies such as fossil fuel energy subsidies – would increase the expected returns from R&D in low-carbon technologies. Future increases in carbon prices, if they are properly anticipated, will have powerful effects on R&D spending and clean technology diffusion. For instance, setting a world carbon price path to stabilise* CO_2 *concentration at 450 ppm and overall GHG concentration at about 550 ppm* CO_2eq *in 2050 is estimated to quadruple energy R&D expenditures and investments in installing renewable power generation.*
- *R&D aimed at improving the energy efficiency of existing technologies would have only limited effects on GHG stabilisation costs, while R&D focused on developing major new low-carbon technologies could lower costs drastically if successful. These results highlight the importance of developing new carbon-free technologies in the non-electricity sectors, in particular the transport sector where the abatement potential of commercially available options is smaller.*
- *Despite the R&D incentives it generates, putting a price on GHG emissions does not address all the market imperfections currently undermining R&D and technology deployment. A complementary R&D policy will therefore be important for reducing the costs of stabilising* CO_2 *concentrations worldwide, helping to overcome market failures and to share knowledge across borders. For example, a global R&D fund to subsidise R&D and/or low-carbon technology deployment could further reduce mitigation costs, if it was in addition to pricing carbon. A strong carbon price signal will be required, not only to provide sufficient private incentives for innovation, but also to encourage producers and consumers to switch to low carbon technologies.*

Introduction

Any cost-effective policy framework to address climate change should foster efficient R&D, innovation and the diffusion of greenhouse gas (GHG) emission-reducing technologies. Technological progress will need to achieve two goals:

- *To bring down the cost of available or emerging emission-reducing technologies.* In most of the key emitting economic activities, emerging low-carbon technologies are significantly costlier than the fossil fuel based technologies they would displace.[1] This will remain the case in the short term, even with a moderate carbon price (IEA, 2008b). For instance, the average cost of reducing emissions through a typical portfolio of low-carbon technologies in electricity, industry, transport and buildings has been estimated to exceed USD 80 per tonne of CO_2 in 2005, reaching over USD 140 in non-electricity sectors (Anderson, 2006).
- *To expand the pool of available technologies and increase their mitigation potential.* Currently, the scope and scale of low-carbon technologies envisaged for the future are rather limited

(Anderson, 2006). Most are specific, rather than general purpose, in nature, and their potential use is restricted to a narrow range of economic activities (*e.g.* wind, solar and nuclear energy for power generation; hydrogen and bio-fuels for transport etc.). Furthermore, there remain constraints (*e.g.* energy storage) on the extent to which emissions from any industry could be abated through the use of one single option. For these reasons, a broad portfolio of technological options will probably have to be involved in mitigating climate change (*e.g.* Pacala and Socolow, 2004).[2]

This chapter describes recent trends in energy-related R&D spending and examine private sector incentives for boosting innovation under different emission-reduction scenarios and associated carbon price paths. The potential role of R&D investment in the development of new technologies is explored, especially in the context of constraints to the expansion of existing low-carbon technologies such as nuclear power and carbon capture and storage (CCS). Finally, taking into account the market failures which hamper private-sector R&D incentives, the options for public policies to support R&D investments are highlighted.

5.1. Recent spending trends in energy-related R&D

Speeding up the emergence and deployment of low-carbon technologies will ultimately require increases in – and reallocation of – the financial resources channelled into energy-related R&D. Average public energy-related R&D expenditure has declined dramatically across the OECD since it peaked in the early 1980s (Figure 5.1, Panel A), although spending varies greatly across countries (Figure 5.1, Panel B). While no comprehensive data exist on private sector energy-related R&D, available evidence suggests that its share in overall private R&D spending is low compared with other sectors and has been decreasing over the past two decades (Doornbosch and Steenblik, 2007; IEA, 2008b).[3] Past declines in public and private R&D spending have been partly attributed to the sustained fall in oil prices following the second oil shock, which reduced research incentives and contributed – along with concerns about safety, waste disposal and proliferation – to the gradual scaling down of public nuclear programmes.

More broadly, climate change mitigation will require increased spending at all stages of the technology development process, ranging from R&D to demonstration, deployment, and ultimately diffusion. Most importantly, empirical evidence suggests that most emerging low-carbon energy technologies are subject to sizeable "learning effects", *i.e.* their costs fall as experience accumulates (*e.g.* IEA, 2000; McDonald and Schrattenholzer, 2001; Neij *et al.* 2003a, 2003b). For example, learning rates – the percentage reduction in unit investment costs for each doubling of cumulative investment – in the order of 10% to 20% have typically been reported for wind and solar power technologies. Thus, significant amounts may have to be spent on deploying low-carbon technologies before they can become competitive at market prices. Nevertheless, there are large uncertainties surrounding the magnitude and even the nature of learning effects, and their policy implications are far from obvious, as discussed below.

Figure 5.1. Public energy-related R&D expenditures in OECD countries

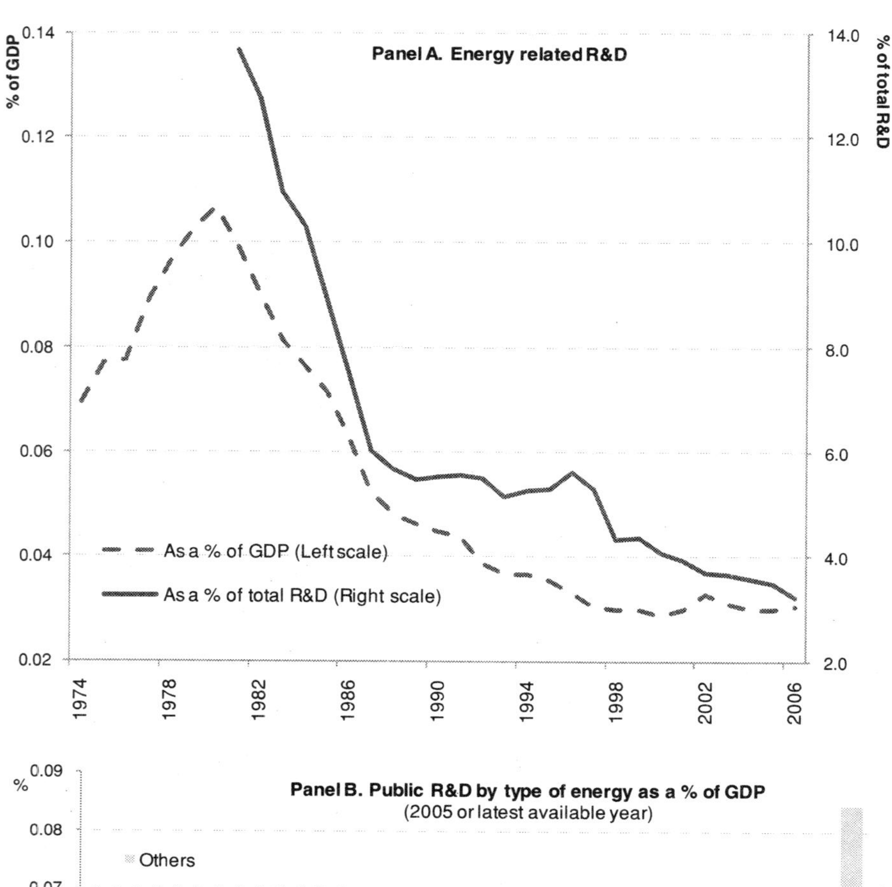

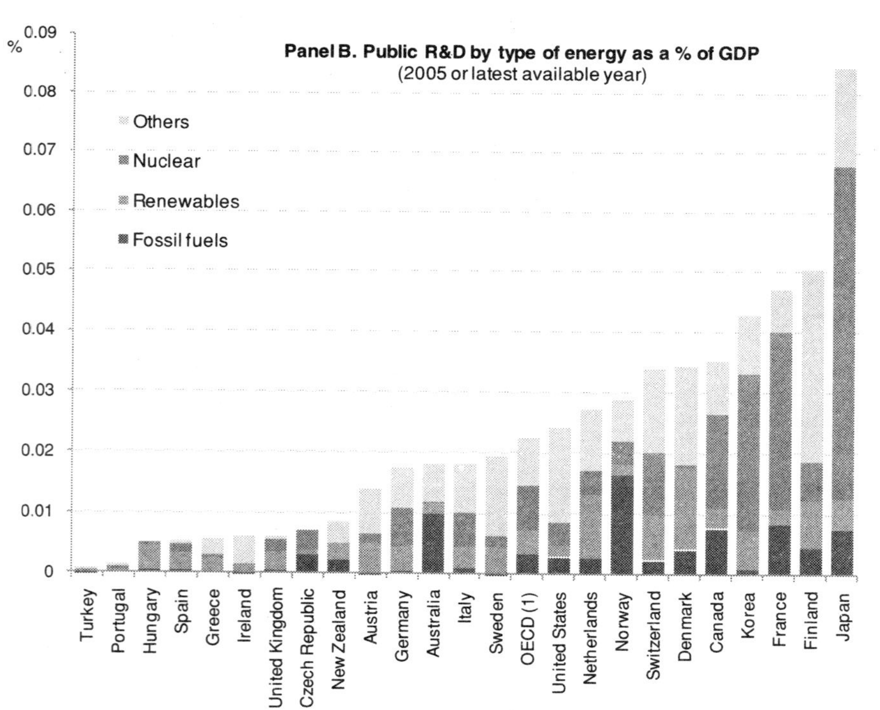

1. Unweighted average of OECD countries less non-IEA member countries (Iceland, Mexico, Poland and Slovak Republic). Due to lack of data, Belgium and Luxembourg are also excluded.

Source: IEA database.

5.2. Policy instruments to stimulate R&D and technology deployment

5.2.1. Dynamic impact of price-based instruments in promoting technology adoption

Pricing GHG emissions – using instruments, including the removal of fossil fuel subsidies, that involve charging for these emissions – would increase the expected returns from R&D in low-carbon technologies. Given the phenomenon of learning effects, pricing also reduces the expected cumulative deployment costs needed for existing climate-friendly technologies to become competitive. The effects of emission pricing on expected returns are likely to be largest for technologies like CCS which yield no private financial gain as they affect only the *carbon intensity* of energy (GHG emissions per unit of energy), not energy *efficiency* (number of units of energy per unit of output). More broadly, emission pricing gives emitters a continuing incentive to develop or use emissions-reducing technology. This is the "dynamic efficiency" of price-based mechanisms.[4] However, as discussed below, the credibility of the price signal also matters, since investing in R&D and/or installing new technology entails sunk costs. In practice, empirical evidence has found private energy-related R&D and innovation at the firm level to be responsive to past fluctuations in energy prices (Popp, 2002; Johnstone *et al.* 2008). The fairly strong correlation until recently between fluctuations in oil prices and public R&D spending suggests that governments also respond to price incentives.

5.2.2. Quantifying the effects of carbon pricing on induced technological change and mitigation costs

The World Induced Technological Change Hybrid (WITCH) model has been used to assess the quantitative impact of carbon pricing on R&D and technology deployment, and the extent to which the technological change induced by the carbon price – referred to as Induced Technological Change (ITC) – may ultimately reduce emission abatement costs. Unlike ENV-Linkages, WITCH incorporates an explicit and endogenous mechanism through which policy incentives influence technological progress (Bosetti *et al.* 2006, 2007, 2009a, Box 5.1).[5] The simulations confirm the incentive power of carbon pricing. For instance, setting a world carbon price path to stabilize CO_2 concentration at 450 ppm and overall GHG concentration at about 550 ppm CO_2eq[6] in 2050 is estimated to quadruple energy R&D expenditures and investments in installing renewable power generation, compared with the baseline scenario (Figure 5.2). These effects grow larger over time and/or as concentration targets become more stringent, reflecting a higher CO_2 price. In fact, because marginal abatement costs rise disproportionately with emission reductions, investment in technology also rises disproportionately with the stringency of the emission reduction objective. A related finding is the need for a strong long-term carbon price signal to foster investment in low-carbon R&D and technology deployment today. Indeed, under similar carbon price levels, R&D investment is found to be noticeably higher under a 550 ppm CO_2eq GHG (450 ppm CO_2 only) concentration objective, reflecting higher expected future increases in carbon prices, than under a 650 ppm CO_2eq (550 ppm CO_2 only) scenario (Figure 5.3).

Figure 5.2. Estimated response of R&D and renewable power generation deployment under alternative world GHG emission price scenarios (650 ppm and 550 ppm GHG concentration stabilisation scenarios)

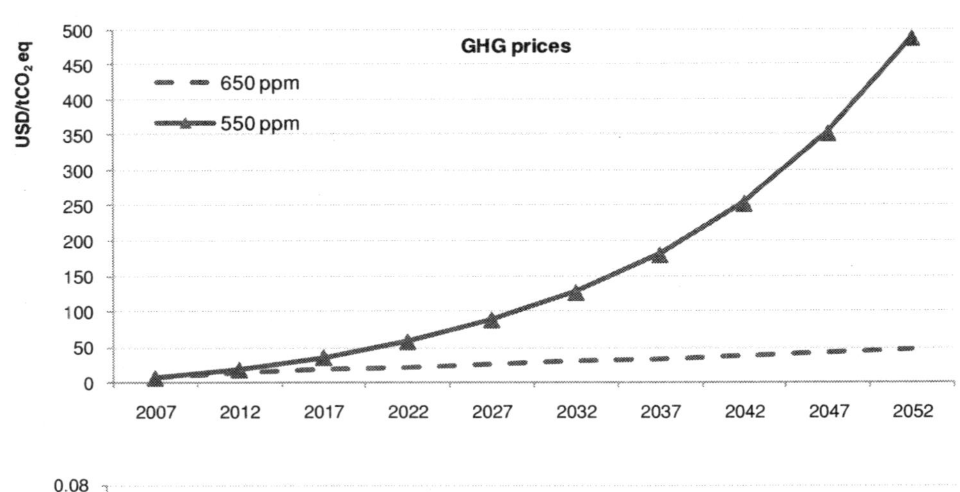

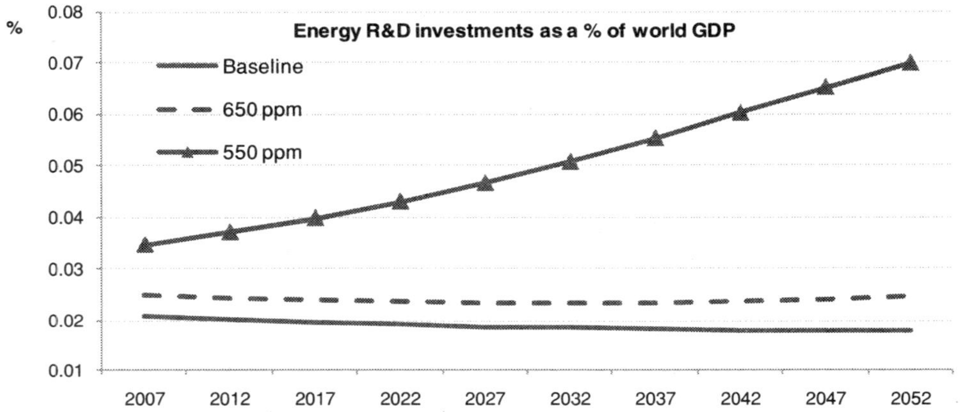

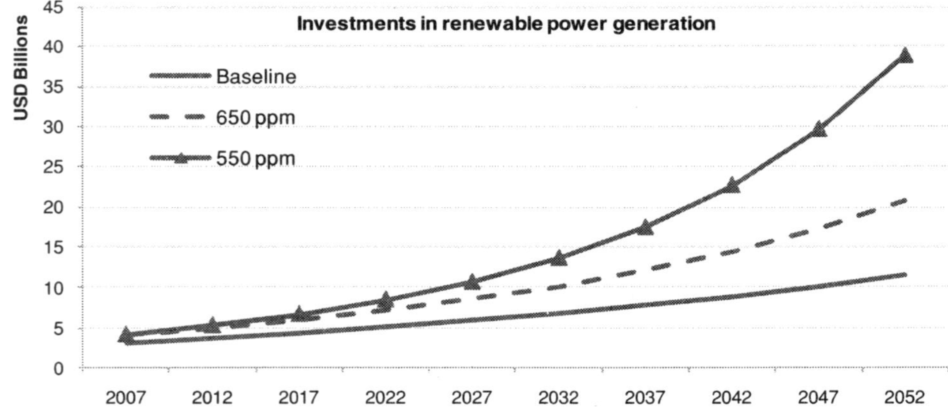

1. Emissions of non-CO_2 gases are not covered by the model used in this analysis and are, therefore, excluded from these simulations. The 550 ppm greenhouse gas concentration stabilisation scenario run here is in fact a 450 ppm CO_2 only scenario and greenhouse gas prices are CO_2 prices. Stabilisation of CO_2 concentration at 450 ppm corresponds to stabilisation of overall greenhouse gas concentration at about 550 ppm.

Source: WITCH model simulations.

Figure 5.3. World energy R&D investment at given GHG emission prices under 650 ppm and 550 ppm GHG concentration stabilisation scenarios

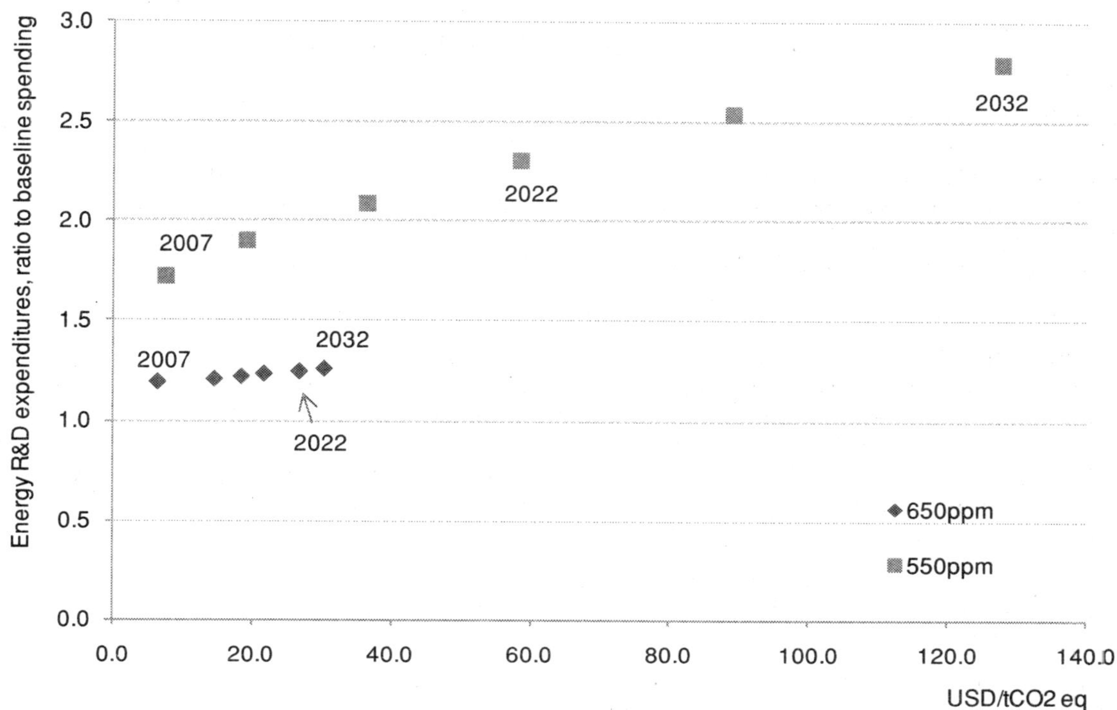

1. Emissions of non-CO_2 gases are not covered by the model used in this analysis and are therefore excluded from these simulations. The 550 ppm greenhouse gas concentration stabilisation scenario run here is in fact a 450 ppm CO_2 only scenario and greenhouse gas prices are CO_2 prices. Stabilisation of CO_2 concentration at 450 ppm corresponds to stabilisation of overall greenhouse gas concentration at about 550 ppm.

Source: WITCH model simulations.

However, the analysis suggests that ITC associated with higher investment in R&D and technology deployment may have only modest effects on mitigation costs, especially under less stringent CO_2 concentration objectives. This can be inferred from the limited increase in the cost estimate of a 550 ppm CO_2eq GHG (450 ppm CO_2 only) concentration scenario when the ITC channel is shut down by forcing R&D to remain at its baseline level and assuming there are no LBD effects (Figure 5.4). Pricing carbon in this model curbs emissions primarily by encouraging the shift towards less carbon-intensive production and consumption patterns, while impacts on ITC are found to be comparatively smaller, for two main reasons:

i) In the electricity sector, low-carbon options already exist today, including nuclear energy and, to a lesser extent, CCS. Both are projected to account for an increasing share of the future energy mix under a rising carbon price (Figure 5.5). If, for technological, political or safety reasons, the uptake of nuclear energy and CCS was constrained, investments in R&D and renewable power generation would be increased, but at the same time overall mitigation costs would rise, because of restricted access to some relatively cheap abatement opportunities (Figure 5.6). Thus, exploiting all currently available technological options may be at least as important as fostering new ones through R&D investment if the overall costs of addressing climate change are to be contained.

ii) Decreasing marginal impacts of R&D on energy efficiency and fading learning effects in renewable energies ultimately limit the gains to be reaped from ITC.

Box 5.1 Key features of the WITCH model

The WITCH model incorporates a detailed representation of the energy sector into an inter-temporal growth model of the economy. The model allows technology-related issues to be studied within a general equilibrium framework. Also, following earlier work by Nordhaus and Boyer (2000) and Popp (2004), world countries are grouped into 12 forward-looking regions that interact strategically to determine their optimal R&D and investment strategies in the presence of environmental externalities – expected future climate change damage is explicitly taken into account – and technology spillovers. The model covers CO_2 emissions but does not incorporate other GHGs.

Four main channels through which ITC and technology spillovers may arise are considered in the analysis:

i. Higher public R&D spending increases energy-related knowledge and thereby improves energy efficiency, with high but diminishing social returns. These returns are entirely appropriated by each region, *i.e.* it is implicitly assumed that intellectual property rights (IPRs) internalise externalities at the regional level. However, energy-related knowledge capital in one region partly spills over to other geographical areas (Bosetti *et al.* 2008, for details). Whilst only public R&D is modelled in the current version of WITCH (due to a lack of data), private R&D would be expected to respond in a similar way to the incentives associated with climate change mitigation policies.

ii. Learning-by-doing (LBD) gradually reduces the cost of several low-carbon technologies in the electricity sector, namely wind and solar power. Learning effects apply to *world* cumulative capacity, thereby generating international spillovers.

iii. The cost of wind and solar technologies, as well as of coal-based electricity with CCS, is also reduced through public research, again with diminishing returns. There are limitations to the use of CCS, however, including the exhaustibility of repository sites and imperfect capture.

iv. In some of the simulations run specifically for this book, R&D and LBD are also assumed to bring some "backstop" technologies (new technologies) into the electricity and/or non-electricity sectors. This allows for the possibility that investment in R&D may not only improve current technologies but could also foster major technological breakthroughs that would add to the portfolio of existing replacements for high-carbon technologies. These backstop technologies are likely to combine new technologies not currently penetrating the market, including advanced nuclear technologies in the electricity sector, and electric and hydrogen-fuel-cell vehicles in the non-electricity sector. Incorporating into the model the impacts of R&D and learning-by-doing on the investment cost of these "backstop" technologies relies partly on past experience with solar, wind and nuclear power (as reflected in the estimates of "two-factor" learning curves in the empirical literature, Bosetti *et al.*, 2009a).

While the calibration of parameters is based on best available empirical evidence, it should be acknowledged that wide uncertainties surround some of these, including the elasticity of R&D to energy prices, social returns to R&D, the creation and diffusion process of new technologies, learning rates, and the magnitude of international spillovers. Therefore, while the key policy findings presented below are qualitatively robust, caution should be exerted when interpreting the quantitative results (for further results, including some sensitivity analysis, Bosetti *et al.*, 2009a).

5.2.3. Carbon pricing and the emergence of breakthrough technology

The previous analysis focused on incremental R&D aimed at improving energy efficiency and the diffusion of *existing* low-carbon technologies. But mitigation policy could also promote the development and deployment of major *new* low-carbon technologies that would, in the long run, replace existing

 THE ECONOMICS OF CLIMATE CHANGE MITIGATION – ISBN: 978-92-64-05606-0 – © OECD 2009

technologies on a wide scale. The cost implications of the possible future development and diffusion of such "backstop" technologies are explored below.

Insofar as one motivation for developing backstop technologies in the electricity sector would be the existence of limitations to the deployment of already existing technologies, nuclear power installed capacity is assumed to be constrained at present levels throughout most of the analysis. Indeed, in the absence of such constraints there would be little need to develop new technologies in the electricity sector, at least in the context of the WITCH model. Therefore, the following three alternative scenarios were considered under the objective of stabilising long-run GHG concentration at 550 ppm CO_2eq (450 ppm CO_2 only):

- Two backstop technologies emerge in the electricity and non-electricity sectors, respectively.
- Only an electricity backstop emerges.
- Only a non-electricity backstop emerges, in which case no constraints are put on nuclear energy.

The simulations presented below assumed that all agents have perfect knowledge about future backstop availability.

Figure 5.4. Projected world GDP costs under 550 ppm GHG concentration stabilisation scenarios, with and without induced technological change

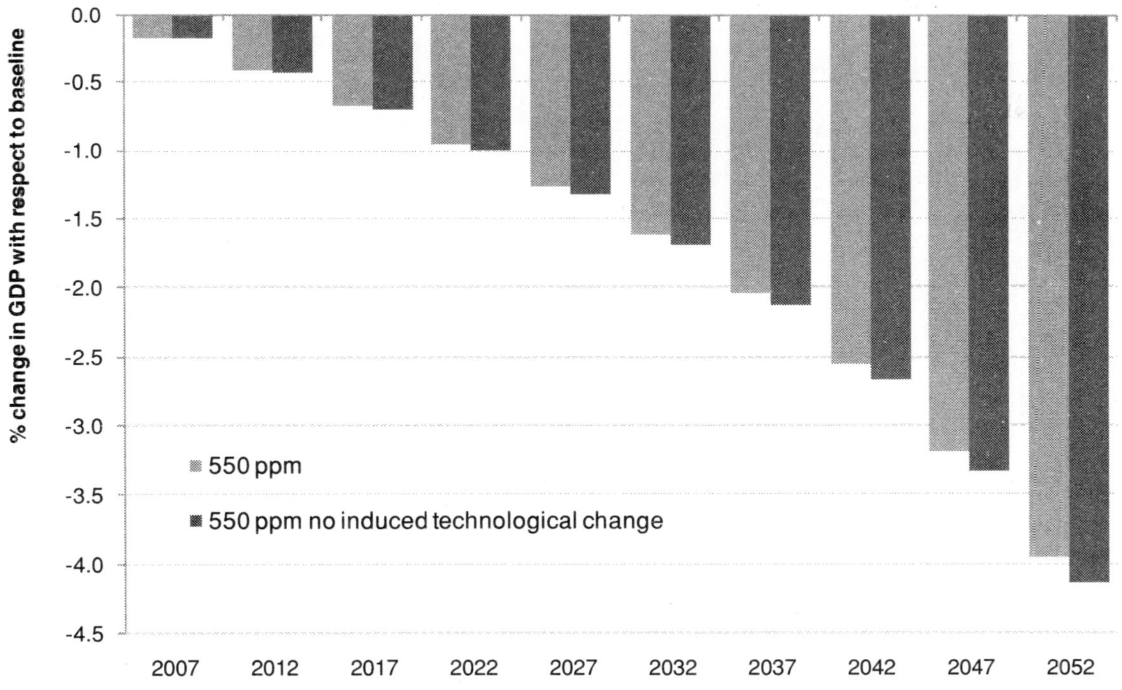

1. Emissions of non-CO_2 gases are not covered by the model used in this analysis and are therefore excluded from these simulations. The 550 ppm greenhouse gas concentration stabilisation scenario run here is in fact a 450 ppm CO_2 only scenario and greenhouse gas prices are CO_2 prices. Stabilisation of CO_2 concentration at 450 ppm corresponds to stabilisation of overall greenhouse gas concentration at about 550 ppm.

Source: WITCH model simulations.

Figure 5.5. Projected energy technology mix in the electricity sector under baseline, 650 ppm and 550 ppm GHG concentration stabilisation scenarios

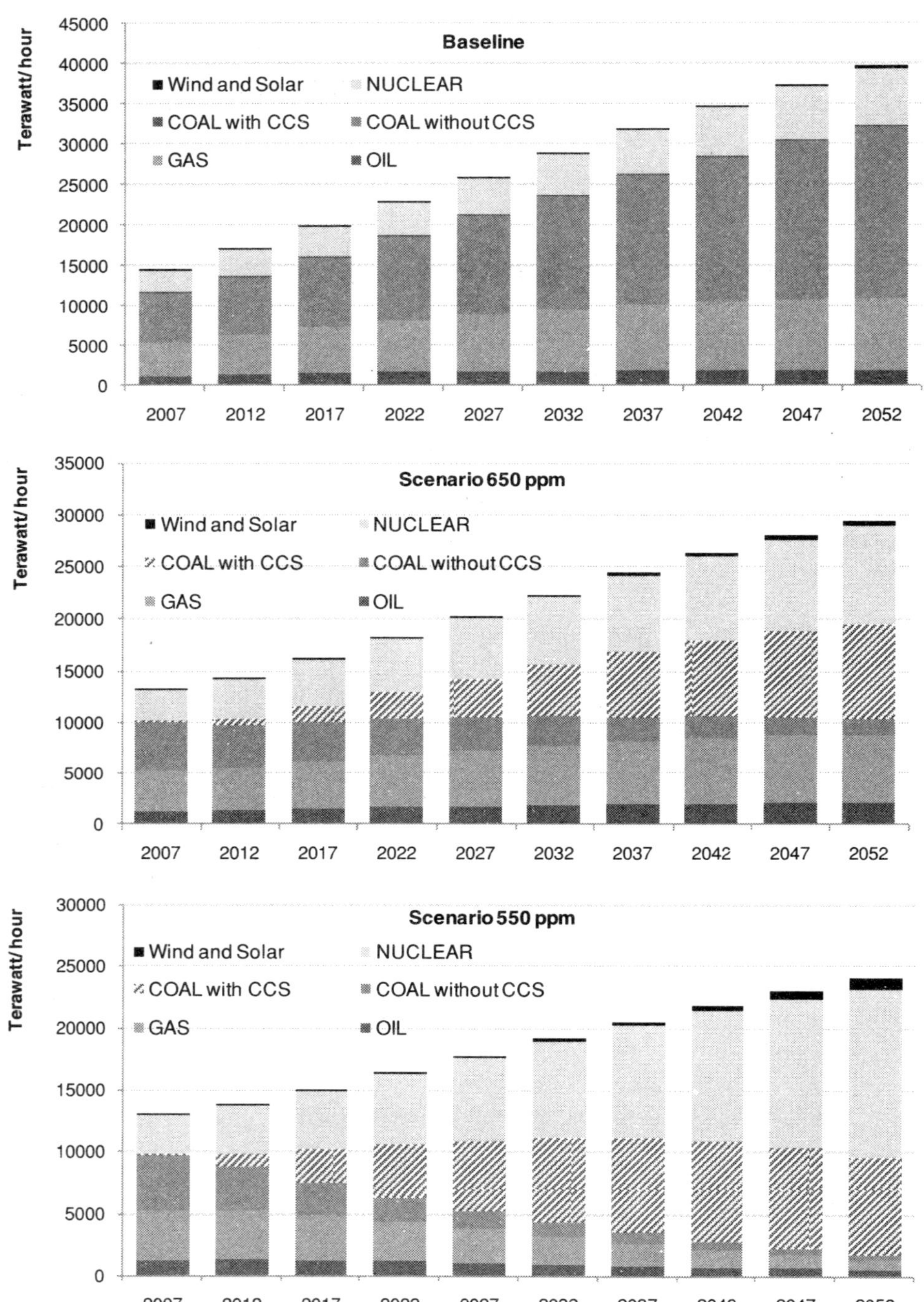

1. Emissions of non-CO_2 gases are not covered by the model used in this analysis and are therefore excluded from these simulations. The 550 ppm greenhouse gas concentration stabilisation scenario run here is in fact a 450 ppm CO_2 only scenario and greenhouse gas prices are CO_2 prices. Stabilisation of CO_2 concentration at 450 ppm corresponds to stabilisation of overall greenhouse gas concentration at about 550 ppm.

Source: WITCH model simulations.

Figure 5.6. Projected world GDP costs under 550 ppm GHG concentration stabilisation scenarios, with and without constraint on nuclear energy and CCS

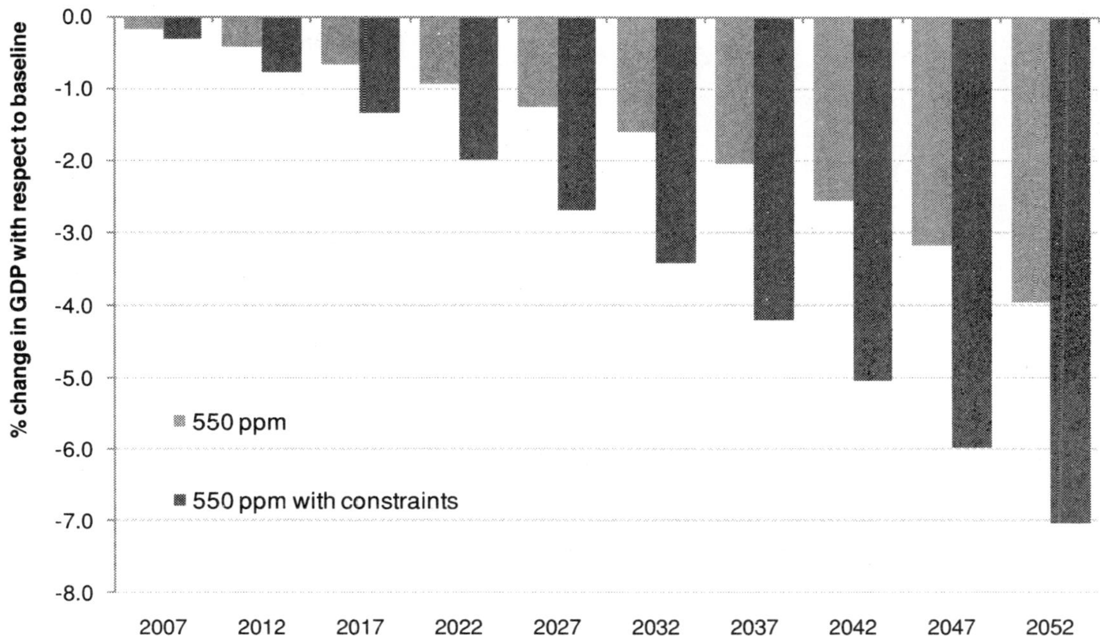

1. Emissions of non-CO_2 gases are not covered by the model used in this analysis and are therefore excluded from these simulations. The 550 ppm greenhouse gas concentration stabilisation scenario run here is in fact a 450 ppm CO_2 only scenario and greenhouse gas prices are CO_2 prices. Stabilisation of CO_2 concentration at 450 ppm corresponds to stabilisation of overall greenhouse gas concentration at about 550 ppm.

Source: WITCH model simulations.

Unlike most of the literature, it is not assumed that backstop technologies will emerge without dedicated investments. More realistically, they become available in the future only if adequate R&D investment costs are previously incurred. As a result, under a world carbon price scenario targeting 550 ppm GHG concentration, the future availability of backstop technologies in the electricity and non-electricity sectors is estimated to substantially increase global energy R&D investments over the coming decades (Figure 5.7). This is especially the case at the start of the modelling period (*i.e.* when the carbon pricing policy is announced and implemented), with energy R&D expenditures rising to about 0.12% of global GDP, above their 1980 peak level of 0.08% of GDP. The shape of the R&D spending path reflects the nature of investment in breakthrough technologies. This involves very high marginal returns at the beginning, which then decline gradually as the R&D stock is built up and the potential fades for further cost reductions through additional R&D investments – especially once the technology becomes available and economically competitive. The cost of the backstop technologies follows an inverted S-shaped path: R&D brings costs down rapidly in the early phases, when backstops remain very expensive. After 2030-2040, further cost declines occur mainly through LBD, as the technologies are deployed.

Figure 5.7. Projected world energy R&D investments under a 550 ppm GHG concentration stabilisation scenario, with and without backstop technologies

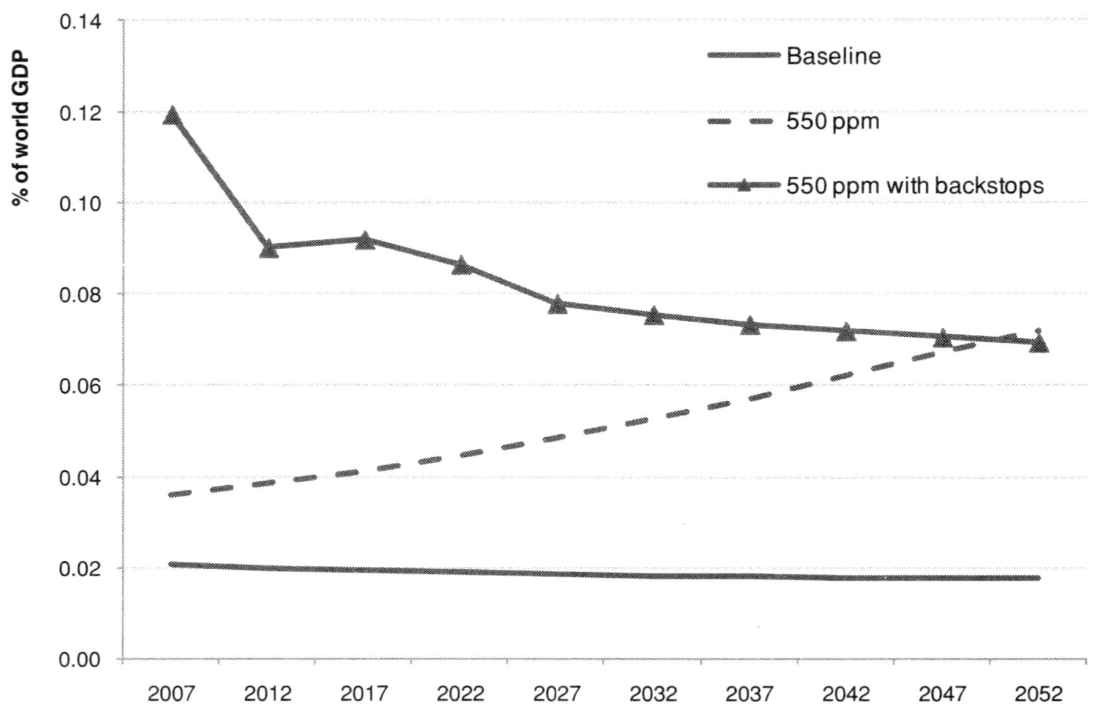

1. Emissions of non-CO_2 gases are not covered by the model used in this analysis and are therefore excluded from these simulations. The 550 ppm greenhouse gas concentration stabilisation scenario run here is in fact a 450 ppm CO_2 only scenario and greenhouse gas prices are CO_2 prices. Stabilisation of CO_2 concentration at 450 ppm corresponds to stabilisation of overall greenhouse gas concentration at about 550 ppm.

Source: WITCH model simulations.

The share of backstop technologies in the production of energy increases rapidly in the simulations. The presence of backstop technology in the electricity sector would offer a substitute for the large deployment of nuclear power capacity as projected in the previous section (Figure 5.5). The backstop in the non-electricity sector mainly relaxes the energy savings constraint that would otherwise be needed to reach the emission target.

Compared with the previous section, where the 550 ppm GHG concentration target was to be achieved without the help of new technologies, R&D investments in backstop technologies are estimated to crowd out part of R&D in energy efficiency. The electricity backstop technology would also reduce the need for investments in wind and solar power generation.[7] This would mainly be the case in the second half of the century, however, when the backstop technology becomes cost effective. In the first decades, investments in wind and solar are projected to be actually higher in the backstop case, reflecting the constraint imposed on nuclear power generation and the time lag needed for the backstop electricity technology to become competitive (Figure 5.8).

Figure 5.8 Investment in wind and solar power generation under a 550 ppm GHG concentration stabilisation scenario, with and without backstop technologies

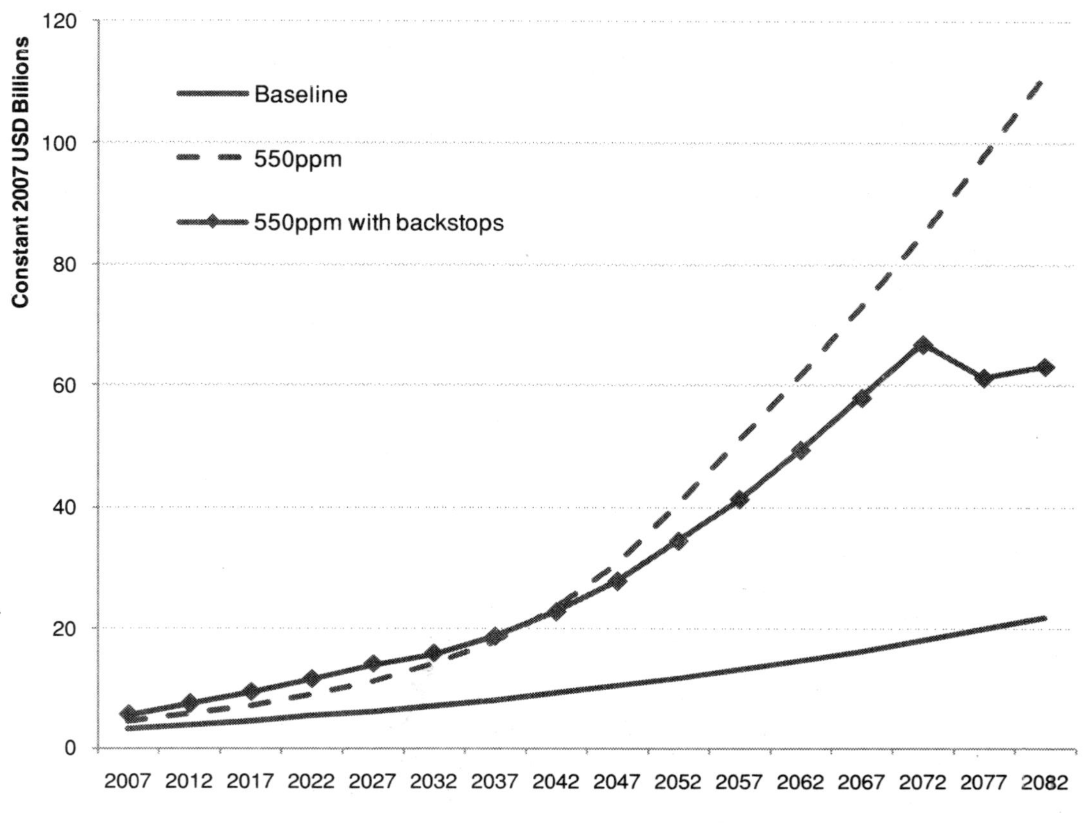

1. Emissions of non-CO_2 gases are not covered by the model used in this analysis and are therefore excluded from these simulations. The 550 ppm greenhouse gas concentration stabilisation scenario run here is in fact a 450 ppm CO_2 only scenario and greenhouse gas prices are CO_2 prices. Stabilisation of CO_2 concentration at 450ppm corresponds to stabilisation of overall greenhouse gas concentration at about 550ppm.

Source: WITCH model simulations.

The possibility of investing in breakthrough technologies is estimated to greatly reduce the level and steepness of the carbon price path needed to meet the 550 ppm GHG concentration target (Figure 5.9, Panel A). This is the case essentially at relatively distant horizons, however, as carbon prices behave in a roughly similar way with and without backstop technologies up to 2025. This latter point indicates that regardless of the possibility of developing breakthrough technologies in the electricity and non-electricity sectors, a strong carbon price signal is still needed over the next few decades in order to meet stringent emission reduction pathways at least cost. Finally, at distant horizons – especially beyond mid-century – the costs of meeting the 550 ppm GHG concentration target are projected to be significantly reduced by the availability of backstop technologies (Figure 5.9, Panel B). However, this comes at the cost of higher GDP losses in the coming decades, due to the large increase in R&D effort needed to raise the productivity of the backstops.

Figure 5.9. Projected world GDP costs and GHG emission price levels under 550 ppm GHG concentration stabilisation scenario, with and without backstop technologies

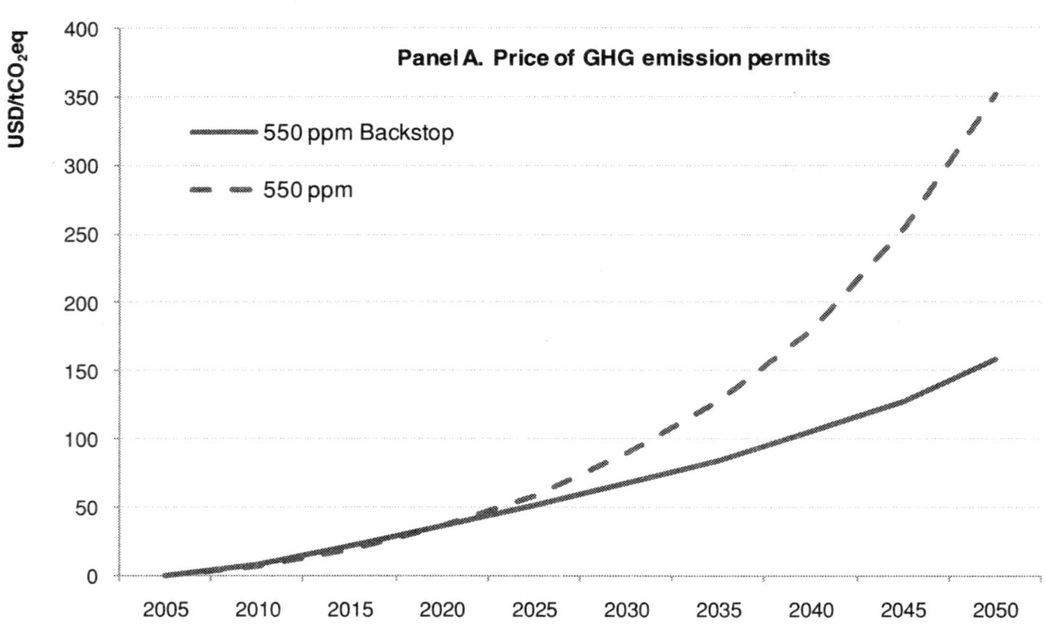

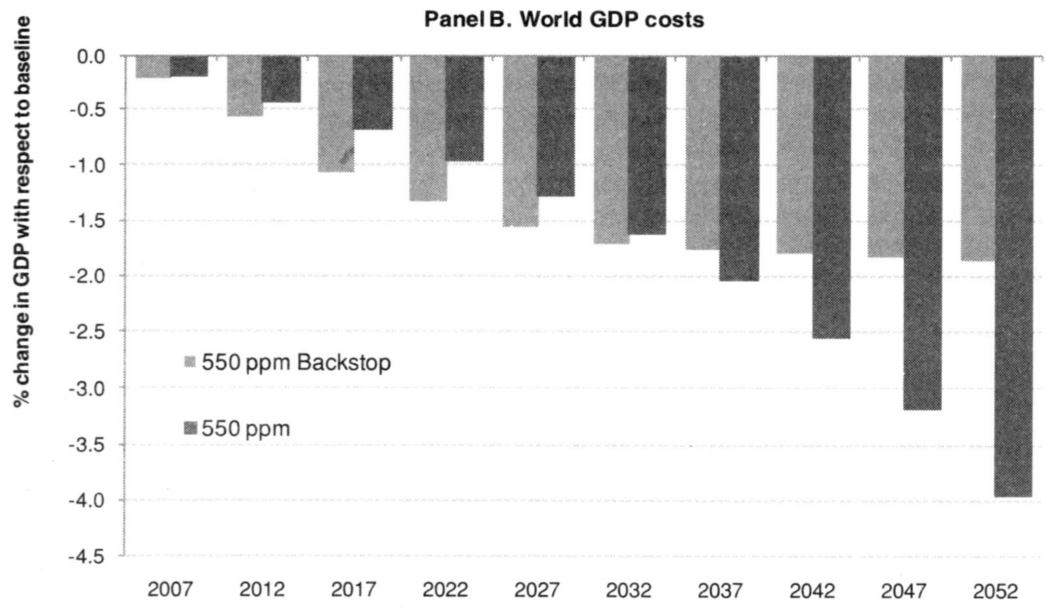

1. Emissions of non-CO_2 gases are not covered by the model used in this analysis and are therefore excluded from these simulations. The 550 ppm greenhouse gas concentration stabilisation scenario run here is in fact a 450 ppm CO_2 only scenario and greenhouse gas prices are CO_2 prices. Stabilisation of CO_2 concentration at 450 ppm corresponds to stabilisation of overall greenhouse gas concentration at about 550 ppm.

Source: WITCH model simulations.

THE ECONOMICS OF CLIMATE CHANGE MITIGATION – ISBN: 978-92-64-05606-0 – © OECD 2009

The backstop technology in the non-electricity sector is found to have more of an impact on mitigation costs than its electricity counterpart (Figure 5.10). In the simulation where only the electricity backstop is assumed to be available, the costs of meeting the 550 ppm GHG concentration target rise marginally, compared with a 550 ppm GHG concentration stabilisation scenario without backstops. This only partly reflects the assumed constraint on the expansion of nuclear power generation, since releasing that constraint would merely bring costs in line with a no-backstops scenario. However, the more nuclear energy and/or the availability of CCS are constrained, the more profitable it would become to search for new power generation technologies. By contrast, in a simulation where only the non-electricity backstop is assumed to be available, costs are drastically reduced, and in fact are not far above the estimated costs under a scenario where both backstops are available. These results highlight the importance of developing carbon-free technologies in the non-electricity sector, where the abatement potential of currently commercially available mitigation options is comparatively smaller than in the electricity sector.

Figure 5.10. The impacts of electricity and non-electricity backstops on projected world GDP costs under 550 ppm GHG concentration stabilisation scenario

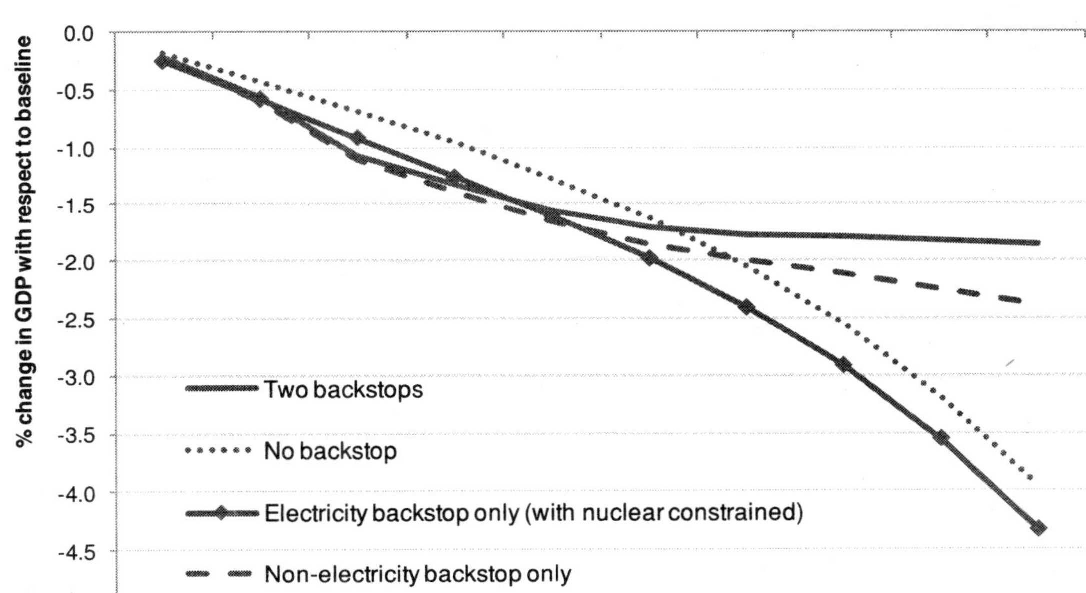

1. Emissions of non-CO_2 gases are not covered by the model used in this analysis and are therefore excluded from these simulations. The 550 ppm greenhouse gas concentration stabilisation scenario run here is in fact a 450 ppm CO_2 only scenario and greenhouse gas prices are CO_2 prices. Stabilisation of CO_2 concentration at 450 ppm corresponds to stabilisation of overall greenhouse gas concentration at about 550 ppm.

Source: WITCH model simulations.

5.2.4. Other policies to encourage R&D and technology deployment

Despite the R&D incentives it generates, putting a price on GHG emissions does not address all the market imperfections undermining R&D and technology deployment. Some of these imperfections are common to all R&D areas, but the following seem to be magnified in climate change mitigation:

- The gap between the expected social and private returns from R&D and technology adoption may be widened by the political uncertainty surrounding future climate policy, which in turn fundamentally reflects the lack of credible devices through which current governments can commit future ones. This issue is often less acute in other public policy areas, either because timescales are shorter or because policies are better established.

- Given the potentially large welfare consequences of any major breakthrough in technological progress – *e.g.* in the area of electricity production – IPR protection may not be sufficiently credible to private investors, who may expect governments to deprive them of any major innovation rent *a posteriori* and, therefore, would be reluctant to invest in this type of R&D.[8]

- Market failures and policy distortions specific to the electricity sector may explain the low levels of R&D compared with other industries. In particular, existing infrastructure can creates network effects that may act as entry barriers to new technologies. For instance, most national grids would not be suited to receive electricity from many small renewable electricity sources, while large scale renewable projects may also encounter problems if located too far from existing grids.[9] Finally, low market competition and distortions such as energy subsidies may also be keeping R&D spending low.[10]

- Adding to these imperfections and distortions, the country and/or sector coverage of price-based instruments is unlikely to be comprehensive, at least in the medium term, thereby increasing the gap between social and private returns, and providing a second-best case for R&D policies.

These factors suggest the need for specific policies aimed at boosting climate-friendly R&D, beyond ensuring an appropriate overall innovation framework (for details, see OECD, 2006c, and Jaumotte and Pain, 2005), removing fossil fuel subsidies and increasing competition in energy markets.[11] Beyond the use of standard tools such as public R&D, research subsidies or grants, there has been growing interest recently in rewarding innovation through the use of "innovation prizes" (Box 5.2), as these may address some limitations of other instruments (Newell and Wilson, 2005). It is also possible that an international R&D policy might be justified given that climate change mitigation is of global benefit, and that R&D knowledge can spill over international borders. For instance, a global fund could be established for helping with technology transfers and rewarding innovations, *e.g.* by buying out the associated patents or through other mechanisms.

Box 5.2 Fostering R&D and innovation through the use of prizes

The use of "inducement prizes" to reward successful innovation has a long history and has experienced a resurgence in recent years, not least due to highly publicised examples in the space and vaccine industries.[1] Such prizes could also be envisaged for climate change mitigation, *e.g.* through (or as a complement to) the global funds that already exist or are about to be set up to facilitate technology transfers.

Prizes have a number of features that make them a potentially useful R&D policy tool. Unlike subsidies and grants, they address governments' lack of information about the likely returns to R&D by shifting the risk of failure to researchers, which may be warranted in the case of applied R&D (see below). Furthermore, they entail low administrative barriers to entry and only limited risks lobbying by private interests. In theory, prizes could increase R&D spending at a lower cost to the government than subsidies and grants, and would even be temporarily costless as they are only paid in case of success.[2] Compared with patents, prizes are potentially less distortive provided the social value of the invention is certain and the distortions associated with prize financing are smaller than the welfare loss from monopoly power under patents (Wright, 1983).

Prizes may have several other attractive features for climate change mitigation. Most importantly, they could help alleviate the political uncertainty surrounding future carbon prices and the potential lack of credibility of IPRs, both of which undermine R&D incentives. In addition, unlike domestic R&D policy instruments, international prizes would pool risks and rewards across countries. Finally, unlike other international instruments (*e.g.* a global R&D fund allocating subsidies across countries), they may avoid political competition for domestic research funding across national governments.

Prizes have a number of limitations, however. In particular, they tend to stimulate applied rather than basic R&D, for at least two reasons (Newell and Wilson, 2005): (1) the social value of innovation is harder to determine in advance for major technological breakthroughs than for specific technological outputs, making it more difficult to determine the appropriate size of the prize;[3] (2) information asymmetry – as governments may be less informed about future technology prospects than researchers – and the associated risk of allocating subsidies and grants to the wrong type of technology can be large for applied R&D, while in basic science the incentives of governments and researchers tend to be better aligned, as the latter have career incentives to advance fundamental research. Also, like patents, prizes can mean that research efforts are duplicated, although these can be mitigated *e.g.* by pre-selecting firms in the context of a multi-stage selection process.

Prize design also matters greatly for R&D incentives. Policymakers can enhance the credibility of their commitment by setting the funds aside, or by purchasing an insurance policy that secures prize payment in case of success. Moreover, in order to minimise judicial uncertainty, the winning conditions need to be defined precisely, which again may be easier for specific technological outputs (*e.g.* specific achievements in CCS, nuclear fission, renewable power generation or hydrogen vehicles) than for broader advances in science. Also, the size of the prize should depend on whether the purpose of policymakers is only to boost R&D or to foster technology transfers as well. In the latter case, one option might be to buy out, in advance, any future patent rights through a higher prize. Along the same lines, while prizes are typically provided in cash, advanced market commitments may be used to encourage uptake when there is no private market for the invention, for example in some developing countries which do not put a price on carbon.[4] Developed countries might commit in advance to finance the implementation of prize-winning technologies in developing countries, which would stimulate both R&D and technology transfers.

1. For an extensive discussion of innovation inducement prizes and concrete policy recommendations to scale them up in the US context, including for climate change mitigation, see National Research Council (2007).
2. In the presence of a "common pool" of knowledge, prizes (or patents) that reward successful researchers with the full social return of innovation would induce excessive research spending, as competitive firms do not internalise the negative impact of their own expenditures on the probability that other firms make a discovery. Therefore, the prize needed to achieve an optimal level of R&D is *less* than the full social return of innovation, and therefore less than the optimal R&D subsidy (see in particular Wright, 1983).
3. From this perspective, patents have an informational advantage, as their market value varies with *ex-post* unforeseen changes in returns to research. The prize amount could be optimised by letting contestants themselves propose (and compete on) the size of the prize, in order to reveal their information about research costs and returns (Che and Gale, 2003).
4. For a detailed discussion of advanced market commitments in the case of vaccines, see Kremer (2001a, 2001b).

Figure 5.11. Projected CO_2 emissions and concentration under a global R&D policy operating in isolation

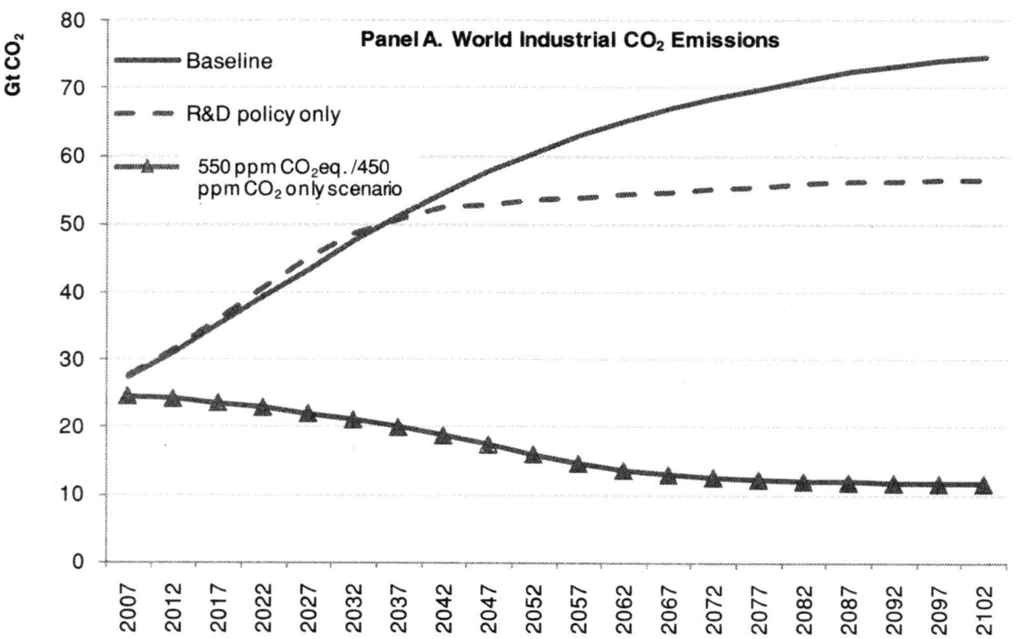

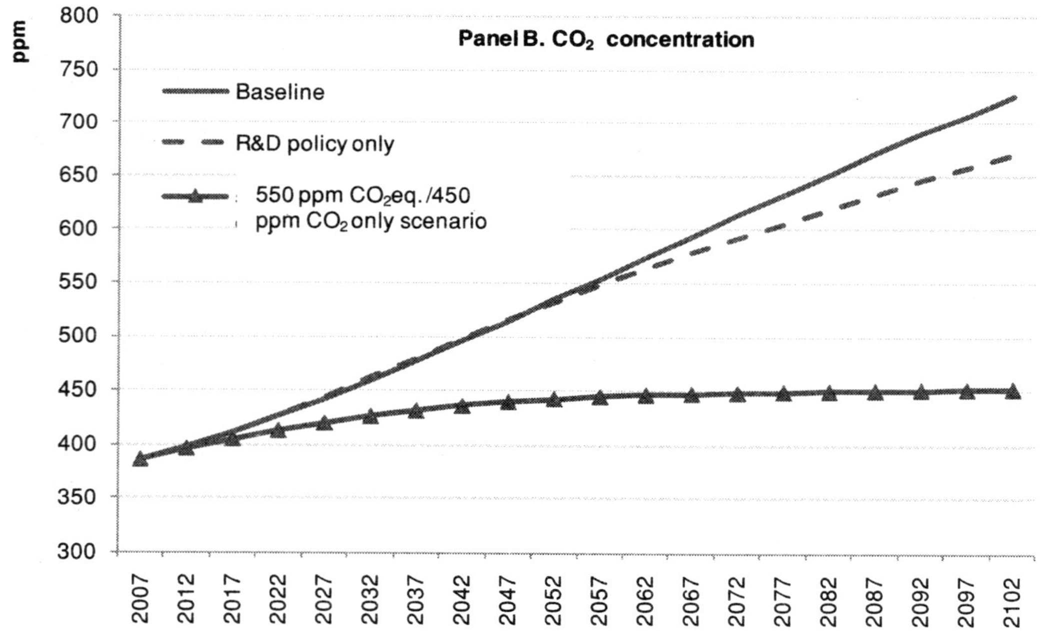

1. Emissions of non-CO_2 gases are not covered by the model used in this analysis and are therefore excluded from these simulations.

Source: WITCH model simulations.

WITCH model simulations suggest tentatively that a global R&D fund to subsidize R&D and/or low-carbon technology deployment could further reduce mitigation costs, if it was in addition to pricing carbon. However, the optimal size of such a fund and its effects are found to be very small, unless R&D investment in new (backstop) technologies is assumed to yield large international spillovers. This partly reflects the assumption in WITCH that social returns are almost entirely appropriated by each region, resulting in rather small international spillovers. Further research about the existence, nature and magnitude of international spillovers might be needed, not least in view of the ongoing debate about how to value some countries' efforts to increase R&D and facilitate technology transfers in the context of a global climate policy agreement. Indeed, from a theoretical perspective, only the returns to public support for R&D and deployment that are not captured by the country itself – *i.e. international* R&D and learning spillovers – should be eligible to be valued in the context of a global agreement.

In the presence of learning spillovers such as learning-by-doing effects, carbon pricing and R&D policies may not be enough to ensure adequate deployment of existing low-carbon technologies (*e.g.* Jaffe *et al.* 2003, 2005). This may be particularly the case in the electricity sector, where network effects and the cumulative nature of knowledge make it difficult to displace existing technologies. As well, as there is essentially no difference in nature between electricity produced from fossil fuels and from other low-carbon sources, market demand for low-carbon energy may remain negligible until it actually becomes competitive, thereby hampering the learning process. This contrasts with a number of other goods (*e.g.* high-technology electronic and computer goods and cars), where "niche markets" exist for new, expensive products (Stern, 2007, Chapter 16). It has also been argued that without policy intervention to speed up the deployment of low-carbon technologies, high-carbon energy systems might be installed in the meantime, as major long-term infrastructure investments are expected over the coming years in power generation, transport and buildings, notably in large developing countries (IEA, 2006, 2007c; OECD, 2008c).

Public support for installing existing technologies also raises a number of concerns, including the risk of locking-in the wrong technologies (Chapter 2).[12] At a minimum, a clear exit strategy should be announced in advance, as the withdrawal of public support may face strong opposition. Finally, optimal subsidies have been found to be small under plausible learning rate assumptions (see *e.g.* Fischer and Newell, 2007). Yet most countries already subsidise renewable electricity heavily, with implicit prices per tonne of CO_2 abated sometimes exceeding EUR 250 for wind power and EUR 1 000 for photovoltaics (OECD, 2004). Thus, the case for further national policy action seems rather limited.

5.2.5. Will investing in R&D work in the absence of carbon pricing?

Another important policy issue is whether, and at what cost, higher R&D expenditures alone might address climate change if no price were put on carbon. WITCH model simulations strongly suggest that world spending on energy-related R&D *alone*, regardless of its magnitude, would not be able to tackle climate change. Even implausibly high expenditure, *e.g.* 1 percentage point of world GDP, or 30 times more than current levels, would have little effect. This reflects the absence of substitution towards less carbon intensive production and consumption that would have occurred in response to a carbon price during the first decades, along with the lags required for the new technologies to penetrate the market.[13] Figure 5.11 illustrates this finding. The model assumes a hypothetical global R&D fund is gradually built up over the coming decades to spend ultimately 0.08% of world GDP annually, an amount that would roughly correspond to the early-1980s peak level of public energy R&D spending within the OECD. Three optimistic assumptions were made about how the fund would be spent: i) R&D investments in the two electricity and non-electricity backstop technologies would be subsidized (Section 5.3.1); ii) these spending would not be at the expense of domestic R&D investments (in reality, countries might reduce their own R&D spending if major subsidies were received from an international fund and/or provided elsewhere); and iii) the fund is financed through a lump sum tax, *i.e.* the potential distortions arising from fund-raising are omitted. Even under these favorable conditions, this stylized global R&D policy is found only to stabilize world emissions in the middle of the century at over twice their current level (Figure 5.11, Panel A).[14] As a result, CO_2 concentration rises continuously, being only roughly 50 ppm below its baseline scenario level at the end of the century (Figure 5.11, Panel B). In fact, it appears that no global R&D policy of any size operating in isolation will stabilize concentration during this century.

Notes

1. Emerging technologies include, inter alia: for power generation: wind and solar power, the next generation of nuclear power, or carbon capture and storage (CCS); for transport: advanced biofuels and electric and hydrogen-fuel-cell vehicles; for industry: CCS and a range of industrial energy technologies to improve fuel efficiency and reduce reliance on fossil fuels; for buildings and appliances: a variety of (mostly) incremental improvements in insulation techniques, lighting and cooling systems or the energy efficiency of appliances (IEA, 2008b).

2. Having a broad range of low-cost technological options would not only reduce future abatement costs but also their sensitivity to emission-reduction objectives. Thus it would hedge against the risk associated with the need for greater than expected efforts to tackle climate change (Stern, 2007, Chapter 16).

3. In power generation, R&D spending as a share of total turnover was about eight times lower than in the manufacturing sector as a whole. This is consistent with disaggregated sectoral analysis for the United States (Alic *et al.* 2003).

4. For a comparison of R&D and deployment incentives under various instruments to reduce GHG emissions, Chapter 2.

5. Technology assumptions have been shown to be critical determinants of differences in the GDP and welfare costs of mitigation across available studies (Barker *et al.* 2002, 2006; Fischer and Morgenstern, 2006). For an overview of recent models featuring ITC, Edenhofer *et al.* (2006).

6. This is the optimal world carbon price path under the non-cooperative solution of the model when a 450 ppm long-run CO_2 concentration target is imposed (for details, Box 5.1 and Bosetti *et al.*, 2009a). Emissions of non-CO_2 gases are not covered by the WITCH model and are therefore excluded from the simulations. However, stabilisation of CO_2 concentration at 450 ppm roughly corresponds to stabilisation of overall GHG concentration at 550 ppm.

7 By definition, investments in nuclear power generation are also crowded out in the simulations.

8. Such concerns have been put forward as an explanation for relatively low private research on vaccines against major worldwide diseases such as malaria, tuberculosis or HIV (Kremer, 2001a, 2001b).

9. Network effects also exist in road transport, where high penetration of low-carbon technologies (*e.g.* electricity and hydrogen-fuel-cell vehicles, biofuels) would likely require new infrastructure, as current infrastructure (*e.g.* fuel stations) is tailored to fossil fuel technologies.

10. The cumulative nature of knowledge may also increase uncertainty about returns to R&D. This is because the ultimate penetration of any path-breaking innovation hinges more crucially than in other sectors on a series of additional incremental innovations and learning gains, which are largely unpredictable (*e.g.* Stern, 2007, Chapter 16).

11. For instance, a theoretical model based on US electricity sector data found that optimal R&D and renewable subsidies could lower by over a third the CO_2 emissions price needed to achieve a 5% cut in US electricity sector emissions, and could bring down the overall cost of the policy package to

zero, due to the positive spillovers generated by the technology-support policies (Fischer and Newell, 2007).

12. See the discussion in Jaffe *et al.* (2003).

13. Focusing on the electricity sector only, Fischer and Newell (2007) find technology-support policies to be the costliest of all abatement policy options, due to: (i) their failure to exploit cheap abatement opportunities that already exist today; and (ii) to the time and investments needed for new technologies to become available.

14. This finding is qualitatively in line with earlier studies (*e.g.* Buchner and Carraro, 2005).

ISBN: 978-92-64-05606-0
The Economics of Climate Change Mitigation
Policies and Options for Global Action beyond 2012

Chapter 6

Regional Incentives for Global Action

This chapter investigates which countries are needed to achieve an ambitious GHG stabilisation target, and identifies the economic incentives that countries have to participate in global action. It identifies the size of the so-called free-rider incentives, whereby countries have a greater incentive to stay outside a global mitigation coalition and benefit from the mitigation actions of others than to participate. It assesses the possibilities to enhance participation incentives by taking co-benefits of mitigation policies (e.g. reduced local air pollution and improved energy security) into account. Finally, the role of financial transfers, specifically the allocation of emission reduction targets across countries, is highlighted as an instrument to stimulate participation.

Key Messages

- *Ambitious global emission reduction is economically rational at the global level, in particular when non-market impacts and the risks of inaction are factored in. Achieving an ambitious GHG stabilisation target will, however, require significant action by all developed countries and the major developing ones. Smaller coalitions would not achieve that target, even if they were to bring their emissions down to zero, and their mitigation costs would become excessively high.*
- *Incentives to participate in mitigation action are likely to be lower in countries where the costs of action are relatively high and/or the expected damages from climate change are relatively low, unless international financial transfers or other support is provided. Given the differences in incentives among countries, and the large global environmental and economic costs that would result from low levels of participation, well-designed mechanisms for sharing the costs of action are needed to ensure that all major emitters participate.*
- *For large developing countries, the co-benefits of mitigation action* (e.g. *reduced local air pollution and increased energy security) will be significant, but alone will not provide sufficient participation incentives unless accompanied by some financial transfers. For developed countries, the costs of such transfers might be rationalised by the various co-benefits of tackling climate change.*
- *To be cost-effective, international financial transfers should be made primarily through market mechanisms, essentially via credits generated to meet binding emission reduction commitments across countries. For example, emission permit allocation rules could be designed to shift at least some of the burden of the costs of action away from countries that may have only limited incentives to participate and/or limited financial resources.*
- *Compared with a harmonised world carbon tax or full permit-auctioning with ETSs, developing countries are projected to gain significantly from permit-allocation rules under which their emission rights cover their business-as-usual emissions or are inversely related to their contribution to past emission levels. Developing countries would also benefit from rules based on population size or GDP per capita, albeit to a somewhat lesser extent. All of these rules generally impose significant costs on developed countries, although the costs vary widely from country to country.*

Introduction

Building political support for international co-operation at the global level will be essential if ambitious GHG mitigation targets are to be achieved. This chapter investigates the main options and bottlenecks in the process of negotiating an international climate agreement. It first analyses the incentives for countries to participate in an environmentally effective and economically feasible international agreement (Section 6.1). It then explores which regions need to be involved if action is to be environmentally effective, and assesses the incentives for countries to voluntarily participate in an international coalition to mitigate climate change. The section highlights the large and complicating role of free-rider incentives in achieving an effective, feasible and stable international agreement.

There are clear links between climate change and other policy domains, such as local air pollution and energy security. This is because action to reduce GHG emissions can also have positive effects (co-benefits) on these other areas. However, while outdoor local air pollution can be substantially reduced by GHG emission reduction, on their own these co-benefits are unlikely to be sufficient to motivate the larger developing countries to join a global agreement. This is partly because direct local

THE ECONOMICS OF CLIMATE CHANGE MITIGATION – ISBN: 978-92-64-05606-0 – © OECD 2009

air pollution control policies are typically cheaper than indirect action via GHG mitigation. Furthermore, over the medium term and/or for less stringent long-term emission reduction objectives, these co-benefits may be lower in developing countries than within the OECD. This is because the cheapest GHG abatement opportunities in developing countries are initially found in the electricity sector, rather than the transport sector, and the human health benefits from emission cuts from the electricity sector appear to be smaller. These issues are further explored in Section 6.2.

More ambitious world mitigation action will need to include greater commitments by developing country emitters. This can be achieved gradually, for example through implicit and/or explicit international financial transfer mechanisms across countries to support increased action in developing countries. Section 6.3 investigates how such transfers can be achieved through allocating emission reduction commitments.

6.1. Broad-based international mitigation and incentives for action

Future climate policies will need to meet ambitious global mitigation objectives. To this end, a successful international climate policy framework will ultimately involve a coalition of countries that is:

i) environmentally effective (has the technical potential to achieve a given world target even if non-participating countries take no mitigation action) and economically feasible (can meet the target without entailing excessively high carbon prices and mitigation costs);

ii) *as a whole* welfare-enhancing to deliver an emission cut that is sufficient to achieve ambitious global mitigation action; and

iii) stable, *i.e.* provides each member country with sufficient incentives to participate.

All three issues are explored in this section.

6.1.1. Which regions are needed for an environmentally effective coalition?

The World Induced Technological Change Hybrid (WITCH) model (Bosetti *et al.* 2006, 2007, 2009a, 2009b; see Box 6.1) was used to identify "potentially effective coalitions" or PECs for achieving a given world target, and then to study the incentives for the main emitting regions to participate in the coalition. WITCH has two major strengths for this analysis: *i)* it belongs to the class of so-called integrated assessment models (IAMs), which means it incorporates explicitly the gains from emission reductions (avoided damage); *ii)* it has a game-theoretic structure, which means it captures some of the strategic aspects of international relations (see Box 6.1 and Bosetti *et al.* 2009b for details). The "business-as-usual" (BAU) scenario (Box 6.1) used in this analysis assumes that the 12 world regions do not co-operate on emission reductions. A coalition is then defined as a PEC if it can technically achieve the target without reducing its own emissions below zero, even if non-participating regions do not act – *i.e.* their emissions continue along their BAU path. Being a PEC is a necessary, but not sufficient, condition for reaching the target because zero emissions are implausible in the foreseeable future,[1] and because of the carbon leakage and free-riding incentives such a large abatement effort would generate, raising emissions in non-participating regions above their BAU levels.

The illustrative target simulated here is to stabilise global GHG concentrations at 550 ppm CO_2eq over the long term. Meeting more stringent targets would require larger coalitions than the PECs identified below. Thus, the identified coalition should be seen as the minimum needed to meet any target equal to or below 550 ppm CO_2eq. Based on the IPCC's Fourth Assessment Report (IPCC, 2007), reaching this target would imply an approximate 30% cut in world emissions from 2000 levels by 2050, and a 50% cut by 2100.

Box 6.1 Analysing climate coalitions: theoretical concepts and implementation in the WITCH model

While the focus of the analysis in Chapter 5 using the WITCH model was on technology (Box 5.1 in Chapter 5), the model's game-theoretic structure allows it to be used to analyse the financial incentives for countries to participate and remain in climate coalitions. It was thus used to explore three different assumptions:

i. A non-cooperative framework: each of the 12 world regions is assumed to set its future emission path today in order to maximise its own welfare (defined as the present value of the logarithm of per capita consumption), taking other regions' choices as given.[1] This is the BAU scenario for this analysis. In this scenario, little abatement effort is made because each region only takes into account the future damage it will incur when setting its emission path, but not the damage it will cause to others.

ii. A co-operative framework: a coalition bringing together some (or possibly all) regions sets emission levels so as to maximise the joint welfare of the coalition, taking into account the damage incurred by the coalition as a whole. This induces the coalition to set emissions below the non-cooperative BAU level.[2] By contrast, regions that do not participate in the coalition are assumed to behave in a non-cooperative manner, *i.e.* they "free ride" on the mitigation action of the coalition.

iii. A cost-effectiveness framework: In both the non-cooperative and cooperative frameworks, the model is run in cost-benefit mode, meaning that the emission path chosen by each region or coalition is a result of the objective to maximise welfare. Therefore the implied world emission path may or may not meet any particular target, such as the 550 ppm CO_2eq GHG concentration target considered throughout this section. However, the model can also be run in cost-effective mode, in which case an exogenous target is assumed, and the coalition considered achieves that target at least cost. An international ETS is assumed to be implemented by the coalition, as well as a specific rule for allocating permits across member regions.

The incentives for countries to participate and the stability of climate change mitigation coalitions can best be examined in cost-benefit mode, although some basic insights about individual regions' gains and losses when participating and not participating can still be established in cost-effective mode. Previous literature on international environmental agreements in a non-cooperative framework highlights that a coalition should be profitable in order to be stable (See *e.g.* Carraro *et al.* 2006; Chander and Tulkens, 2008). Profitability, *i.e.* the condition that the welfare of the coalition as a whole should be larger than the sum of its members' welfare in the non-cooperative (BAU) scenario, will typically be met in cost-benefit mode, where coalitions internalise the climate externality in an optimal manner.[3] The coalition is stable, or self-enforcing, if the welfare of each participating region is larger or equal to the welfare it would obtain from withdrawing from the coalition and free riding on other participants' abatement efforts.[4] The coalition is potentially stable if it can be turned into a stable coalition through a set of self-financed – *i.e.* not greater than the coalition's surplus – financial transfers across participating regions.

Unlike in previous literature, the stability property here is explored only for coalitions that are both potentially effective (*i.e.* that have the potential to meet a 550 ppm CO_2eq GHG concentration target by 2050 and/or 2100) and that are politically relevant. This means that coalitions that exclude some developed countries have not been considered. For this subset of coalitions, the analysis examines not only their stability, but also whether they find it optimal (in cost-benefit mode) to cut emissions to meet (at least) the illustrative 550 ppm CO_2eq target.

1. More precisely, WITCH being an optimal growth model, each region sets the future path of key economic variables (saving, investment in alternative energy inputs, investment in R&D and deployment of low-carbon technologies…etc), which in turn results in an emission path and a (shadow) carbon price (see Bosetti *et al.* 2009b).

2. Coalitions are also assumed to internalise international energy-related R&D spillovers (see Bosetti *et al.* 2009b).

3. By contrast, the profitability condition may not necessarily be met in cost-effective mode, where the gains from avoided climate change may or may not exceed the abatement costs incurred to meet the imposed emission constraint. For instance, if assigned an emission target that is vastly more stringent than its optimal one, a coalition might not be profitable.

4. Only internal stability is considered here. Stable coalitions should in fact also be externally stable, *i.e.* non-participating regions should not have an incentive to join in. If they do, only larger coalitions may be both internally and externally stable.

Table 6.1. Potentially effective coalitions (PECs) for meeting a 550 ppm CO_2eq GHG concentration target by 2050 and 2100 will have to include most large emitters[1]

Panel A. PECs in 2050

Must participate	Not required to participate
	Any combination of the following regions:
1. Developed countries,[2] Latin America, Non-EU Eastern Europe (including Russia), South East Asia, Middle East and North Africa	Africa, South Asia (Including India), China
2. Developed countries,[2] Non-EU Eastern Europe (including Russia), China, Middle East and North Africa	Africa, South Asia (Including India), South East Asia, Latin America
3. Developed countries,[2] Non-EU Eastern Europe (including Russia), China, South East Asia	Africa, South Asia (Including India), Latin America, Middle East and North Africa
4. Developed countries,[2] China, South East Asia, Middle East and North Africa	Africa, South Asia (Including India), Non-EU Eastern Europe (including Russia), Latin America
5. Developed countries,[2] Latin America, China	Africa, South Asia (Including India), Non-EU Eastern Europe (including Russia), Middle East and North Africa, South East Asia
6. Developed countries,[2] Latin America, South Asia (including India), South East Asia, Middle East and North Africa	Africa, China, Non-EU Eastern Europe (including Russia)
7. Developed countries,[2] Non-EU Eastern Europe (including Russia), South Asia (including India), South East Asia, Middle East and North Africa	Africa, China, Latin America
8. Developed countries,[2] Latin America, Non-EU Eastern Europe (including Russia), South Asia (including India)	Africa, China, Middle East and North Africa, South East Asia
9. Developed countries,[2] South Asia (including India), China, South East Asia	Africa, Non-EU Eastern Europe (including Russia), Middle East and North Africa, Latin America
10. Developed countries,[2] South Asia (including India), China, Middle East and North Africa	Africa, Non-EU Eastern Europe (including Russia), South East Asia, Latin America
11. Developed countries,[2] South Asia (including India), China	Africa, Latin America, South East Asia, Middle East and North Africa, Non-EU Eastern Europe (including Russia)

Panel B. PECs in 2100

Must participate	Not required to participate
	Any combination of the following regions:
1. Developed countries,[2] Non-EU Eastern Europe (including Russia), South Asia (including India), China, South East Asia, Middle East and North Africa	Africa, Latin America
2. Developed countries,[2] Latin America, Non-EU Eastern Europe (including Russia), South Asia (including India), China, South East Asia	Africa, Middle East and North Africa
3. Developed countries,[2] Latin America, South Asia (including India), China, Middle East and North Africa	Africa, Non-EU Eastern Europe (including Russia), South East Asia

Note: Each row features one type of PEC. For instance, the first row of Panel A indicates that one type of PEC includes at a minimum all regions in the left column, along with some (or none) of the regions in the right column.

1. For the detailed composition of each region see: http://www.feem-web.it/witch/model.html
2. Developed countries include Australia, Canada, New Zealand, Japan, Korea, United States, Western EU countries and Eastern EU countries.

Source: WITCH model simulations.

The analysis here shows that for the 550 ppm CO_2eq global GHG concentration target to be technically feasible, emission reductions must be made by virtually all the large emitters during the first half of the century. In particular, this would include all developed countries and either China or India by 2050, unless *all* other developing regions (except Africa) reduce their emissions below BAU levels (Table 6.1, Panel A).[2] Furthermore, most developing regions would also need to take action during the second half of the century, with the possible exception of Africa (Table 6.1, Panel B).

Table 6.2. Economically feasible coalitions for meeting a 550ppm CO_2eq GHG concentration target by 2050 and 2100 will have to include almost all large emitters[1]

Panel A. Economically feasible coalitions in 2050

Must participate	Not required to participate
	Any combination of the following regions:
1. Developed countries,[2] Latin America, Non-EU Eastern Europe (including Russia), South Asia (including India), China	Africa, South East Asia, Middle East and North Africa
2. Developed countries,[2] Latin America, South Asia (including India), China, Middle East and North Africa	Africa, South East Asia, Non-EU Eastern Europe (including Russia)
3. Developed countries,[2] Non-EU Eastern Europe (including Russia), South Asia (including India), China, South East Asia, Middle East and North Africa	Africa, Latin America
4. Developed countries,[2] Latin America, Non-EU Eastern Europe (including Russia), South Asia (including India), South East Asia, Middle East and North Africa	Africa, China
5. Developed countries,[2] Latin America, Non-EU Eastern Europe (including Russia), China, South East Asia, Middle East and North Africa	Africa, South Asia (including India)

Panel B. Economically feasible coalitions in 2100

Must participate	Not required to participate
	Any combination of the following regions:
1. Developed countries,[2] Latin America, Non-EU Eastern Europe (including Russia), South Asia (including India), China, South East Asia, Middle East and North Africa	Africa

Note: Each row features one type of PEC. For instance, the first row of Panel A indicates that one type of PEC includes at a minimum all regions in the left column, along with some (or none) of the regions in the right column.

1. For the detailed composition of each region see: http://www.feem-web.it/witch/model.html.
2. Developed countries include Australia, Canada, New Zealand, Japan, Korea, United States, Western EU countries and Eastern EU countries.

Source: WITCH model simulations

However, because a PEC is only one condition for achieving the target, and since more stringent targets (*e.g.* a 450 ppm CO_2eq target) would require larger global cuts than assumed here, in practice most regions of the world – and definitely all large emitters – will have to reduce their emissions below BAU over the coming decades, if ambitious climate mitigation objectives are to be met. This is confirmed by the analysis of economically feasible coalitions, *i.e.* of those coalitions under which the

WITCH model can actually meet a 550 ppm CO_2eq target through a single (coalition-wide), feasible carbon price, without mitigation costs becoming excessively high.[3] Even though mitigation costs are typically low in this version of the model due to the assumption that new technologies will emerge gradually over the coming decades (Box 5.1 and Bosetti *et al.* 2009*a*), economically feasible coalitions would also need to include all large emitting regions, except either China or India (but not both) by 2050, and all world regions except Africa by 2100, as shown in Table 6.2.

6.1.2. What incentives do countries have to participate in a mitigation coalition?

A coalition will not only need to be potentially effective and economically feasible, but also gain from achieving the target. Furthermore, each member must have enough incentive to participate in the coalition. Incentives will ultimately depend on a wide range of economic and political factors, not all of which can be captured by a simple economic model. Nevertheless, useful insights can still be gained by focusing on economic incentives. In the WITCH model these include damage avoided and the abatement costs incurred both within and outside a coalition.

Individual countries' incentives to participate

There are three major incentives for individual countries to participate:

i) *The expected impacts of climate change.* As a general rule, the literature shows that developing countries are likely to be affected more by climate change (expressed in terms of GDP) than developed countries (Figure 6.1, Panel A), although there would likely be significant local or sub-regional variations within each country.[4] Of the developing countries, Africa appears to be more exposed to the impacts of climate change than South Asia (including India) which, in turn, would be more affected than China. Within the developed countries, Western Europe would suffer greater damage than the United States in aggregate, which in turn would be more vulnerable than the OECD Asia-Pacific countries and Canada. Finally, non-EU Eastern Europe (including Russia) would be least affected by climate change, and might even benefit under moderate temperature increases over the coming few decades. However, these estimates do not reflect the latest scientific evidence, and thus may underestimate the market impacts of climate change (Hanemann, 2009) and especially the non-market impacts (*e.g.* on the environment, and to a lesser extent on health) and the risk of catastrophic events, which is likely to be a major contributor to overall damage (IPCC, 2007; Stern, 2007). Therefore, the analysis here considers not only the baseline (low damage) case, but also a high damage scenario which roughly takes into account non-market impacts and catastrophic events by doubling the climate impacts of the low damage case. This raises damage estimates to levels closer to (but still below) those featured in Stern (2007) (Figure 6.1, Panel B).

ii) *The influence of future impacts on current policy decisions.* Since most of the impacts of climate change are expected to occur in the future, how current governments value them has an important effect on their incentives to take action.[5] Here, two different annual discount rates are used to value the welfare of future generations – 0.1% (low case) and 3% (high case) – in line with Stern (2007) and Nordhaus and Boyer (2000), respectively (and see Bosetti *et al.* 2009b).

iii) *The costs of mitigation policies.* In general, the higher the overall carbon intensity of a country or region's output, the larger the economy's abatement costs under a global carbon tax (or a world ETS with full permit auctioning), and the smaller its incentive to participate in a climate coalition. A summary of regional mitigation costs under a range of world carbon tax scenarios in WITCH indicates that developing regions (China, South-East Asia, Africa and, to a somewhat lesser extent, South Asia, including India, and Latin America) would incur larger costs than developed countries in the absence of explicit or implicit financial transfers (Figure 6.2; see also Chapter 5).[6] Economies which are both carbon-intensive and which produce fossil fuels (non-EU Eastern Europe including Russia, the Middle East and North Africa) face the largest costs from broad-based mitigation action.

Achieving a broad international climate coalition

Bringing together the incentives created by damage, discounting and abatement costs, the model analysis confirms that ambitious global mitigation action would be economically rational in the high-damage/low-discounting case, in line with Stern (2007). A fully co-operative, welfare-maximising "grand coalition" involving all the regions would cut world emissions by over 25% by 2050 relative to 2005 levels, and keep overall GHG concentrations below 550 ppm CO_2eq by the end of the century (Figure 6.3). Moreover, some other factors that were omitted from the analysis could lead the world to undertake larger cuts, such as the damage expected beyond 2100, the co-benefits from mitigation action and possibly the risk of catastrophic events. While the latter have been taken into account here to an extent, a precautionary approach might justify even stronger mitigation action upfront (Weitzman, 2007a; 2007b).

Smaller PECs that do not fully internalise the climate externality might not have sufficient incentives to meet this target. Moreover, even the grand coalition itself might not have sufficient incentives to meet the target if the welfare of future generations is highly discounted (high-discounting case) or non-market climate impacts and risks are not fully taken into account (low-damage case) (Figure 6.4).

The analysis also shows that buying in all major emitting regions will be challenging. While ambitious mitigation action is profitable to the group of countries as a whole, the grand coalition is not stable in the absence of financial transfers. Compared with the (non-cooperative) BAU scenario, most world regions would already gain from being in the grand coalition by 2050 in the high-damage case, and all would benefit by 2100 (Figure 6.5). However, all regions would gain *less* from participating than from staying outside and free riding on the abatement efforts of others, assuming the rest of the coalition went forward with action without them. Regions with flatter marginal abatement cost curves and/or flatter marginal damage curves have larger incentives to free ride, because they would have to contribute more to the coalition's abatement effort and/or would benefit less. This explains why non-EU Eastern Europe (including Russia), the Middle East and China are found to gain more from staying outside a coalition than Western Europe or, to a somewhat lesser extent, the United States, Japan and South East Asia.[7] Russia loses from mitigation action both as a carbon-intensive economy and a fossil fuel producer, while benefiting significantly less than most other countries from avoided climate change impacts as it is less affected by climate change.

Figure 6.1. Selected regional and aggregate estimates of the damage caused by climate change

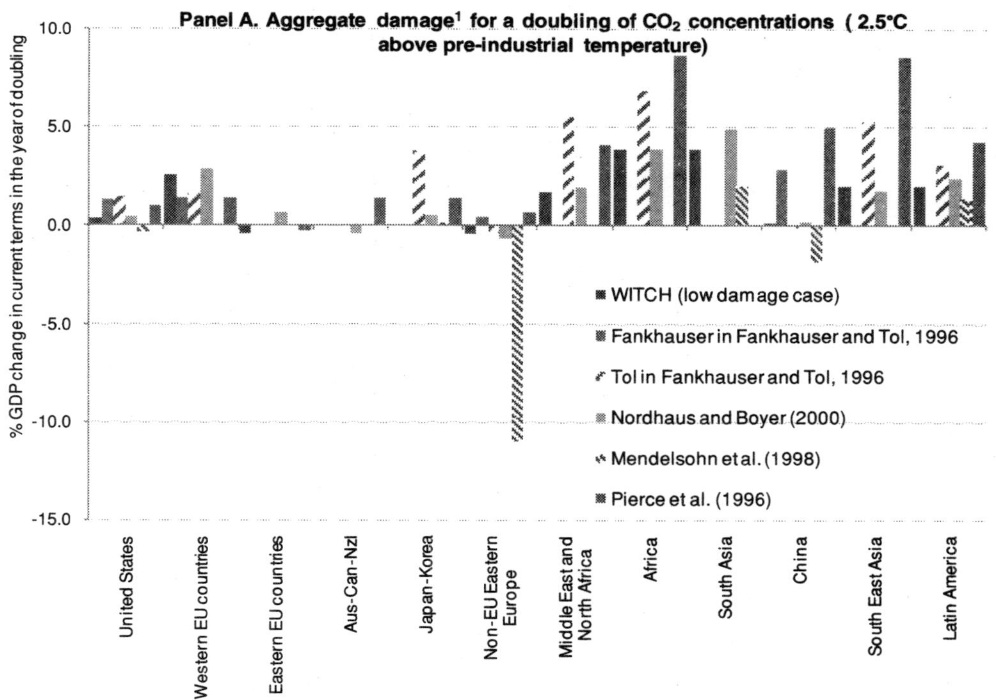

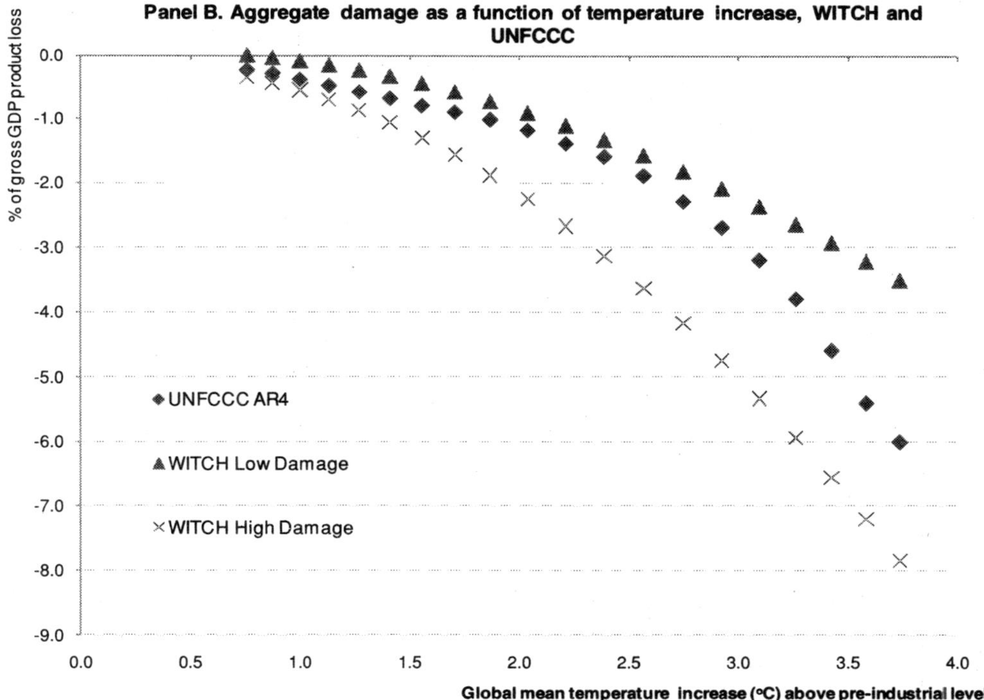

1. Damages are net from adaptation.

Sources: Fankhauser and Tol (1996); Tol (2005b); UNFCCC (2007a), WITCH model simulations.

Figure 6.2. WITCH model estimates of regional abatement costs under different world carbon tax scenarios[1]

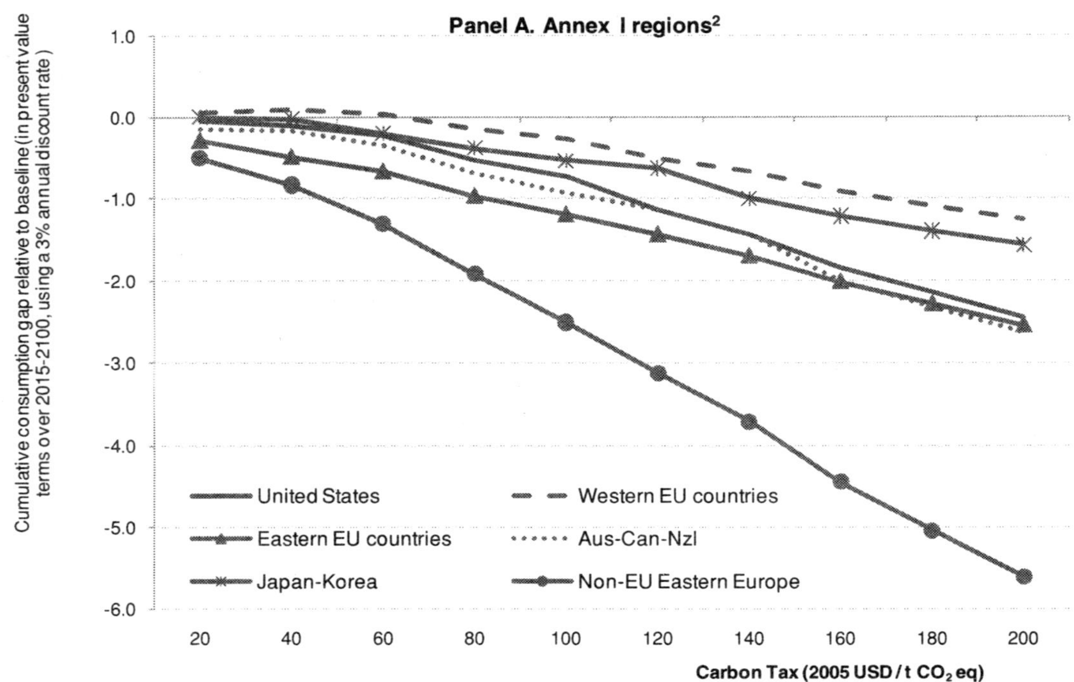

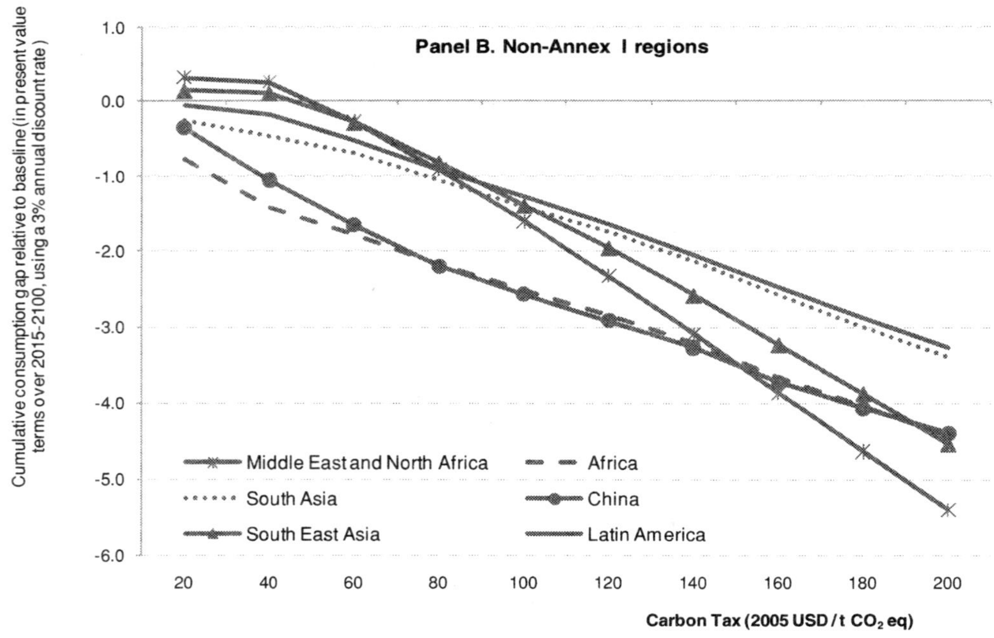

1. In each scenario, the carbon tax is assumed to remain constant over time in present value terms, using a 3% annual discount rate.
2. Korea is grouped with Japan in the WITCH model, but is not an Annex I country.

Source: WITCH model simulations.

Figure 6.3. Global action will lead to much lower optimal GHG emission and concentration paths, assuming high damage and low discounting rates

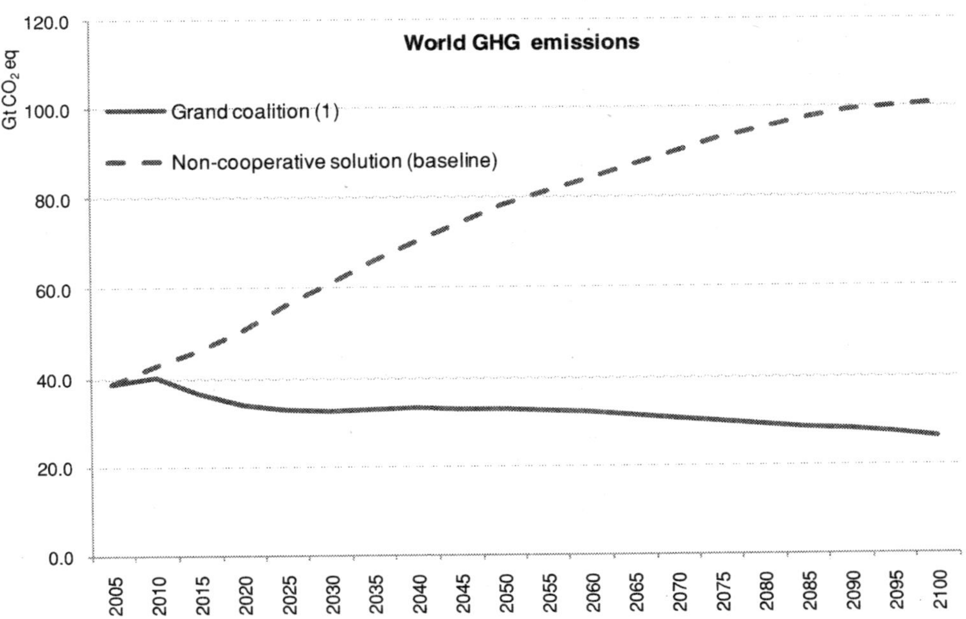

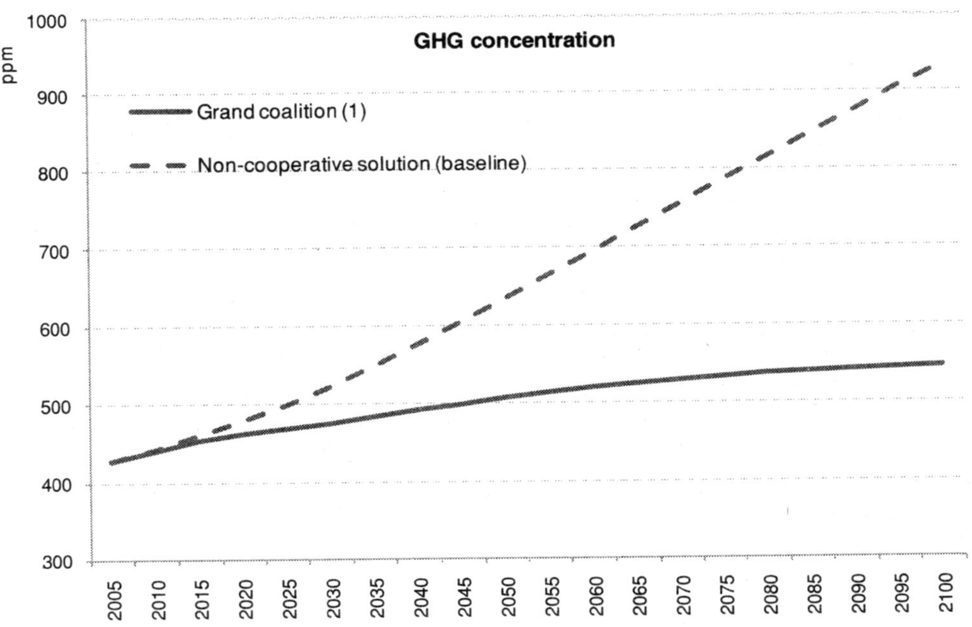

1. The grand coalition is defined as a coalition bringing together all world regions into mitigation action.

Source: WITCH model simulations.

Figure 6.4. Alternative damage and discounting assumptions will significantly affect the optimal GHG emission paths with international co-operation

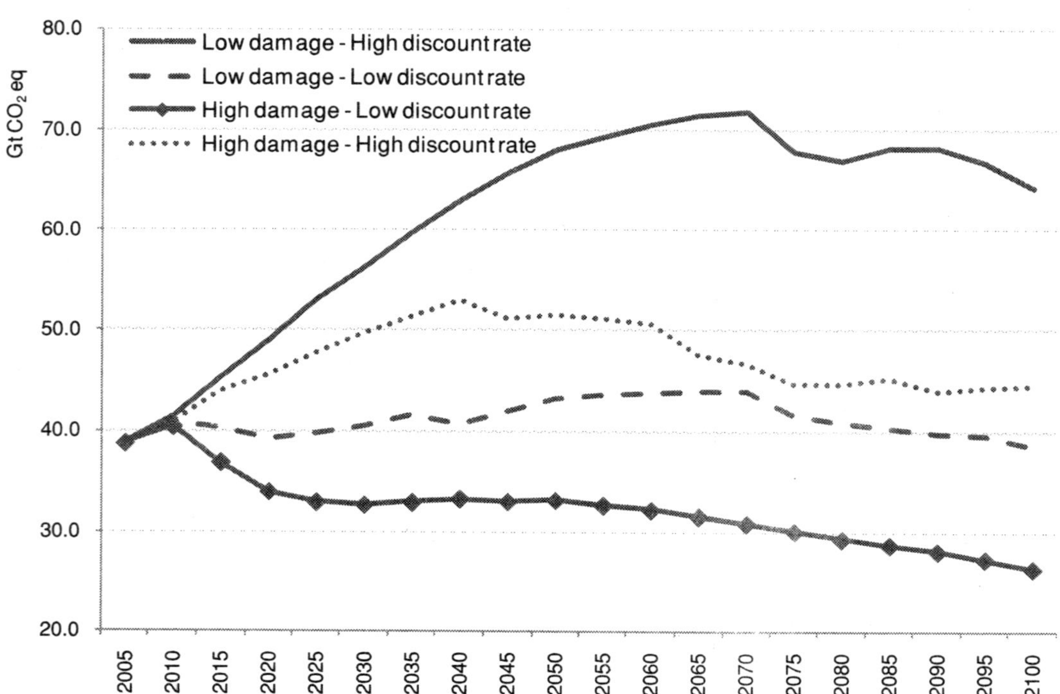

Source: WITCH model simulations.

International support for mitigation action could be broadened through financial transfers from regions that gain most from co-operation to those that gain less or might even lose (see *e.g.* Carraro *et al.* 2006; Chander and Tulkens, 2007; Finus *et al.* 2006; Nagashima *et al.* 2009). A stable international agreement might ultimately be achieved if a set of transfers could be found that would ensure that all signatory countries are better-off participating than not participating. However, even under the favourable high-damage/low-discounting assumptions, no such set of transfers was found in the analysis here, either for the grand coalition or for any smaller PEC (see Bosetti *et al.* 2009b for details) as the gains from co-operation are insufficient to overcome all free-rider incentives. Thus, building up a self-enforcing international framework covering all the main emitters is likely to be complex. This is in line with the above-mentioned literature, which in a similar game-theoretic framework typically finds international climate coalitions to be unstable or, when stable, to deliver only limited emission cuts because they are not PECs and/or have insufficient incentives to undertake large abatement efforts when not all countries are participating.

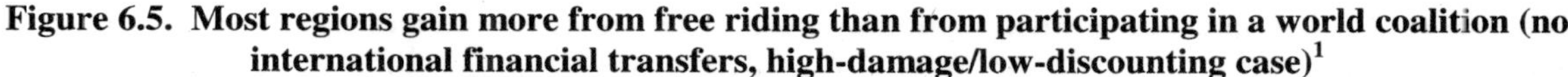

Figure 6.5. Most regions gain more from free riding than from participating in a world coalition (no international financial transfers, high-damage/low-discounting case)[1]

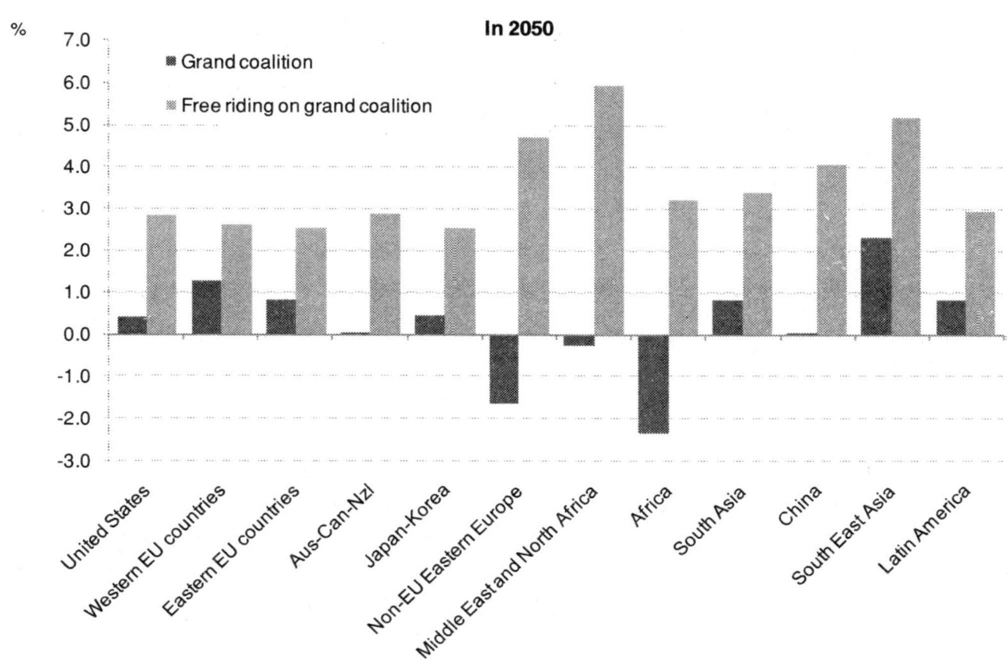

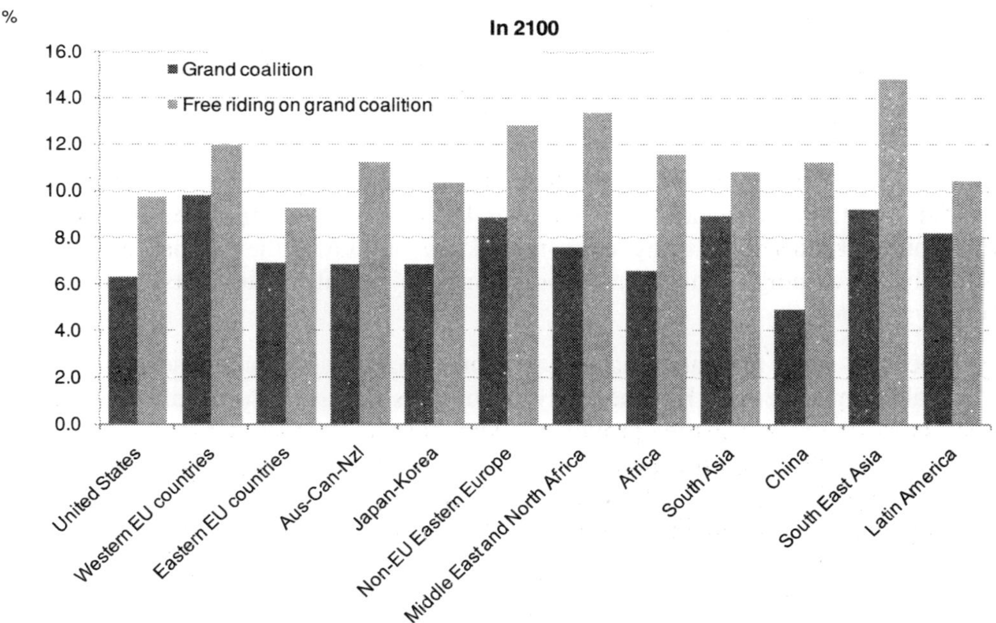

1. WITCH being an integrated assessment model, the damages from climate change explicitly affect GDP and consumption. Furthermore, not only the market, but also the non-market impacts of climate change are taken into account in the "high-damage case" featured here. This explains why all countries are found to gain from a grand coalition against climate change by 2100, compared with a BAU scenario.

Source: WITCH model simulations.

However, further analysis with the model reveals that if developed countries as a group were prepared to incur a permanent consumption loss from world mitigation action, the prospects for a broad and stable international coalition would vastly improve. For instance, a permanent reduction in (the discounted value of) the consumption levels of advanced economies by 3% (relative to BAU) could be enough to produce a stable grand coalition in the high-damage/low-discounting case. That is, all other regions would receive enough financial support to prevent free riding, thereby bringing them into an agreement. However, to be cost-effective, such large financial transfers would have to be made primarily through market mechanisms, essentially via credits generated to meet binding emission reduction commitments across countries.

Limitations of the analysis

All these findings should be interpreted with caution, because the analysis is subject to a number of limitations:

- Even though some sensitivity analysis has been carried out to assess the robustness of the main results, it should be acknowledged that the model-based analysis relies on strong assumptions, (see Bosetti *et al.* 2009b). In particular, there are wide uncertainties in practice surrounding future emission trends,[8] the market and non-market impacts of climate change, the likelihood and impacts of catastrophic risks, and the cross-country distribution of these damages and risks. Furthermore, different negotiation processes than assumed here could occur, which might yield different results (see Bosetti *et al.* 2009b). For instance, a major emitting country may have greater incentives to participate than was found here if it expects its withdrawal to prevent the formation of any coalition.
- The underlying framework only considers immediate, irreversible and self-enforcing participation in an international mitigation coalition, which excludes other possible bargaining options, *e.g.* delayed participation, renegotiation, sanctions or joint negotiation in multiple areas (*e.g.* climate and international trade).
- Removal of fossil fuel subsidies, one of the few policies to potentially yield both climate and economic benefits (see Section 4.1 in Chapter 4), is also omitted from the analysis. But because phasing out subsidies could bring an economic gain and lower the carbon intensity of a number of (mainly developing) countries, it could improve incentives to participate in international mitigation action.
- The co-benefits from mitigation action, *e.g.* for human health, energy security or biodiversity, are not taken into account. But the analysis suggests that such co-benefits are large, although the participation incentives they provide are tempered by the fact that some of these co-benefits could be reaped through direct policy action. In any case, the co-benefits may well be sufficient to offset eventual losses that advanced economies might be willing to incur in order to bring about a broad and stable coalition of participating countries. This issue will be explored in more detail in the next section.

6.2. Enhancing participation incentives through co-benefits of mitigation policies

There is a potentially large and diverse range of co-effects from climate change mitigation policies, which would lower the net costs of emission reductions and strengthen the incentives for countries to participate in a global agreement. Two important co-effects are discussed below: *i)* the reduction in local air pollution (LAP), which affects among others human health and crop yield; and *ii)* implications for energy security. There are other co-benefits of GHG mitigation policy, however, such as for ecosystems and biodiversity, which are not examined here.

Local air pollution co-benefits of mitigation policies

The participation incentives provided by local air pollution (LAP) co-benefits depend on: *i)* their size; and *ii)* the relative cost of achieving the same level of reduction in LAP through direct policies. Ideally, given that there are also co-benefits from pursuing LAP control on GHG emissions, policies to control GHG and LAP would be jointly pursued and optimised (see Bollen *et al.*, 2008, 2009). However, most studies have focused on LAP control co-benefits that stem from GHG mitigation policies. Their main conclusion is that GHG mitigation could yield large short-term benefits in terms of reduced human health risks, and that these benefits might cover a significant part of the GHG mitigation costs (Figure 6.6; OECD 2000; 2001). However, little is currently known about the incentive power of these co-benefits. In this analysis, an extension of the Model for Evaluating the Regional and Global Effects of GHG Reduction Policies (MERGE) was used to examine the co-benefits of climate mitigation policies. This only includes outdoor LAP and its health impacts (Bollen *et al.* 2008, 2009). The analysis covers the main pollutants which affect health,[9] with the important exception of tropospheric ozone.[10] The model was used to simulate the costs and benefits of GHG and LAP policies in a general equilibrium, dynamic, multi-regional and multi-sectoral framework.

Figure 6.6. Review of the co-benefits of reducing GHGs at different GHG emission prices, 2010

(USD/tonne of CO_2 eq.[1])

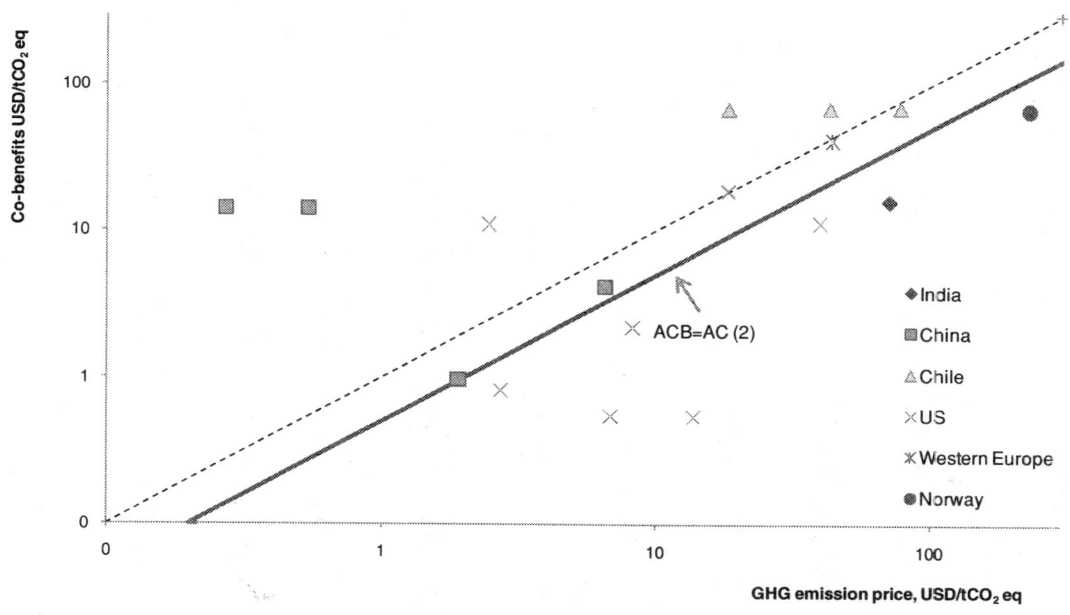

1. For each country, observations represent estimates from various studies and/or for various carbon prices. The base year for estimates is 1996 or the latest available year.
2. The line ACB=AC indicate situation where the average co-benefit is equal to the average cost of abatement. It assumes that abatement costs are a square function of emission reductions; average costs can then be computed as one half of marginal costs (i.e the carbon price). Points above this line indicate situations where the average co-benefit is higher than the average cost.

Source: OECD 2000, 2001.

Figure 6.7. The impact of reduced local air pollution through GHG mitigation policies on the % of premature deaths avoided will vary widely across regions[1]

(Differences from the baseline in %)

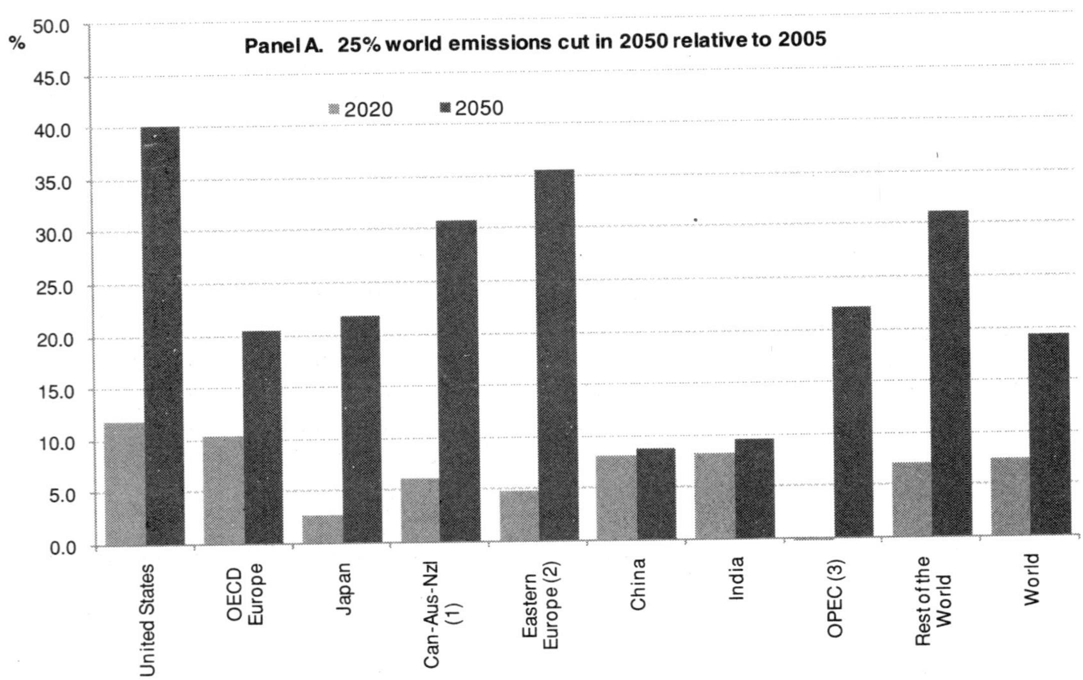

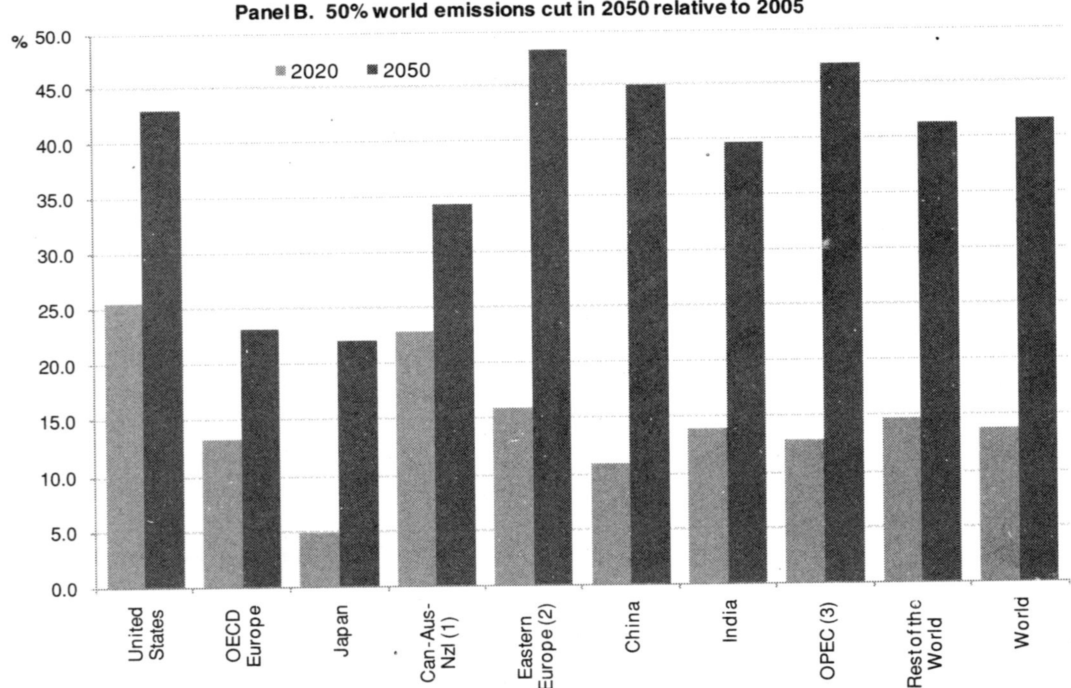

1. Canada, Australia and New Zealand are in the same geographical area in the MERGE model.
2. Including Russia.
3. Including Mexico

Source: Bollen *et al.* (2008).

Overall, the global health co-benefits of climate mitigation are found to be large, and to offset a sizeable share of GHG mitigation costs. Somewhat surprisingly, assuming a global carbon price and under world emission cuts of 25% (relative to 2005), the percentage decline in premature deaths induced by GHG mitigation policies is estimated to be smaller in China and India than in OECD countries (Figure 6.7, Panel A). This is partly because local air pollution in the OECD is mainly stemming from transport, whereas outside the OECD a major source is coal burning by households. Moreover, compared with OECD countries, the cheaper GHG abatement opportunities in developing countries over the next 20 years will be in the electricity sector, rather than in the transport sector, and emission reduction technologies have less impact on LAP in the former than in the latter. Also, human exposure to LAP is usually larger when pollution comes from small point sources (cars and houses) than from large-scale point sources such as power plants. However, for more stringent emissions cuts or over longer horizons, co-benefits ultimately become higher in many non-OECD countries than in their OECD counterparts, as cheaper CO_2 abatement opportunities in the electricity sector in non-OECD countries are exhausted and OECD countries run out of options for reducing LAP through GHG mitigation policies, especially in the transport sector (Figure 6.7, Panel B).

Figure 6.8. Heath co-benefits in 2020 per tonne of CO_2 equivalent and GHG emission prices

USD per tonne of CO_2 eq.

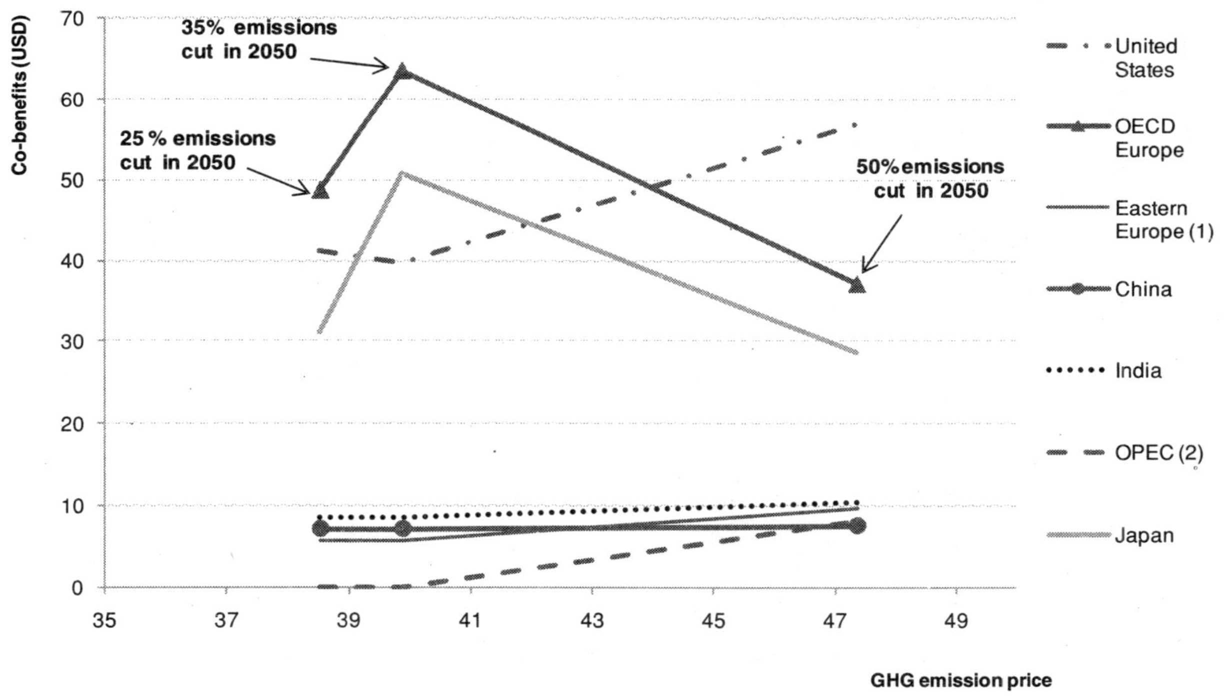

Note: Co-benefits per ton of CO_2eq reflect an average co-benefit while the carbon price reflects the marginal cost of abatement, which exceeds the average cost. Therefore, their values are not directly comparable.

1. Including Russia.
2. Including Mexico.

Source: Bollen *et al.* (2008).

To compare the co-benefits to the cost of mitigation policies, the number of avoided premature deaths needs to be converted into a monetary equivalent. This conversion is based on an explicit assumption about the value of statistical life (VSL). Here, the premature deaths from long-term exposure to air pollution is valued at USD 1 million in Europe in 2000, which is the median value across a range of studies (Holland *et al.* 2004). For other regions and years, this value is adjusted according to their GDP per capita gap relative to Europe in 2000 (for details and sensitivity analysis, see Bollen *et al.*, 2009). As a result, the health co-benefits of mitigation policies per tonne of carbon in monetary units are lower in non-OECD countries than in their OECD counterparts, although they are projected to increase somewhat over time with income growth and urbanisation (Figure 6.8). Given the valuation assumptions and the fact that GDP per capita is projected to remain higher in China than in India, co-benefits are found to be higher in China than in India by 2050. While the average health co-benefit per tonne of carbon cannot be directly compared to the carbon price, which is the marginal cost of abatement and as such exceeds the average cost, the analysis suggests that co-benefits could cover a sizeable part of mitigation costs. Finally, under a uniform carbon price scenario, emission reductions would be larger in non-OECD countries, and as a result co-benefits would also be larger when expressed in percentage points of GDP (Figure 6.9).

Figure 6.9. The health co-benefits of reducing GHG emissions by 50% in 2050 are substantial

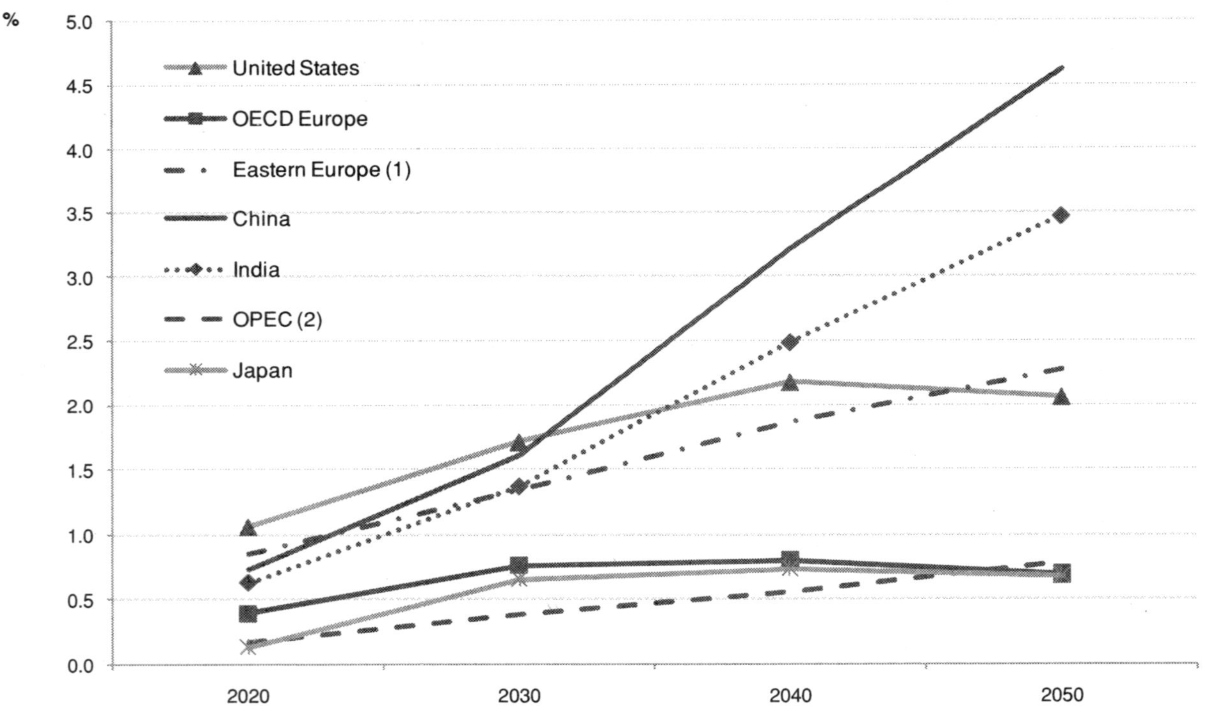

1. Including Russia.
2. Including Mexico.

Source: Bollen *et al.* (2008).

However, while health co-benefits are found to be large and to offset a sizeable share of GHG mitigation costs, they alone are unlikely to provide sufficient incentives for wide participation in a global GHG mitigation agreement in the medium-term (Figure 6.10). Over a longer horizon (*e.g.* to 2100), the gains from GHG mitigation are expected to be large and to outpace mitigation costs. The more limited medium-term incentives are because the cost of achieving the same level of LAP reduction through direct policies is estimated to be low, thereby reducing the incentive to reduce LAP indirectly via GHG mitigation (see Bollen *et al.*, 2009).[11] This finding should be interpreted with care, however, given the various uncertainties surrounding the baseline projection for local pollutant emissions, and the link between average pollutant concentration and the number of deaths. Furthermore, as in the rest of the literature, these estimates omit the possible co-effects of GHG mitigation on indoor air pollution (cooking smoke) from biomass and coal, which could be significant (but either positive or negative).

Figure 6.10. Co-benefits only partially improve incentives for participating in a global climate change agreement to reduce GHG emissions by 50% in 2050[1]

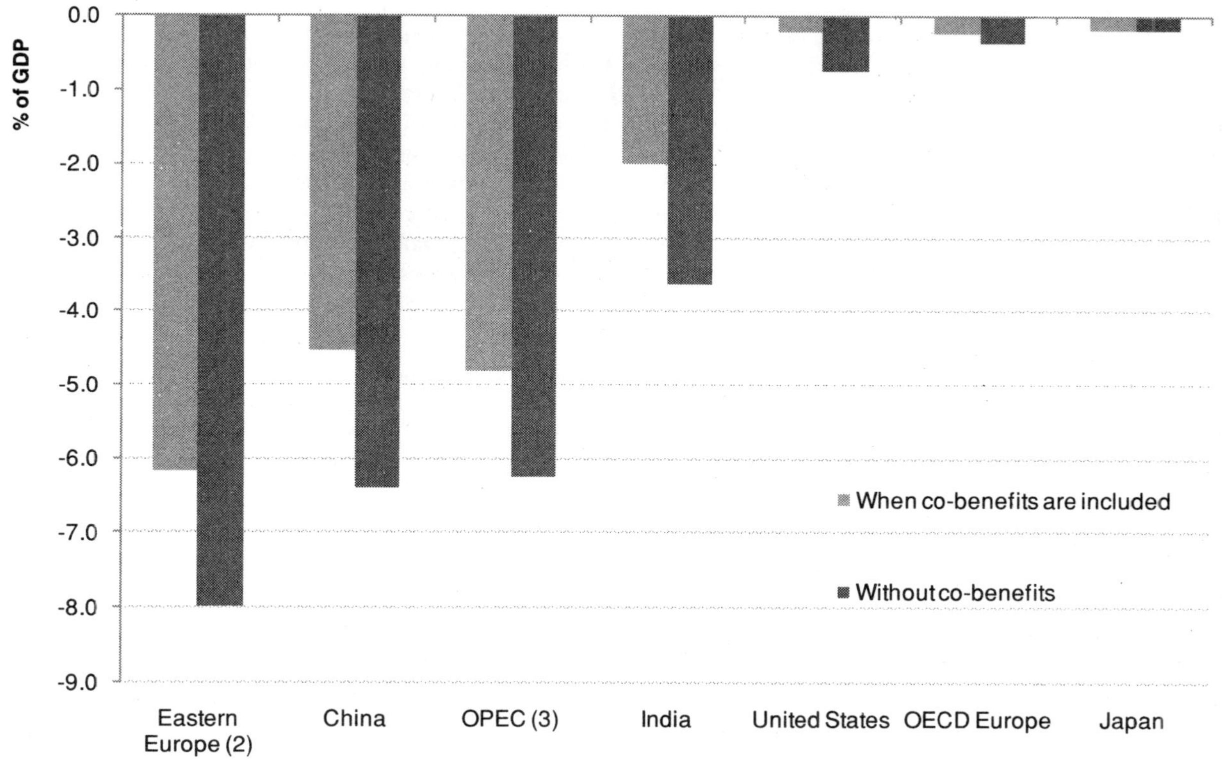

1. "Without co-benefits" is the return from GHG mitigation policy when co-benefits are not included, or the difference between the benefits in terms of avoided global climate change and the cost of mitigation policy. "When co-benefits are included" is the return from GHG mitigation policy when co-benefits are included, i.e the difference between the benefit in terms of both avoided global climate change and local air pollution and the cost of mitigation policy to which the opportunity gain of not having to achieve the same level of LAP reduction through direct policies is then added.
2. Including Russia.
3. Including Mexico

Source: Bollen *et al.* (2008).

The energy security implications of mitigation policies

By reducing economies' reliance on fossil fuels, mitigation action may also improve energy security. Energy security can be broadly defined as a low risk of disruption to energy supply, both in terms of physical availability and price stability (*e.g.* Bohi and Toman, 1996; Box 6.2).

Box 6.2 Energy security

Given that oil and coal markets have been liberalised in OECD and many non-member countries, any physical shortage is likely to be short lived, as prices ultimately adjust. Furthermore, in fairly integrated global oil and coal markets, all countries essentially face similar import prices, regardless of the geographical source of their imports. In the case of natural gas, longer-lasting physical shortages may still occur where national prices are regulated or pegged to the price of oil under long-term contracts, as in a number of European countries. Furthermore, the geographical location of the disruption can matter for gas because gas-pipeline infrastructure is inflexible, so that any supply loss cannot always readily be offset by an increase in supply from other sources. If gas markets increasingly function like oil and coal markets as they are further liberalised and liquefied natural gas gains prominence, energy insecurity would depend primarily on the overall energy intensity of the economy, as well as on overall import dependence and the fuel mix, with some fossil fuels being more prone to price volatility than others. Governments have used a variety of tools – *e.g.* the co-ordinated use of emergency oil stocks – to deal with short-term energy security problems. However, these do little to tackle longer-term energy security concerns, stemming in particular from inelastic supplies and high concentration of world fossil fuel sources in the hands of a small number of producers. This increases the risk of large unexpected price shifts, *e.g.* as a result of political events. This is primarily an issue for oil, as the Organization of the Petroleum Exporting Countries' (OPEC) share in world output is projected to rise significantly over the next three decades in the absence of any further policy action. It is also an issue for gas (IEA, 2007c).[1]

1. However, no cartel structure currently exists in world gas markets, and concentration is projected to decline from levels that are already lower than in the oil market – at least when OPEC is considered as a single oil producer. In the case of coal, the marginal cost of production rises only slowly with global output, due to ample world reserves. The resulting high world supply elasticity is expected to limit the risk of long-lasting price shocks (IEA, 2007a).

Climate change mitigation would be expected to improve long-term energy security in three main ways: *i)* by slowing the depletion of oil reserves in non-OPEC regions it would curb the projected rise in the OPEC market share and thereby reduce the potential for large unforeseen shifts in world oil prices (see Box 6.2);[12] *ii)* by reducing economies' energy and fossil fuel intensity, it would soften the macroeconomic impact of any future price shocks; and *iii)* by fostering greater use of renewable and nuclear energy, and the development of alternative energy sources more broadly, mitigation may also lead to greater energy risk diversification. Such energy security gains are likely to vary across countries, depending on their overall fossil fuel intensity; the diversity of their energy mix (especially their reliance on more volatile oil); the extent to which local production protects them (with terms of trade gains then partly offsetting any macroeconomic cost from price spikes); or their degree of resilience to macroeconomic shocks. However, given that pricing carbon induces firms to shift away from more carbon-intensive coal towards less carbon-intensive oil and gas, gains in the energy security of large coal producers and consumers (*e.g.* Australia, United States, China, India, Indonesia and South Africa) might be lower.[13]

OECD ENV-Linkages simulations provide a preliminary, incomplete illustration of the energy security benefits of world emission cuts. A world carbon price scenario necessary for achieving an illustrative 550 ppm CO_2eq GHG (450 ppm CO_2 only) stabilisation target would significantly reduce fossil fuel intensity (Figure 6.11). This would enhance the reductions in fossil fuel intensity already projected in the baseline scenario, reflecting future expected improvements in energy efficiency. It would be somewhat smaller for oil and gas than for coal, reflecting both greater incentives to shift away from coal and more limited substitution options for oil and/or gas in the non-electricity sector. However, the risk of oil price shocks is expected to be the most significant source of energy insecurity over the coming decades.

Figure 6.11. Projected fossil fuel intensities under baseline and 550 ppm GHG concentration stabilisation scenarios[1]

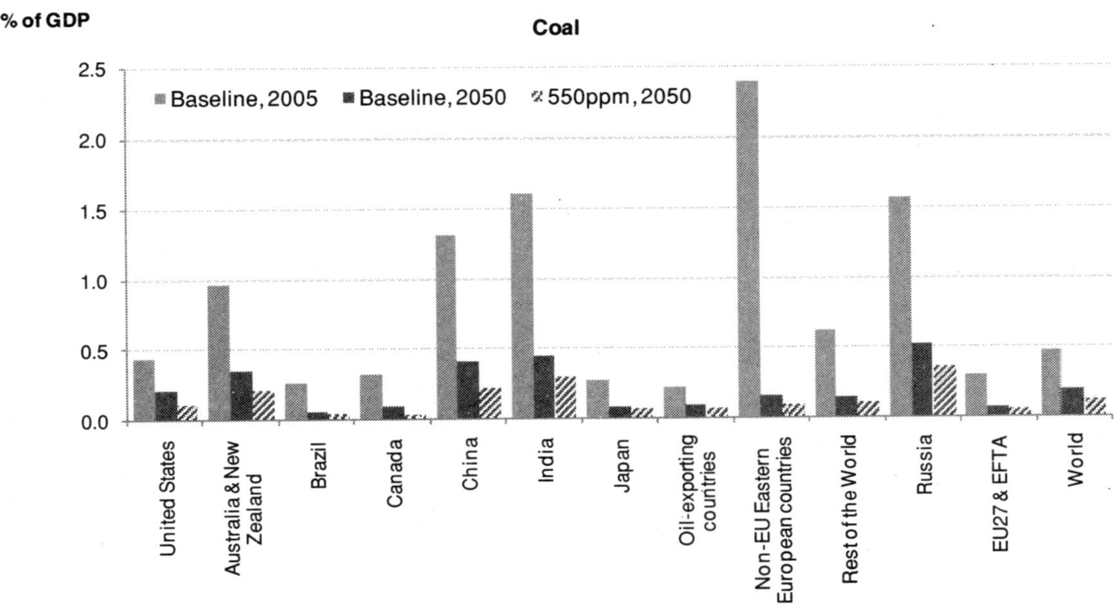

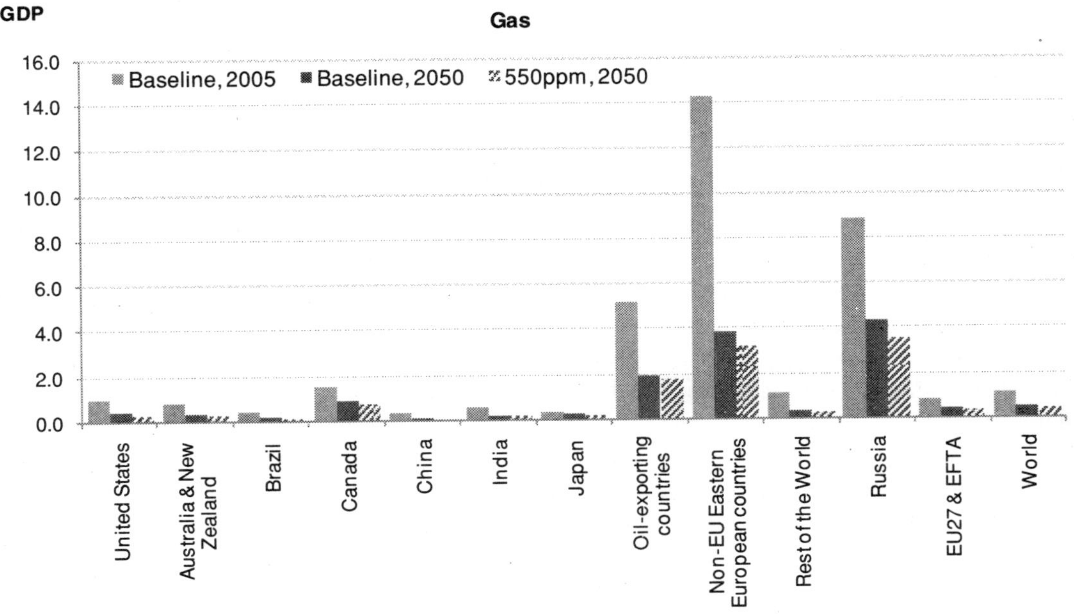

Figure 6.11 continued on next page

Figure 6.11. Projected fossil fuel intensities under baseline and 550 ppm GHG concentration stabilisation scenarios

(continued)

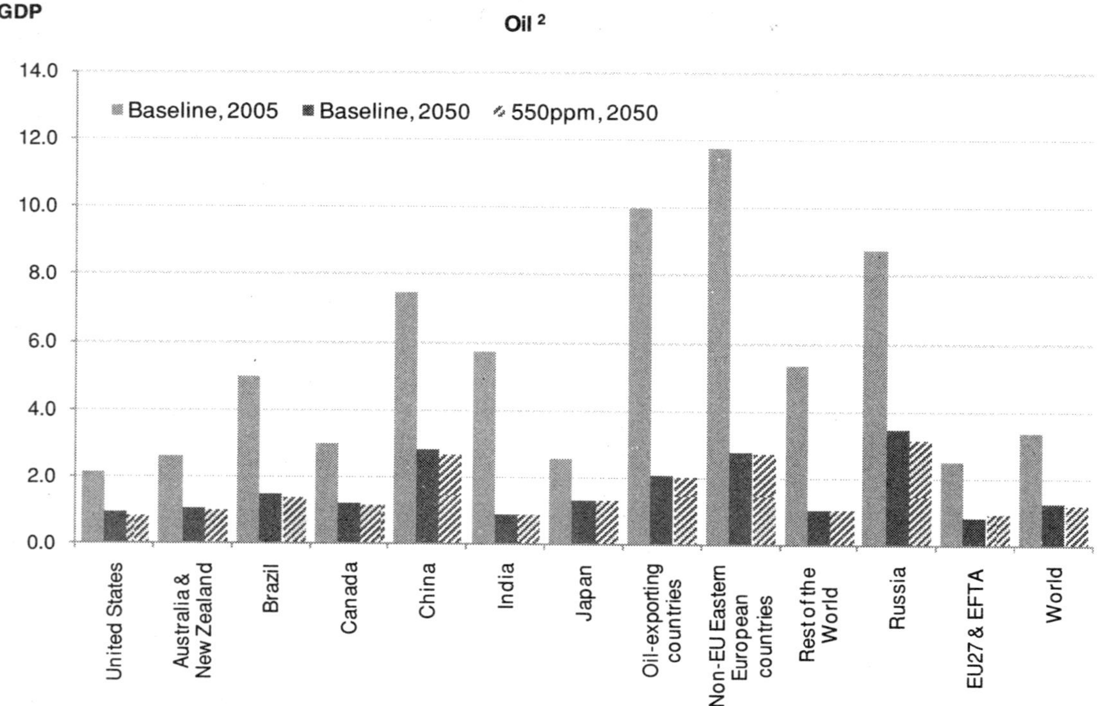

1. Energy intensity, defined as Domestic demand as a % of GDP in 2050.
2. Refined oil only.

Source: OECD ENV linkages model.

In assessing individual countries' mitigation incentives, it is important to account for the free-riding incentives associated with the world public good nature of energy security. Indeed, international action by a sufficiently large group of countries to curb their demand for fossil fuels would lower future world prices and market concentration, thereby benefiting non-participants. On the other hand, preliminary evidence suggests that free riding does little to reduce macroeconomic exposure to fossil fuel price shocks. For instance, a 50% cut in Annex I country emissions by 2050 would only marginally affect fossil fuel intensity in China and India, as the impact from reduced world prices would be offset by a rise in demand (Figure 6.12). In comparison, a 50% cut in world emissions involving action by China and India – here through a world carbon price – would have a much greater impact on the fossil fuel intensity of these two countries, and therefore on their vulnerability to oil price shocks, all other things being equal.

Figure 6.12. Projected fossil fuel intensities in world regions under different mitigation policies[1]

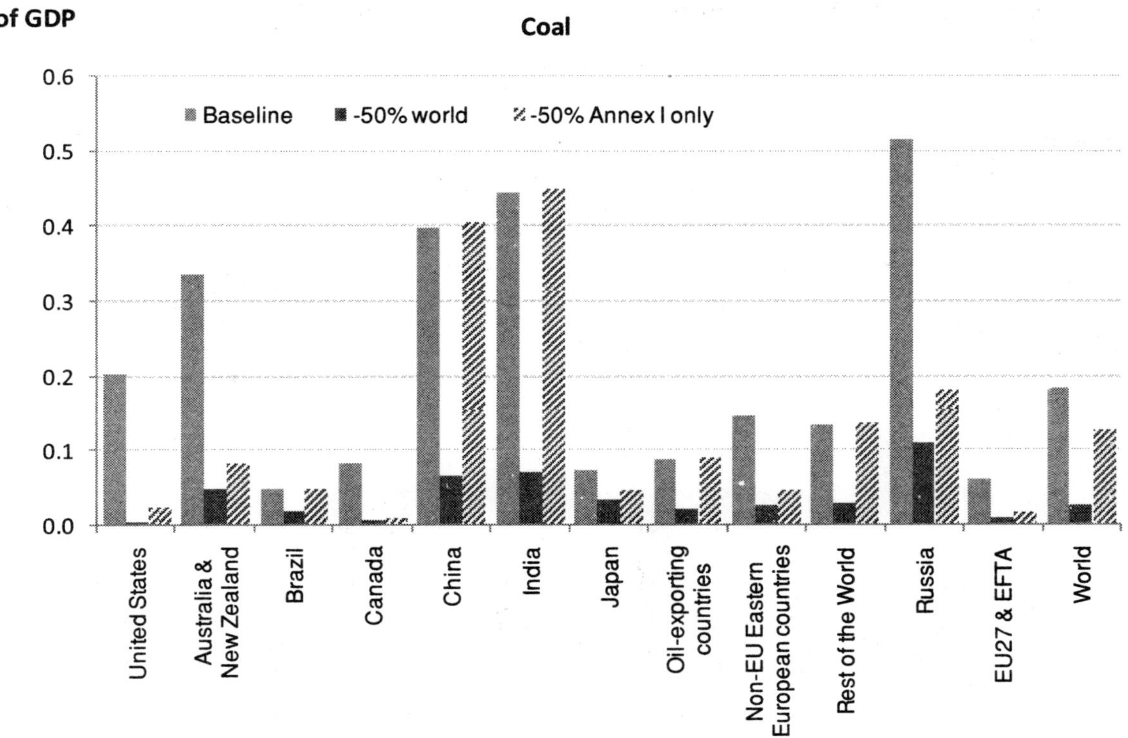

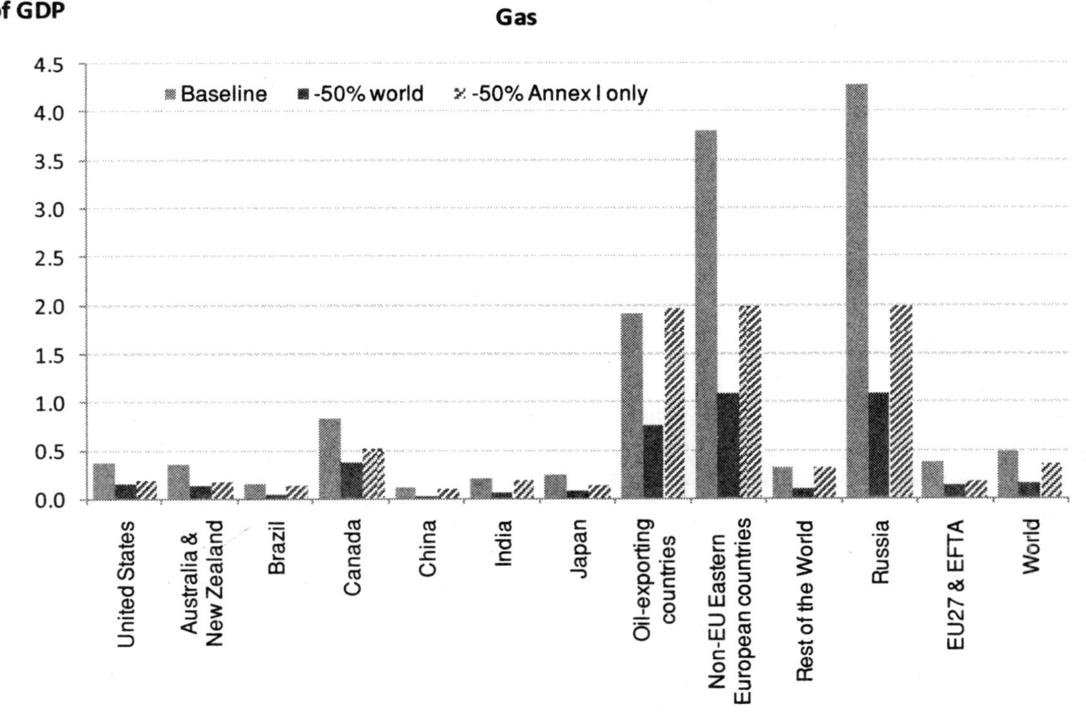

Figure 6.12 continued on next page

Figure 6.12. Projected fossil fuel intensities in world regions under different mitigation policies

(continued)

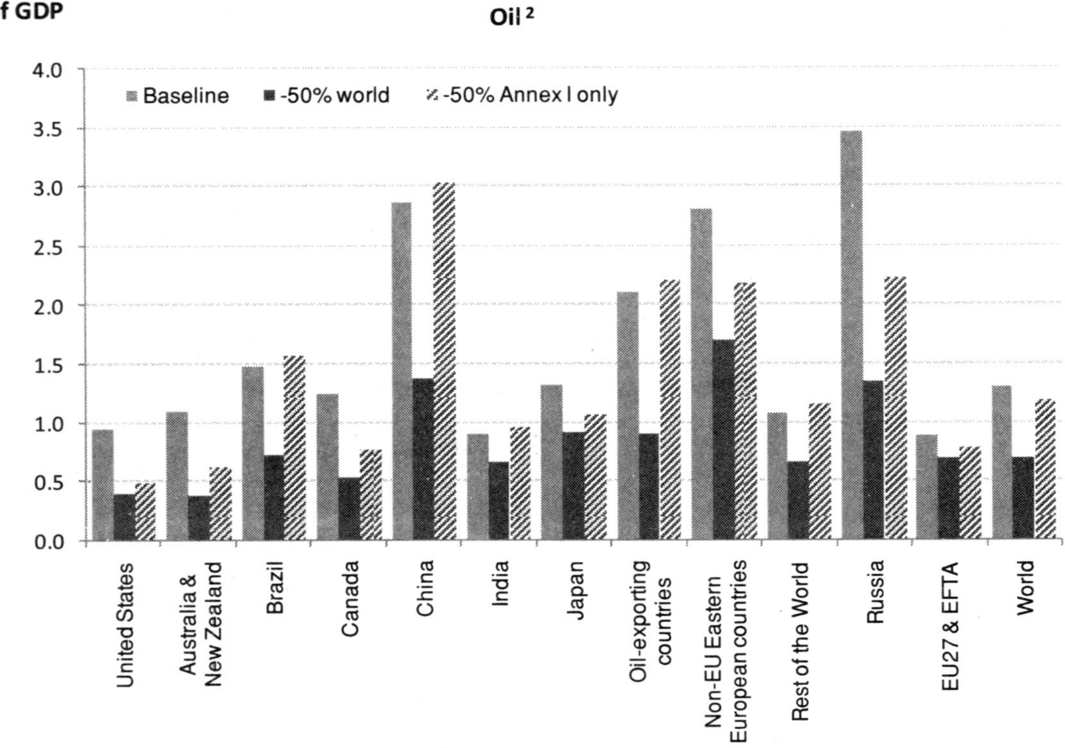

1. Energy intensity, defined as Domestic demand as a % of GDP in 2050.
2. Refined oil only.

Source: ENV linkages model.

6.3. Enhancing participation incentives through financial transfers

Achieving the UNFCCC's ultimate objective, *i.e.* stabilising GHG concentrations in the atmosphere at a level that would prevent dangerous anthropogenic interference with the climate system, will require ambitious emissions cuts in both developed and developing countries. As shown in Section 6.1, however, the large coalitions of countries needed to achieve sufficient emission reductions will be difficult to establish immediately. One condition for enhancing mitigation action in developing countries will be the establishment of implicit and/or explicit international financial transfers to support their action.

International financing mechanisms will have to evolve to encourage developing countries to increase their GHG mitigation actions. This may be achieved as follows:

- Gradual tightening of the sectoral and/or national baselines negotiated in the context of scaled-up CDMs or sectoral crediting approaches, followed by their conversion into binding sectoral caps. This evolution could be supported by international financial flows if these sectoral caps are implemented through the creation of domestic sectoral ETS that would be linked to economy-wide ETS in developed countries.
- Adoption of national emission caps. Financial incentives for this evolution could occur through the way in which emission reduction commitments are allocated or negotiated across countries. This disconnects who takes action – ensuring mitigation action takes place wherever it is least cost – from who pays for that action. Emission allocation rules could therefore be designed to shift at least some of the burden of the costs of action away from developing countries and/or countries that may have only limited incentives to participate.

Thus, to explore the impact of different allocation rules on the gains from participating in a world agreement, the illustrative 550 ppm CO_2eq scenario using the WITCH model was assessed under six simple rules:

i) Full permit auctioning (equivalent to a world carbon tax).

ii) Grandfathering, under which emission rights are allocated based on each country's share of global emissions in 2005.

iii) A per capita rule, under which the same amount of allowances is granted to every human being.

iv) An ability-to-pay rule that allocates allowances every year to each person in inverse proportion to the country's GDP per capita ratio in relation to the world average.[14]

v) A historical responsibility rule that grants allowances to each region in inverse proportion to its percentage contribution to cumulative world CO_2 emissions between 1900 and 2004 (Figure 6.13);[15] and

vi) A business-as-usual rule under which the amount of allowances allocated to non-Annex I regions covers their projected BAU emissions, close to what would happen under a well-functioning crediting mechanism with very generous baselines. This rule implies that Annex I regions set their cap at whatever level is required to meet the 550 ppm CO_2eq target – implying a negative emission level objective by 2035, given the fast projected BAU emission growth in most developing countries.[16]

The costs and gains of international mitigation action vary drastically across different allocation rules for each world region, reflecting the wide differences in their net permit exports (Figures 6.14 and 6.15). By 2050, compared with a full permit auctioning (equivalent to a world carbon tax) scenario, developed regions and non-EU Eastern Europe (including Russia) are projected to lose significantly under the historical responsibility and even more so under the "BAU" allocation rules (Figure 6.14, Panel A). Both rules also become increasingly stringent over time (Figure 6.14, Panel B). By contrast, developed regions and non-EU Eastern Europe (including Russia) gain from grandfathering (compared to full permit auctioning).

Figure 6.13. Contribution of each world region to cumulative world emissions between 1900 and 2004[1]

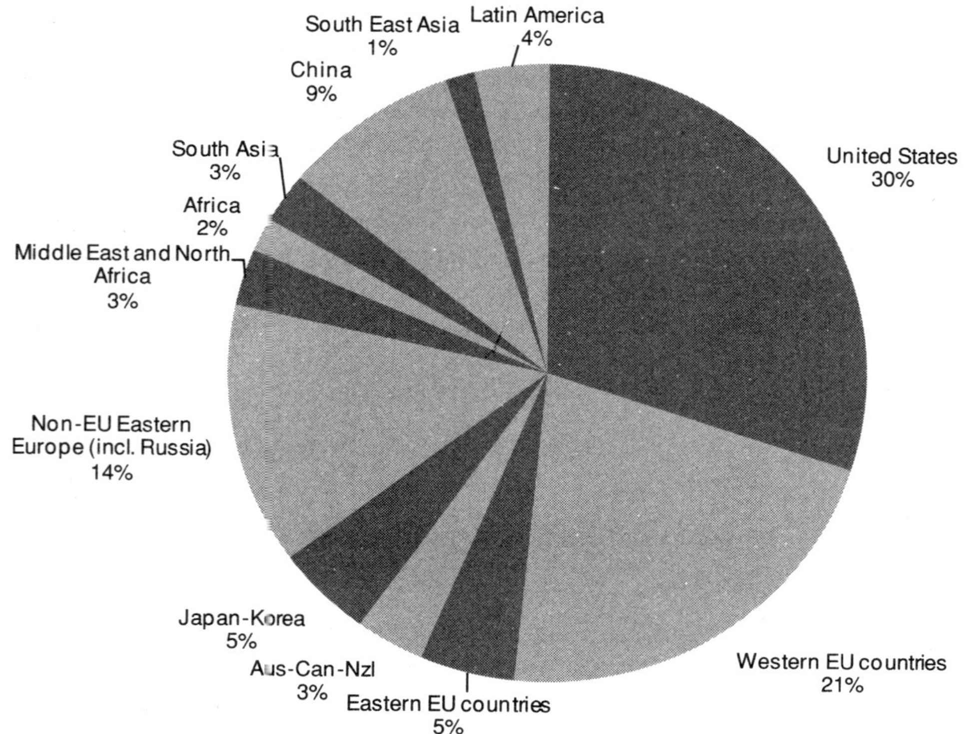

1. Excluding emissions from Land Use, Land-Use Change and Forestry.

Source: World Resources Institute (WRI).

Conversely, developing countries gain most from the BAU rule and to a lesser extent the historical responsibility allocation rule with the exception of Africa, which benefits most from an ability-to-pay rule, due to low income per capita levels. An equal-per-capita rule benefits South Asia (including India) but not China, reflecting faster projected demographic growth and lower carbon intensity in the former region. Overall, given the varied outcomes of these different scenarios, a combination of these simple allocation rules might help achieve any given distribution of mitigation costs across countries.

One result not shown here is that compared with BAU, developing regions incur smaller mitigation costs (as a per cent of BAU consumption, including the market and non-market impacts of climate change and catastrophic risks) on average for the different rules than their developed counterparts. This reflects the larger benefits from avoided climate change in developing countries, especially in the high-damage case considered here. By 2100, all developing regions are even found to *gain* from international mitigation action *regardless* of the allocation rule, compared with a BAU scenario. However, as stressed in Section 6.1, countries might gain from an agreement but still not have sufficient incentives to participate if the gain from opting out is perceived to be larger. Such free-riding incentives cannot be explored under alternative permit allocation rules, because the WITCH model can only be run in cost-effective mode in this case (see Box 6.1 and Bosetti *et al.* 2009b). Free-riding analysis requires the model to be run in cost-benefit mode, because one determinant of a country's decision to join a coalition is the optimal emission target the (remaining) coalition would set if it decided to stay outside.

Figure 6.14. Permit allocation rules substantially influence the costs of mitigation action in Annex I regions

(Difference in consumption levels relative to a full permit auctioning scenario, in %)

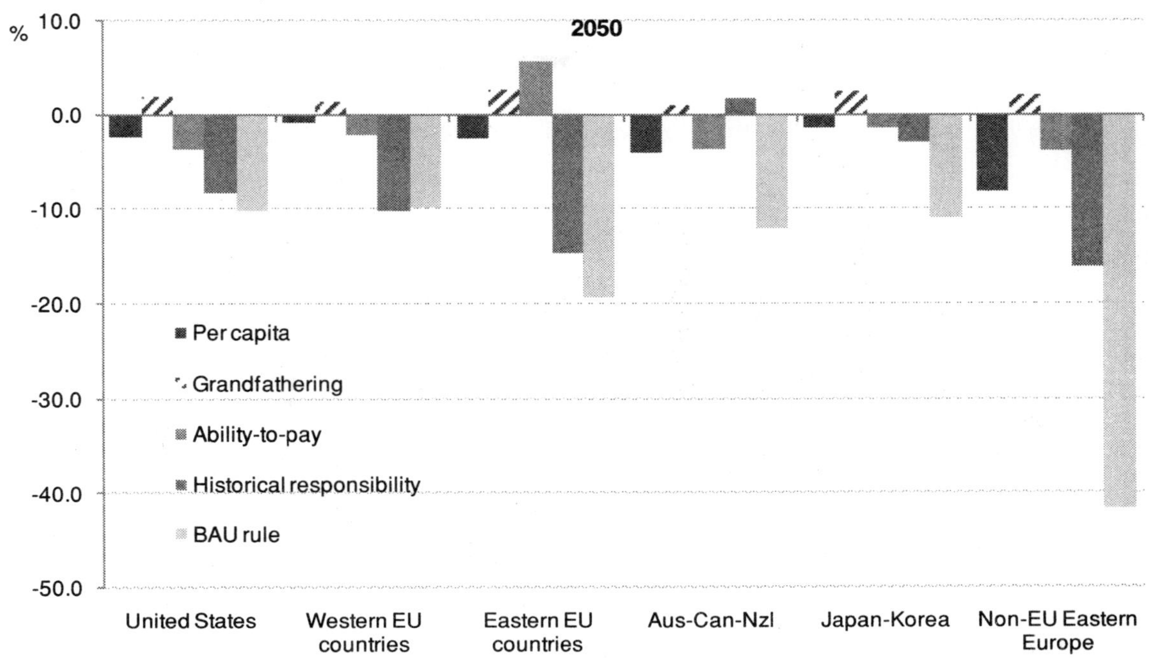

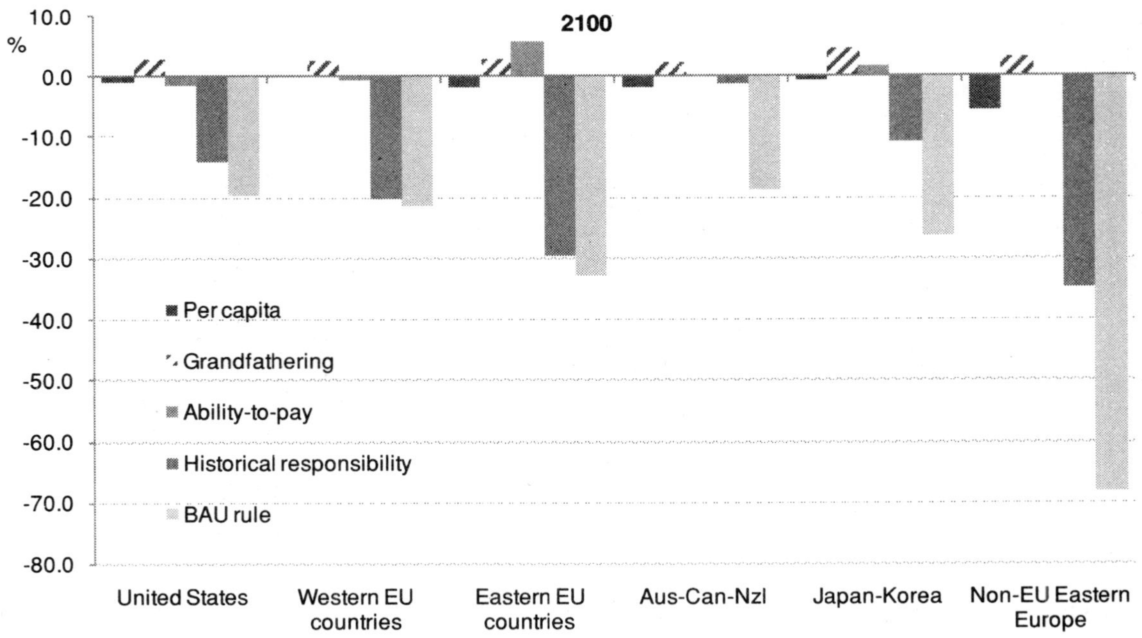

Source: WITCH model simulations.

Figure 6.15. Permit allocation rules substantially influence the costs of mitigation action in non-Annex I regions

(Difference in consumption levels relative to a full permit auctioning scenario, in %)

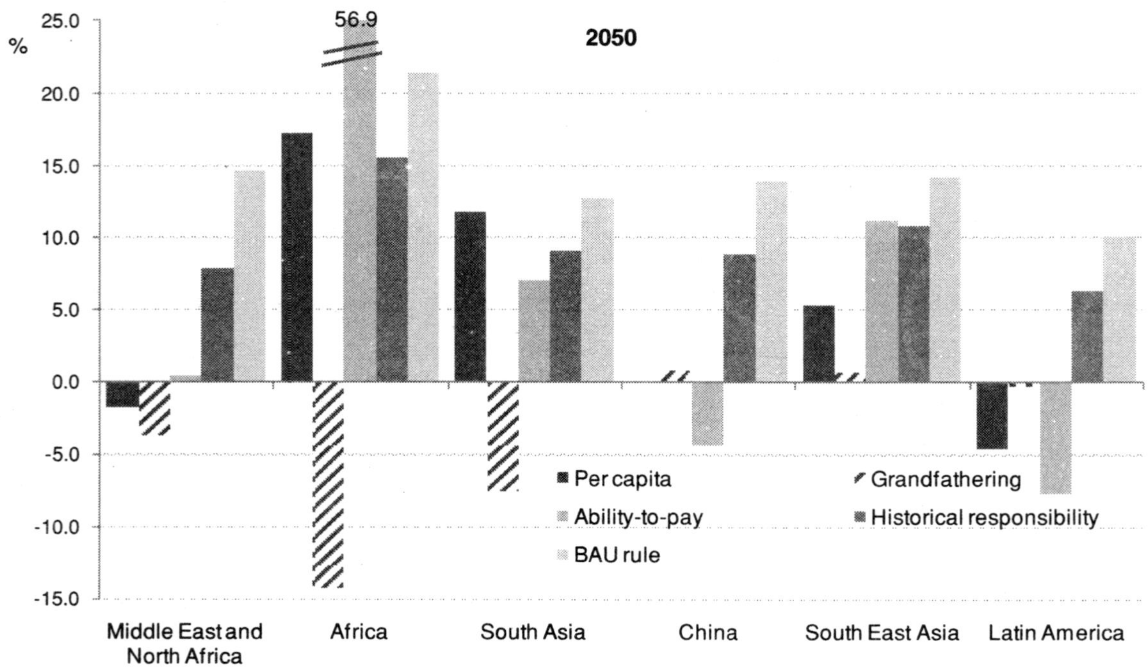

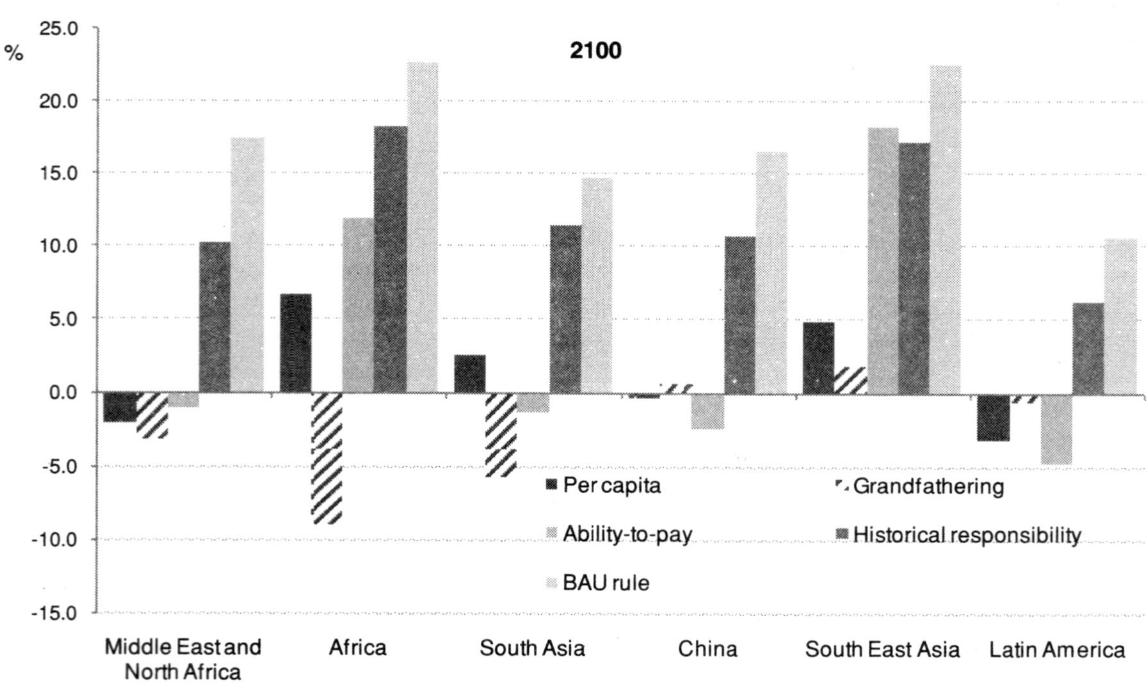

Source: WITCH model simulations.

THE ECONOMICS OF CLIMATE CHANGE MITIGATION – ISBN: 978-92-64-05606-0 – © OECD 2009

Notes

1. Zero emissions do not strictly represent a technical lower bound, however, because negative emissions could be achieved in principle through afforestation/reforestation.

2. Coalitions that exclude some developed countries are not considered in the analysis, as they are assumed to have little political relevance in practice.

3. Excessively large emission cuts over-stretch the limits of the WITCH model – and any other model, including ENV-Linkages – and imply "explosive" carbon prices and mitigation costs.

4. For more detailed analysis, see the 4th Assessment Report of the IPCC, 2007; Nordhaus and Boyer, 2000; and Jamet and Corfee-Morlot, 2009.

5. The usual framework for performing such valuation is the "Ramsey rule", which states that in an infinite horizon, single good, deterministic optimal growth model, the rate for discounting future consumption is: Social discount rate = $\mu *g$ + pure utility discount rate, where μ is the elasticity of the marginal utility of income and g is the future growth rate of the economy. Therefore the social discount rate depends on two main factors: *i)* future economic growth, which lowers the incentive of (poorer) current generations to pay the cost of addressing climate change; and, *ii)* the weight current generations assign to the welfare of future ones, *i.e.* the so-called pure utility discount rate. The former implies lower incentives for high-growth emerging countries than for their developed counterparts. The latter shapes the incentives of all. There is a longstanding controversy regarding both, in particular the pure utility discount rate (Weitzman, 2001). Consistent with a long line of economists (*e.g.* Ramsey, 1928; Harrod, 1948; Solow, 1974), Stern (2007) argues on ethical grounds for a near-zero value, while others dismiss this assumption on the grounds that it is inconsistent with actual individual behaviour (*e.g.* Nordhaus, 2007; Weitzman, 2007a). Therefore two values are considered, while μ equals 1.

6. These regional GDP cost estimates exclude the GDP impact of damage, so as to focus only on abatement costs.

7. In this framework, non-EU Eastern Europe (including Russia) and the Middle East lose more from being highly carbon intensive than from being fossil fuel producers, because they can expect the coalition to cut world emissions significantly – and thereby to exert downward pressure on world fossil fuel prices – regardless of whether they participate. However, an unexplored option is that fossil fuel producers might instead collude and behave strategically, cutting output and raising fuel prices, thereby internalising the carbon price.

8. For instance, projected world BAU emission growth is somewhat higher in WITCH than in the OECD model ENV-Linkages (100% versus 85% over the period 2005-2050).

9. The model includes fine particulate matter ($PM_{2.5}$) from the combustion of solid or liquid fuels in both rural and urban areas – which account for a large amount of the health damages of outdoor LAP – as well as secondary aerosols (SO_2, NOx) from the combustion of oil and coal and NH3 from agriculture.

10. The impact of ozone on health is not treated as a co-benefit but is included in the damages from climate change. The impacts of climate change are represented in a stylised way through region-specific market and non-market damages functions. Non-market damages depend on the average global temperature level and include the damages from exposure to high ozone concentrations.

11. However, for stringent levels of LAP reductions, structural adjustments would be needed that would incidentally lead to GHG emissions reductions. More broadly, there are synergies and higher returns

from controlling both GHG and LAP and from maximising the benefits across these areas (see Bollen *et al.,* 2008; 2009).

12. This is only true if expectations of future carbon price increases do not induce OPEC producers to raise output – and thereby deplete their reserves – more than assumed over the coming decades (see above).

13. However, the broad expansion of CCS would change this situation, as it would make it possible for countries to cut their emissions while continuing to rely heavily on coal.

14. There is no straightforward way to implement an ability-to-pay rule in practice. It has been applied here in three steps. First, the amount (X_i) of world allowances that each region *i* would receive if allocation was proportional to the ratio of GDP per capita to the world average is computed as $\frac{\text{total world allowances}}{\text{world population}} * \frac{\text{GDP per capita of region i}}{\text{average world GDP per capita}} * (\text{population of region i})$

Secondly, the inverse ($1/X_i$) of this amount is computed for each region. Unlike the sum of X_i, the sum of ($1/X_i$) is not equal to total world emissions. Therefore, in a third step, a normalisation is applied, *i.e.* each region's share (in %) of total world allowances is computed as $\frac{(1/X_i)}{\sum_i \{1/X_i\}}$.

15. This also requires a normalisation along the lines of the ability-to-pay rule (see footnote above).

16. The overall Annex I cap is assumed to then be allocated across Annex I regions on a per-capita basis.

ISBN: 978-92-64-05606-0
The Economics of Climate Change Mitigation
Policies and Options for Global Action beyond 2012

Chapter 7

Building Political Support for Global Action

This chapter reviews the climate policy instruments that are already in use or that are planned to start in the near future. This provides a basis for investigating how political support can be built up for global action. It compares mitigation costs and emission reductions (comparability of effort) across countries for a wide range of carbon price levels. It investigates whether the emission reduction targets for 2020 that have been declared or suggested by different countries are sufficient to achieve a pathway consistent with an ambitious GHG stabilisation target. It discusses options for international support, such as financial support for mitigation action in developing countries, technology transfer and support for adapting to a changing climate.

Key Messages

- *Most developed countries have implemented a variety of policy instruments to limit GHG emissions, and many more policies are currently planned or under consideration, including in a growing number of developing countries. While earlier policies such as standards for electric appliances and taxes for oil consumption have often been brought in primarily for other purposes (e.g. reduced dependence on foreign energy), they do contribute to lower GHG emissions. More recent policies directly aimed at mitigating climate change include market-based instruments such as carbon taxes and emissions trading schemes (ETS), which are already in place in several OECD countries including all EU member states. In some instances, these instruments are delivering encouraging results and the experience serves as a basis for learning and lessons for other countries as they design similar instruments.*

- *Other types of policies, such as subsidies to first generation biofuels in the European Union, the United States and Canada may also contribute to limit GHG, but do so at a much higher cost than market-based alternatives, calling into question their appropriateness as a tool to mitigate climate change.*

- *Both total costs and emission reductions achieved for a given uniform carbon price vary substantially across regions. For several countries/regions, such as Australia and New Zealand, Canada and the United States, carbon prices of at least USD 50 per tonne of CO_2eq would be required if emissions are to return to 1990 levels by 2020. The analysis illustrates that comparability of efforts across countries will depend on the indicator used and might imply quite different emission targets.*

- *In the lead up to the UNFCCC Conference of Parties in Copenhagen at the end of 2009, several countries and the European Union have adopted, declared or suggested emission reduction targets for 2020. A preliminary assessment of these targets indicates that they would be insufficient to prevent temperatures from increasing by more than 2°C above pre-industrial levels, which is the objective recently supported by major developing and developed countries. Somewhat less ambitious stabilisation targets (such as 3°C) might still be achievable, but even that would imply far more significant efforts after 2020, at a higher cost. Hence, if ambitious objectives are to be achieved at a reasonable cost, enhanced commitments and broader cooperation will be required, including by developing countries.*

- *One way to do so is by improving international transfer mechanisms across countries. To that end, a variety of options can be envisaged, not least the scaling-up of public finances for capacity building for mitigation action. Financing can also stimulate action where the coverage of emission sources is small and/or there are large market imperfections, such as in the area of R&D and technology transfers. A first step in this regard would be to remove policies that work against the international deployment of clean technology, such as the barriers to foreign trade and investment and the weak intellectual property rights. Financing for adaptation to climate change will also be important for developing countries.*

Introduction

The previous chapters have showed that broad participation in an agreement with ambitious global action is both essential and difficult to reach. The current chapter takes stock of what is already being done. Section 7.1 reviews the instruments that are currently in use globally and focuses especially on the coverage of emissions trading schemes. The overview clearly shows the rapidly evolving climate policies that are implemented or under consideration in most developed countries. Section 7.2 assesses the developed countries' already declared or suggested targets, and finds that these would result in a reduction of emissions in Annex I countries of 9% to 14% by 2020 relative to 1990 levels. This would be clearly insufficient to put world GHG emissions on a pathway to stabilising concentrations at even moderately ambitious levels (*e.g.* a 550 ppm CO_2eq pathway). Section 7.3 focuses on policies that can build support for action across regions, including international financial and technology transfers to support developing regions. Such devices include not only market-based mitigation financing tools (*e.g.* via the crediting mechanisms discussed above), but also direct public funding of mitigation action; international financing of R&D, technology transfers and support for adaptation to climate change; as well as various ways for allocating binding emission targets across countries over the longer term.

7.1. A review of the instruments currently in use

Many countries have implemented some of these instruments either to directly limit GHG emissions or to limit local air pollutants, but with some indirect impact on GHG emissions. For instance, most countries have technology or performance standards for electrical appliances and buildings, as well as taxes on oil consumption. OECD countries have also introduced a wide range of support to low-emission technology deployment, especially in the electricity sector. This support includes fiscal incentives, quota-based schemes or public procurement and infrastructure policies. Perhaps the two most prominent recent instruments have been feed-in tariffs and tradable green certificates. Feed-in tariffs are essentially a fixed price support per unit of electricity produced that is guaranteed over a certain period. These have operated in *e.g.* Germany, Spain, and Denmark (until recently). Tradable green certificates are provided against a requirement that a fixed share of electricity be generated from renewable sources. They include allowances for trading among firms and have been used in *e.g.* Australia, Italy and the United Kingdom. In principle, and in the absence of uncertainty, both instruments could be designed to be equivalent. In practice, given that they provide price guarantees over relatively long periods, feed-in tariffs may be less efficient, as price support fails to adjust spontaneously to cost changes. Also, price support can differ across technologies, while tradable certificates are usually more neutral.[1]

Government support for biofuel production can be substantial (Table 7.1) and has risen drastically in recent years. If policies remain unchanged, this support could reach a total of about USD 25 billion per year in the European Union, the United States and Canada between 2013 and 2017 (OECD, 2008d).[2,3] Available evidence suggests that the implicit costs of ethanol subsidies typically exceed USD 300 per tonne of CO_2 avoided, and sometimes reach much higher levels. For example, a recent OECD study estimates that support policies to current – so-called first-generation – biofuels in the European Union, the United States and Canada could come at a cost equivalent of about USD 960-USD 1 700 per tonne of CO_2 saved (OECD, 2008d).[4] Biodiesel subsidies are lower, but still far above average estimates of the (marginal) social cost of CO_2 or the CO_2 price levels currently prevailing in the EU-ETS.[5] Furthermore, such estimates do not account for any indirect effects of biofuel subsidies on emissions from land use changes – not least deforestation – that may result from induced pressures on land and food prices, and they ignore the additional social cost from other potential negative environmental externalities.[6]

Table 7.1. Applied tariffs on undernatured ethyl alcohol are substantial in several countries, 2007

	Applied MFN tariff (local currency or ad valorem rate)	Ad valorem equivalent pre-tariff unit value of EUR 0.50/litre	Exceptions (in addition to other WTO member economies with which country has a free-trade agreement) or notes
Australia	5% + AUD 38.143/litre	52%	United States, New Zealand
Brazil	0%	0%	Lowered from 20% in March 2006
Canada	CAD 0.0492/litre	6%	Free Trade Agreement partners
European Union	EUR 19.2/hectolitre	38%	European Free Trade Association countries, developing countries in General System of Preferences
Switzerland	CHF 35 per 100kg	34%	EU, developing countries in General System of Preferences
United States	2.5% + USD 0.51/gallon	22%	Free Trade Agreement partners, Caribbean Basin Initiative partners

Source: OECD International Transport Forum (2007).

Market instruments such as taxes and emissions trading schemes (ETSs) have also been introduced in several countries or regions and are planned or under discussion in other ones. In most cases, the purpose is to help countries to meet their obligations under the Kyoto protocol. Countries that have developed market instruments have generally favoured ETSs over a carbon tax. There are good reasons for this choice, as discussed in Chapter 2, in particular the higher political acceptability of ETSs. In addition, with ETSs spreading internationally, there are opportunities to link such schemes together and to have access to the CDM. Both options would lower the cost of achieving country/region level emission reductions targets (Chapter 4). Nonetheless, energy/carbon taxes have been introduced in several European countries, including, Finland, Norway, the Netherlands, Sweden and Switzerland and is under discussion in France, but in these cases they are seen as a complement to the ETS rather than as a substitute for it.

The EU ETS, which is now in the middle of its first commitment period, is the largest system in place (Chapter 4). The system has successfully led to the emergence of a carbon price but it has also encountered a number of problems. It therefore provides useful lessons for emerging emissions trading schemes (Box 7.1). Apart from the EU ETS and the recently launched New Zealand emissions trading schemes, other schemes in place are sub-national (Table 7.2). A number of other countries are currently designing or discussing some form of ETS, including most Annex I countries as well as a number of non-Annex I countries, notably Mexico and South Korea. Although existing ETSs are largely different in their design, they do share some characteristics:

- There are few formal links among existing ETSs, other than between some European country schemes such as the Norwegian ETS and the EU ETS, although the Kyoto protocol allows countries with commitments to trade the allowances that have been assigned to them under the protocol (assigned amount units).
- In all schemes, a significant share of permits is allocated for free, although most schemes plan to gradually introduce auctioning.

 THE ECONOMICS OF CLIMATE CHANGE MITIGATION – ISBN: 978-92-64-05606-0 – © OECD 2009

- Most schemes allow part of the emission reduction to be achieved outside of the scheme through the use of a crediting mechanism, but the rules governing the use of offsets differ between schemes.

Box 7.1 Lessons from the European Union Emissions Trading Scheme

The EU-ETS was introduced in 2005 as a tool to help EU countries meet their obligations under the Kyoto protocol. After a three-year trial period (Phase I, 2005-2007), a commitment period (Phase II) is running from 2008 until 2012 to coincide with the commitment period of the Kyoto protocol, and is scheduled to continue beyond that horizon. The scheme covers emissions from energy-intensive industrial sectors, representing around half of European emissions.

The trial period aimed to develop the infrastructure and provide a first experience with an international cap-and-trade system covering GHG emissions. It was not intended to reduce GHG emissions, especially as it quickly turned out that the amount of emission rights issued only slightly constrained overall emissions. The system has successfully led to the emergence of a carbon price and the volume of transactions has steadily increased since 2005. Nonetheless, it has also encountered a number of problems, and from this perspective provides useful lessons for the design of emissions trading schemes.

Lack of banking provisions and price volatility

Both spot and future price fluctuations have been very large under the EU-ETS, and the gap between both prices has also been highly volatile (Figure 7.1). In April 2006, several member states reported 2005 emissions to be below market expectations, causing excess supply in the spot market for allowances. Because banking between the trial and the first commitment period was not allowed,[1] the spot price fell close to zero, while the future price – which is determined by expectations of future supply and demand for allocations – remained stable. Had banking been allowed, as is the case under Phase II, allowances would have been stored for future use and the spot price collapse would have been avoided.

The impact of price fluctuations on firms' decisions under Phase I was mitigated by the development of derivative markets. A firm that seeks to purchase rights to cover its emissions or hedge against the risk of unexpected emission changes can either purchase allowances in the spot market or purchase a future contract due in the compliance year, *i.e.* the year when allowances have to be surrendered. Transaction volumes steadily increased on both primary and derivative markets since the inception of the scheme, with transactions in the future market being driven more by financial considerations (hedging and speculation) than by the need for compliance. Although over-the-counter trading remains the dominant form of trading, one-third of trade now takes place on exchanges. The main exchange, the London Exchange ECX, provides a range of derivatives including futures, options and swaps. Evidence suggests there has been no lack of intermediaries to facilitate trading among parties and that the market developed in a fashion similar to other financial and commodity markets (Ellerman and Joskow, 2008; Uhrig-Homburg and Wagner, 2008).

Allocation rules and perverse emission-reduction incentives

The allocation of emission rights to individual emitters, which was left to member countries, raised a number of concerns:

- Not only were permits typically allocated based on recent emissions levels, but individual emitters expected this "grandfathering" rule to continue to apply in future phases, thereby undermining emission reduction incentives compared with a situation where allowances would have been allocated once and for all (Neuhoff *et al.* 2006).
- All member states guaranteed a certain volume of free allowances to new entrants on the basis of their expected emissions.2 While this provision was intended to boost competition by compensating new entrants for the cost of purchasing allowances, it may also have created incentives to set up fossil fuel power plants and bias technology choices towards more CO_2-intensive options (Buchner *et al.* 2006; Matthes and Ziesing, 2008).

Box 7.1 continued on next page

Box 7.1 Lessons from the European Union Emissions Trading Scheme

(continued)

- Virtually all industries received enough allowances to fully cover their emissions, with the exception of the electricity sector. The two main reasons for constraining the electricity sector were its lack of exposure to international competition and the existence of cheap abatement opportunities, typically by switching from coal to natural gas.

The EU-ETS is a downstream system (*i.e.* applied at the point of emission) that covers the main energy-intensive sectors. The threshold for inclusion in the ETS (determined by heat input) is very low, hence a large number of small installations with a low contribution to emissions are included. This raises data collection and monitoring problems, as well as sizeable transaction costs (Buchner *et al.* 2006). In particular, reporting and verification requirements impose costs on small installations that are disproportionate to their emissions. Perhaps more importantly, the downstream nature of the scheme could be an important barrier to extending the scheme to other, currently non-covered, emission sources. One answer to these problems might be to move towards an upstream scheme covering refineries, gas terminals, coal mines etc.[3] This would lower overall transaction costs and expand the coverage of carbon pricing, with small installations facing similar emission abatement incentives than under a downstream scheme provided carbon prices upstream are fully passed onto them.

Figure 7.1. Carbon price fluctuations in the European Union Emission Trading Scheme have been large

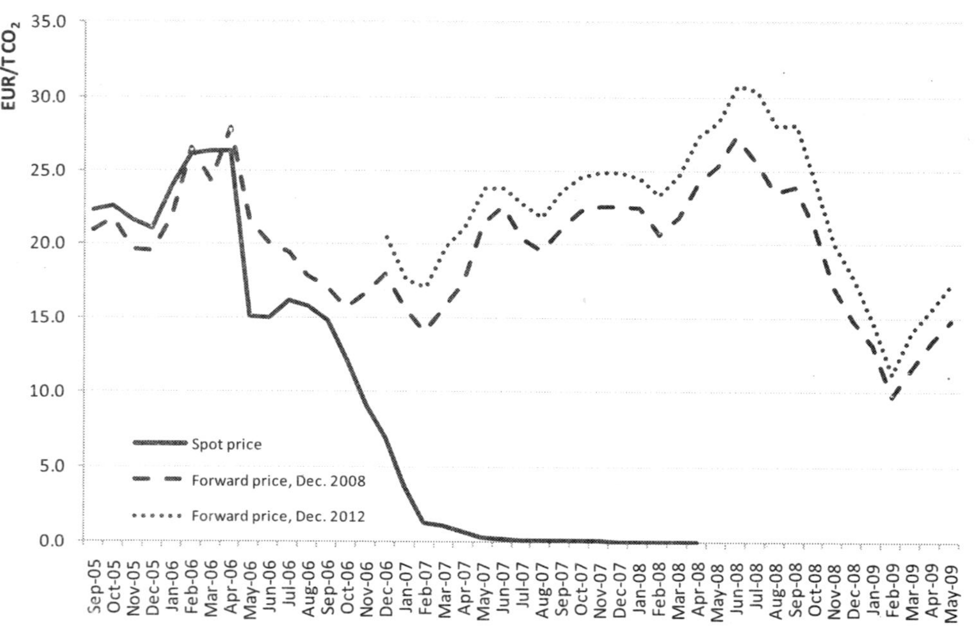

Source: Caisse des dépôts (2009).

1. Banking is the ability to transfer an emission right from one period to another one in the future. The reason that banking was not allowed was to prevent any compliance failure during the trial period to spill over into the second trading period, thereby reducing the chances of meeting the Kyoto reduction target.
2. The proportion of free allowances allocated to new entrants varied from 0.5% in Germany and Poland to 6.5% in the United Kingdom.
3. Imported fossil fuels would also be covered.

Even though several ETSs have developed internationally (Table 7.2), the share of world emissions currently covered and the size of emission reduction commitments are far from sufficient to stabilise GHG concentration at a safe level. Therefore future commitments by major emitters will be key to determine which target will be achievable and at what cost. Furthermore, it will be worth looking at how these schemes can be linked and expanded to ultimately achieve a global carbon price.

Table 7.2. Many emissions trading schemes exist or are projected

Countries/regions	Status	Start date	Main features
EU	In place	2005	• The EU ETS was introduced as a tool to help EU countries to meet their obligations under the Kyoto protocol target and is now planned to be extended after to 2012 to meet the EU target (to reduce GHG emissions by 20% by 2020 compared with 1990 levels). • The scheme was piloted during a trial period (2005-2007) and continued with the first commitment period (2008-2012). It covers half of European emissions and the coverage is planned to be extended. • Free allowances have been granted for the trial period but auctioning is gradually developed in the second and third phases. • Banking of permits was not allowed during the trial period but is allowed for the following periods. • Countries can use emission credits from third countries (JI/CDM credits) but there are some constraints on the amount of emission reductions that can be achieved through these mechanisms.
Norway	In place	2005	Participation in EU ETS from 2008
Switzerland, voluntary emissions trading	In place	2008	• Switzerland introduced a CO_2 tax for fossil fuels in 2008. • A voluntary ETS has also been introduced and firms that decide to participate in the ETS are exempt from the tax. Allowances have been allocated for free according to the 2008-2012 target negotiated within the Kyoto Protocol.
United Kingdom, national	Planned	2010	• A UK Emissions Trading Scheme was operating between 2002 and 2006. The United Kingdom is part of the EU ETS, but a national scheme is planned in order to cover CO_2 emissions that are not already covered by the EU ETS.
Malta, Cyprus, Slovenia, Estonia, Latvia, Lithuania, Bulgaria, Romania	In place	2005 (except Bulgaria & Romania which joined in 2007)	Participating in EU ETS
Liechtenstein	In place	2008	Linking to EU ETS through the European Free Trade Association (EFTA); also linked to Swiss trading system

Table 7.2 continued on next page

Table 7.2. Many emissions trading schemes exist or are projected

(continued)

United States			
Regional GHG initiative (RGGI), covering ten North-eastern and Mid-Atlantic states	In place	2009	• CO_2 emissions from the power sector have to be reduced by 10% by 2018. • The majority of allowances are auctioned. • Offsets can be used but are limited to a number of projects within states participating in the scheme and outside the capped electric power generation sector.
Voluntary Chicago Climate Exchange (CCX)	In place	2003	• CCX is a voluntary cap and trade system. CCX emitting members make a voluntary but legally-binding commitment to meet annual GHG emission reduction targets. Those who reduce below the targets have surplus allowances to sell or bank; those who emit above the targets comply by purchasing a CCX carbon financial instrument. • In Phase I (2003-2006), members committed to reduce emissions by at least 1% a year, for a total reduction of 4% below the baseline. In Phase II (2007-2010), CCX members commit to a reduction schedule that requires 2010 emission reductions to be at least 6% below the baseline.
California	Planned	2010	• The Global Warming Solutions Act signed in 2006 caps GHG emissions at 1990 levels by 2020. Against this background, California has released plans for the introduction of an emissions trading scheme in 2012 and is working closely with other states and provinces in the Western Climate Initiative (WCI) to design a regional cap-and-trade programme (see below). • Regulations to implement the cap-and-trade system would need to be developed by beginning of 2011.
Western Climate Initiative (WCI)[1],	Planned	2010-2020 depending on state	• The target is to lower GHG emissions by 15% from 2005 levels by 2020 • When fully implemented in 2015, the programme is expected to cover nearly 90% of the GHG emissions in WCI states and provinces. • Each member state/province has the flexibility to decide how best to allocate allowances. At least 10% of allowances at the start of the programme, increasing to at least 25% by 2020, will have to be auctioned. • Offsets can be used under certain conditions.
Midwestern Regional GHG Reduction Accord[2]	Planned		• The target and design of this ETS has yet to be decided. However, the Advisory Group recommends a 20% emission cut by 2020 relative to 2005 levels, and a 80% cut by 2050.
Federal	Under discussion	Federal Waxman-Markey proposed for 2012	• At the time of writing, this federal bill was passed by the House of Representatives and is under discussion at the Senate. The exact target and design features of the proposed ETS are not yet known. However, assessment of the draft bill by Environmental Protection Agency and the Pew Center on Global Climate Change suggests that the target would be to reduce emissions by less than 20% below 2005 levels by 2020. • A significant amount of this reduction could be achieved through offsets and a relatively large of allowances would be granted for free, at least in the short-run.

Table 7.2 continued on next page

Table 7.2. Many emissions trading schemes exist or are projected

(continued)

Canada, national	Under discussion		• A national scheme is under discussion
Alberta	In place	2007	• Alberta facilities that emit more than 100 000 tonnes of greenhouse gases a year have to reduce their emissions intensity by 12% by 2010 (relative to 2007 levels), to stabilise emissions by 2020 and then to reduce them by 14% in 2050 relative to 2005 levels. • Facilities can meet their targets by reducing their emissions, buying Alberta-based credits or contributing to a fund (the Climate Change and Emissions Management Fund), which invests in various areas, including energy conservation and efficiency, carbon capture and storage, development of carbon offset projects and climate change adaptation.
Mexico	Planned		• Implementation of a national cap-and-trade scheme has been initiated in 2009 • Several states are observers of the WCI (see above).
Japan			
Japan's Voluntary Emissions Trading System JVETS	In place	2005	• This scheme allows companies to voluntarily pledge to reduce emissions each year by a certain amount (20% in 2007) relative to their average over the previous three years. • One-third of the cost of new facilities to reduce emissions is borne by the government. Firms that fail to achieve their objective must purchase credits for those that have achieved larger-than-targeted reductions or return the subsidy to the government. • At this stage, the participating companies in JVETS account for less than 1% of CO_2 emissions from the industrial sector.
Tokyo emissions trading scheme	Planned		• Supposed to start in 2010
New Zealand	In place	2008-2012 depending on sector	• The New Zealand ETS includes the forestry sector. It is planned to be extended to other sectors progressively and to cover most sectors by 2013. • The target is defined by the Kyoto protocol and targets for post-2012 will have to be decided. The agricultural and energy-intensive sectors would mostly receive free allocations until 2019 and then allowances would be progressively auctioned.
Australia	Under discussion	National 2010	• The introduction of the proposed ETS has been postponed and the design features and targets of the scheme are still under discussion.
NSW/ACT	In place	NSW/ACT 2003	• The act requires individual electricity retailers and certain other parties who buy or sell electricity in NSW to meet mandatory benchmarks based on the size of their share of the electricity market. The benchmark progressively dropped to represent a reduction, in 2007, of 5% below the Kyoto Protocol baseline year of 1989-90. Emissions per capita will then have to be stabilised at this level until 2021.
Korea	Under discussion		• Legislation proposed in 2008, discussing 2020 target.

1. The Western Climate Initiative includes seven US states and four Canadian provinces: Arizona, California, Montana, New Mexico, Oregon, Utah, Washington, and British Columbia, Manitoba, Ontario, Quebec.
2. The accord involves 9 Midwestern governors and 2 Canadian premiers, who have signed on to participate or observe in the *Midwestern Greenhouse Gas Reduction Accord.*

7.2. Comparing mitigation costs and emission reductions across countries

"Common but differentiated responsibilities and respective capabilities" are a key principle of the UNFCCC and undoubtedly will guide decision-making on the commitments and actions that different countries take on to address climate change. Against this background, the aim of this section is to assess the environmental and economic impacts of different emission reduction targets or carbon prices for Annex I countries.

Based on simulations using the ENV-Linkages model, Figure 7.2 shows the emissions reductions that would be achieved in Annex I countries or regions (in terms of percentage change compared to 1990 emission levels) for a variety of carbon taxes applied across all Annex I countries. This is plotted against the total cost of this action in terms of GDP loss for each country/region.[7,8] This exercise facilitates comparing the economic costs of different mitigation efforts across countries, assuming a cost-effective distribution of efforts (*i.e.* a uniform carbon tax). It may, therefore, help inform the discussion on country commitments, along with other indicators that may be relevant for deciding the distribution of the costs of global mitigation action across countries.[9] Both total costs and emission reductions achieved for a given uniform carbon price vary substantially across regions. For several countries/regions (Australia and New Zealand, Canada, the United States), carbon prices of at least USD 50 per tonne of CO_2eq would be required if emissions are to return to 1990 levels by 2020. The curves in Figure 7.2 illustrate that comparability of efforts across countries will depend upon the indicator used and might imply quite different emission targets.

A similar analysis can also be used to assess the targets that Annex 1 countries have already announced or suggested. Box 7.2 describes how the targets are assessed and translated into simulation scenarios. Table 7.3 presents the impacts of these scenarios. Panel A reflects the minimum commitments that developed countries have pledged. The scenario with ambitious Annex I action (Panel B) further assumes full linking of ETSs between Annex I countries. Both scenarios assume there is access to CDM offsets, but use of these is limited to 20% of emission reduction requirements.[10]

Implementing the unilaterally committed emission targets (panel A) would reduce Annex I countries' emissions in 2020 by 17% compared with BAU, or 5% below their 1990 levels; including the credits from offsets, the reduction in Annex I emissions amounts to 9% from 1990. The more ambitious targets presented in panel B lead to larger emission reductions within Annex I (-8% from 1990 levels).[11] Including credits from offsets, these imply a reduction of 14% from 1990 levels in Annex I countries. Given the projected growth in BAU emissions in non-Annex I countries, world emissions in 2020 would still rise above their 2005 levels, with 24% and 22% in the unilateral commitments and Annex I ambitious action scenarios, respectively (compared to +35% in the BAU projection). These reductions are insufficient to put emissions onto a concentration stabilisation pathway of 450 ppm CO_2eq. Indeed, the IPCC 2007 mitigation assessment suggests that reductions by Annex I countries as a group of at least 25% from 1990 levels would be required to achieve this, and "substantial deviation from baseline" in many non-Annex I countries before 2020 (Gupta *et al.*, 2007). Although inter-temporal flexibility in the pathways and overshooting options might still make ambitious stabilisation targets achievable, it would be at a much higher cost after 2020.

Figure 7.2. For many Annex I countries, substantial carbon taxes are required to let emissions in 2020 return to 1990 levels

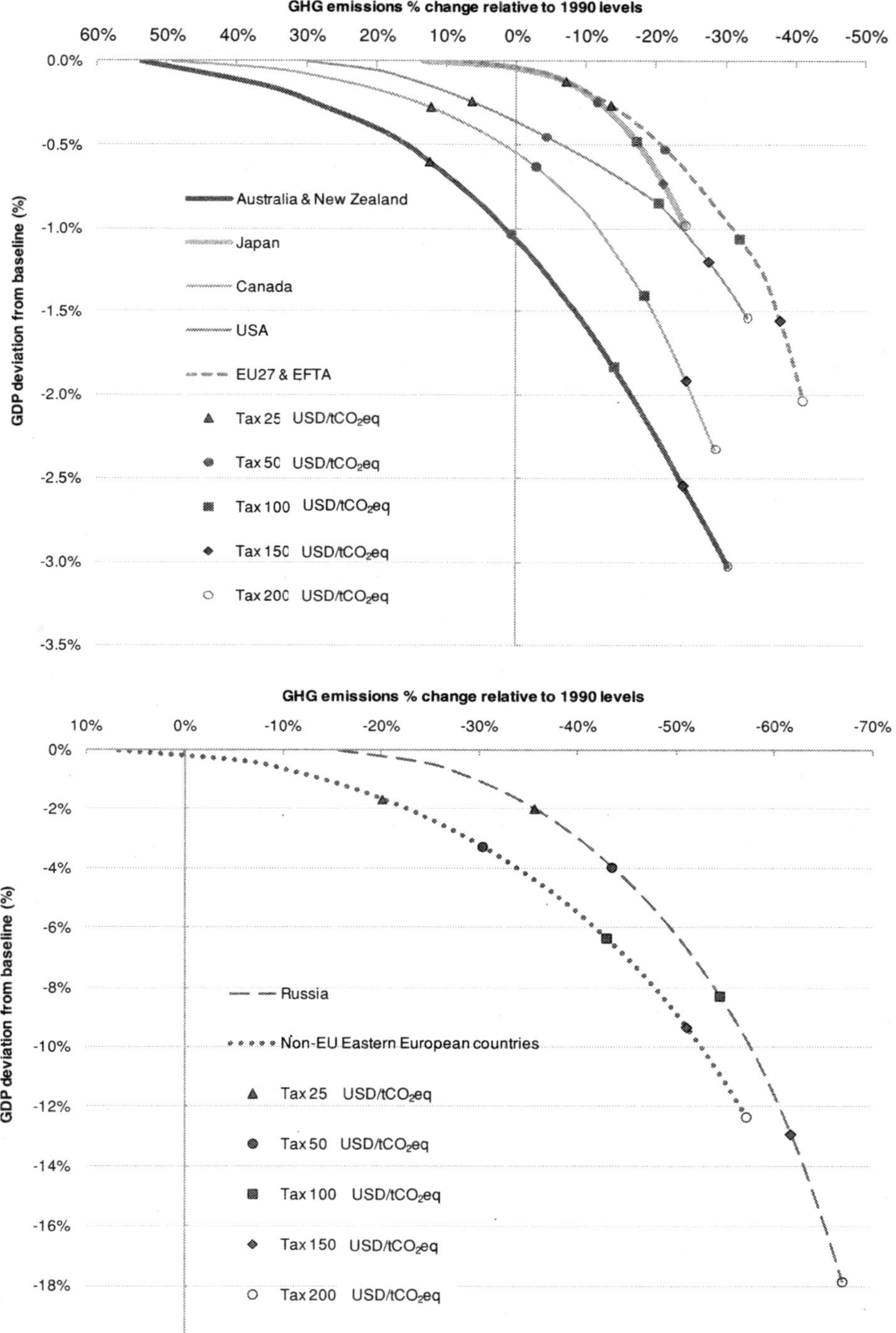

Note: Simulation for EU27 & EFTA does not include the EU-ETS.

Source: OECD, ENV-Linkages model.

Box 7.2. Assessing developed countries' declared or suggested emission reduction targets for 2020

The declared or suggested targets are rapidly evolving as the UNFCCC 15th Conference of Parties in Copenhagen draws nearer. The targets as investigated here reflect the situation as of July 2009, and are expressed as required changes in emissions in 2020 from 1990 levels. As several countries have announced a range of targets, depending on the level of ambition by other regions, three scenarios are assessed, based on the following assumptions:

Region	Unilateral commitments	Annex 1 ambitious action	Justification through declared or suggested country targets
Australia & New Zealand	+10%	0%	Australia -5% to -15% from 2000; New Zealand -50% by 2050
Canada	0%	0%	-20% from 2006
EU27 & EFTA	-20%	-30%	EU27 and Switzerland -20% to -30% from 1990; Norway -30% from 1990; Iceland -15% from 1990
Japan	-8%	-8%	-15% from 2005 domestic reductions; offsets are additional to this
Russia	-10%	-20%	-10% to -20% from 1990; not yet decided
United States	0%	0%	Waxman-Markey bill -17% from 2005 (covering 85% of emissions); Obama/Stern "return to 1990 levels"
Non-EU Eastern European Countries	-18%	-18%	Ukraine -20% from 1990; Belarus -5% to -10% from 1990; both "under consideration"
Brazil	No target	No target	No target announced
China	No target	No target	Ambitious target on energy intensity not translated into national cap on emissions
India	No target	No target	No target announced
Middle East	No target	No target	No target announced
Rest of the World	No target	No target	South Africa "peak emissions between 2020 and 2025"; Korea will announce target later this year

7.3. Policies to build global support for action

Achieving the UNFCCC's ultimate objective, *i.e.* stabilising GHG concentrations in the atmosphere at a level that would prevent dangerous anthropogenic interference with the climate system, will require ambitious emissions cuts in both developed and developing countries. As shown in Chapter 6, however, the large coalitions of countries needed to achieve sufficient emission reductions will be difficult to establish immediately. Intermediate, transitory arrangements will therefore be needed in the interim. Chapter 4 has highlighted the instruments that could be used to help build a global carbon price across countries and sectors gradually, in order to increase participation in mitigation action to sufficient levels. Over time, actions to reduce emissions will need to be scaled-up across all countries, including through increasingly ambitious mitigation actions by developing country emitters. Eventually, many of the intermediate arrangements described in the preceding chapters might develop into sectoral or national caps covering a large proportion of global emissions.

Table 7.3. Simulation of declared or suggested country targets

Panel A. Unilateral commitments, 20% offsets, no linking

Region	2020					
	Carbon price (USD/tCO_2)	GDP % deviation	Household equivalent real income[1]	GHG emissions deviation		
				MtCO_2 eq.	% relative to BAU2020	% relative to base year [2]
Australia & New Zealand	23.0	-0.5	-0.7	-227	-25.8	20.4
Brazil	0.4	0.0	0.0	-23	-1.7	27.6
Canada	32.8	-0.4	-2.3	-254	-28.6	11.1
China	0.4	0.0	-0.1	-372	-2.8	76.3
EU27 & EFTA	22.8	-0.2	-0.4	-868	-16.1	-16.0
India	0.4	0.1	0.3	-69	-1.9	61.5
Japan	65.9	-0.3	-0.3	-328	-23.0	-8.0
Middle East [3]	0.4	-0.3	-1.5	-55	-1.3	43.1
Non-EU Eastern European countries	16.0	-0.9	-2.0	-283	-19.8	-12.6
Rest of the World	0.4	0.0	-0.1	-177	-1.9	34.2
Russia	-0.2	-0.1	-1.3	50	1.9	-10.4
United States	33.3	-0.3	-0.5	-1724	-20.7	7.0
Annex I		-0.3	-0.5	-3634	-17.3	-4.6
Non-Annex I		0.0	-0.2	-697	-2.2	53.5
World		-0.2	-0.4	-4331	-8.2	23.8

Table 7.3 (Panel B) continued on next page.

Panel B. Ambitious Annex I action, 20% offsets, with linking

Region	2020					
	Carbon price (USD/tCO_2)	GDP % deviation	Household equivalent real income[1]	GHG emissions deviation		
				MtCO_2 eq.	% relative to BAU2020	% relative to base year [2]
Australia & New Zealand	29.9	-0.7	-1.0	-249	-28.3	16.4
Brazil	0.9	0.0	0.0	-21	-1.5	27.8
Canada	29.9	-0.3	-2.1	-238	-26.8	13.9
China	0.9	0.0	-0.1	-488	-3.6	74.7
EU27 & EFTA	29.9	-0.3	-0.7	-991	-18.3	-18.3
India	0.9	0.1	0.3	-71	-1.9	61.4
Japan	29.9	-0.1	-0.1	-261	-18.4	-2.4
Middle East	0.9	-0.3	-1.5	-56	-1.3	43.1
Non-EU Eastern European countries	29.9	-1.7	-2.5	-373	-26.1	-19.5
Rest of the World	0.9	0.0	-0.1	-170	-1.9	34.3
Russia	29.9	-2.1	-2.2	-635	-24.5	-33.6
United States	29.9	-0.3	-0.5	-1599	-19.2	9.0
Annex I		-0.3	-0.6	-4346	-20.7	-8.5
Non-Annex I		0.0	-0.2	-806	-2.5	53.0
World		-0.2	-0.5	-5152	-9.7	21.7

1. Hicksian "equivalent real income variation" defined as the change in real income (in percentage) necessary to ensure the same level of utility to consumers as in the baseline projection.
2. Due to data availability constraints, the base year is 1990 for Annex I regions and 2005 for non-Annex I regions (Brazil, China, India, Middle East, and Rest of the world). Global deviation is based on 2005 data for all regions.

Source: OECD, ENV-Linkages model.

One condition for enhancing mitigation action in developing countries will be the establishment of implicit and/or explicit international financial transfers to support their action. Indeed, the Bali Action Plan (UNFCCC, 2007b) explicitly refers to finance, technology and capacity-building support for GHG mitigation actions. This section discusses the framework conditions that can support action by developing countries and secure broader political engagement in global mitigation. These include financing to support mitigation, international technology transfers, R&D and support for adaptation in countries vulnerable to the impacts of climate change. They come in addition to the allocation of emission reduction commitments, which could be used to raise incentives for developing countries, as discussed in Chapter 6.

THE ECONOMICS OF CLIMATE CHANGE MITIGATION – ISBN: 978-92-64-05606-0 – © OECD 2009

7.3.1. International financial support for mitigation

Several of the market instruments already discussed in previous chapters, such as a scaled-up CDM or possible sectoral crediting mechanisms, would provide private financing and/or technological support for mitigation action in developing countries. The market value of CERs transferred through CDM reached over USD 8 billion in 2007. This amount is estimated to rise to over USD 12 billion under the illustrative scenario discussed in Section 4.3 of Chapter 4 (where Annex I countries cut their emissions by 20% by 2020, and up to 50% of offset credits are allowed to be used to meet their domestic commitments). This estimate is on the low side, however, since it assumes a low price of future CERs as a result of the implementation of a perfect scaled-up CDM.

Further international financial support already exists through direct public funding for mitigation actions in developing countries, especially in the form of funds. However, these public financing devices remain fragmented and limited in size compared to the amount of funding generated by the CDM and, even more so, given estimates of the future financing required to meet ambitious global mitigation scenarios. As a result, a number of proposals have been made recently to scale up public finances for mitigation (Box 7.3). The required increase in public funding is hard to determine for two reasons. First, it will ultimately reflect countries' incentives and willingness to distribute the costs of global action via such funds, rather than through other, possibly more cost-effective devices.[12] Second, in theory the (optimal) amount of financing would depend on the degree of ambition and effectiveness of market mechanisms such as ETS, a scaled-up CDM and/or sectoral approaches. The smaller the coverage of emission sources and/or the larger the market imperfections left unaddressed by market mechanisms – *e.g.* in the areas of R&D and technology transfers – the greater the case for increasing public mitigation funding. Rationalising existing funds, and targeting areas that are unlikely to benefit from adequate private financing, will be needed to ensure that public funds are spent in a cost-effective manner.

Box 7.3. Direct public financing mechanisms for mitigation in developing countries and options for the future

Direct public funding to support mitigation actions in developing countries already exists in different forms:

- A number of multilateral funds are currently operating, mostly under the UNFCCC or in the form of special climate change funds run by multilateral development banks, primarily the World Bank. Current annual funding available for mitigation under the UNFCCC is about USD 1 billion. In particular, the Global Environmental Facility (GEF) is the UNFCCC's key financial mechanism for both mitigation and adaptation, and finances mitigation activities through three specific funds (UNFCCC, 2009): i) the Trust Fund, which is accessible to all countries; ii) the Special Climate Change Fund, accessible to non-Annex I countries only; and, iii) the Least-Developed Countries Fund, specifically dedicated to least- developed countries. The World Bank currently manages over USD 2 billion in ten carbon funds and facilities, and over USD 6 billion in its recently launched Climate Investment Funds.[1] Together, these funds are expected to provide annual funding in the order of USD 1.5 billion between 2009 and 2012.
- An increasing number of bilateral initiatives have also emerged recently, such as Japan's Cool Earth Partnership, which is expected to deliver USD 2 billion in annual funding over the coming years, essentially for mitigation actions in developing countries. For REDD-related activities, bilateral funding is projected to substantially exceed multilateral financing.[2]

Box 7.3 continued on next page.

Box 7.3. Direct public financing mechanisms for mitigation in developing countries and options for the future

(continued)

- Finally, some support to mitigation action and capacity building in developing countries is currently provided through bilateral and multilateral assistance. Climate-change specific bilateral official development assistance by the 23 members of the OECD's Development Assistance Committee amounted to slightly less than USD 4 billion in 2006, accounting for about 5% of overall public aid (OECD-CRS database).

A number of proposals have been made recently to scale up public finances for mitigation. Mexico has proposed creating a world fund of at least USD 10 billion in capital – an amount that would exceed the combined size of the GEF and the Clean Technology Fund – to gather and scale up existing funds in both the technology transfer and adaptation areas (Mexico, 2008). All countries, other than LDCs, would contribute into the fund, but developing countries would be able to draw more from the funds than what they contribute. Switzerland proposed a USD 2 uniform global carbon tax for all annual emissions in excess of 1.5t CO_2, whose revenues would be partly remitted to an international fund depending on GDP per capita. Norway suggested that a small portion of Assigned Amount Units could be auctioned by an appropriate international institution. Developing countries have also been active in this area, with China suggesting setting up a Multilateral Technology Acquisition Fund that would be mainly financed by developed countries through their R&D budgets, energy taxes and/or fiscal revenues from carbon pricing (China, 2009).

One open issue is whether earmarking fiscal revenues levied on the carbon market – *e.g.* from permit auctioning in regions covered by emission trading schemes or from the CDM, as would be the case under some proposals – would be an appropriate way to scale up multilateral funds. On the one hand, there is no reason to expect that linking funding to the (nominal) size of carbon markets over a few years would deliver optimal and predictable financial flows, especially in a context where carbon prices could remain volatile. On the other hand, compared with direct funding by governments, such financing mechanisms may be seen as less discretionary – and, therefore, more credible – and possibly more acceptable to the electorates of developing countries as well as those of developed countries. Should earmarking be pursued, one option might be to phase it out gradually as other financing arrangements through the overall budgets of governments in developed countries are put in place.[3]

---

1. The Climate Investment Funds were launched with financial contributions from the United States, the United Kingdom and Japan. They comprise two funds that will operate in the areas of mitigation, technology transfers and – to a lesser extent – adaptation: i) the Clean Technology Fund, to support the demonstration, deployment and transfer of technologies to cut emissions of GHGs and other pollutants; and ii) the Strategic Climate Fund, which will include programmes for climate resilience, greening energy access and sustainable forestry. Significant bilateral initiatives have been taken by the United Kingdom (ETF-IW), Germany (International Climate Initiative), Australia (IFCI), Spain (UNDP-Spain MDG Achievement Fund) and the European Commission (GCCA). See UNFCCC (2009) for details.

2. The largest recent bilateral initiatives in this area include Norway's Climate and Forest Initiative and the Brazilian Development Bank's Amazon Fund, which combined have over USD 2 and 1 billion under management, respectively, and have pledged over USD 0.4 and 0.1 billion in annual funding for the coming years. Multilateral financing through the UN-REDD Programme and the World Bank's Forest Carbon Partnership Facility is comparatively very small (less than USD 0.35 billion managed overall).

3. Another issue which has been raised in the context of the Mexico Proposal is whether emission cuts achieved through the fund should yield CERs. This might raise serious additionality concerns, however, as the certification authority would have to check additionality relative to a situation where these cuts might have been partly achieved via the CDM, rather than compared to business-as-usual emissions. The CDM will itself continue to raise an additionality issue, even in a scaled-up form.

7.3.2. Broadening political support for action through technology transfer and R&D

Other tools for supporting and broadening participation in global mitigation action include frameworks to support international technology transfer and deployment and support for R&D.

A framework to support technology transfer and diffusion

Scaling up the demonstration, transfer and deployment of emission-reducing technologies across countries will be needed to mitigate climate change at least cost (Chapter 5). The three major channels through which technologies spread internationally are international trade, foreign direct investment (FDI) and licensing (Maskus, 2000; 2004).[13] While there are almost no data on international transfers of low-carbon technologies through each of these three channels, international patent data can be a fairly useful indicator, because an innovating firm only patents an invention when it plans to exploit it commercially (OECD, 2008a). Recent OECD work in this area highlights the following (Dechezleprêtre *et al.* 2008; OECD, 2008a):

- Developed countries account for the bulk of innovation in low-carbon technologies, with the United States, Japan and Germany patenting over two-thirds of all inventions. However, large emerging countries such as China are already among the leaders in some areas (Table 7.4; Brewer, 2007). By contrast, least-developed countries are neither inventors nor recipients, and appear to face the most acute barriers to technology transfers. There is, therefore, wide heterogeneity across developing countries themselves.
- International transfers of patented low-carbon technologies have yet to pick up significantly. While the rate of technology transfer for climate mitigation technologies – measured by the share of inventions that are patented at least in two countries (OECD, 2008a) – has picked up since the mid-1990s, this has merely reflected the general trend towards technology internationalisation (Figure 7.3, Panel A). Furthermore, despite a significant increase since the late 1990s, North-South technology transfers remain small compared with North-North flows (Figure 7.3, Panel B).

There are two main justifications for public intervention in international technology transfer and deployment: *i)* market imperfections and policy distortions in recipient countries may prevent profitable technological opportunities from being taken up; and *ii)* financial support for technology transfer and deployment is one policy device for lowering developing countries' mitigation costs, thereby supporting their participation in an international agreement. However, policymakers should proceed carefully in this area, as forcing technology diffusion through policy is not necessarily a cost-effective way to reduce GHG emissions (*e.g.* Stoneman and Diederen, 1994). Cross-country differences in the take-up of advanced technologies partly reflect structural factors, including firm size, expected returns and risks from the technology adopted, market structure, access to information, production factor quantities and prices (*e.g.* existence of natural resources that allow large-scale use of renewables), human capital, the existence of suitable infrastructure (*e.g.* gas or CO_2 transport pipelines) and/or R&D.[14] For instance, lower prices of labour relative to capital justify at least to some extent the more limited use of labour-saving technologies in developing countries.

Table 7.4. Top 10 inventors of climate-related technologies, 1998-2003

Country	Rank	Average % of world inventions	Most important technology classes (decreasing order)
Japan	1	40.8	All technologies
United States	2	12.8	Wind, solar, hydro, methane, buildings
Germany	3	12.7	Biomass, ocean, waste, CCS, wind, solar
China	4	5.8	Cement, geothermal, solar, hydro, methane
South Korea	5	4.6	Lighting, ocean, hydro, biomass, cement
Russia	6	4.2	Geothermal, cement, hydro, CCS, ocean
France	7	2.4	Cement, CCS, buildings, biomass, hydro
United Kingdom	8	1.9	Ocean, biomass, wind, methane
Canada	9	1.5	Hydro, wind, CCS, ocean
Brazil	10	1.1	Ocean, building

Source: Dechezleprêtre *et al.,* 2008.

Figure 7.3. International technology transfer trends, 1978-2008

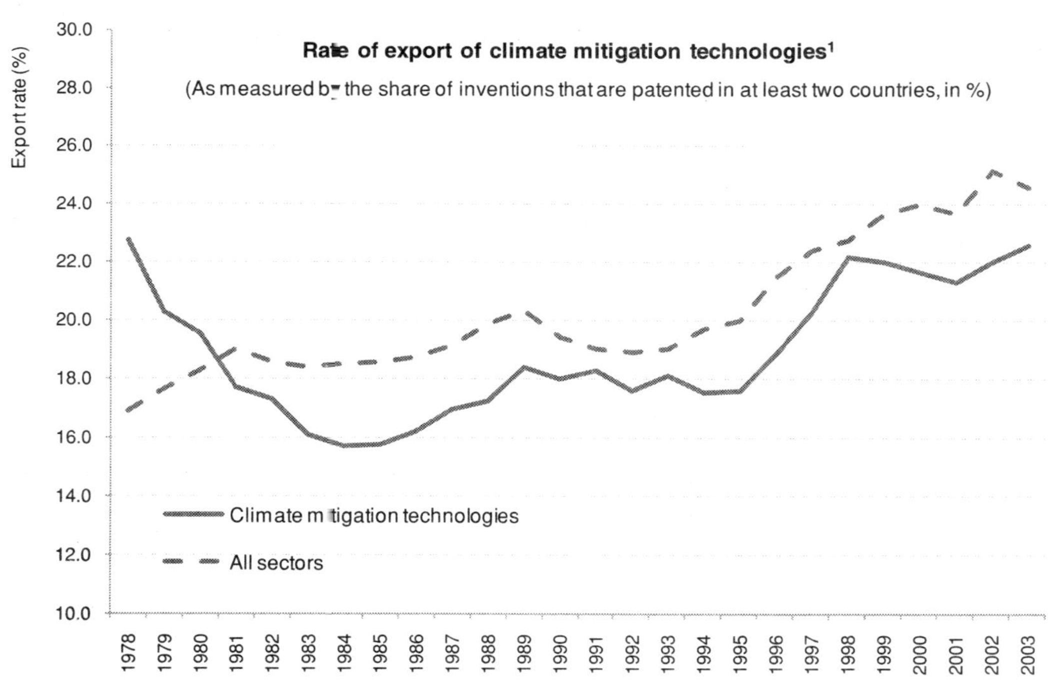

Figure 7.3 continued on next page.

Figure 7.3. International technology transfer trends, 1978-2008

(continued)

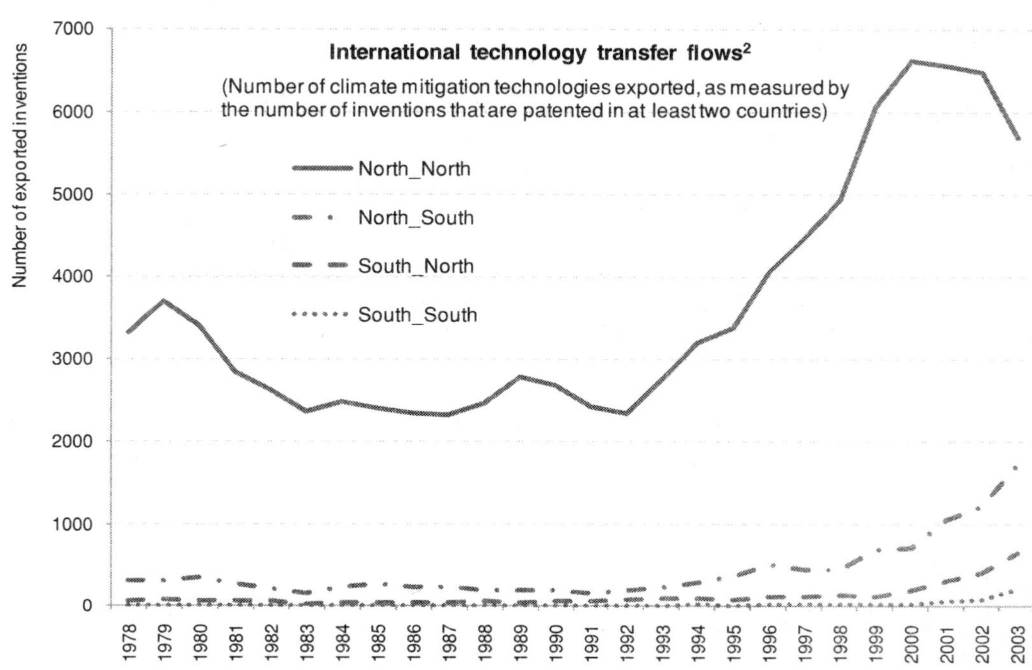

1. Climate mitigation technologies cover 13 fields: 6 renewable energy technologies (wind, solar, geothermal, ocean energy, biomass and hydropower), waste use and recovery, methane destruction, climate-friendly cement, energy conservation in buildings, motor vehicle fuel injection, energy-efficient lighting and carbon capture & storage (CCS).
2. North and south countries denote Annex I and non-Annex I countries, respectively.

Source: Dechezleprêtre *et al.* (2008).

Removing three main types of policy distortion would facilitate international technology transfer and deployment, particularly in developing countries:

- *Lack of a carbon price:* removing fossil fuel subsidies and pricing carbon would boost local firms' adoption incentives, especially for technologies like carbon capture and storage that yield no private return and are therefore unlikely to be transferred and adopted otherwise. Pricing carbon would also encourage governments themselves to facilitate technology transfers, by investing in infrastructure, human capital, or enforcing IPRs. One way – albeit an imperfect one – to provide such price incentives is through the CDM. From this perspective, scaling up the CDM along the lines discussed in Chapter 4 (Section 4.3) would increase financial flows and technology transfers to developing countries on a much larger scale than under the current framework. Recent OECD analysis of 13 climate mitigation technologies and 100 countries between 1985 and 2004 found that the overall size of CDM projects implemented in the recipient country had a significant positive impact on technology transfers (Hascic and Johnstone, 2009).

- *Barriers to international trade and foreign direct investment:* openness to international trade can facilitate the transfer and deployment of technologies embodied in goods – especially capital goods. Tariffs typically exceed 15% on an *ad valorem* basis for energy-efficient electrical appliances or renewable-energy products and technologies. There is therefore room for lower tariffs on a wide range of goods and technologies relevant to climate change mitigation in developing countries, and for lower non-tariff barriers – at least via greater harmonisation of criteria and tests for energy-efficiency requirements – in their OECD counterparts (Steenblik, 2005; Steenblik *et al.* 2006).[15] Furthermore, there are technical barriers to trade in a number of areas; these could be reduced by harmonising technical standards (IEA, 2007d). Also of importance are barriers to trade in services; the deployment of many mitigation technologies requires a wide range of consulting, engineering or construction services (*e.g.* renewable power generation or energy-efficient buildings). FDI restrictions also undermine deployment, as multinational firms play a major role in international technology transfers. An opportunity to liberalise trade in some climate-friendly goods and services currently exists at the multilateral level within the context of the Doha Round.

Figure 7.4. Patent rights index, 2005

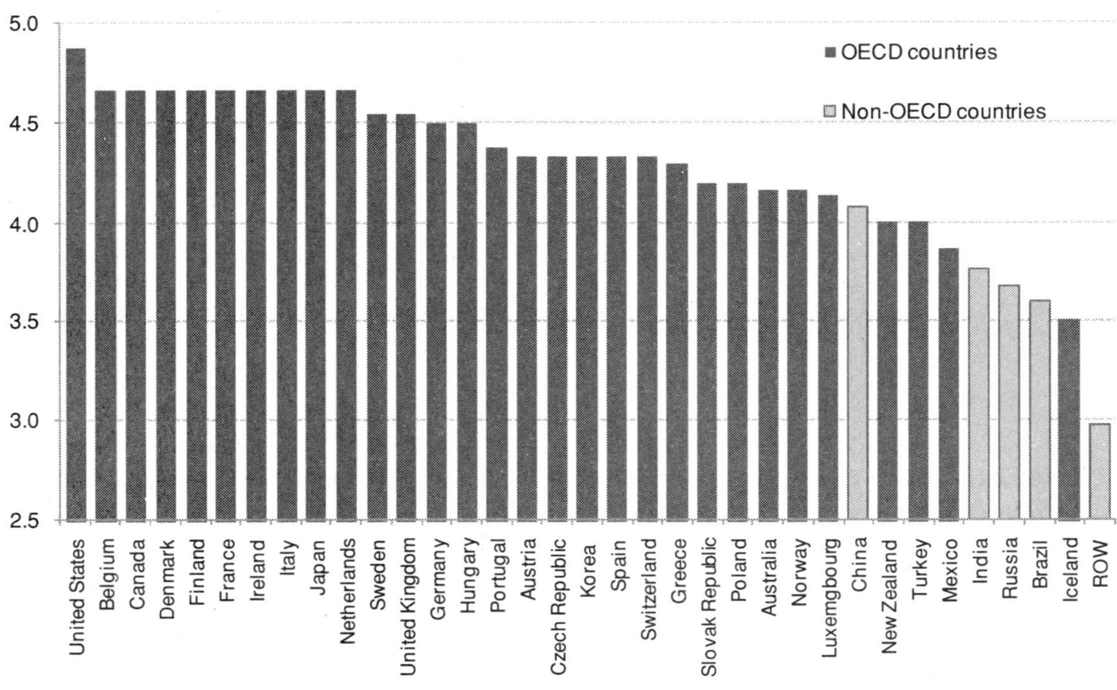

1. For each country, the value of the index is computed as the sum of scores assigned in five areas: membership in International Treaties, sectoral coverage of patent rights, absence of restrictions, enforcement and duration of protection. Scores in each of these individual areas are between 0 and 1.

Source: Park and Lippoldt (2008).

 THE ECONOMICS OF CLIMATE CHANGE MITIGATION – ISBN: 978-92-64-05606-0 – © OECD 2009

- *Absence or lack of enforcement of intellectual property rights (IPRs):* establishing and enforcing IPRs are critical to providing adequate incentives for private firms to invest in climate-friendly R&D (Chapter 5). However, the impact of IPRs on technology transfers is more ambiguous. On the one hand, by reducing imitation, stricter IPRs can expand the market, *i.e.* they increase patent holders' perceived demand for their technology and therefore their incentives to license and/or undertake FDI (*e.g.* Arora *et al.*, 2001). On the other hand, overly stringent IPRs create market power and thus may induce inventors to raise prices, thereby discouraging transfers (*e.g.* Correa, 2005). In practice, evidence suggests that stricter IPRs in recipient countries increase incoming technology transfers (*e.g.* Maskus, 2004; Park and Lippoldt, 2008), including of low-carbon technologies (Dechezleprêtre *et al.* 2008). Patent rights are currently less protected in many developing countries than in their developed counterparts (Figure 7.4). They could be strengthened, along with technical assistance and financial support from developed countries, *e.g.* in the context of international sector-wide approaches, and/or through existing or new multilateral funds (Box 7.3).[16] An alternative that would still maintain adequate R&D incentives might be for developed countries to cover IPR-related costs (licensing fees, royalties etc) or even buy out patents on key transferable technologies (*e.g.* Newell, 2008).[17]

International technology transfer and deployment may not only be hampered by policy distortions, but also by genuine market imperfections. This suggests the need for international support beyond creating incentives through the international carbon market and reducing barriers to trade and FDI in climate-friendly goods, services and technologies. The following market imperfections need to be addressed:

- *Learning spillovers and network externalities* in the deployment of existing technologies, especially in the electricity sector (Chapter 5). Major long-term infrastructure investments are expected over the coming years in power generation, transport and buildings, notably in large developing countries (IEA, 2006, 2007b; OECD, 2008c). These might risk locking-in high-carbon energy systems in the absence of policy intervention. While renewable electricity is already heavily subsidised across most OECD countries, there may be a case for providing subsidies in key developing countries, which in some cases enjoy lower deployment costs and/or greater potential for cost declines through learning-by-doing – *e.g.* in solar power generation (IEA, 2005). However, in order to be cost-effective, these subsidies would have to be accompanied by the removal of existing subsidies on fossil fuel power generation in developing countries.
- *Poor information on available technology on the part of recipients*, which may prevent optimal transfers from being made. Buyers' access to information might be improved through a mix of demonstration projects, advertising campaigns, labelling schemes or subsidies to technological consulting services.
- *Financial market imperfections,* such as short-term credit constraints and the incompleteness of insurance markets to cover investment risks. These problems are magnified by existing uncertainty about future climate policy at both local and global levels, which unduly raises the costs and risks of adopting low-carbon technology. This might justify loan guarantees, which along with concessional loans and grants, will be one of the main financing mechanisms under the Clean Technology Fund (Box 6.3). However, identifying financial market imperfections is not straightforward, and policy design in this area can be subject to government failure (*e.g.* Adams and Von Pischke, 1992).

Multilateral funds to support international technology transfers (Box 7.3) could be scaled up and rationalised to address these market imperfections in a technology-neutral way. If the deployment of particular technologies is to be subsidised, experience with the GEF suggests that targeting fairly mature technologies has the largest impact on international technology diffusion, possibly reflecting the greater absorptive capacity for such technologies (Christoffersen *et al.* 2002). There may also be a (second-best) case for mainly subsidising technology diffusion to least developed countries which do not price carbon and continue to have limited access to CDM financing in the near future.

Finally, as a burden-sharing device, public support to international technology transfer and deployment may also go beyond addressing policy distortions and market imperfections. For instance, it might support actions like boosting human capital (*e.g.* nuclear engineer or reservoir geologist university and training programmes), infrastructure (*e.g.* support to pipeline infrastructure to transport natural gas, biofuels or CO_2, promotion of grid interconnection schemes that support renewable power generation, shift to public transportation in urban areas) and/or complementary R&D in the energy production sector (*e.g.* by offering firms in developed countries similar fiscal incentives to carry out R&D in climate mitigation technologies at home and abroad).[18] One challenge with such an approach is to provide cost-effective and technology-neutral support, given the risks of government failure.

Support for R&D

Chapter 5 highlighted the large potential impact of R&D policies in bringing down the medium- and long-term global mitigation costs–especially basic R&D on major new abatement technologies, primarily in the non-electricity sector. While pricing carbon and setting up appropriate innovation and regulatory frameworks are key to providing the necessary incentives, they are unlikely to be enough given the magnitude of the market imperfections involved in climate change mitigation. Therefore, there is a case for specific policies to boost climate-friendly basic R&D. Given the global public good nature of mitigation, some co-ordination at the international level would be justified. However, this issue has received only limited attention thus far, at least compared with other international climate policy areas such as technology transfers and adaptation, where international policy devices have already been set up and proposals for scaling them up have proliferated. This may reflect to some extent the priority put by countries on domestic (as opposed to international collaborative) R&D policies. It might also stem from two unfavourable political economy features of such policies: *i)* benefits would be reaped in the distant future, while costs would be borne upfront; and, *ii)* countries' basic R&D efforts are hard to value, and thereby difficult to incorporate in the context of a global climate policy agreement.

Long-term and large-scale technologies that entail sizeable costs and risks, and which have little short-term commercial value, seem well-suited for sharing international costs and tasks. Current collaboration on fusion power (the International Thermonuclear Experimental Reactor project) and hydrogen fuel cells (the International Partnership for the Hydrogen Economy) illustrates this (*e.g.* De Coninck *et al.* 2008).[19] Such international collaboration also already exists in the form of IEA Implementing Agreements, which cover a range of climate-related technologies. These experiences could be scaled up and/or expanded to a range of other basic research fields. As regards applied R&D, one option might be to supplement the usual R&D subsidies and grants with internationally co-ordinated innovation inducement prizes (Box 5.2, Chapter 5). In any event, ways are needed to ensure that any increase in R&D spending at the international level is not at the expense of domestic R&D spending cuts. One solution might be to set climate-related R&D spending targets for each country (*e.g.* a given share of GDP), rather than as an addition to existing investment, and possibly to exclude private sector R&D from the accounting, as it may be difficult to distinguish from research in other areas (De Coninck *et al.* 2008).[20]

7.3.3. Support for developing countries to adapt to climate change

Some degree of climate change is already inevitable due to cumulative past emissions and technologies currently in place. Countries and individuals will need to adapt to these changes, *i.e.* to reduce the damage involved, and to take advantage of any new opportunities it presents. Least-developed countries are particularly vulnerable, both because their economies are more directly dependant on climate-sensitive natural resources and because of their limited capacity to adapt to the impacts of climate change.

Financing the costs of adaptation by least developed countries is likely to be an important element of a post-2012 climate change agreement, and will help engage these countries in mitigation action over the longer run. A consensus around the magnitude of the overall adaptation costs, however, remains somewhat premature. This reflects serious methodological issues (*e.g.* lack of integrated cost-benefit analysis, including some accounting for risk, to determine optimal adaptation spending) and data limitations (*e.g.* lack of explicit mapping between cost estimates and specific adaptation activities, incomplete coverage, extrapolations at the global level based on local evidence; OECD, 2008f). Nevertheless, available estimates point to annual adaptation costs in the developing world in the tens of billions of dollars annually over the coming decades, the bulk of which would be incurred when infrastructure is renewed (World Bank, 2006; Stern, 2007; UNDP, 2007; UNFCCC, 2007a).

To bridge the gap between available resources for adaptation and future adaptation costs, considerable efforts are being made to scale up international financing for adaptation. The creation of an Adaptation Fund, confirmed at the 2008 14th Conference of Parties to the United Nations Framework Convention on Climate Change (COP14 of UNFCCC) in Poznan, is a significant step in this direction. The fund is financed through a 2% levy on the sale of emission credits generated by emission-saving projects undertaken in developing countries under the CDM. The future size of the fund will therefore partly depend on the extent to which the CDM is scaled up. While the Adaptation Fund is expected to significantly increase available resources, it may nevertheless remain small compared with adaptation financing needs. For instance, under the illustrative scenario already discussed above where Annex I countries cut their emissions by 20% by 2020, with the possibility of using up to 50% of offset credits to meet their domestic commitments, the 2% tax is found to yield only about USD 250 million by 2020 (in 2005 USD), reflecting the likely low price of future CERs under successful scaling up. At the time of writing a variety of other innovative mechanisms to scale up adaptation financing are also being proposed; many relying on earmarking of some share of the proceeds from auction revenues from GHG emissions permits.

Significant efforts are also being made to better integrate adaptation within development aid efforts, national policy and budgetary processes, sectoral and local policies (OECD, 2009). Although mitigation involves a clearer public good than adaptation, there is also some local – and, in some cases, even global – public good component involved in many key adaptation actions, such as the preservation of ecosystems, the protection of coastal areas and rivers, water management and supply systems, or agricultural crop research. As a result, the private sector is unlikely to deliver adequate spending on adaptation, making a case for government intervention. Some interventions should primarily focus on setting up market incentives for, and/or removing existing policy distortions to, efficient adaptation. Examples include developing water markets and removing water use subsidies, and pricing – explicitly or, where unfeasible, implicitly through regulation – the adaptation benefits of forests (for example in terms of soil quality and watershed protection) and the services provided by ecosystems (biodiversity, landscape preservation) (OECD, 2008f). In other cases, government intervention may primarily involve increased public spending, for instance on physical infrastructure (*e.g.* sea walls, flood defenses), or on particular institutional arrangements (*e.g.* catastrophe bonds to insure extreme risks, disaster relief).

One policy challenge at both local and international levels will be to scale up adaptation financing for least-developed countries, while at the same time alleviating potential "moral hazard" problems. These may arise if firms, households and/or governments under-invest in adaptation action either because their climate-related risks are fully insured, or because they expect to be bailed out in the event of disaster. In an international policy context, such concerns might be alleviated for instance through fixed, "lump sum" transfers to co-finance local public spending on adaptation (infrastructure investment, catastrophe bond emissions, etc.), along with explicit "no bail-out" clauses.

Notes

1. There is also some evidence that tradable certificates may have stimulated not only technology deployment but also innovation. Based on patent data for a panel of 25 countries over the period 1978-2003, Johnstone et al. (2008) found significant impacts on patenting from tradable certificates, but not from feed-in tariffs.

2. This figure does not take into account mandatory blending requirements. While these boost biofuel consumption, the implicit support they provide to domestic output is not straightforward and depends partly on the comparative costs of local biofuels, fossil fuels and imported biofuels; the latter being typically inflated by tariff and non-tariff barriers (see below).

3. Government support amounting to about USD 1 billion also exists in Brazil, but ethanol from sugarcane grown in this country is currently by far the cheapest biofuel produced (OECD Roundtable on Sustainable Development, 2007).

4. As a matter of comparison, the price of CO2 in the EU-ETS fluctuated between about USD 30 and USD 45 during the first half of 2008.

5. For instance, the implicit subsidy from the excise tax exemption for biodiesel in high-tax European countries is equivalent to several thousand EUR per car, on the basis of average kilometres driven over a car's lifetime (Steenblik, 2007).

6. These include soil acidification, toxicity of agricultural pesticides and biodiversity loss.

7. This was simulated through a multilateral carbon tax in all Annex I regions and by varying the level of the tax. Therefore, for any individual Annex I region we assume that all other Annex I regions implement the same carbon tax and there is no carbon tax in the non-Annex I regions. Relaxing that assumption, *i.e.* assuming different carbon prices across countries, would generate different costs. This is because the cost of mitigation action in one particular country depends in part on the actions taken in other countries. However, further simulations show that these second-order impacts of actions by other regions are limited, and do not change the qualitative findings.

8. For consistency in this exercise, but in contrast to the other simulations with the ENV-LINKAGES model, the existence of the EU-ETS is not assumed in the baseline for this analysis. Moving the EU-ETS to the baseline results in an upward shift of the line for the EU27 & EFTA in Figure 7.2 by 0.3% points (because of lower costs for any given tax rate). For low carbon tax levels, the curve also shifts to the right: according to the model simulations the projected baseline emissions in 2020 for the EU27 & EFTA are some 5.5% below 1990 levels due to the EU-ETS, compared with 7% above 1990 in the absence of the EU-ETS.

9. For an analysis of these indicators, see Karousakis *et al.* (2008).

10. In line with the other simulations it is assumed that the CDM is scaled up to include all sectors, and that transaction costs are ignored, *i.e.* the results assume a cost-effective supply of CERs.

11. The availability of the offsets implies that reductions achieved domestically are smaller than the imposed target. Linking also affects regional reductions.

THE ECONOMICS OF CLIMATE CHANGE MITIGATION – ISBN: 978-92-64-05606-0 – © OECD 2009

12. The governance structure may matter in this regard, with developing countries possibly more likely to support global than bilateral funds, over which donor countries typically have greater control (Hall *et al.* 2008). In any event, developing countries may have only limited incentives to contribute, at least if such funds substitute – rather than complement – emission reductions that might have been achieved through the CDM and other crediting mechanisms.

13. Other important channels include: uncompensated imitation, *e.g.* through reverse engineering; the international mobility of qualified staff; and information collected from patent applications, professional journals, etc.

14 For a survey and some analysis of policy implications in a climate mitigation policy context, see *e.g.* Blackman, 1999.

15. Preliminary OECD research points to significant negative effects of import tariffs on international transfers of climate mitigation technologies (Dechezleprêtre et al. 2008). More indirect evidence (World Bank, 2007) finds that removing barriers would have large effects on international trade between developed and developing countries in renewable energy, "clean" coal and efficient lighting.

16. This may require enhanced co-ordination between the UNFCCC, the World Trade Organization (WTO) – through its Agreement on Trade-Related Aspects of Intellectual Property Rights (TRIPS) – and the World Intellectual Property Organization (WIPO).

17. Compulsory licensing has sometimes been put forward as yet another policy alternative, but compared with strengthening IPRs, this approach would likely be more detrimental to R&D and innovation.

18. For recent empirical evidence on the effectiveness of such policies, see Dechezleprêtre *et al.* (2008).

19. Examples in other areas include the International Space Station or the European particle accelerator (Large Hadron Collider).

20. Provided this crowding-out effect is addressed, Barrett (2006, 2007b) argues that international co-operation may actually be far easier to achieve in R&D than in mitigation, for instance through a built-in rule that ties each country's contribution to a co-ordinated international R&D effort to that of others.

References

Achard, F., *et al.* (2004), "Improved Estimates of Net Carbon Emissions from Land Cover Change in the Tropics for the 1990s", *Global Biogeochemical Cycles*, Vol. 18, No. 2.

Adams, D. and J. von Pischke (1992), "Microenterprise Credit Programs: Déjà Vu", *World Development,* Vol. 20, No. 1.

Aldy, E. and R. Stavins (2008), "Economic Incentives in a New Climate Agreement", *Issue Paper,* The Harvard Project on International Climate Agreements.

Alic, J., D. Mowery and E. Rubin (2003), "US Technology and Innovation Policies: Lessons for Climate Change", *Report for the Pew Center on Global Climate Change*, Arlington, VA.

Anderson, D. (2006), "Costs and Finance of Abating Carbon Emissions in the Energy Sector", Background Report for the Stern Review, Imperial College, London.

Arora, A., A. Fosfuri and A. Gambardella (2001), *Markets for Technology: The Economics of Innovation and Corporate Strategy,* MIT Press, Cambridge, Massachussets.

Arquit Niederberger, A. and R. Fecher (2006), "Demand-Side Energy Efficiency Promotion Under the Clean Development Mechanism: Lessons Learned and Future Prospects", *Energy for Sustainable Development,* Vol. 10, No. 4.

Arrow, K.J., and A.C. Fisher (1974), "Environmental Preservation, Uncertainty, and Irreversibility", *Quarterly Journal of Economics* No. 88, pp. 312–19.

Babiker, M. (2005), "Climate Change Policy, Market Structure and Carbon Leakage", *Journal of International Economics,* Vol. 65, No. 2.

Bakker, A., *et al.* (2007), "Carbon Credit Supply Potential Beyond 2012: A Bottom-up Assessment of Mitigation Options", Energy Research Centre of the Netherlands Report *ECN-E—07-090.*

Barker, T., M. Qureshi, and J. Köhler (2006), "The Costs of Greenhouse Gas Mitigation with Induced Technological Change: A Meta-Analysis of Estimates in the Literature, *Tyndall Centre for Climate Change Research Working Paper* No. 89.

Barker, T., J. Köhler, and M. Villena (2002), "The Costs of Greenhouse Gas Abatement: A Meta-Analysis of Post-SRES Mitigation Scenarios", *Environmental Economics and Policy Studies,* Vol. 5, No. 2.

Baron, R., B. Buchner and J. Ellis (2009), "Sectoral Approaches and the Carbon Market", OECD/IEA, Paris, forthcoming.

Baron, R. and S. Bygrave (2007), "Linking Tradable Permit Systems for Greenhouse Gas Emissions: Opportunities, Implications and Challenges," International Emissions Trading Association.

Baron, R. and J. Ellis (2006), "Sectoral Crediting Mechanisms for Greenhouse Gas Mitigation: Institutional and Operational Issues", *COM/ENV/EPOC/IEA/SLT(2006)4*, OECD/IEA, Paris.

Baron, R. (2000), "An Assessment of Liability Rules for International GHG Emissions Trading," OECD/IEA, Paris.

Barrett, S. (2007a), "Proposal for a New Climate Change Treaty System", *The Economists' Voice*, Vol. 4, No. 3.

Barrett, S. (2007b), "A Multitrack Climate Treaty System", in J. Aldy and R. Stavins (eds), *Architectures for Agreement: Addressing Global Climate Change in the Post-Kyoto World,* Cambridge University Press, Cambridge.

Barrett, S. (2006), "Climate Treaties and "Breakthrough" Technologies", *American Economic Review,* Vol. 96, No. 2.

Bassanini, A. and R. Duval (2006), "Reassessing the Role of Policies and Institutions for Labour Market Performance: A Consolidated Analysis", *OECD Economics Department Working Papers* No. 486, Paris.

Baumol, W. and W. Oates (1988), *The Theory of Environmental Policy,* Cambridge University Press, Cambridge.

Biglaiser, G., J. Horowitz and J. Quiggin (1995), "Dynamic Pollution Regulation", *Journal of Regulatory Economics,* Vol. 8, No. 1.

Blackman, A. and W. Harrington (2000), "The Use of Economic Incentives in Developing Countries: Lessons from International Experience with Industrial Air Pollution", *Journal of Environment and Development,* Vol. 9, No. 1.

Blackman, A. (1999), "The Economics of Technology Diffusion: Implications for Climate Policy in Developing Countries", *Resources for the Future Discussion Paper* No. 99-42.

Bohi, D. and M. Toman (1996), *The Economics of Energy Security*, Kluwer Academic Publishers, Massachussets.

Bohm, P. and C. Russell (1985), "Comparative Analysis of Alternative Policy Instruments", in A. Kneese and J. Sweeney (eds.), *Handbook of Natural Resource and Energy Economics*, Vol. 1, North Holland, Amsterdam.

Bollen, J., *et al.* (2009), "Co-benefits of Climate Change Mitigation Policies: Literature Review and New Results", *OECD Economics Department Working Papers*, No. 693, Paris.

Bollen, J., *et al.* (2008), "Co-Benefits of Climate Policy", PBL Report No. 500116005, PBL, Bilthoven, the Netherlands.

Bollen, J., T. Manders and P. Veenendaal (2005), "Caps and Fences in Climate Change Policies, Trade-Offs in Shaping Post-Kyoto", *MNP Report* 500035003/2005, Bilthoven, Netherlands.

Bollen, J., A. Gielen and H. Timmer (1999), "Clubs, Ceilings and CDM: Macroeconomics of Compliance with the Kyoto Protocol", *Energy Journal,* Vol. 20, Special Issue.

Bosetti, V., *et al.* (2009a), "The Role of R&D and Technology Diffusion in Climate Change Mitigation: New Perspectives Using the WITCH Model", *OECD Economics Department Working Papers,* No. 664, Paris.

Bosetti, V., *et al.* (2009*b*), "The Incentives to Participate in and the Stability of International Climate Coalitions: A Game-Theoretic Analysis Using the WITCH Model", *OECD Economics Department Working Papers* No. 702, Paris.

Bosetti, V., *et al.* (2008), "International Energy R&D Spillovers and the Economics of Greenhouse Gas Stabilisation", *Energy Economics,* Vol. 30, No. 6.

Bosetti, V., E. Massetti and M. Tavoni (2007), "The WITCH Model: Structure, Baseline, Solutions", *FEEM Working Paper Series* No. 10-2007, Fondazione Eni Enrico Mattei, Milan.

Bosetti, V., *et al.* (2006), "WITCH: A World Induced Technical Change Hybrid Model", *The Energy Journal, Special Issue on Hybrid Modelling of Energy-Environment Policies: Reconciling Bottom-up and Top-down*: pp. 13-38.

Bosi, M. and J. Ellis (2005), "Exploring Options for Sectoral Crediting Mechanisms", *COM/ENV/EPOC/IEA/SLT(2005)1,* OECD, Paris.

Bovenberg, A., L. Goulder and M. Jacobsen (2008), "Costs of Alternative Environmental Policy Instruments in the Presence of Industry Compensation Requirements", *Journal of Public Economics,* Vol. 92, No. 5.

Bradley, R., *et al.* (2007), *Slicing the Pie: Sector-Based Approaches to International Climate Arrangements, Issues and Options*, World Resources Institute, Washington D.C.

Brewer, T. (2007), "Climate Change Technology Transfer: International Trade and Investment Policy Issues in the G8+5 Countries", *Paper prepared for the G8+5 Climate Change Dialogue.*

Buchanan, J. (1969), "External Diseconomies, Corrective Taxes, and Market Structure", *American Economic Review,* Vol. 59, No. 1.

Buchner, B., C. Carraro and D. Ellerman (2006), "The Allocation of European Union Allowances. Lessons, Unifying Themes and General Principles", MIT Global Change Forum, Report No. 140.

Buchner, B. and C. Carraro (2005), "Economic and Environmental Effectiveness of a Technology-based Climate Protocol", *Climate Policy,* Vol. 4, No. 3.

Burniaux, J-M, *et al.* (2009), "The Economics of Climate Change Mitigation : How to Build the Necessary Global Action in a Cost-effective Manner", *OECD Economics Department Working Papers* No. 701, Paris.

Burniaux, J-M. and J. Chateau (2008), "An Overview of the OECD ENV-Linkages Model", *OECD Economics Department Working Papers* No. 653, Paris.

Burniaux, J-M. and J. Oliveira Martins (2000), "Carbon Emission Leakages: a General Equilibrium View", *OECD Economics Department Working Papers* No. 242, Paris.

Burniaux, J-M., J.P. Martin and J. Oliveira-Martins (1992), "The Effect of Existing Distortions in Energy Markets on the Costs of Policies to Reduce CO_2 Emissions: Evidence from GREEN", *OECD Economic Studies*, No. 19, Winter, Paris.

Burtraw, D., D. Kahn and K. Palmer (2006), "Dynamic Adjustment to Incentive Based Policy to Improve Efficiency and Performance", *mimeo,* Resources for the Future, Washington D.C.

Caisse des Dépots (2009), "Tendances Carbone, The Monthly Bulletin on the European Carbon Market", No. 38, July.

Capoor, K. and P. Ambrosi (2008), *State and Trends of the Carbon Market 2008,* The World Bank, Washington D.C.

Capoor, K. and P. Ambrosi (2006), *State and Trends of the Carbon Market 2006,* IETA and World Bank, Washington D.C.

Carraro, C., J. Eyckmans and M. Finus (2006), "Optimal Transfers and Participation Decisions in International Environmental Agreements", *Review of International Organisations,* Vol. 1, No. 4.

Castles, I. and D. Henderson (2003a), "Economics, Emission Scenarios and the Work of the IPCC", *Energy and Environment,* Vol. 14, No. 4.

Castles, I. and D. Henderson (2003b), "The IPCC Emission Scenarios: an Economic-Statistical Critique", *Energy and Environment,* Vol. 14, No. 2-3.

Chander, P. and H. Tulkens (2008), "Cooperation, Stability and Self-Enforcement in International Environmental Agreements: A Conceptual Discussion", in R. Guesnerie (ed.) *The Design of Climate Policy*, MIT Press, Cambridge, Massachussets.

Chander, P. and H. Tulkens (2007), "Climate Coalitions: A Theoretical and Computational Appraisal", *Département des sciences économiques de l'Université catholique de Louvain, Discussion Paper* No. 2007-6.

Che, Y-K. and I. Gale (2003), "Optimal Design of Research Contests", *American Economic Review,* Vol. 93, No. 3.

China (2009), "China's Views in the Fulfillment of the Bali Action Plan and the Components of the Agreed Outcome to be Adopted by the Conference of the Parties at its 15th Session", *Working Paper,* February.

Christoffersen, L., *et al.* (2002), *The First Decade of the GEF: Second Overall Performance Study*, Global Environment Facility, Washington D.C.

Congressional Budget Office (2008), "Options for Offsetting the Economic Impact on Low- and Moderate- Income Households of a Cap-and-Trade Program for Carbon Dioxide Emissions", Letter to the Honorable Jeff Bingaman, US Congress, Washington D.C.

Correa, C. (2005), "Can the TRIPS Agreement Foster Technology Transfer to Developing Countries? ", in K. Maskus and J. Reichman (eds), *International Public Goods and Transfer of Technology Under a Globalized Intellectual Property Regime,* Cambridge University Press, Cambridge.

Cropper, M. and W. Oates (1992), "Environmental Economics: A Survey", *Journal of Economic Literature,* Vol. 30, No. 2.

Dasgupta, P. (2007), "Commentary: The Stern Review's Economics of Climate Change", *National Institute Economic Review,* Vol. 199, No. 1.

Dechezleprêtre, A., *et al.* (2008), "Invention and Transfer of Climate Change Mitigation Technologies on a Global Scale: A Study Drawing on Patent Data", *mimeo,* Mines ParisTech / CERNA /Agence Française de développement.

De Coninck, H., *et al.* (2008), "International Technology-Oriented Agreements to Address Climate Change", *Energy Policy,* Vol. 36, No. 1.

DeFries, R., *et al.* (2005), "Monitoring Tropical Deforestation for Emerging Carbon Markets" in P. Mountinho and S. Schwartzman (eds.), *Tropical Deforestation and Climate Change,* IPAM and Environmental Defense, Belem, Brazil and Washington D.C.

DeFries, R., *et al.* (2002), "Carbon Emissions from Tropical Deforestation and Regrowth Based on Satelite Observations for the 1980s and 1990s", *PNAS*, Vol. 99, No. 22.

De la Chesnaye, F. and J. Weyant (eds) (2006), "Multi-Greenhouse Gas Mitigation and Climate Policy", *The Energy Journal*, Special Issue.

De Mooij, R. (1999), "The Double Dividend of Environmental Tax Reform", in J.C. van der Bergh (ed.), *Handbook of Environmental and Resource Economics*, Cheltenham, Edward Elgar, UK.

Denicolo, V. (1999), "Pollution-Reducing Innovations Under Taxes or Permits", *Oxford Economic Papers,* Vol. 51, No. 1.

Dixit, A and R. Pindyck (1994), "Investment Under Uncertainty", Princeton University Press, Princeton New Jersey.

Dixon, A., *et al.* (2008), *Integration of REDD into International Carbon Market: Implications for Future Commitments and Market Regulations,* Report prepared for the New Zealand Ministry of Agriculture and Forestry.

Doornbosch, R. and R. Steenblik (2007), "Biofuels: Is the Cure Worse than the Disease?", *OECD Round Table on Sustainable Development, SG/SD/RT(2007)3,* OECD, Paris.

Downing, P. and L. White (1986), "Innovation in Pollution Control", *Journal of Environmental Economics and Management,* Vol. 13, No. 1.

Duval, R. and C. de la Maisonneuve (2009), "Long-Run GDP Growth Scenarios for the World Economy", *OECD Economics Department Working Papers* No. 663, Paris.

Dudek, D. and A. Golub (2003), "Intensity Targets: Pathway or Roadblock to Preventing Climate Change While Enhancing Economic Growth", *Climate Policy* No. 3 (S2), pp. S21–S28.

Easterly, W. and R. Levine (2001), "It's Not Factor Accumulation: Stylized Facts and Growth Models", *World Bank Economic Review,* Vol. 15, No. 2.

ECCP (2007), European Climate Change Platform Meeting Report, October.

Edenhofer, O., C. Flachsland and R. Marschinski (2007), "Towards a Global CO_2 Market: An Economic Analysis", Potsdam Institute for Climate Impact Research.

Edenhofer, O., *et al.* (2006), "Induced Technological Change: Exploring its Implications for the Economics of Atmospheric Stabilisation", *The Energy Journal, Special Issue on Endogenous Technological Change and the Economics of Atmospheric Stabilisation,* Vol. 27.

Eliasch, J. (2008), Eliasch Review - Climate Change: Financing Global Forest, The Stationery Office Limited on behalf of the Controller of Her Majesty's Stationery Office, Surrey, U.K.

Ellerman, D. and P.L. Joskow (2008), "The European Union's Emissions Trading System in Perspective", *Document prepared for the Pew Center on Global Climate Change.*

Ellis, J. and S. Kamel (2007), "Overcoming Barriers to Clean Development Mechanism Projects", *COM/ENV/EPOC/IEA/SLT(2007)3,* OECD, Paris.

Ellis, J (2006), "Issues Related to a Programme of Activities under the CDM", *COM/ENV/EPOC/IEA/SLT(2006)3,* OECD, Paris.

Ellis, J. and D. Tirpak (2006), "Linking GHG Emission Trading Systems and Markets," OECD/IEA, http://www.oecd.org/dataoecd/45/35/37672298.pdf.

Enqvist, P-A. (2007), "A Cost Curve for Greenhouse Gas Reduction", *McKinsey Quarterly*, No. 1.

EPRI (2007), "Interactions of Cost-Containment Measures and Linking of Greenhouse Gas Cap-and-Trade Programs", *September Climate Brief*, Palo Alto, (http://globalclimate.epri.com/Briefs.html).

Eto, J., *et al.* (1994), *The Cost and Performance of Utility Commercial Lighting Programmes,* Lawrence Berkeley Laboratories, Berkeley, CA.

Fankhauser, S. and R.S.J. Tol (1996), The Social Costs of Climate Change. The IPCC Assessment Report and Beyond, *Mitigation and Adaptation Strategies for Global Change*, Vol. 1, No. 4, pp. 385-403.

Fankhauser, S. (1995), Valuing Climate Change – The Economics of the Greenhouse (EarthScan, London).

Fearnside, P. (2000), "Global Warming and Tropical Land-Use Change: Greenhouse Gas Emissions from Biomass Burning, Decomposition and Soils in Forest Conversion, Shifting Cultivations and Secondary Vegetation", *Climatic Change*, Vol. 46, No. 1.

Figueres, C. and M. Philips (2007), "Scaling up Demand-side energy Efficiency Improvements through Programmatic CDM", *ESMAP Technical Paper No. 120/07*, Carbon Finance Unit, World Bank.

Finus, M., E. van Ierland and R. Dellink (2006), "Stability of Climate Coalitions in a Cartel Formation Game", *Economics of Governance,* Vol. 7, No. 3.

Fischer, C. and R. Mogenstern (2008), "Metrics for Evaluating Policy Commitments in an Fragmented World: The Challenges of Equity and Integrity", *Harvard Project on International Climate Agreements Discussion paper No. 08-17*, Belfer Center for Science and International Affairs, Harvard Kennedy School.

Fischer, C. and R. Morgenstern (2006), "Carbon Abatement Costs: Why the Wide Range of Estimates?", *The Energy Journal*, Vol. 27, No. 2.

Fischer, C. and R. Newell (2007), "Environmental and Technology Policies for Climate Mitigation", *Journal of Environmental Economics and Management,* Vol. 55, No. 2.

Fischer, C., I. Parry and W. Pizer (2003), "Instrument Choice for Environmental Protection when Technological Innovation is Endogenous", *Journal of Environmental Economics and Management,*Vol. 45, No. 3.

Fisher, B., *et al.* (2007), "Issues Related to Mitigation in the Long Term Context" in Climate Change 2007: Mitigation, in B. Metz *et al.* (eds.), *Contribution of Working Group III to the Fourth Assessment Report of the Intergovernmental Panel on Climate Change (IPCC),* Cambridge University Press, Cambridge, United Kingdom and New York, NY USA.

Flachsland, C., *et al.* (2008a), "Developing the International Carbon Market: Linking Options for the EU ETS," Potsdam Institute for Climate Impact Research.

Flachsland, C., R. Marschinski, and O. Edenhofer (2008b), "Global Trading *versus* Linking: Architectures for International Emissions Trading," Potsdam Institute for Climate Impact Research.

Fullerton, D. and S. West (2000), "Tax and Subsidy Combinations for the Control of Car Pollution", *NBER Working Paper* No. 7774.

Geres, R. and A. Michaelowa (2002), "A Qualitative Method to Consider Leakage Effects from CDM and JI projects", *Energy Policy,* Vol. 30, No. 6.

Girard, P. and A. Fallot (2006), "Review of Existing and Emerging Technologies for the Production of Biofuels in Developing Countries", *Energy for Sustainable Development,* Vol. 10, No. 2.

Goulder, L., *et al.* (1999), "The Cost-effectiveness of Alternative Instruments for Environmental Effectiveness in a Second-Best Setting", *Journal of Public Economics,* Vol. 72, No. 3.

Goulder, L. and S. Schneider (1999), "Induced Technological Change and the Attractiveness of CO_2 Abatement Policies", *Resource and Energy Economics,* Vol. 21, Nos. 3-4.

Goulder, L. (1995), "Environmental Taxation and the Double Dividend: A Reader's Guide", *International Tax and Public Finance,* Vol. 2, No. 2.

Grieg-Gran, M. (2008), "The Cost of Avoiding Deforestation", Update of the Report prepared for the Stern Review of the Economics of Climate Change International Institute for Environment and Development, London.

Grieg-Gran, M. (2006), "The Costs of Avoiding Deforestation", Report prepared for the Stern Review of the Economics of Climate Change, International Institute for Environment and Development, London.

Grubb, M. and K. Neuhoff (2006), "Allocation and Competitiveness in the EU Emissions Trading Scheme: Policy Overview", *Climate Policy* No. 6, Vol. 1.

Guellec, D. and B. van Pottelsberghe (2004), "From R&D to Productivity Growth: Do the Institutional Settings and the Source of Funds of R&D Matter?", *Oxford Bulletin of Economics and Statistics,* Vol. 66, No. 3.

Gupta, S., *et al.* (2007), "Policies, Instruments and Co-operative arrangements", in B. Metz, *et al.* (eds.), *Climate Change 2007: Mitigation. Contribution of Working Group III to the Fourth Assessment Report of the Inter-Governmental Panel on Climate Change*, Cambridge University Press, Cambridge.

Hahn, R. and R. Stavins (1991), "Incentive-Based Environmental Regulation: A New Era from an Old Idea?", *Ecology Law Quarterly,* Vol. 18, No. 1.

Haites, E., and F. Mullins (2001), "Linking Domestic and Industry Greenhouse Gas Emission Trading Systems", EPRI, IEA and IETA report.

Haites, E., and Xueman Wang (2006), "Ensuring the Environmental Effectiveness of Linked Emissions Trading Schemes, http://www.margaree.ca/papers/Linking%20Trading%20Schemes-2006-05.pdf.

Hall, D., *et al.* (2008), "Policies for Developing Country Engagement", *Harvard Project on International Climate Agreements Discussion Paper* No. 2008-15, Cambridge, Massachussets.

Hall, R. and C. Jones (1999), "Why Do Some Countries Produce So Much More Output than Others?", *Quarterly Journal of Economics,* Vol. 114, No. 1.

Hanemann, M. (2009), "The Economics of Climate Change Reconsidered", *mimeo.*

Hanks, J. (2002), "Voluntary Agreements, Climate Change and Industrial Energy Efficiency", *Journal of Cleaner Production,* Vol. 10, No. 2.

Harrod, R. (1948), "*Towards a Dynamic Economics: Some Recent Developments of Economic Theory and Their Application to Policy",* MacMillan, London.

Hascic, I. and N. Johnstone (2009), "The Kyoto Protocol and International Technology Transfer: An Empirical Analysis Using Patent Data", *mimeo.*

Hassett, K. and G. Metcalf (1995), "Energy Tax Credits and Residential Conservation Investment: Evidence from Panel Data", *Journal of Public Economics,* Vol. 57, No. 2.

Helm, D. (2005), *Climate Change Policy,* Oxford University Press, Oxford.

Helm, D., C. Hepburn and R. Mash (2004), "Time-Inconsistent Environmental Policy and Optimal Delegation", *Oxford University Department of Economics Discussion Paper* No. 175.

Helm, C. (2003), "International Emissions Trading with Endogenous Allowance Choices", *Journal of Public Economics,* Vol. 87.

Henderson, D. (2005), "The Treatment of Economic Issues by the Intergovernmental Panel on Climate Change", *Energy and Environment,* Vol. 16, No. 2.

Henry, C. (1974), "Investment Decisions Under Uncertainty: the Irreversibility Effect", A*merican Economic Review No.* 64, pp. 1006–12.

Hertel, T., S. Rose and R. Tol (2008), "Land Use in Computable General Equilibrium Models: An Overview", in: T. Hertel, S. Rose and R. Tol (eds.), *Economic Analysis of Land Use in Global Climate Change Policy.*

Hinostroza, M., *et al.* (2007), "Potentials and Barriers for End-Use Energy Efficiency Under Programmatic CDM", *CD4CDM Working Paper No. 3,* UNEP RISO Centre.

Hoel, M. and L. Karp (2001), "Taxes and Quotas for a Stock Pollutant with Multiplicative Uncertainty", *Journal of Public Economics,* Vol. 82, No. 1.

Holland, M., *et al.* (2004), Final Methodology Paper (Volume 1) for the Clean Air for Europe Programme (CAFE), European Commission, DG Environment, AEAT/ED51014/Methodology, Issue 4, Brussels, Belgium.

Hoogwijk, M., *et al.* (2008), *"Sectoral Mitigation Potentials : Bottom Up and Top Down Comparison Project",* Netherlands Environmental Assessment Agency (available at www.mnp.nl).

Houghton, R. (2008), "Carbon Flux to the Atmosphere from Land-Use Changes: 1850-2005", in TRENDS: A Compendium of Data on Global Change. Carbon Dioxide Information Analysis Center, Oak Ridge National Laboratory, U.S. Department of Energy, Oak Ridge, Tennessee.

Houghton, R. (2003), "Revised Estimates of the Annual Net Flux of Carbon to the Atmosphere from Changes in Land Use and Land Management 1850-2000", *Tellus B*, Vol. 55, No. 2.

Houghton, R. (1999), "The Annual Net Flux of Carbon to the Atmosphere from Changes in Land Use 1850-1990", *Tellus B*, Vol. 51, No. 2.

Hourcade, J.C. and P. Shukla (2001), "Global, Regional and National Costs and Ancillary Benefits of Mitigation", in IPCC (eds.), *Third Assessment Report of the Intergovernmental Panel on Climate Change,* Cambridge University Press, New York.

IEA (2008a), *World Energy Outlook,* Paris.

IEA (2008b), *Energy Technology Perspectives*, Paris.

IEA (2007a), *Climate Policy Uncertainty and Investment Risk,* Paris.

IEA (2007b), *Mind the Gap,* Paris.

IEA (2007c), *World Energy Outlook*, Paris.

IEA (2007d), *International Standards to Develop and Promote Energy Efficiency and Renewable Energy Sources*, Paris.

IEA (2006), *World Energy Outlook,* Paris.

IEA (2005), *Deploying Climate-Friendly Technologies through Collaboration with Developing Countries,* Paris.

IEA (2000), *Experience Curves for Energy Technology Policy,* Paris.

IEA (1999), World Energy Outlook, Looking at Energy Subsidies: Getting the Prices Right, OECD/IEA, Paris.

IMF (2008), *World Economic Outlook*, International Monetary Fund, April.

IPCC (2007), *Fourth Assessment Report of the Intergovernmental Panel on Climate Change*, Cambridge University Press, New-York.

IPCC (1995), *Second Assessment Report of the Intergovernmental Panel on Climate Change*, Cambridge University Press, New-York.

Jaffe, J. and R. Stavins (2007), "Linking Tradable Permit Systems for Greenhouse Gas Emissions: Opportunities, Implications, and Challenges", IETA report.

Jaffe, A., R. Newell and R. Stavins (2005), "A Tale of Two Market Failures: Technology and Environmental Policy", *Ecological Economics*, Vol. 54, Nos. 2-3.

Jaffe, A., R. Newell and R. Stavins (2003), "Technological Change and the Environment", in K-G. Mäler and J. Vincent (eds.), *Handbook of Environmental Economics*, Vol. 1, North Holland, Amsterdam.

Jaffe, A. and R. Stavins (1995), "Dynamic Incentives of Environmental Regulations: The Effects of Alternative Policy Instruments on Technology Diffusion", *Journal of Environmental Economics and Management,* Vol. 29, No. 3.

Jakeman, G. and B.S. Fisher (2006), "Benefits of Multi-Gas Mitigation: An Application of the Global Trade and Environment Model (GTEM), Multi-Gas Mitigation and Climate Policy", *The Energy Journal* No. 27, Vol. 3, pp. 323–342.

Jamet, S. (2009), "Carbon Price Uncertainty and Firms Investment Decisions: A Theoretical Analysis", *OECD Economics Department Working Papers,* forthcoming, Paris.

Jamet, S. and J. Corfee-Morlot (2009), "Assessing the Impacts of Climate Change: A Literature Review", *OECD Economics Department Working Papers* No. 693, Paris.

Jaumotte, F. and N. Pain (2005), "Innovation Policies and Innovation in the Business Sector", *OECD Economics Department Working Papers* No. 459, Paris.

Johansson, A, *et al.* (2008), "Taxation and Economic Growth", *OECD Economics Department Working Papers* No. 620.

Johnston, A. (2006), "Free Allocation of Allowances under the EU Emissions Trading Scheme: Legal Issues", *Climate Policy,* Vol. 6, No. 1.

Johnstone, N., I. Hascic and D. Popp (2008), "Renewable Energy Policy and Technological Innovation: Evidence Based on Patent Counts", *NBER Working Paper* No. 13760.

Jotzo, F. and J. Pezzey (2007), "Optimal Intensity Targets for Greenhouse Gas Emissions Trading Under Uncertainty", *Environmental and Resource Economics,* Vol. 38, No. 2.

Jung, C., K. Krutilla and R. Boyd (1996), "Incentives for Advanced Pollution Abatement Technology at the Industry Level: An Evaluation of Policy Alternatives", *Journal of Environmental Economics and Management,* Vol. 30, No. 1.

Kallbekken, S., L. Flottorp and N. Rive (2007a), "CDM Baseline Approaches and Carbon Leakage", *Energy Policy,* Vol. 35, No. 8.

Kallbekken, S. (2007b), "Why the CDM will Reduce Carbon Leakage", *Climate Policy,* Vol. 7, No. 3.

Karousakis, K., B. Guay and C. Philibert (2008), "Differentiating Countries in terms of Mitigation Commitments, Actions and Support", *COM/ENV/EPOC/IEA/SLT(2008)2,* OECD, Paris.

Karousakis, K. and J. Corfee-Morlot (2007), "Financing Mechanisms to Reduce Emissions from Deforestation: Issues in Design and Implementation", OECD/IEA, Paris.

Keeler, A. and A. Thompson (2008), "Industrialized-Country Mitigation Policy and Resource Transfers to Developing Countries: Improving and Expanding Greenhouse Gas Offsets", *Discussion Paper 2008-05,* Harvard Project on International Climate Agreements, Cambridge, Massachussets.

Kennedy, P. and B. Laplante (1999), "Environmental Policy and Time Inconsistency: Emissions Taxes and Emissions Trading", in E. Petrakis, E. Sarzetakis and A. Xepapadeas (eds.), *Environmental Regulation and Market Power: Competition, Time Inconsistency and International Trade,* Northampton, Edward Elgar, UK.

Keohane, R. and K. Raustiala (2008), "Toward a Post-Kyoto Climate Change Architecture: a Political Analysis", *The Harvard Project on International Climate Agreements Discussion Paper* No. 08-01.

Keohane, N. (2001), Essays in the Economics of Environmental Policy, Ph.D. Dissertation, Harvard University.

Keohane, N. (1999), "Policy Instruments and the Diffusion of Pollution Abatement Technology", *mimeo,* Harvard University.

Kerr, S. and R. Newell (2004), "Policy-Induced Technology Adoption: Evidence from the U.S. Lead Phasedown", Journal of Industrial Economics, Vol. 51 No. 3.

Kerr, S. and D. Maré (1998), "Transaction Costs and Tradable Permit Markets: The United States Lead Phasedown", *mimeo,* Motu Economic and Public Policy Research.

Kindermann, G., *et al.* (2008), "Global Cost Estimates of Reducing Carbon Emissions through Avoided Deforestation", *PNAS*, Vol. 105, No. 30.

Kindermann, G., *et al.* (2006), "Predicting the Deforestation Trend under Different Carbon Prices", *Carbon Balance and Management*, Vol. 1, No. 15.

Kolstad, C. (2006), "The Simple Analytics of Greenhouse Gas Emission Intensity Reduction Targets", *Energy Policy,* Vol. 33, No. 17.

Kremer, M. (2001a), "Creating Markets for New Vaccines: Part I: Rationale", in B. Jaffe, J. Lerner and S. Stern (eds.), *Innovation Policy and the Economy,* Vol. 1, MIT Press, Cambridge, Massachussets.

Kremer, M. (2001b), "Creating Markets for New Vaccines: Part II: Design Issues", in B. Jaffe, J. Lerner and S. Stern (eds.), *Innovation Policy and the Economy,* Vol. 1, MIT Press, Cambridge, Massachussets.

Levine, M., *et al.* (1994), *Energy Efficiency, Market Failures and Government Policy,* Lawrence Berkeley Laboratory and Oak Ridge Laboratory, Berkeley, CA.

Maeda, A. (2003), "The Emergence of Market Power in the Emission Rights Markets: The Role of Initial Permit Distribution", *Journal of Regulatory Economics,* Vol. 24, No. 3.

Malhi, Y. and J. Grace (2000), "Tropical Forest and Atmospheric Carbon Dioxide", *Trends in Ecology and Evolution*, Vol. 15, No. 8.

Marcu, M. and W. Pizer (2003), "Special Supplement on Defining and Trading Emission Targets", *Climate Policy,* Vol. 3, Supplement 2.

Marschinski, R. and F. Lecocq (2006), "Do Intensity Targets Control Uncertainty Better than Quotas? Conditions, Calibration and Caveats", *World Bank Policy Research Working Paper* No. 4033.

Maskus, K. (2004), "Encouraging International Technology Transfer", *ICSTD/UNCTAD Issue Paper* No. 7, UNCTAD-ICSTD Project on IPRs and Sustainable Development.

Maskus, K. (2000), *Intellectual Property Rights in the Global Economy,* Institute for International Economics, Washington D.C.

Matthes, F.C. and H.-J. Ziesing (2008), "Die Entwicklung des deutschen Kraftwerksparks und die aktuelle Debatte um die künftige Strombedarfsdeckung", Öko-Institut Discussion Paper 2008, available at:
http://www.oeko.de/oekodoc/722/2008-196-de.pdf?PHPSESSID=u3nhgdkbn8h6kt4783js54pd62

McDonald, A. and L. Schrattenholzer (2001), "Learning Rates for Energy Technologies", *Energy Policy* Vol. 29, No. 4, pp. 255-261.

McKibbin, W. (2007),"Climate Change Policy: From National to International", 2006 Sir Lesley Melville Lecture. Lowy Institute for International Policy Perspectives.

McKibbin, W. and P. Wilcoxen (2007), "A Credible Foundation for Long Term International Cooperation on Climate Change", in J. Aldy and R. Stavins (eds.), *Architectures for Agreement:*

Addressing Global Climate Change in the Post-Kyoto World, Cambridge University Press, Cambridge.

McKibbin, W. and P. Wilcoxen (2006), "A Credible Foundation for Long-Term International Cooperation on Climate Change," Lowy Institute.

McKibbin, W. and P. Wilcoxen (2002), Climate Change Policy After Kyoto: A Blueprint for a Realistic Approach, Brookings Institution, Washington D.C.

McKinsey & Company (2009), "Pathways to a Low-Carbon Economy: Version 2 of the Global Greenhouse Gas Abatement Cost Curve", McKinsey & Company.

Mendelsohn, R., M. Schlesinger and L. Williams (2000), "Comparing Impacts Across Climate Models" *Integrated Assessment*, 2000:1.

Mendelsohn, R.O., *et al.* (1998), "Country-specific Market Impacts of Climate Change", *Climatic Change* No. 45, Vol. 3-4, pp. 553–569.

Mexico (2008), "World Climate Change Fund (Green Fund): Mexico's Proposal under the Bali Action Plan", *Working Paper,* 5 June.

Milliman, S. and R. Prince (1989), "Firm Incentives to Promote Technological Change in Pollution Control", *Journal of Environmental Economics and Management,* Vol. 17, No. 3.

Mollicone, D., *et al.* (2003), "Land Use Change Monitoring in the Framework of the UNFCCC and its Kyoto Protocol", Report on Current Capabilities of Satellite Remote Sensing Technology, European Community Luxembourg.

Montero, J-P. (2005), "Pollution Markets with Imperfectly Observed Emissions", *RAND Journal of Economics,* Vol. 36, No. 3.

Montero, J-P. (2002), "Permits, Standards, and Technology Innovation", *Journal of Environmental Economics and Management,* Vol. 44, No. 1.

Nagashima, M., *et al.* (2009), "Stability of International Climate Coalitions – A Comparison for Transfer Schemes", *Ecological Economics,* Vol. 8, No. 4.

Nakicenovic, N., *et al.* (2000), *Special Report on Emission Scenarios. Working Group III, Intergovernemental Panel on Climate Change (IPCC)*, Cambridge University Press, Cambridge.

National Research Council (2007), *Innovation Inducement Prizes at the National Science Foundation,* National Academies Press, Washington D.C.

Neij, L., P. Andersen and M. Durstewitz (2003a), "The Use of Experience Curves for Assessing Energy Policy Programmes", in IEA (eds), *Experience Curves: Tool for Energy Policy Analysis and Design*, Proceedings of joint European Union/International Energy Agency Workshop, Paris.

Neij, L., *et al.* (2003b), "Experience Curves: A Tool for Energy Policy Assessment", *Environmental and Energy Systems Studies*, Lund University, Sweden.

Nepstad, D., *et al.* (2007), "The Costs and Benefits of Reducing Carbon Emissions from Deforestation and Forest Degradation in the Brazilian Amazon", Woods Hole Research, Falmouth, MA.

Neuhoff, K., K.K. Martinez and M. Sato (2006), "Allocation, Incentives and Distortions: the Impact of EU ETS Emissions Allowance Allocations to the Electricity Sector", *Climate Policy* No.°6.

New Carbon Finance (2009), "The Impact of Forestry on the Global Carbon Market", 25 February.

Newell, R. (2008), "International Climate Technology Strategies", *Harvard Project on International Climate Agreements Discussion Paper* No. 2008-12, Cambridge, Massachussets.

Newell, R. and N. Wilson (2005), "Technology Prizes for Climate Change Mitigation", *Resources for the Future Discussion Paper* No. 05-33.

Newell, R. and W. Pizer (2003), "Regulating Stock Externalities Under Uncertainty", *Journal of Environmental Economics and Management,* Vol. 45, No. 2.

Nordhaus, W. (2007), "A Review of the Stern Review on the Economics of Climate Change", *Journal of Economic Literature*, Vol. 45, No. 3.

Nordhaus, W.D. and J. Boyer (2000), "Warming the World: Economic Models of Global Warming", The MIT Press.

Nordhaus, W.D. (1991), "To Slow or Not to Slow: The Economics of the Greenhouse Effect", *Economic Journal,* No. 101 pp. 920–937.

OECD, (2009), *Integrating Climate Change Adaptation into Development Co-operation: Policy Guidance*, Paris.

OECD (2008a), *Costs of Inaction on Key Environmental Challenges*, Paris.

OECD (2008b), *OECD Environmental Outlook to 2030*, Paris.

OECD (2008c), *Infrastructure Investment: Links to Growth and the Role of Public Policies,* Paris.

OECD (2008d), *Biofuel Support Policies: An Economic Assessment*, Paris.

OECD (2008e), "Eco-Innovation: Environmental Policy Design and Technology Transfer", *ENV/EPOC/WPNEP(2008)6,* Paris.

OECD (2008f), "Economic Aspects of Adaptation to Climate Change: An Assessment of Costs, Benefits and Policy Instruments", *ENV/EPOC/GSP(2008)7,* Paris.

OECD (2007a), "Environmentally Related Taxes and Tradable Permits in Practice", *COM/ENV/EPOC/CTPA/CFA(2007)31,* Paris.

OECD (2007b), "Instrument Mixes for Environmental Policy", *ENV/EPOC/WPNEP(2006)9/REV2,* Paris.

OECD (2007c), *Financial Market Trends*, No. 94, Paris.

OECD (2006a), "Sensitivity analysis in ENV-Linkages", *ENV/EPOC/GSP(2006)6*, Paris

OECD (2006b), *The Political Economy of Environmentally Related Taxes*, Paris.

OECD (2006c), *Economic Policy Reforms: Going for Growth,* Paris.

OECD (2004), *Sustainable Development in OECD Countries*, Paris.

OECD (2003), *Voluntary Approaches for Environmental Policy: Effectiveness, Efficiency and Usage in Policy Mixes*, Paris.

OECD (2001), "The Commitment Period Reserve", *Information Paper, COM/ENV/EPOC/IEA/SLT(2001)13*, http://www.oecd.org/dataoecd/50/20/2468753.pdf, Paris.

OECD (2000), *Ancillary Benefits and Costs of Greenhouse Gas Mitigation*, Paris.

OECD (1999), *Action Against Climate Change: The Kyoto Protocol and Beyond*, Paris.

OECD International Transport Forum (2007), *Biofuels: Linking Support to Performance*, Paris.

OECD Roundtable on Sustainable Development (2007), "Biofuels: Is the Cure Worse than the Disease?", *Round Table on Sustainable Development, SG/SD/RT(2007)3,* Paris.

Ogonowski, M., *et al.* (2007), "Reducing Emissions from Deforestation and Degradation: The Dual Markets Approach", Center for Clear Air Policy, August.

Olson, M. (1965), *The Logic of Collective Action*, Harvard University Press, Cambridge, Massachusetts.

Palmer, K., W. Oates and P. Portney (1995), "Tightening Environmental Standards: The Benefit-Cost or the No-Cost Paradigm?" *Journal of Economic Perspectives,* Vol. 9, No. 4.

Park, W., and D. Lippoldt (2008), "Technology Transfer and the Economic Implications of the Strengthening of Intellectual Property Rights in Developing Countries", *OECD Trade Policy Working Papers,* No. 62.

Parry, I. (1998), "Pollution Regulation and the Efficiency Gains from Technological Innovation", *Journal of Regulatory Economics,* Vol. 14, No. 3.

Pacala, S. and R. Socolow (2004), "Stabilization Wedges: Solving the Climate Problem for the Next 50 Years with Current Technologies", *Science,* Vol. 305, No. 5686, pp. 968-972.

Perez, R. (2007), "Towards a Generalized System of Environmental Tariffs?", *mimeo*, United Nations.

Pezzy, J. and A. Park (1998), "Reflections on the Double Dividend Debate: The Importance of Interest Groups and Information Costs", *Environmental and Resource Economics,* Vol. 11, Nos. 3-4.

Philibert, C., J. Ellis and J. Podkanski (2007), "Carbon Capture and Storage in the CDM", *COM/ENV/EPOC/IEA/SLT(2007)10,* OECD, Paris.

Philibert, C. (2005), "New Commitment Options: Compatibility with Emissions Trading", *mimeo*, International Energy Agency, Paris (http://www.iea.org/textbase/papers/2005/cp_commitment.pdf).

Pigou, A. (1920), *The Economics of Welfare*, Macmillan &Company, London.

Pindyck, R. (2007), "Uncertainty in Environmental Economics", *Review of Environmental Economics and Policy*, Vol. 1, Issue 1, Winter, pp. 45–65.

Piris-Cabezas, P. and N. Keohane (2008), "Reducing Emissions from Deforestation and ForestDegradation: Implications for Carbon Market", Environmental Defense Fund, Washington D.C.

Pizer, W. (2002), "Combining Price and Quantity Controls to Mitigate Global Climate Change", *Journal of Public Economics,* Vol. 85, No. 3.

Plantinga, J. and K. Richards (2008), "International Carbon Sequestration in a Post Kyoto Agreement", Harward Kennedy School, Cambridge Massachusetts.

Point Carbon (2007), "Issues in the International Carbon Market, 2008-2012 and Beyond", Study for New Zealand Emissions Trading Group.

Popp, D. (2004), "ENTICE: Endogenous Technological Change in the DICE Model of Global Warming", *Journal of Environmental Economics and Management,* Vol. 48, No. 1.

Popp, D. (2002), "Induced Innovation and Energy Prices", *American Economic Review* Vol. 92, No. 1, pp. 160–180.

Porter, M. and C. van der Linde (1995), "Toward a New Conception of the Environment-Competitiveness Relationship", *Journal of Economic Perspectives,* Vol. 9, No. 4.

Ramsey, F. (1928), "A Mathematical Theory of Saving", *Economic Journal,* Vol. 38, No. 152.

Rao, S. and K. Riahi (2006), "The Role of Non-CO_2 Greenhouse Gases in Climate Change Mitigation: Long Term Scenarios for the 21st Century", *The Energy Journal*, No. 3, pp. 177-200.

Rehdanz, K. and R.S.J. Tol (2005), "Unilateral Regulation of Bilateral Trade in Greenhouse Gas Emission Permits", *Ecological Economics*, Vol. 54, pp. 397-416.

Reilly, J., *et al.* (2007), "Global Economic Effects of Changes in Crops, Pasture, and Forests Due to Changing Climate, Carbon Dioxide, and Ozone", *Energy Policy*, Elsevier, Vol. 35(11), pp. 5370-5383.

Reinaud, J. and C. Philibert (2007), "Emissions Trading: Trends and Prospects", OECD/IEA, Paris, http://www.oecd.org/dataoecd/60/38/39725657.pdf.

Riahi, K., A. Grubler, and N. Nakicenovic (2006), "Scenarios of Long-Term Socio-Economic and Environmental Development Under Climate Stabilization", *Technological Forecasting and Change*, Special Issue, No. 74 pp. 8-9.

Roberts, M. and M. Spence (1976), "Effluent Charges and Licenses Under Uncertainty", *Journal of Public Economics,* Vol. 5, No. 3-4.

Russell, C. and W. Vaughan (2003), "The Choice of Pollution Control Policy Instruments in Developing Countries: Arguments, Evidence and Suggestions", in H. Folmer and T. Tietenberg (eds.), *The*

International Yearbook of Environmental and Resource Economics, 2003/2004, Cheltenham, Edward Elgar, UK.

Sathaye, J., *et al.* (2006), "GHG Mitigation Potential Costs and Benefits of Global Forests", *Energy Journal*, Vol. 27 (Multi-Greenhouse Gas Special Issue).

Sawa, A. (2008), "A Sectoral Approach as an Option for a Post-Kyoto Framework", Discussion Paper 08-23, The Harvard Project on International Climate Agreements.

Schelling, T. (2007), "Climate Change: the Uncertainties, the Certainties, and What They Imply About Action", *The Economists' Voice,* Vol. 4, No. 3.

Schmalensee, R. (1994), "The Costs of Environmental Protection", in M. Kotowski (ed.), *Balancing Economic Growth and Environmental Goals*, American Council for Capital Formation, Center for Policy Research, Washington D.C.

Schneider, L. (2007)," Is the CDM Fulfilling its Environmental and Sustainable Development Objectives? An Evaluation of the CDM and Options for Improvement", Report prepared for WWF, Öko-Institut, Berlin.

Schneider, S. and L. Goulder (1997), "Achieving Low-cost Emissions Targets", Nature, Vol. 389, No. 4.

Schwank, O. (2004), Concerns About CDM Projects Based on Decomposition of HFC-23 from HCFC-22 Production Sites, Infras, Zurich.

Sinn, H-W. (2007), "Public Policies Against Global Warming", *NBER Working Paper,* No. 13454.

Sohngen, B., A. Golub and T. Hertel (2008), "The Role of Forestry in Carbon Sequestration in General Equlibrium Models" in: T. Hertel, S. Rose and R. Tol (eds.), *Economic Analysis of Land Use in Global Climate Change Policy.*

Sohngen, B. and R. Mendelsohn (2003), "An Optimal Control Model of Forest Carbon Sequestration", *Americal Journal of Agricultural Economics*, Vol. 85, No. 2.

Sohngen, B., R. Mendelsohn and R. Sedjo (1999), "Forest Management, Conservation and Global Timber Market", *Americal Journal of Agricultural Economics*, Vol. 81, No. 1.

Solow, R.M. (1974), "The Economics of Resources or the Resources of Economics", *American Economic Review*, Vol. 64, No. 2.

Sorrell, S. and J. Sijm (2003), "Carbon Trading in the Policy Mix", *Oxford Review of Economic Policy,* Vol. 19, No. 3.

Sorrell, S. (2002), "The Climate Confusion: Implications of the EU Emissions Trading Scheme for the UK Climate Change Levy and Climate Change Agreements", Science and Technology Policy Research (SPRU), University of Sussex, Brighton, UK.

Sorrell, S., *et al.* (2000), *Barriers to Energy Efficiency in Public and Private Organisations, Science and Technology Policy Research,* University of Sussex, Brighton, UK.

Stavins, R. (1997), "Policy Instruments for Climate Change: How Can National Governments Address a Global Problem?", *The University of Chicago Legal Forum*, Vol. 1997.

Steenblik, R. (2007), "Subsidies: The Distorted Economics of Biofuels", in OECD/ITF Roundtable, *Biofuels: Linking Support to Performance*, Paris.

Steenblik, R. (2006), "Liberalisation of Trade in Renewable Energy and Associated Technologies: Biodiesel, Solar Thermal and Geothermal Energy", *OECD Trade and Environment Working Paper* No. 2006-01, Paris.

Steenblik, R., S. Vaughan and P. Waide (2006), "Can Energy-Efficient Electrical Appliances be Considered "Environmental Goods?", *OECD Trade and Environment Working Paper* No. 2006-04, Paris.

Steenblik, R. (2005), "Liberalisation of Trade in Renewable-Energy Products and Associated Goods: Charcoal, Solar Photovoltaic Systems, and Wind Pumps and Turbines", *OECD Trade and Environment Working Paper* No. 2005-07, Paris.

Sterk, W., *et al.* (2006), "Ready to Link Up? Implications of Design Differences for Linking Emissions Trading Schemes", Jet-Set Working Paper I/06; Wuppertal Institute.

Stern, N. (2008), "The Economics of Climate Change", *American Economic Review*, Vol. 98, No. 2.

Stern, N. (2007), *The Economics of Climate Change: The Stern Review*, CUP, Cambridge.

Sterner, T. (2003), "Policy Instruments for Environmental and Natural Resource Management, Resources for the Future Press", Washington D.C.

Stiglitz, J. (2006), "A New Agenda for Global Warming", The Economists' Voice, Vol. 3, No. 7.

Stoneman, P. and P. Diederen (1994), "Technology Diffusion and Public Policy", *Economic Journal,* Vol. 104, No. 425.

Strassburg, B., *et al.* (2009), "Reducing Emissions from Deforestation: The Combined Incentives Mechanism and Empirical Simulations", *Global Environmental Change*, in press (DOI 10.1016/j.gloenvcha.2008.11.004).

Tavoni, M., B. Sohngen and V. Bossetti (2007), "Forestry and the Carbon Market Response to Stabilize Climate", *Energy Policy,* Vol. 35, No. 11.

Tol, R.S.J. (2005a) "Adaptation and Mitigation: Trade-Offs in Substance and Methods", *Environmental Science & Policy*, Vol. 8, pp. 572-578.

Tol., R.S.J. (2005b), "The Marginal Damage Costs of Carbon Dioxide Emissions: An Assessment of Uncertainties", *Energy Policy*, No. 33, pp. 2064-2074.

Tol, R. (2002), "New Estimates of the Damage Costs of Climate Change, Part II: Dynamic Estimates", *Environmental and Resource Economics*, Vol. 21, No. 2, pp. 135-160.

Tol, R.S.J. and H. Dowlatabadi (2001), "Vector-Borne Diseases, Development & Climate Change, *The Integrated Assessment Journal*, Vol. 2, pp. 173-181.

Uhrig-Homburg M. and M. Wagner (2008), "Instruments in the EU Emissions Trading Scheme - An Early Market Perspective", *Energy and Environment*, Vol. 19, No. 5, Available at SSRN: http://ssrn.com/abstract=882792.

UNDP (2007), *Human Development Report 2007/2008: Fighting Climate Change: Human Solidarity in a Divided World,* Washington D.C.

UNFCCC (2009), *Investment and Financial Flows to Address Climate Change: An Update.*

UNFCCC (2007a), *Investment and Financial Flows to Address Climate Change: Background Paper,* Bonn.

UNFCCC (2007b), Decision 1/CP.13, FCCC/CP/2007/6/Add. 1.

UNFCCC (2005), "Decision/CMP.1, Modalities and Procedures for a Clean Development Mechanism as Defined in Article 12 of the Kyoto Protocol", in UNFCCC Secretariat, *COP11/MOP1,* UNFCCC, Montreal.

Van Vuuren, DP, *et al.* (2007), "Stabilising Greenhouse Gas Concentrations at Low Levels: An Assessment of Reduction Strategies and Costs", *Climatic Change*, No. 81, pp. 119-159.

Victor, D.G. (2001), *The Collapse of the Kyoto Protocol and the Struggle to Slow Global Warming,* Princeton: Princeton University Press.

Vöhringer, F., T. Kuosmanen and R. Dellink (2006), "How to Attribute Market Leakage to CDM Projects", *Climate Policy,* Vol. 5, No. 5.

Wagner, M. and M. Uhrig-Homburg (2007), "Instruments in the EU Emissions Trading Scheme - An Early Market Perspective", *Energy and Environment*, 2008, Available at SSRN: http://ssrn.com/abstract=882792.

Walter, A., *et al.* (2007), "Market Evaluation: Fuel Ethanol", *Task 40 Sustainable Bio-Energy Trade: Securing Supply and Demand (Deliverable 8),* State University of Campinas (Unicamp), Campinas, Brazil.

Wara, W. and D. Victor (2008), "A Realistic Policy on International Carbon Offsets", *Working Paper No.°74*, Stanford University.

Watkiss, P. and T. Downing (2008), "The Social Cost of Carbon: Valuation Estimates and their Use in IK Policy", *The Integrated Assessment Journal*, Vol. 8, No. 1.

Weitzman, M. (2007a), "A Review of the Stern Review on the Economics of Climate Change", *Journal of Economic Literature*, Vol. 45, No. 3.

Weitzman, M. (2007b), "Structural Uncertainty and the Value of Statistical Life in the Economics of Catastrophic Climate Change", *NBER Working Paper* No. 13490.

Weitzman, M. (2001), "Gamma Discounting", *American Economic Review*, Vol. 91, No. 1.

Weitzman, M. (1974), "Prices vs. Quantities", *Review of Economic Studies*, Vol. 41, No. 4.

World Bank (2008), "State and Trends of the Carbon Market 2008", World Bank Institute, Washington D.C.

World Bank (2007), *International Trade and Climate Change: Economic, Legal and Institutional Perspectives,* The World Bank, Washington D.C.

World Bank (2006), *Clean Energy and Development: Towards an Investment Framework,* The World Bank, Washington D.C.

WRI (2009), *Climate Analysis Indicators Tool* (CAIT), Version 6.0, World Resources Institute, Washington, DC.

Wright, B. (1983), "The Economics of Invention Incentives: Patents, Prizes, and Research Contracts", *American Economic Review* Vol. 73, No. 4.

Yohe, G. (2007), "Prepared Statement of Gary W. Yohe", Weslyan University. U.S. Senate Committee on Resources and Energy, Full Committee Hearing: Stern Review of the Economics of Climate Change.

Yohe, G. (2006), "Some Thoughts on the Damage Estimates Presented in the Stern Review - An Editorial", *Integrated Assessment Journal,* Vol. 6, No. 3.

Zerbe, R. (1970), "Theoretical Efficiency in Pollution Control", *Western Economic Journal,* Vol. 8, No. 4.

ISBN: 978-92-64-05606-0
The Economics of Climate Change Mitigation
Policies and Options for Global Action beyond 2012

Annex 1

Long-Run GDP Growth Framework and Scenarios for the World Economy

Introduction

This annex applies a simple "conditional growth" framework to long-term GDP projections for the world economy that serves as a baseline for the examination of policy scenarios.[1] Baseline economic scenarios have proliferated in recent years in the context of climate change projections, such as those developed by the Intergovernmental Panel on Climate Change (IPCC), which typically assumes a convergence process whereby the income levels of less-developed countries gradually, and at least partially, catch-up to those of more developed economies.[2] The vast majority of projections focus on convergence at the macroeconomic level, in terms of GDP per capita or GDP per worker (the "top-down" approach) while a few others assume some gradual catch-up at the sectoral level (the "bottom-up" approach).[3] In both cases, climate modellers have typically relied on simple assumptions regarding the form and the speed of convergence, without explicitly specifying the policy assumptions underlying their scenarios. This, and the fact that in the IPCC's Special Report on Emission Scenarios (SRES) a large number of possible outcomes are presented as being equally likely, may have contributed to strengthening the impression of uncertainty that is inherent to any long-run world economic projections.[4]

In this annex, special emphasis is put on setting up a theoretical framework that explicitly integrates some of the current theoretical and empirical knowledge regarding the long-run drivers of economic growth. At the same time, reflecting both data constraints and the wide diversity of existing growth theories,[5] a simple and fairly consensual framework is retained, in which GDP per capita depends on technology, investment in physical capital, investment in human capital and the employment rate, and "conditional growth convergence" applies. With this framework at hand, a baseline scenario can be constructed based on explicit assumptions regarding each of the four growth drivers. As well, plausible alternative scenarios can be built up in order to roughly assess the degree of uncertainty surrounding the projections, while still placing some bounds on the future path of world GDP.

Against this background, the annex proceeds as follows. Section A1.1 presents the theoretical framework underlying the long-run GDP projections. Section A1.2 discusses the assumptions made within this framework in order to construct a baseline scenario, including at the sectoral level, and provides the associated GDP projections. Section A1.3 provides the sources of data. The final section presents in table form the results from selected simulations that are discussed in Chapter 4 of the book and illustrated in corresponding figures.

It should be stressed upfront that the projections presented in this annex were built as part of an OECD project carried out in the course of 2008. As a result, they do not incorporate the sharp deterioration in world economic activity and forecasts that occurred during the second half of 2008 and first half of 2009. Factoring in this slowdown would imply a downward revision of world GDP growth over the first 5-10 years of the projection period, but would be expected to have very small, if any, effects over the period up to 2050, at least insofar as long-run potential growth is only marginally affected.

A1.1. Theoretical framework and basic assumptions underlying its empirical implementation

A1.1.1. Theoretical framework

While there is no agreement on any single theoretical model of economic growth, a basic empirical consensus – including previous OECD work – seems to support the so-called "conditional convergence" hypothesis.[6] This hypothesis basically states that a country's growth rate in GDP per capita should be negatively related to the starting level of its GDP per capita conditional on fixed values of other variables, including *inter alia* investment rates in physical and human capital, policies and institutions more broadly, demographics, geography etc. As a result, each country would be expected to converge to its own steady-state level of GDP per capita determined by the above-mentioned variables. Because the latter vary across countries, in the long-run differences would remain in per capita income levels but not in growth rates.

In order to incorporate the conditional convergence hypothesis into the projections, this annex adopts the most widely-used theoretical framework in recent empirical analyses of cross-country disparities in per-capita incomes (Caselli, 2005; Caselli and Coleman, 2006; Easterly and Levine, 2001; Hall and Jones, 1999; Jones, 1997; Klenow and Rodriguez-Clare, 1997; OECD, 2004). Cross-country variation in the levels of output per worker is typically decomposed into parts attributed to the variation in physical and human capital per worker and total factor productivity (TFP). Such exercises have found TFP and – to a lesser extent – human capital to be the main drivers of current disparities in living standards between developed and developing economies.[7] With such decomposition at hand, long-run output per worker scenarios for each country may then be built up by projecting each of the three components (see *e.g.* Jones, 1997).

Concretely, as shown in Box 1, based on a standard aggregate Cobb-Douglas production function with physical capital, human capital, and labour as production factors and labour-augmenting technological progress, and assuming that production function is invariant both across countries and over time, GDP per capita can be decomposed as follows:[8]

$$Y_t / Pop_t = (K_t / Y_t)^{\alpha/(1-\alpha)} A_t h_t (L_t / Pop_t) \quad (1)$$

where K_t/Y_t, A_t, h_t, and L_t/Pop_t denote the capital/output ratio, TFP, human capital per worker and the employment rate (defined here as the ratio of employment to *total* population), respectively, and α is the capital share in aggregate output.

Such decomposition can be performed for a base year, and long-run projections then be made for each of the four components in order to project the future path of GDP per capita.

Box A1.1 Disentangling the long-run drivers of GDP per capita

Consider a standard Cobb-Douglas production function with capital and skilled labour and labour-augmenting (Harrod-neutral) technological progress:

$$Y_t = K_t^{\alpha}(A_t H_t)^{1-\alpha} = K_t^{\alpha}(A_t h_t L_t)^{1-\alpha}$$

where Y, K, H, h, L and A denote output, physical capital, effective labour input, human capital per worker, employment and TFP, respectively. After some basic manipulations, this can be re-written as:

$$Y_t / L_t = (K_t / Y_t)^{\alpha/(1-\alpha)} A_t h_t$$

GDP per capita and GDP can then be written respectively as (with Pop denoting population):

$$Y_t / Pop_t = (Y_t / L_t)(L_t / Pop_t) = (K_t / Y_t)^{\alpha/(1-\alpha)} A_t h_t (L_t / Pop_t)$$

and:

$$Y_t = (Y_t / L_t)(L_t / Pop_t)Pop_t = (K_t / Y_t)^{\alpha/(1-\alpha)} A_t h_t (L_t / Pop_t)Pop_t$$

Cross-country differences in GDP per capita at any point in time can thus be decomposed into four components: [1]

- Capital/output ratios
- Human capital per worker
- TFPs
- Employment rates

1. In principle, hours worked could also be incorporated as another driver of cross-country differences in GDP per capita. In practice, however, this would be feasible only for OECD countries, due to data availability constraints. This factor is therefore omitted from the framework. This means that any cross-country differences in hours worked will ultimately be captured as cross-country differences in TFP, and any TFP convergence scenario will also implicitly include an hours worked convergence scenario.

A1.1.2. Basic assumptions underlying the empirical implementation of the theoretical framework

In order to perform the decomposition featured in equation (1) for a base year, comparable data are needed across countries for labour productivity, TFP, the capital/output ratio, human capital per worker and the employment rate. This in turn implies a number of simplifications to facilitate harmonisation, not least regarding physical capital stocks. Data sources and data construction methodology are described in detail in Section A1.3. The key features of the data are the following:

- Two base years are considered, 1995 and 2005.

- Labour productivity levels are computed for each country as the ratio of GDP in 2005 constant PPP USD to employment, using the latest PPP estimates published within the context of the International Comparison Program (ICP) coordinated by the World Bank (World Bank, 2007). These include noticeable revisions with respect to past estimates, which had been shown to overstate aggregate price gaps and, therefore, to understate PPP income gaps between developed and developing countries.[9] As a result, income gaps between developed and developing countries have been typically revised upwards, with potentially important implications for future world GDP growth within the context of convergence scenarios.[10]

- Capital stocks (in constant 2005 national currency prices) are built up from investment series through the perpetual inventory method, assuming a 5% annual depreciation rate.[11] Long investment time series – dating back at least to the early 1970s – are used, so that capital stock estimates in 1995 and 2005 are largely insensitive to the choice of the initial value.[12] The capital stock estimate is then divided by GDP (also expressed in constant 2005 national currency prices) to obtain the capital/output ratio.

- Human capital stocks are constructed in two steps. In a first step, data on the average number of years of schooling across population aged 25-64 are assembled for a wide range of countries, using primarily the dataset constructed by Cohen and Soto (2007),[13] which in turn is consistent with, but improves on the well-known Barro-Lee dataset.[14] In a second step, the average number of years of schooling across the population is converted into a human capital stock based on an assumption regarding returns to education. Following the seminal paper by Hall and Jones (1999), and relying on microeconomic evidence on returns to schooling for many countries surveyed in Psacharopoulos (1994) and Psacharopoulos and Patrinos (2002), the marginal return to schooling is set equal to 13.4% for the first four years of education, 10.1% for the next four and 6.8% beyond the eighth year.[15] While the magnitude of social returns to education – and of possible externalities to education in particular – remains subject to uncertainty, the general pattern of falling returns by level of education is well established, and a 6.5%-7% average return to upper secondary and tertiary education is fairly consistent with both microeconomic and macroeconomic evidence.[16]

- TFP is then derived from GDP per capita, physical capital stock, human capital stock and employment rate data, re-arranging equation (1) as follows:

  $$A_t = (Y_t / Pop_t) / [(K_t / Y_t)^{\alpha/(1-\alpha)} h_t (L_t / Pop_t)],$$

  where the capital share α is set equal to 1/3.

Results from this decomposition are presented in Table A1.1 for the year 2005. In line with findings from recent literature – which Easterly and Levine (2001) labeled the "new stylised facts of growth", and in contradiction with basic neo-classical growth theory,[17] TFP appears to be the main driver of existing cross-country differences in GDP per capita, especially between developed and developing countries.[18] Human capital is also found to play an important role. This suggests that both these factors are likely to be the major drivers of any long-run convergence scenario.

Table A1.1 Decomposition of cross-country differences in GDP per capita into their broad determinants, 2005[1,2]

(United States = 100)

	GDP PPP per capita	TFP	Human capital	Physical capital	Employment
	Y/Pop	A	h	$(K/Y)^{\alpha/(1-\alpha)}$	L/Pop
United States	100.0	100.0	100.0	100.0	100.0
Canada	83.5	72.0	103.3	105.8	106.0
Japan	72.6	52.6	100.4	130.7	105.1
China	9.8	13.6	57.3	105.2	119.5
India	5.2	12.7	47.7	98.3	87.1
Brazil	20.5	29.3	70.1	103.1	96.8
Russian Federation	28.6	31.5	84.9	97.4	99.3
Australia & New Zealand[3]	78.3	64.1	101.5	114.8	104.5
EU27 & EFTA[3]	64.7	67.8	91.2	114.1	91.3
Rest of the World[3]	12.3	20.9	59.7	103.6	81.7
Total World[3]	22.8	27.9	64.2	104.2	95.8

1. While equal in principle, Y/Pop and the product of A, h, $(K/Y)^{\alpha/(1-\alpha)}$ and L/Pop can differ in practice for two reasons: First, for countries where fossil fuels extraction makes a sizeable share of overall output (Russian Federation and a number of countries in the Rest of the World aggregate), TFP levels were estimated for total output excluding the mining and quarrying sector, for reasons explained in the text. Second, geographical area aggregates are computed as arithmetic averages, while geometric means would have to be used for the equality $Y/Pop = A\ h\ (K/Y)^{\alpha/(1-\alpha)}\ L/Pop$ to hold.
2. The long-term growth framework is applied at the individual country level. The geographical disaggregation of the world economy presented here matches that of the OECD ENV-Linkages model (see Annex 2).
3. Population-weighted arithmetic averages.

Source: Duval and de la Maisonneuve (2009).

A1.2. Baseline economic scenario for the world economy up to 2050

A1.2.1. Assumptions

Until 2008, GDP, investment and employment projections are taken from the *OECD Economic Outlook* for OECD countries as well as for Brazil, China, India and Russia, and from the *IMF World Economic Outlook* for all other countries. This allows some extension of the GDP decomposition presented in Table A1.1 up to 2008. Starting from 2009, scenarios are then drawn for each of the four GDP components for each country up to 2050. These scenarios are described below, followed by a description of the approach adopted for those countries – representing about 10% of world GDP – where the projection framework cannot be applied due to lack of accurate data.

 THE ECONOMICS OF CLIMATE CHANGE MITIGATION – ISBN: 978-92-64-05606-0 – © OECD 2009

TFP growth scenario

Because technology circulates freely across the world at least in the long run, it seems reasonable to expect TFP levels in lagging countries to gradually catch up to those of technological leaders. At the same time, a host of factors, including persistent cross-country differences in policies and institutions, may prevent full convergence. The baseline scenario implicitly assumes that such factors will continue to play a role in the future, albeit to a lower extent than they do today. More concretely, it is assumed that TFP in lagging countries will ultimately converge not to the technological frontier but rather to the (lower) average of TFP levels in "high-TFP" OECD countries. Concretely, the baseline TFP scenario rests on the following assumptions:

- The average TFP level across those OECD countries whose TFP levels stand above the OECD average is calculated for 2005.[19] This TFP level across "high-TFP" economies is then assumed to grow at a 1.5% annual rate between 2009 and 2050.[20] The resulting path is assumed to be the "frontier" towards which all lagging countries converge. The 1.5% TFP growth assumption implies that in the long run, assuming the educational attainment of younger generations ultimately levels off and the capital/output ratio stays constant, labour productivity will also grow at 1.5% a year.
- For lagging countries and up to 2015, recent TFP trends are extrapolated by assuming these countries converge to the above "frontier" at the average rate observed for each country over the period 1995-2005 (set equal to zero if they actually diverged).[21]
- Between 2015 and 2025, the speed of convergence is assumed to converge gradually to a 2% annual rate. This corresponds to the average estimated speed of convergence in GDP per capita across a wide range of datasets and econometric methods reported by Barro and Sala-i-Martin (2004).[22] Applying such speed of convergence to TFP seems reasonable given that TFP is the main driver of cross-country differences in GDP per capita levels and growth rates.[23] Incidentally, this figure is also not inconsistent with the 3% TFP convergence speed estimated in recent OECD work (Nicoletti and Scarpetta, 2003) for a sample of OECD countries.[24]
- Beyond 2025, lagging countries converge to the "frontier" at a 2% annual rate, *i.e.* the TFP gap with respect to frontier closes by 2% each year.

Human capital accumulation scenario

Two main stylised facts stand out regarding world accumulation of human capital, which can be useful for the projection.[25] First, based on the historical dataset by cohorts used in this annex, educational attainment of the 25-29 age group increased on average at a fairly regular pace of about 1.2 years per decade between 1960 and 2000 in less-educated countries.[26] Second, educational attainment has tended to level off in those countries where it was highest, *e.g.* Australia, Switzerland or the United States. A hypothesis that may be drawn from this observation is that the speed of human capital accumulation typically slows as educational attainment increases. The baseline human capital scenario is, therefore, constructed as follows:

- Educational attainment of the 25-29 age group is projected to remain constant in the future in the country where it is currently highest (South Korea, with 14.4 years of education in 2000).
- Up to 2015, recent trends are extrapolated by assuming that all other countries converge to the above "frontier" at their average 1990-2000 speed (set equal to zero if educational attainment actually declined over this period).

- Between 2015 and 2025, the speed of convergence is assumed to converge gradually to the average speed observed in the average world country[27] over the period 1960-2000.
- Beyond 2025, countries converge to the "frontier" at the average speed observed in the average world country over the period 1960-2000.
- Based on this scenario for the 25-29 age group, future educational attainment across the population aged 25-64 is projected through cohort effects, and then converted into a human capital stock based on the returns to education assumptions described above.[28]

Physical capital accumulation scenario

In a world where international capital is at least partly mobile, future physical capital accumulation at the country level should be driven at least partly by real interest rates at the world level, which in turn should reflect the world saving-investment equilibrium. Unfortunately, in the absence of a truly global, integrated world growth framework, world saving trends cannot be factored in the analysis undertaken here, so that their impact on future world investment *via* real interest rates cannot be explored. This is certainly an area for future development of the above framework. Nevertheless, it is still possible to incorporate the fact that capital/output ratios should not diverge permanently across countries in a world of integrated capital markets, as this would imply permanent cross-country differences in the marginal return to capital.[29] This is implemented here as follows:

- The US investment rate path is assumed to gradually stabilise the capital/output ratio at its current level. This implicitly assumes that the United States is on a balanced growth path.
- Investment rates in all other countries are projected to vary in such a way that their capital/output ratios converge gradually to the US level. Full convergence is assumed to be reached only by 2080, *i.e.* beyond the horizon of the scenario presented here.[30]

Employment scenario

The TFP, physical capital and human capital projections need to be combined with an employment projection in order to yield a baseline GDP scenario for each country. Future employment is forecast by decomposing employment into population, the participation rate and the unemployment rate, and then by assuming the following paths for each of these three components:

- Population projections are taken from the baseline United Nations (UN) scenario up to 2050.
- Participation rates are projected in two steps. First, in the top quintile of OECD countries where participation is currently highest,[31] future effective retirement ages are partially indexed to life expectancy, so as to maintain a constant share of life spent in retirement. Second, in all other countries where data by cohorts are available, participation for each age group is assumed to converge gradually to the average of the top quintile.[32] Aggregate participation rates are then projected using the cohort approach presented in Burniaux *et al.* (2003). For those countries where data by cohorts are not available, the convergence assumption is similar but is applied directly to aggregate participation rather than to the participation of each individual age group.
- Unemployment rates are assumed to converge gradually to 5% by 2050.

Baseline scenario for those countries where the framework cannot be applied

The above approach is applied to 76 individual countries covering over 90% of world GDP and world population in 2005. For all other countries, human and/or physical capital data are too scarce or too unreliable to apply the same framework with a reasonable degree of confidence. In a number of cases, for instance, the period over which investment series are available is too short to be able to estimate capital stocks with a reasonable degree of confidence. The approach followed for these countries is to apply to labour productivity the methodology applied to TFP for those countries where the above framework could be applied.[33]

A1.2.2. Sectoral issues

One missing element from most aggregate projections, especially those made within the context of climate policy analysis, is that GDP is seldom endogenised for those areas where fossil fuels extraction makes a sizeable share of overall output. For example, it makes little sense to project future GDP in OPEC countries regardless of the future paths of oil supply. In order to overcome this issue, for those countries where fossil fuels matter, the convergence scenarios described above are in fact applied not to GDP but rather to GDP excluding the mining and quarrying sector.[34] GDP excluding mining and quarrying is projected using the approach described in Section A1.2.1., and the value added in mining and quarrying – and therefore overall GDP – is then determined by running the OECD's global, multi-sector, general equilibrium model ENV-Linkages. With its nested-CES structure featuring a detailed representation of energy inputs at the sectoral level, the model is particularly suitable to project energy supply, demand and prices (see Annex 2).

OECD ENV-Linkages being a multi-sector model, the variables projected in Section A1.2.1 for the economy as a whole are not sufficient to run it, and sectoral assumptions are required. Such assumptions are also useful *per se* because various long-run economic projection exercises have a major sectoral dimension, not least greenhouse gas emission projections. The starting point for projecting sectoral output and value-added growth is that history consistently points to different productivity trends across sectors, as illustrated for instance by the long sector-level productivity growth time series assembled by the Groningen Growth and Development Centre for a wide range of countries (Groningen Growth and Development Centre, 2006; Van Ark, 1996; Timmer *et al.* 2007). Productivity growth has typically been found to be faster in agriculture and manufacturing than in construction, transport and – to an even greater extent – other services. One challenge is, therefore, to build up for each country a sectoral productivity growth scenario that factors in the continuation of these historical patterns while still being consistent with the aggregate productivity growth scenario – excluding the mining and quarrying sector, whose output is determined endogenously by the model – described in Section A1.2.1. This is done here by calibrating sectoral productivity growth in the OECD ENV-Linkages model in such a way that particular *relative* sectoral productivity growth patterns and the aggregate productivity growth scenario (excluding mining and quarrying) *both* hold *ex-post*. The relative sectoral productivity growth patterns are assumed to be the following:

- Recent relative sectoral productivity growth patterns observed in each country over the past 15-20 years[35] are extrapolated in the short run, but they are assumed to converge by 2025 to the average historical patterns observed over 1950-2000 across those 10 OECD countries where long time series exist.[36]
- Average historical patterns apply to all countries beyond 2025. The implicit assumption is that past relative sectoral productivity growth trends across developed countries offer a good indication of the future path developing countries will follow. It is also assumed that past

patterns will continue to hold in developed countries, with faster productivity growth in agriculture and manufacturing than in services. This seems plausible given that no major break has been observed so far in these patterns, although productivity growth in services picked up during the late 1990s and early 2000s in a few developed countries, including the United States.

The approach followed in this annex also addresses the criticisms made recently in the climate change economics literature towards using market exchange rate (MER)-based economic projections. These constitute the vast majority of scenarios published over the past two decades, including in the IPCC SRES (Castles and Henderson, 2003a, 2003b; Henderson, 2005). Price levels expressed in common currency are typically higher in developed countries than in developing ones, due to the "Baumol-Balassa-Samuelson" effect. As a result, current cross-country differences in income per capita levels tend to be over-estimated when MERs are used to convert national GDPs into a common currency. Within the context of any convergence scenario, such over-estimation is likely to translate into an over-estimation of future GDP and greenhouse gas emissions growth, *ceteris paribus*. In the present case, no such problem arises because PPPs, not MERs, are used to compare initial income per capita levels and compute the economic convergence scenario.

A1.2.3. Results

The main features of the baseline economic scenario are presented in Tables A1.2 and A1.3. The baseline scenario in PPP USD (Table A1.2) is roughly in line with – albeit somewhat below – recent OECD projections up to 2025 (Hervé *et al.* 2007). World GDP per capita growth is projected to be higher in PPP USD than in constant 2005 MER USD, due to the smaller weight assigned to fast-growing countries in the latter case. When expressed in constant MER USD, baseline world GDP per capita growth up to 2030 falls roughly in the middle of the 1%-3.1% range provided in the IPCC SRES, which also relies on constant MER USD.

Applying the long-run growth framework also yields a number of interesting country-specific findings, such as the fact that growth could be lower in China than in India over the coming decades. This is because compared with India, China is already fairly capital intensive, has virtually no room for further raising labour force participation, and is bound to face a significant slowdown in population growth.

Table A1.2 Baseline economic scenario: main features[1]

(Average annual growth rates, PPP USD)

Country/region	GDP per worker			GDP per capita			GDP		
	2000-2006	2006-2025	2025-2050	2000-2006	2006-2025	2025-2050	2000-2006	2006-2025	2025-2050
United States	1.7	1.7	1.6	1.6	1.6	1.6	2.6	2.4	2.2
Canada	0.7	2.0	1.7	1.6	1.9	1.6	2.6	2.7	2.1
Japan	1.7	1.9	1.9	1.5	1.7	1.5	1.6	1.5	0.8
China	8.6	6.4	3.7	9.0	6.1	3.3	9.7	6.6	3.2
India	5.0	5.2	4.6	5.6	6.3	5.1	7.3	7.6	5.6
Brazil	0.0	2.5	3.3	1.5	3.0	3.5	2.9	4.0	3.9
Russian Federation	5.4	3.8	2.5	6.7	4.0	2.5	6.2	3.4	1.8
Australia & New Zealand	0.9	2.0	1.7	1.9	2.0	1.6	3.1	2.9	2.1
EU27 & EFTA	1.1	2.1	1.8	1.7	2.3	1.8	2.1	2.4	1.7
Oil-exporting countries	1.9	2.3	3.7	2.9	3.0	4.2	4.8	4.4	5.0
Rest of the World	2.1	3.1	3.5	2.8	3.3	3.7	4.5	4.9	4.7
Total World	2.0	2.5	2.8	2.5	2.8	2.9	3.7	3.8	3.4
Total World in constant 2005 MER USD		1.9	2.3		2.2	2.4		3.2	3.0

1. The long-term growth framework is applied at the individual country level. The geographical disaggregation of the world economy presented here matches that of the OECD ENV-Linkages model (see Annex 2).

Source: Duval and de la Maisonneuve (2009).

Table A1.3 Baseline economic scenario: population and employment projections[1]

(Percentages)

Country/region	Population growth, average annual			Employment rates[2], average		
	2000-2006	2006-2025	2025-2050	2000-2006	2007-2025	2026-2050
United States	1.0	0.8	0.5	60.0	58.5	56.6
Canada	1.0	0.8	0.5	60.3	60.8	57.9
Japan	0.1	-0.3	-0.7	58.2	55.8	51.8
China	0.7	0.5	-0.1	72.6	68.9	60.5
India	1.6	1.2	0.5	61.8	64.3	68.8
Brazil	1.4	1.0	0.4	61.7	64.0	63.6
Russian Federation	-0.5	-0.6	-0.7	54.7	58.0	58.8
Australia & New Zealand	1.2	0.9	0.5	60.5	61.6	58.4
EU27 & EFTA	0.3	0.1	-0.1	51.2	53.5	53.4
Oil-exporting countries	1.8	1.5	0.8	52.6	54.8	55.2
Rest of the World	1.7	1.5	1.0	60.2	60.1	57.8
Total World	1.2	1.0	0.5	61.6	61.6	59.9

1. The long-term growth framework is applied at the individual country level. The geographical disaggregation of the world economy.
2. Defined as employment as a percentage of population aged 15 and over.

Source: Duval and de la Maisonneuve (2009).

A1.3. Data sources and methodology

This Section presents further details on the sources and methodology used to construct the data used in the long-term growth framework.

A1.3.1. Aggregate production in volume

Definition: Real GDP in 2005 constant PPP USD.

Source: OECD Economic Outlook (hereafter, EO); World Bank, Word Development Indicators database (hereafter, WDI) for GDP and World Bank (2007) for 2005 PPP exchange rates;[37] IMF, World Economic Outlook (hereafter, WEO).

Data adjustments: GDPs in local currency are converted in PPP USD for the year 2005, using World Bank PPP estimates. GDPs are then extrapolated backwards to 1995 and forward to 2006 using real GDP growth rates in national currency. Finally, GDPs in constant 2005 PPP USD for the years 2007 and 2008 are obtained by extrapolating 2006 GDP data using projected GDP growth rates as published in EO82 (for OECD countries and Brazil, Russia, India and china) and the October 2007 issue of the WEO (for other countries).

For countries where fossil fuels extraction makes a sizeable share of output, convergence scenarios are applied to GDP excluding the mining and quarrying sector (OPEC countries, Azerbaijan, Kazakhstan, Bahrain, Israel, Jordan, Oman, Syrian Arab Republic, Yemen, Brunei Darussalam, Norway and Russia). The share of this sector in total value added is calculated from the United Nations National Accounts. For most countries, the latest year available was 2005.

A1.3.2. Employment

Labour Force

Definition: Labour force aged 15 and over.

Source: OECD, Labour Force Statistics (hereafter, LFS); OECD Employment Outlook; International Labour Organisation, Labour Force Survey (hereafter ILO); WDI; WEO; EO; for China, Statistical Yearbook 2007; for India, Report no 522, National Sample Survey, National Sample Survey Organisation, Ministry of Statistics and Programme Implementation. Primary sources are LFS for OECD countries, The OECD Employment Outlook for Brazil and the Russian Federation, national sources for China and India, and ILO or WDI for other countries up to 2006 (or the latest available year).

Data adjustments: Over the period 2007-2008, EO and WEO projections are used to extrapolate labour force data for OECD and other countries, respectively. Any missing values over the period 1995-2006 are filled in using alternative data sources available and/or linear interpolation.

Unemployment

Unemployment of individuals aged 15 and over is taken from similar sources as labour force data, and is subject to the same data adjustments.

Employment

Employment is calculated as labour force minus unemployment.

Employment rates are calculated as the ratio of employment to population aged 15 and over.

A1.3.3.Population

Population data are available by cohorts (5-year age groups) and are taken from United Nations population projections.

A1.3.4. Human capital stock

Definition: Average number of years of schooling of population aged 25-64 (then converted into a human capital stock measure, based on explicit assumptions about social returns from education).

Source: Cohen-Soto database; Barro-Lee dataset. The primary source is the Cohen-Soto database, which provides average years of education by 5-years age groups. The average number of years of education across the population aged 25-64 can then be projected by cohorts, based on a single educational attainment scenario for the 25-29 age group.

For some countries, data by cohorts are unavailable (Croatia, Czech Republic, Hong-Kong, Iceland, Pakistan, Poland, Russia, Slovakia, Slovenia and South Africa), The Barro-Lee dataset is then used in those cases, and the average number of years of education across the population aged 25-64 is projected directly.

A1.3.5. Physical capital stock

Definition: Real aggregate capital stock in constant 2005 national currency prices.

Source: WDI, WEO and Statistical Yearbook for Russia.

Data adjustments: Historical real investment and GDP series are taken from WDI and extrapolated up to 2008 using EO82 and October 2007 WEO projections. A capital stock to GDP ratio is then derived using the so-called perpetual inventory method. For a few Eastern European countries where investment series are too short to derive reliable capital stock estimates from the perpetual inventory method, strong assumptions are made regarding the initial value of the capital stock. For Croatia, Czech Republic, Poland, Slovakia and Slovenia, the capital/output ratio is assumed to be similar to that of Hungary (which is available) in 1990, and the perpetual inventory method is applied starting only from 1991 to extrapolate the capital stock up to 2008. For Estonia, Latvia and Lithuania, the capital/output ratio is assumed to be similar to that of Russia in 1995. For Romania, the capital/output ratio is assumed to be similar to that of Bulgaria in 1990.

A1.4. Detail results for selected simulations

This section reproduces in tabular form the results from selected simulations which are reported in various Charts in Chapter 4. The purpose is to provide more detailed information about the precise numbers underlying the scenarios discussed in that chapter. More specifically, Table A1.4 includes the numbers shown in Figures 4.9 and 4.10, Table A1.5 reports those underlying Figure 4.18, and Table A1.6 the numbers reported in Figure 4.19.

Table A1.4 Mitigation policy costs and carbon prices under a 50% emission cut in each Annex I region separately, with and without crediting mechanisms[1]

2020

	Mitigation cost (income equivalent variation relative to baseline, in %)			Price of carbon (USD / t CO_2 eq)		
	Without crediting mechanism	With crediting mechanism (20%)	With crediting mechanism (50%)	Without crediting mechanism	With crediting mechanism (20%)	With crediting mechanism (50%)
Australia & New Zealand	-4.2	-2.1	-0.9	140.8	73.2	19.5
Canada	-6.4	-4.3	-2.1	129.6	61.3	23.2
EU27 & EFTA	-0.5	-0.3	-0.1	60.5	41.7	10.6
Japan	-1.1	-0.4	0.0	180.1	87.5	17.7
Russia	-3.1	-2.1	-0.9	4.8	2.9	1.2
United States	-1.7	-1.1	-0.5	106.5	68.1	28.5
Non-EU Eastern European countries	-3.8	-2.5	-1.2	32.5	19.6	6.7
Non-Annex I				0.0	0.6	3.8

2050

	Mitigation cost (income equivalent variation relative to baseline, in %)			Price of carbon (USD / t CO_2 eq)		
	Without crediting mechanism	With crediting mechanism (20%)	With crediting mechanism (50%)	Without crediting mechanism	With crediting mechanism (20%)	With crediting mechanism (50%)
Australia & New Zealand	-8.2	-3.8	-1.4	404.9	163.3	43.7
Canada	-10.2	-6.3	-2.7	602.8	241.0	65.9
EU27 & EFTA	-2.6	-1.2	-0.4	207.0	107.5	44.4
Japan	-1.5	-0.7	-0.1	213.6	104.5	24.2
Russia	-10.8	-7.1	-3.3	80.9	50.2	19.3
United States	-1.6	-0.9	-0.4	142.8	78.6	31.0
Non-EU Eastern European countries	-18.8	-11.7	-4.9	201.7	111.7	36.1
Non-Annex I				0.0	0.8	4.0

1. The values reported in this table correspond to Figures 4.9 and 4.10 in Chapter 4.

Source: OECD, ENV-Linkages model.

Table A1.5 Mitigation costs under an international ETS in Annex I and binding sectoral caps in non-Annex I regions[1]

(50% cut in Annex I regions and 20% cut in EEIs and power sector in non-Annex I regions by 2050, income equivalent variation relative to baseline, in %)

Country/region	Without any linking	With direct linking within non-Annex I sectoral schemes	With full linking between Annex I economy-wide and non-Annex I sectoral schemes	Without any linking	With direct linking within non-Annex I sectoral schemes	With full linking between Annex I economy-wide and non-Annex I sectoral schemes
		2020			2050	
Australia & New Zealand	-4.2	-4.2	-4.3	-9.0	-8.9	-8.4
Brazil	-0.6	-0.7	-0.6	-0.8	-0.8	-0.8
Canada	-5.7	-5.7	-5.9	-10.6	-10.1	-9.7
China	-4.1	-4.2	-4.0	-3.2	-4.8	-4.6
EU27 & EFTA	-0.4	-0.4	-0.5	-2.5	-2.5	-2.0
India	-9.3	-6.1	-5.4	-8.6	-6.8	-7.5
Japan	-0.1	-0.1	-0.2	-1.0	-1.1	-1.0
Non-EU Eastern European countries	-4.0	-3.9	-3.7	-21.2	-21.0	-20.3
Oil-exporting countries	-9.2	-8.8	-8.5	-10.7	-8.0	-8.6
Rest of the World	-1.2	-1.1	-1.1	-1.3	-1.3	-1.4
Russia	-2.5	-2.5	-2.2	-11.8	-11.7	-12.1
United States	-1.6	-1.6	-1.7	-1.7	-1.7	-1.8
Annex I	-1.2	-1.2	-1.3	-2.9	-2.9	-2.7
Non-Annex I	-3.6	-3.2	-3.1	-3.6	-3.4	-3.5

1. The values reported in this table correspond to Figure 4.18 in Chapter 4.

Source: OECD, ENV-Linkages model.

THE ECONOMICS OF CLIMATE CHANGE MITIGATION – ISBN: 978-92-64-05606-0 – © OECD 2009

Table A1.6 The impact of sectoral crediting on mitigation costs in Annex I and non-Annex I regions[1]

(Under a 20% cut by 2020 and a 50% cut by 2050 relative to 1990 levels in each Annex I region, income equivalent variation relative to baseline, in %)

Country/region	Without sectoral crediting mechanism	With sectoral crediting mechanism covering EIIs and power sector[2]	Without sectoral crediting mechanism	With sectoral crediting mechanism covering EIIs and power sector[2]
	2020		2050	
Australia & New Zealand	-3.6	-2.5	-7.1	-4.5
Brazil	0.0	0.0	-0.1	-0.1
Canada	-5.0	-3.6	-8.2	-5.7
China	-0.1	-0.1	0.0	0.0
EU27 & EFTA	-0.7	-0.2	-2.4	-0.9
India	0.5	0.3	0.6	0.3
Japan	-0.5	-0.3	-1.2	-0.5
Non-EU Eastern European countries	-3.4	-2.4	-19.3	-12.4
Oil-exporting countries	-2.8	-2.0	-3.4	-2.2
Rest of the World	-0.2	-0.1	-0.4	-0.2
Russia	-1.6	-0.7	-10.1	-6.0
United States	-1.6	-1.1	-1.6	-1.1
Annex I	-1.3	-0.8	-2.6	-1.5
Non-Annex I	-0.4	-0.3	-0.5	-0.3

1. The values reported in this table correspond to Figure 4.19 in Chapter 4.
2. With a 20% cap on use of offset credits.

Source: OECD, ENV-Linkages model.

Notes

1. This annex is largely based on Duval and de la Maisonneuve (2009).

2. See in particular Nakicenovic *et al.* (2000).

3. See, for instance, the approach followed by McKibbin *et al.* (2004) using the G-Cubed model. One difficulty with the "bottom-up" approach is that it relies on comparisons of sectoral labour productivity levels across countries which, in turn, requires the use of PPP exchange rates at the sector level. Insofar as these data do not exist for the vast majority of countries, strong assumptions have to be made when constructing them.

4. See Nakicenovic *et al.* (2000), as well as the recent update provided in Fisher *et al.* (2007). Figure 3.2 p.180 in the latter paper indicates that even when ignoring the most extreme scenarios, projected world GDP in 2100 could lie anywhere between less than 100 billion USD 1990 (5th percentile of the distribution of SRES scenarios) and more than 500 billion USD 1990 (95th percentile).

5. See Barro and Sala-i-Martin (2004). For an overview of the potential implications of growth theories for global convergence scenarios, which was the topic of an OECD workshop held on 16 January, 2006, see Vanston (2006).

6. Barro and Sala-i-Martin (2004), OECD (2004).

7. In turn, cross-country differences in levels of TFP and/or human capital may reflect differences in policies and institutions. Analysing such factors goes beyond the scope of the present paper.

8. The constant-returns-to-scale assumption excludes *de facto* the possibility of permanent growth effects of the human capital stock. While some empirical literature hints at endogenous growth effects of human or even physical capital (see *e.g.* Bassanini and Scarpetta, 2004; Bond *et al.,* 2004), this issue remains fairly controversial in practice (*e.g.* Sianesi and Van Reenen, 2003).

9. This is due in part to past estimates relying on the so-called "Geary-Khamis" technique for constructing GDPs in PPPs, which has been shown to overestimate the relative incomes of poor countries. Other available approaches, including the so-called "EKS" method now used for most countries, have been found to be less biased in this regard (at least under homothetic consumer preferences, see Neary, 2004). See World Bank (2007), as well as Nordhaus (2007) for some discussion of this issue within the context of climate models.

10. For instance, GDP per capita levels in China and India for the year 2005 are now estimated to be equal to about 10% and 5% of the US level, respectively, versus 16% and 8% previously, although the revision may also reflect other factors including the use of more recent price survey data.

11. This very simple method was chosen for two reasons: *i)* it allows capital stocks to be constructed for a large number of countries, including many developing countries; *ii)* it allows capital-output ratios to be compared across countries, which is essential in the context of convergence scenarios. However, one drawback of the approach – and one potential source of bias both across countries and over time – is to ignore changes in the relative price of investment, and in particular the trend decline in the price of information and communication technologies. This decline has contributed to the gradual shift to chain-weighting in the National Accounts of most OECD countries.

12. The initial value of the capital stock is computed as $I0/(\delta+g)$, where I0 denotes investment for the first available year, δ is the depreciation rate of the capital stock (set here at 5%) and g is average GDP growth rate between periods 0 and 10. This is the capital stock that would prevail along a balanced growth path where GDP growth and the investment rate would be constant. While applying this common methodology to all countries yields rather crude capital stock series for those

countries where such data are readily available from National Accounts, its key strength within the present context is to vastly expand the set of countries covered and to allow for cross-country comparisons of capital/output ratios.

13. See Cohen and Soto (2007).

14. Barro and Lee (1993, 2001).

15. Formally, it is assumed that human capital per worker can be written as $h_t = e^{\phi(S)}$, where S denotes the number of years of schooling, and φ(S) is chosen to be a piecewise linear function in order to reproduce the three different marginal returns to education used here for three different levels of education. Bils and Klenow (2000) argue that such specification is the appropriate way to incorporate years of schooling into an aggregate production function. An additional year of schooling increases both "effective" labour input in equation (1) and the real wage by 100φ'(S) %, which is the marginal (Mincerian) rate of return to schooling.

16. Meta analysis of microeconomic studies provided by Harmon *et al.* (2003) concludes to an average 6.5% return to schooling across a wide range of OECD countries, datasets and model specifications. Boarini and Strauss (2007) obtain average private internal rates of return to tertiary education of about 8% on average across 21 OECD countries over the period 1991-2005. Based on panel data growth regressions for a sample of OECD countries, Bassanini and Scarpetta (2001) find an implicit 6% marginal (social) rate of return to education at the sample mean of 10 years of average education. This is in line with the implicit 5.9% return found in Gemmel (1996).

17. See *e.g.* Mankiw *et al.* (1992), based on a similar production function to that used in the present paper.

18. Cross-country variance in the logarithm of TFP is found to account for over half of the cross-country variance in the logarithm of GDP per capita.

19. These countries are Austria, Belgium, Canada, Denmark, Finland, France, Greece, Ireland, Italy, the Netherlands, Norway, Spain, Sweden, the United Kingdom and the United States.

20. This is slightly above the 1.3% average annual growth rate over 1990-2006 observed for the United States in the dataset, and yields medium-term potential GDP growth estimates for this country which are consistent with OECD medium-term projections.

21. The dynamic annual equation used is: dln(TFPt) = dln(TFPt*) - β[ln(TFPt-1) - ln(TFPt-1*)], where TFP* is the "frontier" described in the text and β is the average speed of convergence observed over the period 1995-2005.

22. Summing up the evidence, the authors argue p.497 that "one surprising result is the similarity of the speed of β convergence across data sets. The estimates of β are around 2-3% per year in the various contexts".

23. For some decomposition of contributions to cross-country differences in GDP per capita levels, see Table A1.1, as well as Hall and Jones (1999). For some decomposition of contributions to cross-country differences in GDP per capita growth rates, see Easterly and Levine (2001).

24. It may also be worth pointing out that such speed of convergence is also close to that observed for China over the period 1995-2005, and above that observed for India.

25. In line with the theoretical framework adopted, one strong assumption made here is that educational convergence impacts on, but is not influenced by income convergence.

26. This is the average increase across all countries for which data are available, excluding those 15 countries where educational attainment was highest back in 1960.

27. Excluding those 15 countries where educational attainment was highest back in 1960.

28. For those few countries where educational attainment data by cohorts is not available (Czech Republic, Croatia, Hong Kong, Iceland, Pakistan, Poland, Slovak Republic, Slovenia, Russia, South Africa), the projection method was applied directly to the 25-64 age group.

29. The marginal return to capital is equal to $\alpha Y/K$ in the theoretical framework used here.

30. Formally, the investment rate path chosen for each country is the smoothest possible path that meets the constraint that the capital/output ratio is equal to the US level in 2080.

31. These countries are Canada, Denmark, Iceland, New Zealand, Norway and Sweden.

32. Countries for which participation data by cohorts are available include the OECD countries, Brazil, Russia, India and China. Assuming convergence in participation by age group rather than on aggregate allows taking into account permanent cross-country differences in participation that may still be associated with country-specific demographics.

33. Finally, for those (very) few countries and geographical areas where labour productivity data in levels are not available, labour productivity growth is assumed to be equal to average world labour productivity growth over the projection period.

34. These countries are OPEC countries as well as Norway and Russia. In the latter two countries, it also has to be assumed that the capital/output ratio in the mining and quarrying sector is similar to that in the rest of the economy.

35. The exact time span considered varies across countries, depending on the exact period covered by the Groningen Growth and Development Centre databases used here. As well, while sectoral productivity growth data are available for all large emitters and more, many – *e.g.* African and Middle Eastern – countries are not covered. For the latter, the average historical patterns across those 10 OECD countries where long time series exist are assumed to hold throughout the whole projection period.

36. These countries are Denmark, France, Germany, Italy, Japan, the Netherlands, Spain, Sweden, the United Kingdom and the United States.

37. For those few countries where no 2005 PPP exchange rates are published in World Bank (2007), PPP estimates for the year 2000 are used, as published in WDI. The countries concerned are Algeria, the United Arab Emirates and some Central American countries.

References

Barro, R. and J-W. Lee (2001), "International Data on Educational Attainment: Updates and Implications", *Oxford Economic Papers,* Vol. 53, No. 3.

Barro, R. and J-W. Lee (1993), "International Comparisons of Educational Attainment", *Journal of Monetary Economics,* Vol. 32, No. 3.

Barro, R. and X. Sala-i-Martin (2004), *Economic Growth*, second edition, The MIT Press, Cambridge, Massachussets.

Bassanini, A. and S. Scarpetta (2001), "The Driving Forces of Economic Growth: Panel Data Evidence for the OECD Countries", *OECD Economic Studies,* No. 33.

Bassanini, A. and S. Scarpetta (2004), "Does Human Capital Matter for Growth in OECD Countries? A Pooled Mean Group Approach", *Economics Letters,* Vol. 74, No. 3.

Bils, M. and P. Klenow (2000), "Does Schooling Cause Growth?", *American Economic Review,* Vol. 90, No. 5.

Boarini, R. and H. Strauss (2007), "The Private Internal Rates of return to Tertiary Education: New Estimates for 21 OECD countries", *OECD Economics Department Working Papers* No. 591.

Bond, S., A. Leblebicioglu and F. Schiantarelli (2004), "Capital Accumulation and Growth: A New Look at the Empirical Evidence", *Boston College Working Papers* No. 591, Paris.

Burniaux, J-M., *et al.* (2008), "The Economics of Climate Change Mitigation: Policies and options for the Future", *OECD Economics Department Working Papers* No. 658, Paris.

Burniaux, J-M. and J. Chateau (2008), "An Overview of the OECD ENV-Linkages Model", *OECD Economics Department Working Papers* No. 653, Paris.

Burniaux, J-M., R. Duval and F. Jaumotte (2003), "Coping with Ageing: a Dynamic Approach to Quantify the Impact of Alternative Policy Options on Future Labour Supply", *OECD Economics Department Working Papers* No. 371, Paris.

Caselli, F. (2005), "Accounting for Cross-Country Income Differences", in P. Aghion and S. Durlauf (eds.), *Handbook of Economic Growth*, Elsevier, Amsterdam.

Caselli, F. and W. Coleman (2006), "The World Technology Frontier", *American Economic Review,* Vol. 96, No. 3.

Castles, I. and D. Henderson (2003a), "Economics, Emission Scenarios and the Work of the IPCC", *Energy and Environment,* Vol. 14, No. 4.

Castles, I. and D. Henderson (2003b), "The IPCC Emission Scenarios: an Economic-Statistical Critique", *Energy and Environment,* Vol. 14, No. 2-3.

Cohen, D., and M. Soto (2007), "Growth and Human Capital: Good Data, Good Results", *Journal of Economic Growth,* Vol. 12, No. 1.

Duval, R. and C. de la Maisonneuve (2009), "Long-run GDP Growth Scenarios for the World Economy", *OECD Economics Department Working Papers* No. 663.

Easterly, W. and R. Levine (2001), "It's Not Factor Accumulation: Stylized Facts and Growth Models", *World Bank Economic Review,* Vol. 15, No. 2.

Fisher, B., *et al.* (2007), "Issues Related to Mitigation in the Long-Term Context", in B. Metz, O. Davidson, P. Bosch, R. Dave and L. Meyer (eds.), *Climate Change 2007: Mitigation. Contribution of Working Group III to the Fourth Assessment Report of the Inter-Governemental Panel on Climate Change*, Cambridge University Press, Cambridge.

Gemmel, R. (1996), "Evaluating the Impacts of Human Capital Stocks and Accumulation on Economic Growth: Some New Evidence", *Oxford Bulletin of Economics and Statistics,* Vol. 58, No. 1.

Groningen Growth and Development Centre (2006), "Data Sources and Methodology of the 60-Industry Database of the Groningen Growth and Development Centre", Groningen Growth and Development Centre, *mimeo.*

Hall, R. and C. Jones (1999), "Why Do Some Countries Produce So Much More Output than Others?", *Quarterly Journal of Economics,* Vol. 114, No. 1.

Harmon, C., H. Oosterbeek and I. Walker (2003), "The Returns to Education: Microeconomics", *Journal of Economic Surveys,* Vol. 17, No. 2.

Henderson, D. (2005), "The Treatment of Economic Issues by the Intergovernmental Panel on Climate Change", *Energy and Environment,* Vol. 16, No. 2.

Herve, K., I. Koske, N. Pain and F. Sedillot (2007), "Globalisation and the Macroeconomic Policy Environment", *OECD Economics Department Working Papers* No. 552.

Jones, C. (1997), "Convergence Revisited", *Journal of Economic Growth,* Vol. 2, No. 2.

Klenow, P. and A. Rodriguez-Clare (1997), "The Neoclassical Revival in Growth Economics: Has it Gone Too Far?", in B. Bernanke and J. Rotemberg (eds.), *NBER Macroeconomics Annual* 1997, The MIT Press, Cambridge.

Mankiw, G., D. Romer and D. Weil (1992), "A Contribution to the Empirics of Economic Growth", *Quarterly Journal of Economics,* Vol. 107, No. 2.

McKibbin, W., D. Pearce and A. Stegman (2004), "Long-Run Projections for Climate Change Scenarios", *Lowy Institute for International Policy, Working Papers in International Economics* No. 1.04.

Nakicenovic, N., *et al.* (2000), *Special Report on Emission Scenarios. Working Group III, Inter-Governmental Panel on Climate Change (IPCC)*, Cambridge University Press, Cambridge.

Neary, P. (2004), "Rationalizing the Penn World Table: True Multilateral Indices for International Comparisons of Real Income", *American Economic review,* Vol. 94, No. 5.

Nicoletti, G. and S. Scarpetta (2003), "Regulation, Productivity and Growth: OECD Evidence", *OECD Economics Department Working Papers* No. 347.

Nordhaus, W. (2007), "Alternative Measures of Output in Global Economic-Environmental Models: Purchasing Power Parity or Market Exchange Rates?", *Energy Economics,* Vol. 29, No. 3.

OECD (2004), *Sources of Economic Growth*, Paris.

Psacharopoulos, G. (1994), "Returns to Investment in Education: a Global Update", *World Development,* Vol. 22, No. 9.

Psacharopoulos, G., and H. Patrinos (2002), "Returns to Investment in Education: a Further Update", *Education Economics,* Vol. 12, No. 2.

Sala-i-Martin, X., G. Doppelhofer and R. Miller (2004), "Determinants of Long-Term Growth: A Bayesian Averaging of Classical Estimates (BACE) Approach", *American Economic Review,* Vol. 94, No. 4.

Sianesi, B. and J. Van Reenen (2003), "The Returns to Education: Macroeconomics", *Journal of Economic Surveys,* Vol. 17, No. 2.

Timmer, M. and G. de Vries (2007), "A Cross-Country Database For Sectoral Employment And Productivity In Asia And Latin America, 1950-2005", Groningen Growth and Development Centre, *mimeo.*

Van Ark, B. (1996), "Sectoral Growth Accounting and Structural Change in Post-War Europe", in B. Van Ark and N. Crafts (eds.), *Quantitative Aspects of Post-War European Economic Growth*, CEPR/Cambridge University Press, Cambridge.

Vanston, N. (2006), "Summary of a Workshop on Global Convergence Scenarios: Structural and Policy Issues", *OECD Economics Department Working Papers*, No. 483, Paris.

World Bank (2007), *2005 International Comparison Program: Preliminary results*, 17 December, The World Bank, Washington D.C.

ISBN: 978-92-64-05606-0
The Economics of Climate Change Mitigation
Policies and Options for Global Action beyond 2012

Annex 2

An Overview of the OECD ENV-Linkages Model

A2.1. Introduction

The OECD ENV-Linkages General Equilibrium (GE) model is the successor to the OECD GREEN model for environmental studies, which was initially developed by the OECD Economics Department (Burniaux, *et al.* 1992) and is now hosted at the OECD Environment Directorate. GREEN was originally used for studying climate change mitigation policy and culminated in Burniaux (2000). It was developed into the Linkages model, and subsequently became the JOBS/Polestar modelling platform that was used to help underpin the OECD Environmental Outlook to 2020. A version of that model is also currently in use at the World Bank for research in global economic development issues. Previous work using the model includes development of a baseline to 2030 and a study of the consequence of structural change (including some environmental implications) associated with economic growth. Much of the applied work with the model is reported in various chapters of the OECD *Environmental Outlook to 2030* (2008). Exploration of the model's properties and some sensitivity analysis is reported in OECD (2006).

This Annex, which presents a summary description of the ENV-Linkages model rather than a full documentation, is structured as follows. Section A2.2 introduces the model and briefly reviews its key features, its recent developments and the climate policy instruments that can be simulated. Section A2.3 describes the structure of the model and discusses its main equations. Finally, Section A2.4 discusses the calibration method, first to fit the model on base year data, and second to dynamically produce a baseline emissions projection.

A2.2. A brief overview of the ENV-Linkages model

A2.2.1.Key features

The ENV-Linkages model is a recursive dynamic neo-classical general equilibrium model. It is a global economic model built primarily on a database of national economies. In the version of the model used for this book, the model represents the world economy in 12 countries/regions, each with 25 economic sectors (Tables A2.1 and A2.2), including five different technologies to produce electricity (fossil fuel based, nuclear, hydro-electricity, wind & solar technologies and renewable combustibles and waste electricity). Each of the 12 regions is underpinned by an economic input-output table (usually sourced from national statistical agencies). The database has been built and maintained at Purdue University by the Global Trade Analysis Project (GTAP) consortium. A fuller description of the database can be found at Dimaranan (2006). Those tables identify all the inputs that go into an industry, and identify all the industries that buy specific products.

All production in ENV-Linkages is assumed to operate under cost minimisation with an assumption of perfect markets and constant return to scale technology. The production technology is specified as nested CES production functions in a branching hierarchy. The top node thus represents an output – using intermediate goods combined with value-added, on the one hand, and non-CO_2 greenhouse gases (GHG) in sectors that emit these gases as joint-products (see below), on the other hand. This structure is replicated for each output, while the parameterisation of the CES functions may differ across sectors. For non-fossil fuel based electricity technologies, the other inputs bundle slightly differs in the sense that the upper nest combines a factor endowment (specific to the technology) with the value-added/ intermediate goods nest.

Total output for a sector is the sum of two different production streams: resulting from the distinction between production with an "old" capital vintage, and production with a "new" capital vintage. The substitution possibilities among factors are assumed to be higher with new capital than with old capital. In other words, technologies have putty/semi-putty specifications. This will imply longer adjustment of quantities to prices changes. Capital accumulation is modelled as in traditional Solow/Swan neo-classical growth model.

The valued-added bundle is specified as a CES combination of labour and a broad concept of capital. In the "crop" production sector, this capital is itself a CES combination of fertilizer and another bundle of capital-land-energy. The intention of this specification is to reflect the possibility of substitution between intensive and extensive agriculture. In the "livestock" sector, substitution possibilities are between bundles of land and feed, on the one hand, reflecting a similar choice between extensive and intensive livestock production, and of capital-energy-labour bundle, on the other hand. Production in other sectors is characterised by substitution between labour and a bundle of capital-energy (and possibly a sector-specific factor for primary resources).

Household consumption demand is the result of static maximization behaviour which is formally implemented as an "Extended Linear Expenditure System". A representative consumer in each region – who takes prices as given – optimally allocates disposal income among the full set of consumption commodities and savings. Saving is considered as a standard good and therefore does not rely on a forward-looking behaviour by the consumer.

The government in each region collects various kinds of taxes in order to finance a given sequence of government expenditures. Given also a sequence of public savings (or deficits) the government budget is balanced through the adjustment of the income tax on consumer income.

International trade is based on a set of regional bilateral flows. The model adopts the Armington[1] specification, assuming that domestic and imported products are not perfectly substitutable. Moreover, total imports are also imperfectly substitutable between regions of origin. Allocation of trade between partners then responds to relative prices at the equilibrium.

These core elements of ENV-Linkages are similar to those outlined in van der Mensbrugghe (2005) so a full model listing of equations will not be repeated here. The next section outlines some areas where improvements have been made.

A2.2.2. Recent improvements

Given the varied needs of the OECD Environment Directorate, flexibility was deemed essential in building a general-purpose tool for environmental policy analysis. The objective of these changes was therefore to make ENV-Linkages as adaptable as possible to studying different policy issues within a relatively short time horizon. Some of the features include:

- General purpose routines that extract data from various source databases: GTAP database, United Nations Population Prospects, IMF, US-EPA for non-CO_2 greenhouse gases, IEA databases for energy demands and CO_2 emissions associated to fuel combustion, economic baseline drivers such as productivity, labour force participation, etc. This has made it possible to adapt to new versions of databases with little disruption and quick turnaround.
- Development and maintenance of database routines that allow a source file including 96 countries/regions to be maintained. The aggregation routines permit an easy shift between

sectoral and regional aggregations of the model. The procedures automatically generate aggregated data that serve as preliminary projections of the baseline for a model simulation. A high degree of flexibility in the routines permits modification for different applications. Consistency across aggregations in model parameters and calibrations is largely automatic with only residual effort needed to make different aggregations largely equivalent from an economic perspective; *i.e.* that the sum of individual region responses to most policy are nearly equal to the whole of an aggregated region. Nonetheless, some simulation results would be aggregation dependent. For instance, "Armington trade-off" between goods of different /countries/regions would be affected by the retained aggregation.

- For the current purpose, the model has been aggregated into 25 sectors and 12 regions, as reported in Tables A2.1 and A2.2.
- Flexibility has also been developed in changing the model's structure. Some elements of the model may be added or removed in order to focus on specific issues while keeping the model tractable. For example, it is easy to change between an economy that follows a quasi-balanced growth path (where the capital to output ratio is fixed) versus one where it does not. The structure of the energy demand can be modified easily too. In the model currently used, the energy bundle consists of several nests implying different degree of substitution between specific energy sources. International trade shares may be made to evolve over time rather than just respond to price changes – so globalisation can be factored in. Other areas have also been made to be more flexible. The importance of these changes is that the model can be re-specified on relatively short notice to study issues of interest for policy from alternative perspectives.
- Non-CO_2 greenhouse gases are a significant contributor to climate change. Approximately 30% of the human-induced greenhouse effect can be attributed to the non-CO_2 greenhouse gases (though most of this is from methane and nitrous oxide). Burniaux (2000) reported that abating non-CO_2 gases was cheaper in many cases than abating CO_2 from energy. This result has been upheld by other studies that have since been completed (Weyant and de la Chesnaye, 2006). The current version of the model incorporates several emission sources of non-CO_2 gases (methane, nitrous oxide and industrial gases). These gases are introduced by considering an additional nest at the top of the production function including the emissions of these gases in a way similar to Hyman *et al.* (2002).
- The dynamic calibration of the model has been made more flexible. In the construction of a baseline scenario (*e.g.* the central projection made on the basis of a set of exogenous drivers and used as a benchmark for subsequent policy simulations) some trends may be exogenously determined, or left as part of the solution of the model simulation.
- Five alternative technologies to generate electricity have been introduced.

Table A2.1. ENV-Linkages model sectors

Labels	Description
1) Rice	Paddy rice: rice, husked and in the husk.
2) Other crops	Wheat: wheat and meslin
	Other Grains: maize (corn), barley, rye, oats, other cereals
	Veg & Fruit: vegetables, fruits, fruit and nuts, potatoes, cassava, truffles.
	Oil Seeds: oil seeds and oleaginous fruits; soy beans, copra
	Cane & Beet: sugar cane and sugar beet
	Plant fibers: cotton, flax, hemp, sisal and other raw vegetable materials used in textiles
	Other Crops
3) Livestock	Cattle: cattle, sheep, goats, horses, asses, mules, and hinnies; and semen thereof
	Other Animal Products: swine, poultry and other live animals; eggs, in shell, natural honey, snails
	Raw milk
	Wool: wool, silk, and other raw animal materials used in textile
4) Forestry	Forestry: forestry, logging and related service activities
5) Fisheries	Fishing: hunting, trapping and game propagation including related service activities, fishing, fish farms; service activities incidental to fishing
6) Crude Oil	Parts of extraction of crude petroleum & service activities incidental to oil extraction excl. surveying
7) Gas extraction and distribution	Pars of extraction of natural gas & service activities incidental to gas extraction excl. surveying
	distribution of gaseous fuels through mains; steam and hot water supply
8) Fossil Fuel Based Electricity	Coal, Coal gases, Natural gases and oil fired electricity (production, collection and distribution)
9) Hydro and Geothermal electricity	Hydroelectric power and Geothermal electricity
10) Nuclear Power	Nuclear Power
11) Solar& Wind electricity	Solar, Wind, Wave and Tide Electricity
12) Renewable combustibles and waste electricity	wood, wood waste, other solid waste ; industrial waste ; municipal waste ; biogas ; liquid biofuels & waste
13) Petroleum & coal products	Petroleum & Coke: coke oven products, refined petroleum products, processing of nuclear fuel
14) Food Products	Cattle Meat: fresh or chilled meat and edible offal of cattle, sheep, goats, horses, asses, mules
	Pig meat and offal. Preserves and preparations of meat, meat offal or blood, flours
	Vegetable Oils: crude and refined oils of soya-bean, maize, olive, sesame, groundnut, olive seeds
	Milk: dairy products
	Processed Rice: rice, semi- or wholly milled
	Sugar
	Other Food: prepared and preserved fish or vegetables, fruit & vegetable juices, prepared fruits, flours,
	Beverages and Tobacco products

Table A2.1 continued over page.

Table A2.1. ENV-Linkages model sectors

(continued)

15) Other Mining	Other Mining: mining of metal ores, uranium, gems. other mining and quarrying
16) Non-ferrous metals	Non-Ferrous Metals: production and casting of copper, aluminum, zinc, lead, gold, and silver
17) Iron & steel	Iron & Steel: basic production and casting
18) Chemicals	Chemical Rubber Products: basic chemicals, other chemical products, rubber and plastics products
19) Fabricated Metal Products	Fabricated Metal Products: Sheet metal products, but not machinery and equipment
20) Paper & Paper Products	Paper & Paper Products: includes publishing, printing and reproduction of recorded media
21) Non-Metallic Minerals	Non-Metallic Minerals: cement, plaster, lime, gravel, concrete
22) Other Manufacturing	Textiles: textiles and man-made fibers
	Wearing Apparel: Clothing, dressing and dyeing of fur
	Leather: tanning and dressing of leather; luggage, handbags, saddlery, harness and footwear
	Other Transport Equipment: Manufacture of other transport equipment
	Electronic Equipment: office, accounting and computing, radio, television and communication equipment
	Other Machinery & Equipment: electrical machinery, medical, precision and optical, watches
	Other Manufacturing: includes recycling
	Motor Vehicles: cars, lorries, trailers and semi-trailers
	Lumber: wood and products of wood and cork, except furniture; articles of straw and plaiting materials
23) Transport services	Other Transport: road, rail ; pipelines, auxiliary transport activities; travel agencies
	Water transport
	Air transport
24) Services	Trade: all retail sales; wholesale trade and commission trade; hotels and restaurants;
	repairs of motor vehicles and personal and household goods ;
	Water: collection, purification and distribution
	Retail sale of automotive fuel
	Communications: post and telecommunications
	Other Financial Intermediation: includes auxiliary activities but not insurance and pension funding
	Insurance: includes pension funding, except compulsory social security
	Other Business Services: real estate, renting and business activities
	Recreation & Other Services: recreational, cultural and sporting activities, other service activities;
	private households with employed persons
	Other Services (Government): public administration and defense; compulsory social security,
	education, health and social work, sewage and refuse disposal, sanitation and similar activities,
	activities of membership organizations n.e.c., extra-territorial organizations and bodies
25) Construction & Dwellings	Construction: building houses factories offices and roads
	Dwellings: ownership of dwellings (imputed rents of houses occupied by owners)

THE ECONOMICS OF CLIMATE CHANGE MITIGATION – ISBN: 978-92-64-05606-0 – © OECD 2009

Table A2.2. ENV-Linkages model regions

ENV-Linkages regions	GTAP countries/regions
1) Australia & New Zealand	Australia, New Zealand
2) Japan	Japan
3) Canada	Canada
4) United States	United States
5) European Union 27 & EFTA	Austria, Belgium, Denmark, Finland, Greece, Ireland, Luxembourg, Netherlands, Portugal, Sweden, France, Germany, United Kingdom, Italy, Spain, Switzerland, Rest of EFTA, Czech Republic, Slovakia, Hungary, Poland, Romania, Bulgaria, Cyprus, Malta, Slovenia, Estonia, Latvia, Lithuania
6) Brazil	Brazil
7) China	China, Hong Kong
8) India	India
9) Russia	Russian Federation
10) Oil-exporting countries	Indonesia, Venezuela, Rest of Middle East, Islamic Republic of Iran, Rest of North Africa, Nigeria
11) Non-EU Eastern European countries	Croatia, Rest of Former Soviet Union
12) Rest of the world	Korea, Taiwan, Malaysia, Philippines, Singapore, Thailand, Viet Nam, Rest of East Asia, Rest of Southeast Asia, Cambodia, Rest of Oceania, Bangladesh, Sri Lanka, Rest of South Asia, Pakistan, Mexico, Rest of North America, Central America, Rest of Free Trade Area of Americas, Rest of the Caribbean, Colombia, Peru, Bolivia, Ecuador, Argentina, Chile, Uruguay, Rest of South America, Paraguay, Turkey, Rest of Europe, Albania, Morocco, Tunisia, Egypt, Botswana, Rest of South African Customs Union, Malawi, Mozambique, Tanzania, Zambia, Zimbabwe, Rest of Southern African Development Community, Mauritius, Madagascar, Uganda, Rest of Sub-Saharan Africa, Senegal, South Africa.

A2.2.3. Climate policy instruments

For studying the impacts of climate change policy, four types of instruments have been developed:

- GHG taxes, global or specific by sectors, gases or emission sources;
- tradable emission permits (with flexibility between regions and sectors);
- offsets (including the Clean Development Mechanism);
- regulatory policy (modelled as *quantity constraints*)

Taxes and tradable permits are applied on inputs of fossil fuel producing sectors (refined petroleum, natural gas, coal). They are applied, as well, on final demands of fossil based energy. This requires calculating emission coefficients that link base-year quantities of carbon dioxide emissions and base-year constant-dollar quantities. A carbon dioxide emissions database has been developed for GTAP (Lee, 2002) that uses data provided to GTAP by the International Energy Agency. The emission rates for non-CO_2 gases come from US-EPA (2006a). Twenty-seven sources of emissions over the thirty-two censed by US-EPA are implemented in the model.

Regulatory policy has also been introduced in the model through a mechanism imposing a shadow cost on the firm's inputs or capital. It has the effect of changing the marginal cost of particular inputs, or changing the quantity of capital used to produce a given output, but does use market instruments. The analysis requires assumptions concerning the cost of the regulatory policy, but it breaks the link between policy instruments and revenue transfer that is inherent in tax policy and tradable permits.

Factor-income taxes as well as factor taxes and subsidies on factor supply have also been introduced as these instruments are distinguished in the GTAP version 6.2 database.

A2.3. The structure of the model

This section outlines more formally the structure of the ENV-Linkages model. It provides a methodological overview of the model rather than an exhaustive listing of all equations in the model.

A2.3.1. Consumption

Income generated by economic activity ultimately reflects demand for goods and services by final consumers. ENV-linkages represent consumers as being largely similar at a very aggregated level of consumption. As such, the model postulates a representative consumer who allocates disposable income according to preferences among consumer goods and saving. In this version of the model, consumers purchase goods and services as produced by firms (*i.e.* a *transition matrix* to map produced goods into consumer goods is not implemented). The consumption/saving decision is static instead of forward-looking: saving is treated as a "good" and its amount is determined simultaneously with the demands for the other goods, the price of saving being set arbitrarily equal to the average price of consumer goods. This means that consumers are saving a constant proportion of their income and not adjusting that to reflect future events that may impact on income.

Formally, a representative consumer maximises well-being (utility) subject to resource constraints:

$$\begin{gathered} Max \;\; U = \sum_k \mu_k \ln(C_k - \theta_k) + \mu_s \ln(\frac{S}{P_s}) \\ Subject\ to \;\; \sum_k P_k^c\, C_k + S = Y, \quad and \quad \sum_k \mu_k + \mu_s = 1 \end{gathered} \qquad [1]$$

where U represents utility, C is a vector of k consumer goods, P^c is the vector of consumer prices, S represents the value of saving, P_s the relevant price of saving, and Y is total net-of-taxes income (completely allocated between consumption and savings). The parameter θ is the floor level of consumption – its main function is in making the utility function non-homothetic, which is consistent with considerable empirical evidence (*e.g.* Dowrick, *et al.* 2003). Since consumers are not represented with forward-looking behavior, some care needs to be exercised in studying policies that consumers may reasonably be expected to anticipate – either the policy itself or its consequences.

For each country, the consumer's objective function thus gives rise to household private consumptions [2] and saving [3]:

$$C_k = Pop \times \theta_k + \frac{\mu_k}{P_k^c} \times Y^*, \quad where \ \ Y^* = Y^c - Pop \times \sum_k P_k^c \times \theta_k \tag{2}$$

$$S = Y^c - \sum_k P_k^c \times C_k \tag{3}$$

where *Pop* represents population, Y^c represents household disposable income and Y^* is a *supernumerary* income (i.e. income above the subsistence level).

Production

Firms in all sectors minimise the cost of producing the goods and services that are demanded by consumers and other producers (domestic and foreign). Production is represented by constant returns to scale technology.

Figure A2.1 illustrates the typical nesting of the model's sectors (some sectors, like agriculture have a different nesting). The nesting of the electricity production is slightly different and is reported in Figure A2.2.

In Figure A2.1, each node represents a constant elasticity of substitution (CES) production function. This gives marginal costs and represents the different substitution (and complementarity) relations across the various inputs in each sector. Each sector uses intermediate inputs – including energy inputs - and primary factors (labour and capital). In some sectors, primary factors include natural resources, *e.g.* trees in forestry, land in agriculture, etc.

The top-level production nest considers final output as a composite commodity combining emissions of non-CO_2 gases and the production of the sector net of these emissions. In sectors that do not emit non-CO_2 gases, the corresponding emission rate is set equal to zero. For the purpose of calibration, these non-CO_2 gases are valuated using an arbitrary very low carbon price. The following non-CO_2 emission sources are considered: *i)* methane from rice cultivation, livestock production (enteric fermentation and manure management), coal mining, crude oil extraction, natural gas and services (landfills); *ii)* nitrous oxide from crops (nitrogenous fertilizers), livestock (manure management), chemicals (non-combustion industrial processes) and services (landfills); *iii)* industrial gases (SF6, PFC's and HFC's) from chemicals industry (foams, adipic acid, solvents), aluminum, magnesium and semi-conductors production. The values of the substitution elasticities are calibrated such as to fit to marginal abatement curves available in the literature on alternative technology options, (see, for instance, US-EPA (2006b).

Figure A2.1. Structure of production in ENV-Linkages

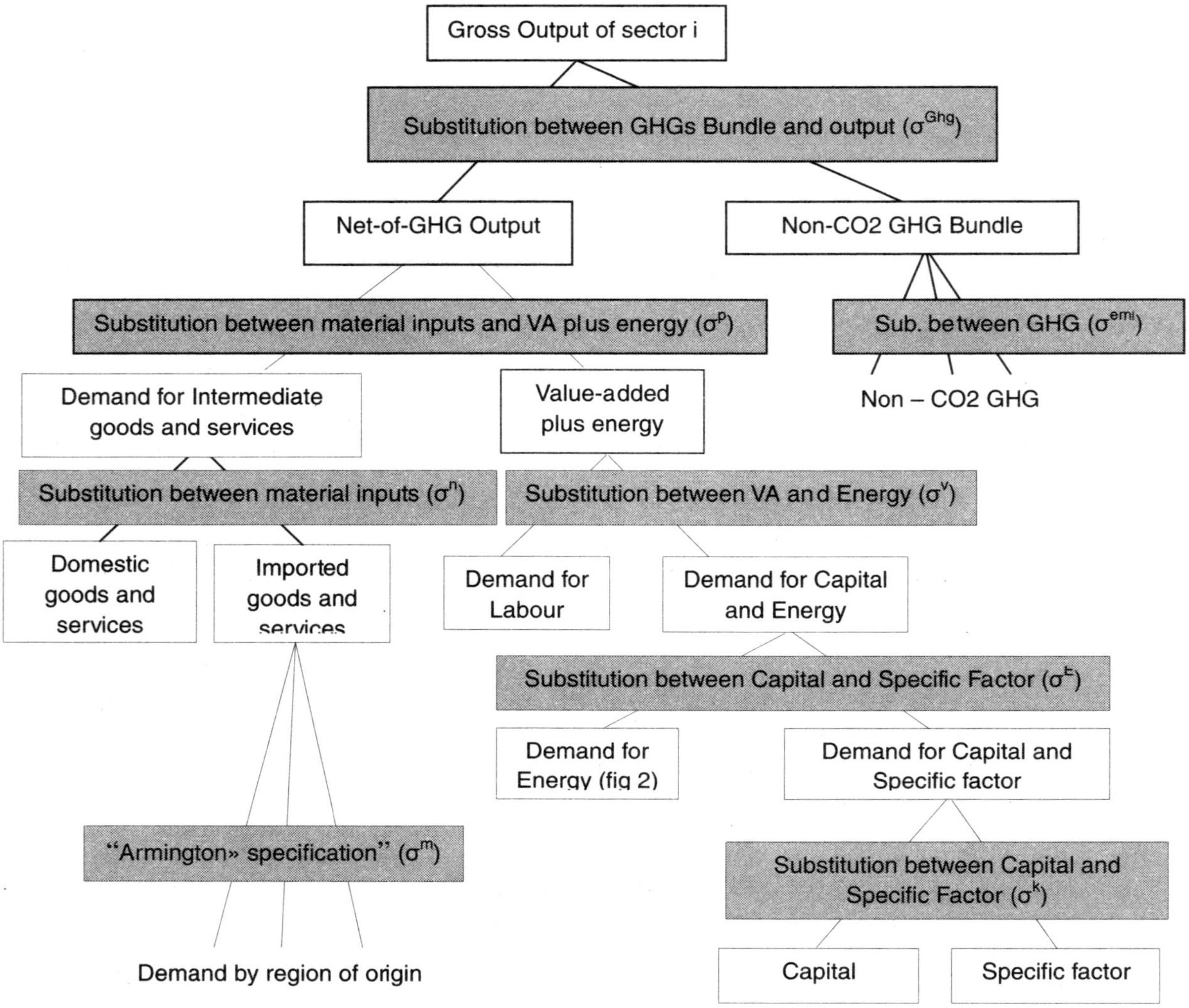

Gross Output of sector i

Substitution between GHGs Bundle and output (σ^{Ghg})

Net-of-GHG Output

Non-CO2 GHG Bundle

Substitution between material inputs and VA plus energy (σ^{p})

Sub. between GHG (σ^{emi})

Non – CO2 GHG

Demand for Intermediate goods and services

Value-added plus energy

Substitution between material inputs (σ^{n})

Substitution between VA and Energy (σ^{v})

Domestic goods and services

Imported goods and services

Demand for Labour

Demand for Capital and Energy

Substitution between Capital and Specific Factor (σ^{E})

Demand for Energy (fig 2)

Demand for Capital and Specific factor

"Armington» specification" (σ^{m})

Substitution between Capital and Specific Factor (σ^{k})

Demand by region of origin

Capital

Specific factor

Note: See Table A2.3 for parameter values.

Figure A2.2. Structure of Electricity production

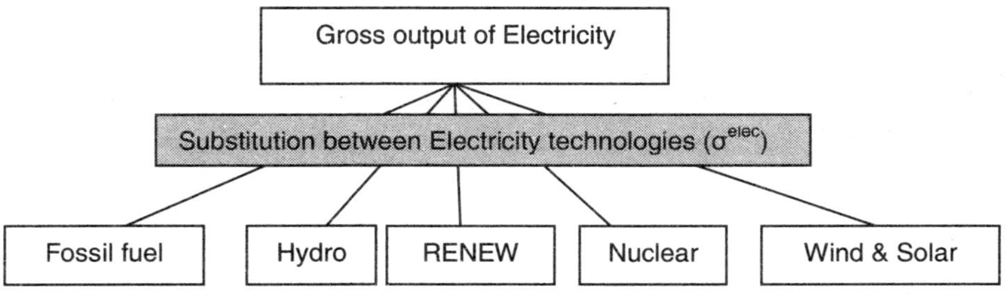

See Figure below for these technologies

Structure of production of non-fossil technologies

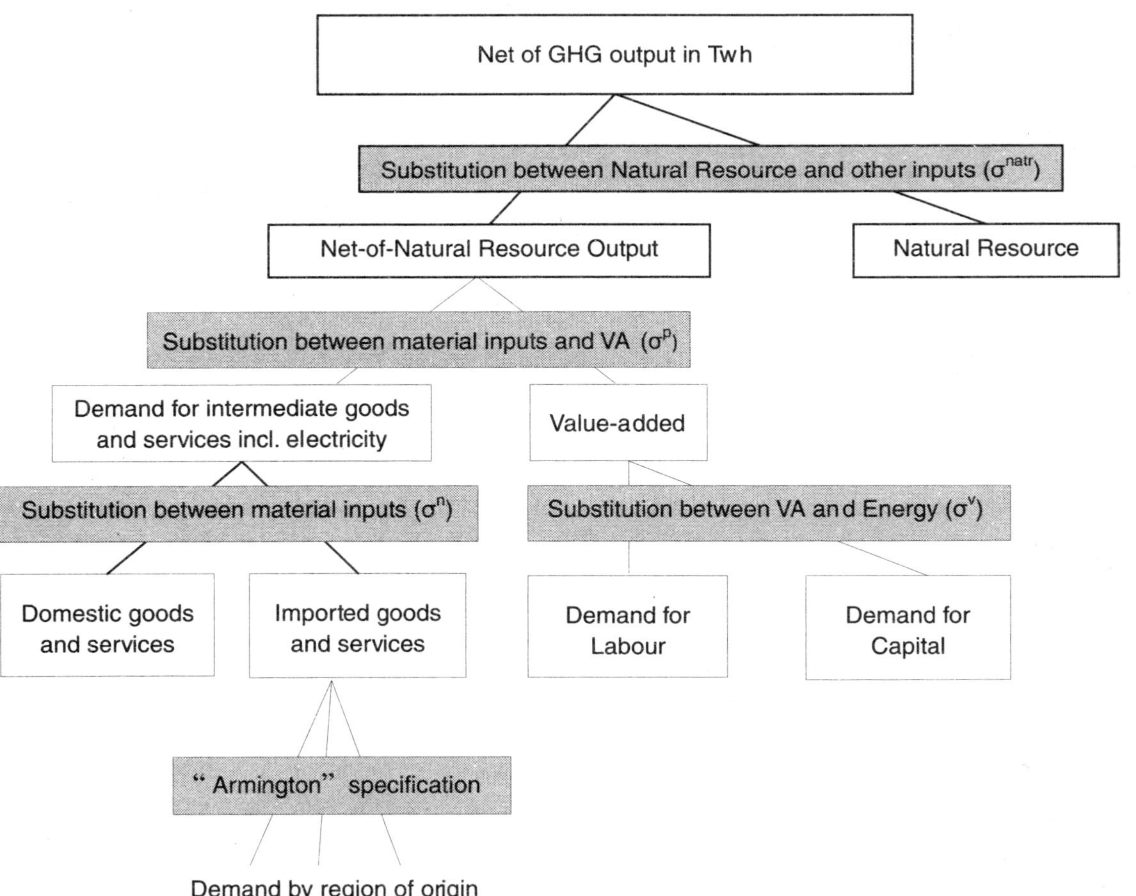

The second-level nest considers the gross output of sector (net of GHGs) as a combination of aggregate intermediate demands and a value-added bundle, including energy. For each good or service, output is produced by different production streams which are differentiated by capital vintage (old and new). Capital that is implemented contemporaneously is new – thus investment impacts on current-period capital; but then becomes old capital (added to the existing stock) in the subsequent period. Each production stream has an identical production structure, but with different technological parameters and substitution elasticities. Letting $X_{i,v}$ represents gross output of sector i (net of GHGs) using capital of vintage v, the equations representing production are derived from first order conditions [4] to [6] of the firm's profit maximisation objective.

$$INT_i = \sum_v \alpha_{i,v}^{INT} \times A_{i,v}^{\sigma_{i,v}^P - 1} \times \left(\frac{VC_{i,v}}{P_i^{INT}} \right)^{\sigma_{i,v}^P} \times X_{i,v} \qquad [4]$$

$$VA_{i,v} = \alpha_{i,v}^{VA} \times A_{i,v}^{\sigma_{i,v}^P - 1} \times \left(\frac{VC_{i,v}}{P_i^{VA}} \right)^{\sigma_{i,v}^P} \times X_{i,v} \qquad [5]$$

$$VC_{i,v} = \frac{1}{A_i} \times \left[\alpha_{i,v}^{INT} \left(P_i^{INT} \right)^{1-\sigma_{i,v}^P} + \alpha_{i,v}^{VA} \left(P_i^{VA} \right)^{1-\sigma_{i,v}^P} \right]^{(1/(1-\sigma_{i,v}^P))} \qquad [6]$$

where INT is the intermediate demand bundle (P^{INT} its price), VA represents value-added (P^{VA} its price), VC is unit variable cost of producing one unit of net of GHGs output (average costs include the cost of capital), A is a technical change term. In order to determine the industry-wide cost that includes both capital vintages, there is an averaging (weighted) of variable costs across the two vintages.

The model includes adjustment rigidities. An important feature is the distinction between old and new capital goods. In addition, old capital is assumed to be only partially mobile across sectors, reflecting differences in the marketability of capital goods across sectors. There is also homogeneity in the use of old and new capital.

In each period, the supply of primary factors (*e.g.* capital, labour, land and natural resources) is usually predetermined On the right hand side of the tree in Figure A2.1 value-added is shown as being composed of a labour input [7] along with a composite capital/energy bundle [8]:

$$L_i = \sum_v \alpha_{i,v}^{L} \times \lambda_i^{\sigma_{i,v}^V - 1} \times \left(\frac{P_{i,v}^{VA}}{W_i} \right)^{\sigma_{i,v}^V} \times VA_{i,v} \qquad [7]$$

$$KE_{i,v} = \alpha_{i,v}^{KE} \times \left(\frac{P_{i,v}^{VA}}{P_{i,v}^{KE}} \right)^{\sigma_{i,v}^V} \times VA_{i,v} \qquad [8]$$

where L represents labour (W its price), λ is the technical progress associated with labour, and KE is the capital-energy bundle (P^{KE} its price). The price of the value-added bundle, for generation v, is:

$$P_{i,v}^{VA} = \frac{1}{A_{i,v}} \times \left[\alpha_{i,v}^{KE} \left(P_{i,v}^{KE} \right)^{1-\sigma_{i,v}^V} + \alpha_{i,v}^{L} \left(\frac{W_i}{\lambda_i} \right)^{1-\sigma_{i,v}^V} \right]^{(1/(1-\sigma_{i,v}^V))} \qquad [9]$$

 THE ECONOMICS OF CLIMATE CHANGE MITIGATION – ISBN: 978-92-64-05606-0 – © OECD 2009

The value-added bundle (VA) is a sub-component of the top level node that produces sectoral net-of-GHGs output X_i. Similar sub-components also exist in formulating the capital and energy bundles. In fact, as shown in Figure A2.1, the capital is bundled with a sector-specific resource when one exists and energy is itself a bundle of different energy inputs.

The structure of electricity production assumes that a representative electricity producer maximizes its profit by using the five available technologies to generate electricity using a CES specification with a large value of the elasticity of substitution (Figure A2.2). The production of the non-fossil electricity technologies (net of GHG and expressed in TeraWatt per hour) has a structure similar than for the other sectors, except a top nesting combining a sector-specific natural resource, on one hand, and all other inputs, on the other hands. This specification aims at controlling the supply of these electricity technologies given the value of the substitution elasticity.

The energy bundle is of particular interest for analysis of climate change issues. Energy, as reported in Figure A2.3, is a composite of fossil fuels and electricity. In turn, fossil fuel is a composite of coal and a bundle of the "other fossil fuels". At the lowest nest, the composite "other fossil fuels" commodity consists of crude oil, refined oil products and natural gas. The value of the substitution elasticities are chosen as to imply a higher degree of substitution among the other fuels than with electricity and coal.

Figure A2.3. Structure of energy demand in ENV-Linkages

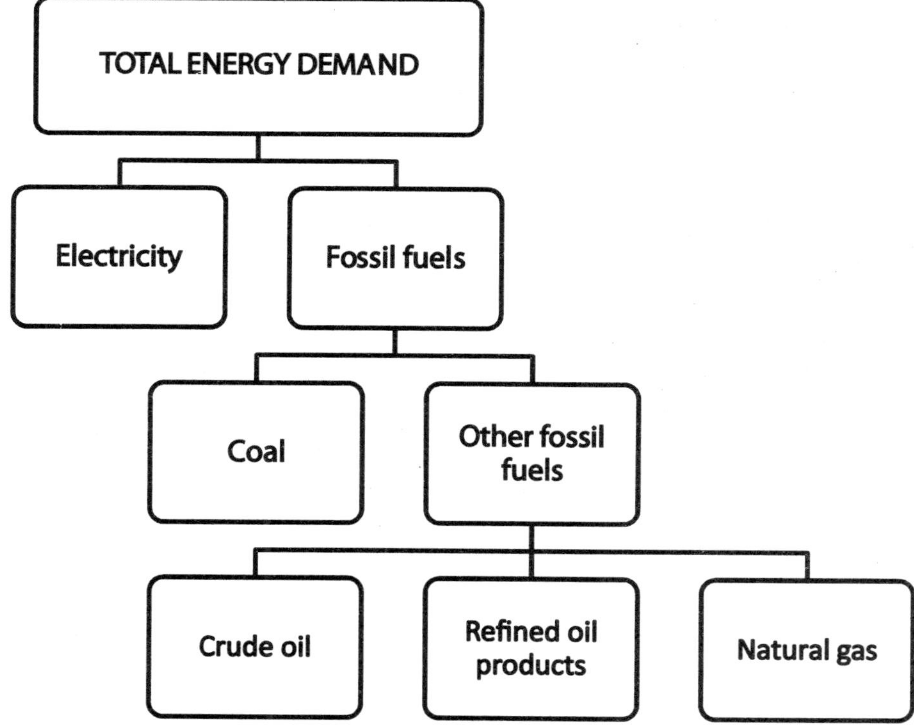

Note: See Table A2.3 for parameter value.

Source: OECD.

Given the dual streams of production (from old and new capital), there is a higher degree of substitutability between energy sources when capital is new, but after one year it becomes a sunk cost and falls to a low level of substitutability among energy sources. Moreover, in the sectors that produce fossil fuels (with the exception of natural gas), there is no substitutability between energy inputs. The low level of substitutability of energy when old capital is present is consistent with empirical findings by Arnberg and Bjorner (2007) who look at plant level changes in energy intensity. However, since this model includes the possibility of changes in industry composition, the overall responsiveness to energy price changes will be higher than these researchers found at plant levels.

Once a sector's optimal combination of inputs is determined from relative prices, sectoral output (included GHGs) prices are calculated assuming competitive supply (zero-profit) conditions.

Investment and Market goods equilibria

This version of the model does not include an investment schedule that relates investment to interest rates. In each period, investment net-of-economic depreciation is equal to the sum of government savings, consumer savings and net capital flows from abroad. Investment as well as government demand use final goods according with a CES specification. Then, the total demand of a good in the economy is equal to the consumer final demand plus the intermediary demands from firms plus the intermediary demands by final good sectors, corresponding to government and investment expenditures.

Market goods equilibria imply that, on the one side, the total production of any good or service is equal to the demand addressed to domestic producers plus exports; and, on the other side, the total demand is allocated, according to the Armington principle, between the demands (both final and intermediary) addressed to domestic producers and the import demand(see below).

Foreign Trade

World trade in ENV-Linkages is based on a set of regional bilateral flows. The basic assumption is that imports originating from different regions are imperfect substitutes Therefore in each region, total import demand for each good is allocated across trading partners according to the relationship between their export prices. This specification of imports - commonly referred to as the Armington specification - formally implies that each region faces a reduction in demand for its exports if domestic prices increase. The Armington specification is implemented using two CES nests. At the top nest, domestic agents choose the optimal combination of the domestic good and an aggregate import good[10]. At the second nest, agents optimally allocate demand for the aggregate import good [12] across the range of trading partners *r'*.

$$XMT_i = \beta_i^m \times \left(\frac{PA_i}{PMT_i} \right)^{\sigma_i^m} \times XA_i \qquad [10]$$

$$PMT_i = \left[\sum_r \beta_{i,r}^W PM_{i,r}^{1-\sigma_{i,r}^w} \right]^{(1/(1-\sigma_i^w))} \qquad [11]$$

where XMT is the bundle of imports of a particular good or service (*PMT* its price) and *XA* represents the aggregate demand for domestically produced and import goods (*PA* is its price).

$$WTF_{r',i} = \beta^{w}_{r',i} \times \left(\frac{PMT_i}{PM^{M}_{r',i}} \right)^{\sigma^{w}_{i}} \times XMT_i \qquad [12]$$

where $WTF_{r'}$ is import of a particular good or service from region *r'*. Its price, $PM_{r'}$, represents the domestic import price (*e.g.* domestic producer price of its partner r' adjusted for export tax or subsidy, transport margin, "iceberg" costs, and domestic tariffs).

Prices

ENV-Linkages is fully homogeneous in prices and only relative prices matter. All prices are expressed relatively to the *numéraire* of the price system that is arbitrarily chosen as the index of OECD manufacturing exports prices. From the point of view of the model specification, this has an impact on the evaluation of international investment flows. They are evaluated with respect to the price of the *numéraire* good. Therefore, one way to interpret the foreign investment flows is as the quantity of foreign saving which will buy the average bundle of OECD manufacturing exports.

The domestic producer price of the good j in the model is defined as a composite index of the average variable cost [6] and the costs of the non-CO_2 GHGs bundle, plus production taxes. The aggregate market prices of a good i (PA) is calculated as a composite index of domestic producer prices and import prices. Then the prices of final or intermediary demands are market prices (PA) plus agent-specific *ad valorem* taxes.

Government and long-term closure

Government collects income taxes, indirect taxes on intermediate and final consumption as well as possible carbon taxes, production taxes, tariffs, and export taxes/subsidies. Aggregate government expenditures are linked to real GDP. Since predicting corrective government policy is not an easy task, the real government deficit is exogenous. The closure of the model implies that some fiscal instrument is endogenous – in order to meet government budget constraint. The fiscal closure rule in ENV-Linkages is that the income tax rate adjusts to offset changes that may arise in government expenditures, or as a result of other taxes. For example, a reduction or elimination of tariff rates is compensated by an increase in household direct taxation, *ceteris paribus*. Alternative closure rules can be easily implemented.

Each region runs a current-account surplus (or deficit), which is fixed (in terms of the model *numéraire*). Closure on the international side of each economy is achieved by having, as a counterpart of these imbalances, a net outflow (or inflow) of capital, which is subtracted from (added to) the domestic flow of saving. These net capital flows are exogenous. In each period, the model equates investment to saving (which is equal to the sum of saving by households, the net budget position of the government and foreign capital flows). Hence, given exogenous sequences for government and foreign savings, this implies that investment is ultimately driven by household savings.

Dynamic Features

The ENV-Linkages model has a simple recursive dynamic structure as agents are assumed to be myopic and to base their decisions on static expectations concerning prices and quantities. Dynamics in the model originate from two endogenous sources: *i)* accumulation of productive capital and *ii)* the putty/semi-putty specification of technology, as well as, from exogenous drivers like population growth or productivity changes.

Capital accumulation and sectoral allocation of capital

At an aggregate level, the basic capital accumulation function equates the current capital stock to the depreciated stock inherited from the previous period plus investment. Differences in sectoral rates of return determine the allocation of investment across sectors. The model features two vintages of capital, but investment adds only to new capital. Sectors with higher investment, therefore, are more able to adapt to changes than are sectors with low levels of investment. Indeed, declining sectors whose old capital is less productive begin to sell capital to other firms (which they can use after incurring some adjustment costs).[2]

The putty/semi-putty specification

The substitution possibilities among production factors are assumed to be higher with the *new* than with the *old* capital vintages – technology has a putty/semi-putty specification. Hence, when a shock to relative prices occurs (*e.g.* tariff removal), the demands for production factors adjust gradually to the long-run equilibrium because the substitution effects are delayed over time. The adjustment path depends on the values of the short-run elasticities of substitution and the replacement rate of capital. As the latter determines the pace at which new vintages are installed, the larger is the volume of new investment, the greater the possibility to achieve the long-run total amount of substitution among production factors.

A2.4. Calibration of the ENV-Linkages model

The process of calibration of the ENV-Linkages model is broken down into three stages. First, a number of parameters are calibrated, given some elasticity values, on base-year (2001) values of variables. This process is referred to as the static calibration. Second, the 2001 database is updated to 2005 by simulating the model dynamically over the period 2001-2005 and static calibration is performed again with price re-normalisation in order to express all variables in 2005 real USD. Third, the baseline projection is obtained by defining a set of exogenous socio-economic drivers (demographic trends, labour productivity, future trends in energy prices and energy efficiency gains) and running the model dynamically again over the period 2005-2050.[3]

A2.4.1.Static calibration of the model

Many key parameters are set on the basis of information drawn from various empirical studies and data sources (elasticities of substitution, income elasticities of demand, supply elasticities of natural resources, etc). Table A2.3 reports some key elasticities used in the current version of the model. Use of these parameters was illustrated in Figures A2.1 and A2.2, as well as by the equations in Section A2.3. Income elasticities of household demand as well as Armington elasticities are taken from the GTAP 6.2 database.

However, the information available on the values of these parameters is insufficient for the model simulation to be able to reproduce base-year data values. Given the modelling choices made with regard to the representation of both behaviours and structural technical relationships, some model parameters must be calculated to fit to the data for the initial year (expressed in 2001 USD) of the version 6 of the GTAP database. As a general rule, the parameters used to do this are those whose impact on the outcomes in terms of variation rates remains limited (scale parameters) or parameters for which there are no empirical studies (CES share coefficients).[4]

Table A2.3. Key parameter values

Key parameter		Value
σ^{Ghg}	Substitution between GHGs bundle and Net-of-GHGs Output	Substitution is from 0.03-0.05 for Agr. Sectors to 0.15-0.3 in some industrial emissions
σ^{p}	Substitution between material inputs and VA plus energy	Substitution between material inputs and VA plus energy is 0, except for new capital in manufacturing where it is 0.1.
σ^{n}	Substitution between material inputs	Substitution between material inputs is 0 for non services and non manufacturing sector and 0.1 for other sectors.
σ^{V}	Substitution between VA and Energy	0.05 for old capital vintages and 0.4 for new vintages in agriculture, forestry and fishing and fossil fuels sectors and varying form 0.2-0.27 (1.8-2.1 in other sectors)
σ^{f}	Substitution between inputs investment and government exp.	0.8
σ^{E}	Substitution between Capital and Energy	0 for old capital vintages, 0.2-0.8 for new vintages, but always 0 in coal and crude oil.
σ^{k}	Substitution between Capital and Specific Factor	Substitution between Capital and Specific Factor is 0
σ^{ELY}	Elasticity between Electricity & Non-electricity energy inputs	0.062 for old capital and 0.5 for new in electricity sector. 0.12 and 1 in other sector except fossil fuel where equals to 0 and chemicals where 0.08 and 0.4.
σ^{Coa}	Elasticity between Coal & Non-Coal bundle	0.03 for old capital and 0.25 for new in electricity sector. 0.12 and 1 in other sector except fossil fuel where equals to 0.
σ^{Ep}	Elasticity between enery inputs in Non-Coal bundle	0.25 for old capital vintages, 2 for new vintages, but always 0 in the energy sectors, except for Electricity
σ^{X}	Armington elasticity, domestic versus imports	Varies from 0.9 to 5depending on sectors, identical across regions. GTAP data is used
σ^{W}	Armington elasticity, import sources	Same as σ^{X}
σ^{M}	Armington elasticity, intermediate goods imports	Same as σ^{X}
σ^{EI}	*Armington elasticity, energy imports*	*Same as* σ^{X}
σ^{elec}	Elasticity between electricity technologies	10
σ^{natr}	Elasticity between specific resource and other inputs	Only for non-fossil electricity technologies, varying form 0.0-0.4

A2.4.2. Dynamic calibration of the model

Ideally, an informed choice of prospective trends in exogenous variables would produce a set of acceptable scenarios. However, it is difficult to cover all these trends comprehensively. Furthermore, this would make comparisons of different alternative scenarios practically unmanageable. Therefore, the approach followed here considers only one single set of exogenous drivers while recognising that alternative sets may potentially generate somewhat different simulation results[5]. The baseline projection allows calculating the values of a number of parameter over time (such as energy efficiency gains, for instance), in order to reproduce the evolution of the exogenous drivers. In any variants or policy simulations, these parameter values are kept constant while all other variables in the model are fully endogenous.[6]

The list of exogenous drivers specified in the baseline projection is the following:

- Demographic projections and employment trends.
- Aggregate average and sectoral labour productivity growth, controlled by calibration of technical progress coefficients embodied in labour.
- Autonomous efficiency gains for capital, land and specific natural resources.
- Autonomous efficiency gains of fertilizers in crops sectors and of the food bundle in livestock rearing.
- Supply of land and natural resources (excepted for fossil fuels sectors).
- International trade margins.
- Shares of public expenditure in real GDP.
- Public savings and flows of international savings.
- Energy demands (projected by using elasticities of demands to GDP), for all kind of fuels demands excepted crude oil, controlled by calibration of the Autonomous Energy Efficiency Improvements (named AEEIs) in energy use, by sector and type of fuel.
- International prices of fossil fuels, controlled by calibration of the potential supply of fossil fuels resources.
- Investment to GDP ratios, controlled by calibration of the marginal propensity to save of the households.
- Non-CO_2 GHGs emissions, controlled by calibration of autonomous efficiency gains in non-CO_2 GHGs emissions, by sector and type of GHGs emissions.
- The share of each type of electricity-producing technology, controlled by calibration of the specific "natural resource".

A2.4.3. Data used for dynamic calibration

Socio-economic variables such as population, apparent labour productivity or investment to GDP ratios are discussed in Duval and De la Maisonneuve (2009).

AEEIs in energy uses have been dynamically calibrated on the basis of elasticities of each kind of energy demand to GDP for 2005-2030 as projected in the IEA's *World Energy Outlook* (2006). These elasticities are assumed to evolve after 2030 in line with their projected trends over the period 2025-2030.

The structure of electricity production between the five alternative technologies is calibrated based on the projections from the IEA's *World Energy Outlook* (2008).

The non-CO_2 greenhouse gases need to be calibrated in the base year database. For this purpose, the price of these emissions is arbitrary set equal to USD 0.5 per ton of CO_2 equivalent in the upper bundle of the gross output. Emissions by source reported in US EPA (2006b) are associated to the sectors of ENV-linkages, and for sake of consistency GHGs levels in 2005 are adjusted to match IEA data. It was not possible to associate all emission sources to an economic activity described in the model.[7] For the period 2005-2020, the non-CO_2 emissions are calibrated on forecasts made by the US EPA by adjusting an autonomous efficiency parameter in the emissions bundle of the production function. After 2020 the trend over the period 2015-2020 is extended, except for agriculture sources of non-CO_2 GHGs emissions where the trend assumed is taken from the *OECD Environmental Outlook* (2008).

The evolution of the international import prices of fossil fuels are also controlled for in the baseline scenario. During the period 2005-2008, the model reproduces the historical evolutions and short run projections made by the IEA for its *World Energy Outlook 2008* report. Over the medium term (2007 to 2030) the crude oil potential reserves in the "oil-exporting countries" (see Table A2.2. for the composition of this region) are calibrated to reproduce the exogenous trajectory of the international crude oil price assumed by IEA (2008). After 2030, the price is assumed to increase by 1% in real terms each year, the calibrated oil reserves of the oil-exporting countries will then gradually decline, reflecting some exhaustion of existing reserves.

In line with IEA projections, the evolution of the international price of natural gas closely follows that of the crude oil price. This is controlled for by adjusting natural gases resources in all producing regions. After 2030, the link between international oil and natural gas prices is projected to be looser, in line with the assumption of a more elastic supply of natural gas in the longer term. The historical surge of the international coal price up to 2008 is introduced by controlling the supply of coal-producing regions. After 2008, the coal price is fully determined by the model mechanisms and remain almost constant in real terms, reflecting the presumption of an elastic coal supply at the world level.

From 2001-2005, current account balances as well as government savings are calibrated to match IMF historical data. After 2005, government deficits (or surplus) as well as current accounts deficits (or surplus) are assumed to gradually vanished (at an arbitrary 2.5% rate of reduction per year). However, the Chinese surplus and US deficit are assumed to disappear less rapidly (only after 2020).

A2.4.4. Dynamic calibration of household preferences

In addition, the parameters relative to household demands (see equations [1] - [3]) need to be recalibrated dynamically in the baseline simulation. The household preferences in ENV-Linkages include a minimum subsistence level of demand for each good that makes the utility function non-homothetic. However, when using the model over a rather long projection horizon, household income increase quite substantially and, if the minimum subsistence demands are not adjusted, income elasticity of demand for all goods converge towards unity. This problem is offset by adjusting the subsistence parameters in the baseline scenario for each period in order to reproduce the desired set of income elasticities.

Moreover in the baseline simulation, income elasticities of demand are evolving over time assuming, a conditional convergence of household preferences (*e.g.* income elasticities of demand for non-energy goods) of the non-OECD countries to the OECD standard, based on relative income per capita.

A2.4.5. Dynamic adjustment of world trade and output structures

In a model like ENV-Linkages that uses so-called Armington specifications to represent international trade flows, countries face downward sloping demand for their exports. Therefore, a fast-growing country would typically experience a decline in its relative factor prices, implying a depreciation of its real exchange rate, *ceteris paribus* (abstracting from the offsetting Balassa-Samuelson effect). This appears inconsistent with past history, which shows that imports from fast-growing countries have typically increased through the creation of new products rather than through price reductions (see in particular Krugman, 1989). In order to capture this historical feature in a simplified manner, the baseline projection further assumes a gradual exogenous increase in the share of non-OECD countries in the overall imports of OECD countries.

In addition, the increase in global competition is accompanied by growth in the use of services in production, in line with the argument advanced in OECD (2005). This is simulated by adjusting dynamically the input-output structure such as to increase the weight of services (in the broad sense of the term) in the composition of the bundle of intermediate goods, for non-agricultural and non-fossil fuels sectors.

A2.4.6. Software and model solution

ENV-Linkages is written in the General Algebraic Modeling System (GAMS) modelling language. GAMS is particularly useful for numerical modelling of linear, nonlinear and mixed integer optimization systems. The software has a number of solvers that can be used for a particular problem and, in many cases, switching between solvers is straightforward. In the past this has proved useful since problems that don't solve with one solution algorithm may solve with another.

For economic problems, GAMS can be particularly useful since it allows problems to be written as mixed complementarity – which specifies inequalities that the solution must meet. This facilitates the solutions to problems involving budgets constraints or homogeneous products being produced by multiple sectors.

A2.4.7. Future Model developments

A number of developments will be introduced into the ENV-Linkages model to enhance its applicability to climate policy analysis.

Carbon capture and storage

Carbon dioxide capture and storage (CCS) is a process for reducing emissions by first extracting CO_2 from flue gas streams (generally from electricity production), fuel processing and other industrial processes, including cement production. Once captured and compressed, the CO_2 is transported by pipeline or tanker to a storage site: generally for injection into suitable geological formation, but sometimes also into deep waters. Numerous studies (*e.g.* IEA, 2004) have looked at the feasibility of CCS and generally concluded that at prices near USD 50 per tonne of CO_2, CCS is feasible for both natural gas and coal combustion. There is an energy penalty that must be paid, and the capital cost is substantial, but there did not appear to be any technical obstacles to implementation. Based on the results of various studies, CCS is implemented in the current version of ENV-Linkages but was not used in the simulations reported in this book.

Land-use change emissions

A potentially important source of GHG emissions that is not going to be implemented at this stage is that associated with land-use change. Achard, *et al.* (2004) reported a large potential for this source, but data are currently very poor and scientific understanding is incomplete. Once the data quality and completeness improve, steps will be taken to incorporate it into the model.

A2.4.8. Concluding remarks

ENV-Linkages is an economic model that continues to evolve for use in environmental policy. It has a rigorous foundation in general equilibrium economics and captures core aspects of the world economy. It thus facilitates exploration and quantification of policy responses to a wide range of government initiatives. For policies such as carbon dioxide taxes, the model is very strong in representing the full array of general equilibrium repercussions that the tax would cause.

Some of the model's limitations in representing economic phenomenon such as endogenous capital mobility and forward-looking behaviour complicate the types of policies that the model can adequately address. For example, future policy action announced today would not affect today's behaviour of firms and consumers in the model. This would lead to overstating the cost of the policy upon actual implementation. On the other hand, insofar as the policy announcement is not fully credible, the model's response to the policy may be more appropriate. This example illustrates the need to present the model's results along with clear discussion of the context in which policy is assumed to operate.

Notes

1. See Armington (1969).

2. Formally, at the sectoral level, the specific accumulation functions may differ because the demand for (old and new) capital can be less than the depreciated stock of old capital. In this case, the sector contracts over time by releasing old capital goods. Consequently, in each period, the new capital vintage available to expanding industries is equal to the sum of disinvested capital in contracting industries plus total saving generated by the economy.

3. The baseline simulation also contains the assumption that the EU Emission Trading System is implemented over the period 2006-2012, assuming a permits price that will rise gradually from 5 to 25 constant USD in 2012 and for the years after.

4. During this calibration stage, all before-tax prices are normalised to unity, which makes it possible, inter alia, to ensure by means of dual cost functions that the sum of CES production function coefficients is equal to one.

5. For instance, differences in projected energy prices in the baseline scenario may affect the economic costs of policy scenarios, although by a marginal extent. For more on sensitivity analysis to baseline scenario, see OECD (2006).

6. For instance, in the baseline scenario, the technical progress embodied in labour is calibrated to reproduce given GDP trends. In contrast, in any policy variants, GDP is fully endogenous given this technical progress calculated in the baseline scenario.

7. Non-CO_2 emissions from forest and savannas' burning are not introduced. They correspond to less than 5% of the non-CO_2 emissions reported by the US EPA.

References

Achard, F., H.D. Eva, P. Mayaux, H.-J. Stibig and A. Belward (2004), "Improved Estimates of Net Carbon Emissions from Land Cover Change in the Tropics for the 1990s", *Global Biogeochem. Cycles*, Vol. 18.

Armington, P. (1969), "A Theory of Demand for Products Distinguished by Place of Production," *IMF Staff Papers*, Vol. 16, pp. 159-178.

Arnberg, S. and T.B. Bjorner (2007), "Substitution Between Energy, Capital and Labour Within Industrial Companies: A Micro Panel Data Analysis", *Resource and Energy Economics*, 2007, Vol. 29, No. 2, pp. 122-136.

Burniaux, J-M. (2000), "A Multi-Gas Assessment of the Kyoto Protocol', *OECD Economics Department Working Papers* No. 270.

Burniaux, J-M., G. Nicoletti and J. Oliveira Martins (1992), "GREEN: A Global Model for Quantifying the Costs of Policies to Curb CO_2 Emissions", *OECD Economic Studies*, 19 (Winter).

Dimaranan, B.V., Editor (2006). *Global Trade, Assistance, and Production: The GTAP 6 Data Base*, Center for Global Trade Analysis, Purdue University.

Dowrick, S., Y. Dunlop, and J. Quiggin (2003), "Social Indicators and Comparisons of Living Standards", *Journal of Development Economics*, 2003, Vol. 70.

Duval, R. and C. de la Maisonneuve (2009), "Long-Run GDP Growth Framework and Scenarios for the World Economy", *OECD Economics Department Working Papers, No.663*, forthcoming.

Hyman, R.C., J.M. Reilly, M.H. Babiker, A. De Masin, and H.D. Jacoby (2002), "Modeling Non-CO_2 Greenhouse Gas Abatement", *Environmental Modeling and Assessment*, Vol. 8, No. 3, pp. 175-86.

IEA (2008), *World Energy Outlook 2008*, Paris.

IEA (2006), *World Energy Outlook 2006*, Paris.

IEA (2004), *Prospects for CO_2 Capture and Storage*, Paris.

Krugman, P. (1989), "Differences in Income Elasticities and Trends in Real Exchange Rates", *European Economic Review,* Vol. 33, No. 5.

Lee, H-L. (2002), "An Emission Data Base for Integrated Assessment of Climate Change Policy Using GTAP", *Draft GTAP Working Paper,* Center for Global Trade Analysis, Purdue University, West Lafayette, Indiana.

OECD (2008), *OECD Environmental Outlook to 2030*, Paris.

OECD (2006), "Sensitivity Analysis in ENV-Linkages", *ENV/EPOC/GSP(2006)6*, Paris.

OECD (2005), "Trade and Structural Adjustment", Paris.

US EPA (2006a), "Global Anthropogenic Non-CO_2 Greenhouse Gas Emissions: 1990-2020", United States Environmental Protection Agency, Washington D.C., June, Revised.

US EPA (2006b), "Global Mitigation of Non-CO_2 Greenhouse Gases", United States Environmental Protection Agency, Washington D.C., June.

van der Mensbrugghe, D. (2005), "Linkage Technical Reference Document Version 6.0", Development Prospects Group, The World Bank, Washington, January 2005.

Weyant, J. and F. de la Chesnaye (eds.) (2006), "Multigas Mitigation and Climate Change", *Energy Journal,* special issue.